2018
青岛统计年鉴

QINGDAO STATISTICAL YEARBOOK

（总 第39期 VOL.39）

青 岛 市 统 计 局
国家统计局青岛调查队 编
QINGDAO MUNICIPAL STATISTICS BUREAU
NBS SURVEY OFFICE IN QINGDAO

中国统计出版社
China Statistics Press

图书在版编目（CIP）数据

青岛统计年鉴 .2018/ 青岛市统计局，国家统计局青岛调查队编 .-- 北京：中国统计出版社，2018.8
ISBN 978-7-5037-8545-0

Ⅰ. ①青… Ⅱ. ①青… ②国… Ⅲ. ①统计资料 – 青岛 –2018– 年鉴Ⅳ . ① C832.523-54

中国版本图书馆 CIP 数据核字（2018）第 160597 号

青岛统计年鉴 -2018

作　　者 / 青岛市统计局　国家统计局青岛调查队
责任编辑 / 陈越月
装帧设计 / 中闻集团青岛印务有限公司
出版发行 / 中国统计出版社
地　　址 / 北京市丰台区西三环南路甲 6 号　邮政编码 /100073
电　　话 / 邮购（010）63376909　书店（010）68783171
网　　址 / http://csp.stats.gov.cn
印　　刷 / 中闻集团青岛印务有限公司
经　　销 / 新华书店
开　　本 / 890mm × 1240mm　1/16
字　　数 / 1110 千字
印　　张 / 26.125
版　　别 / 2018 年 9 月第 1 版
版　　次 / 2018 年 9 第 1 次印刷
定　　价 / 280.00 元

如有印装差错，由本社发行部调换。

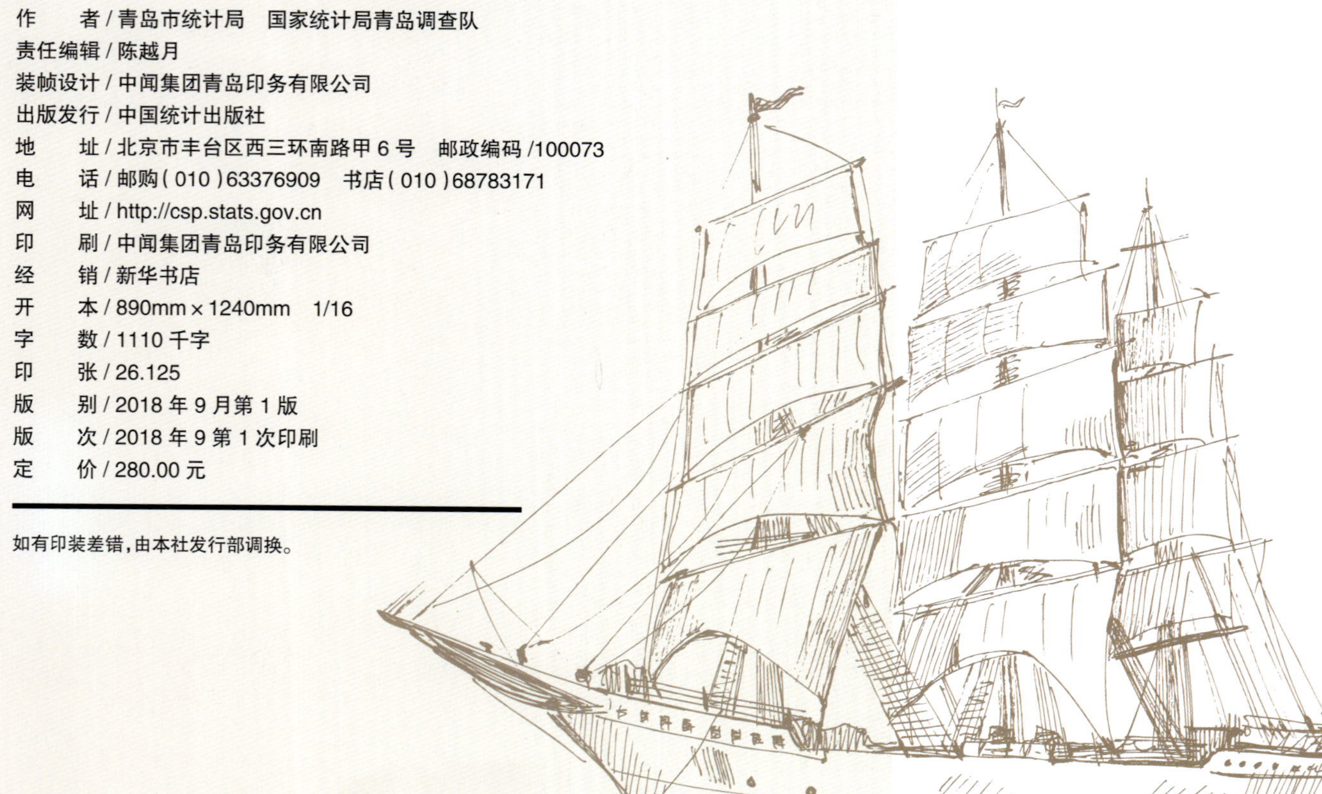

全市生产总值构成（%）

Composition Of Gross Domestic Product（%）

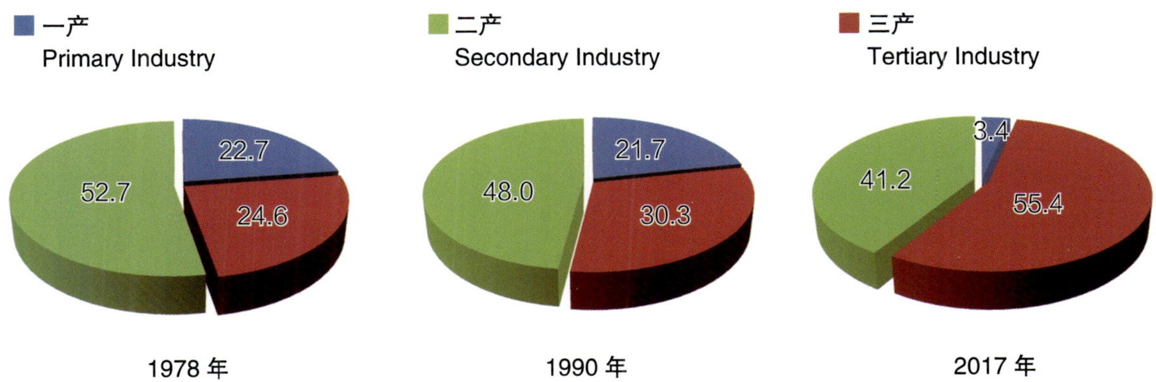

全市生产总值（亿元）

Gross Domestic Product（100 million yuan）

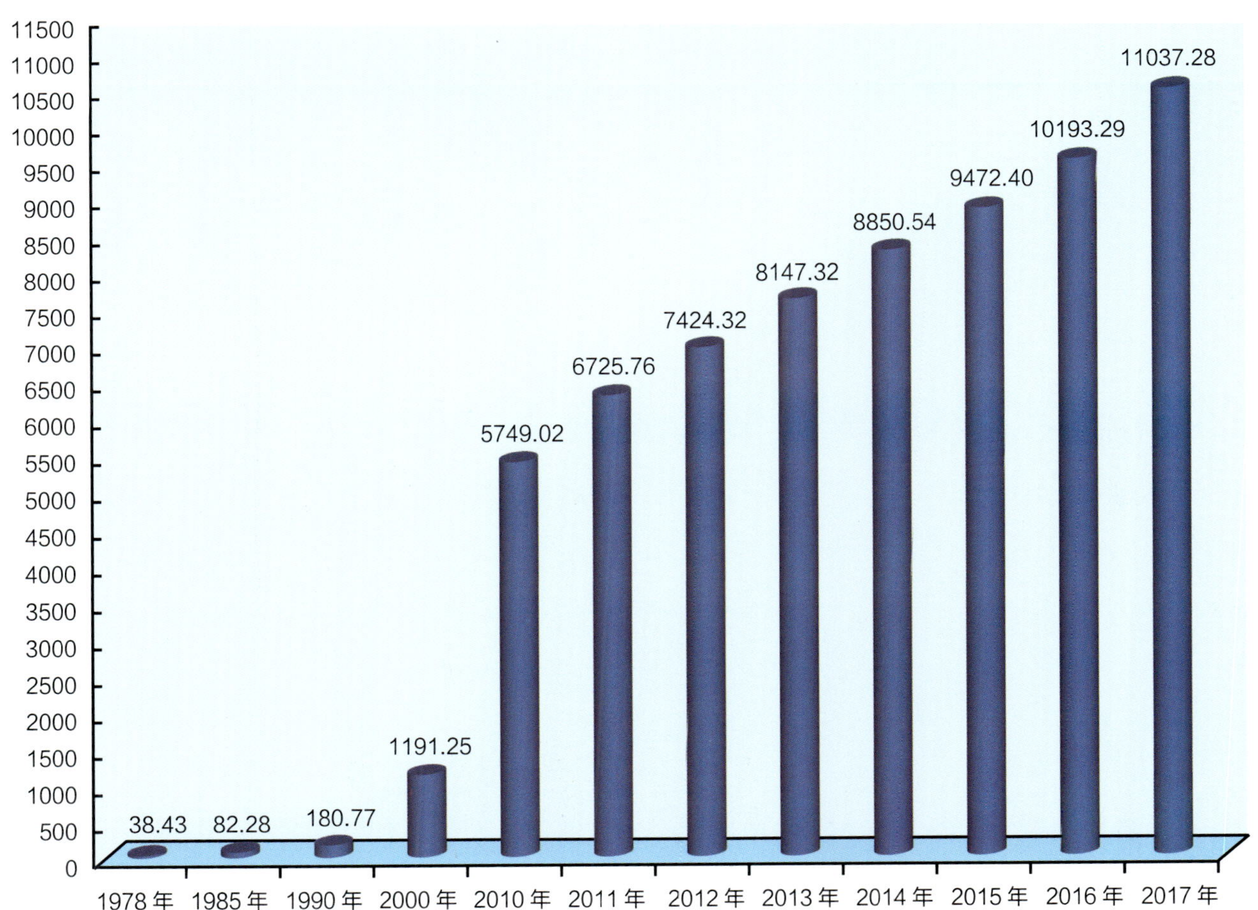

农林牧渔业总产值（亿元）

Gross Output Value Of Agriculture（100 million yuan）

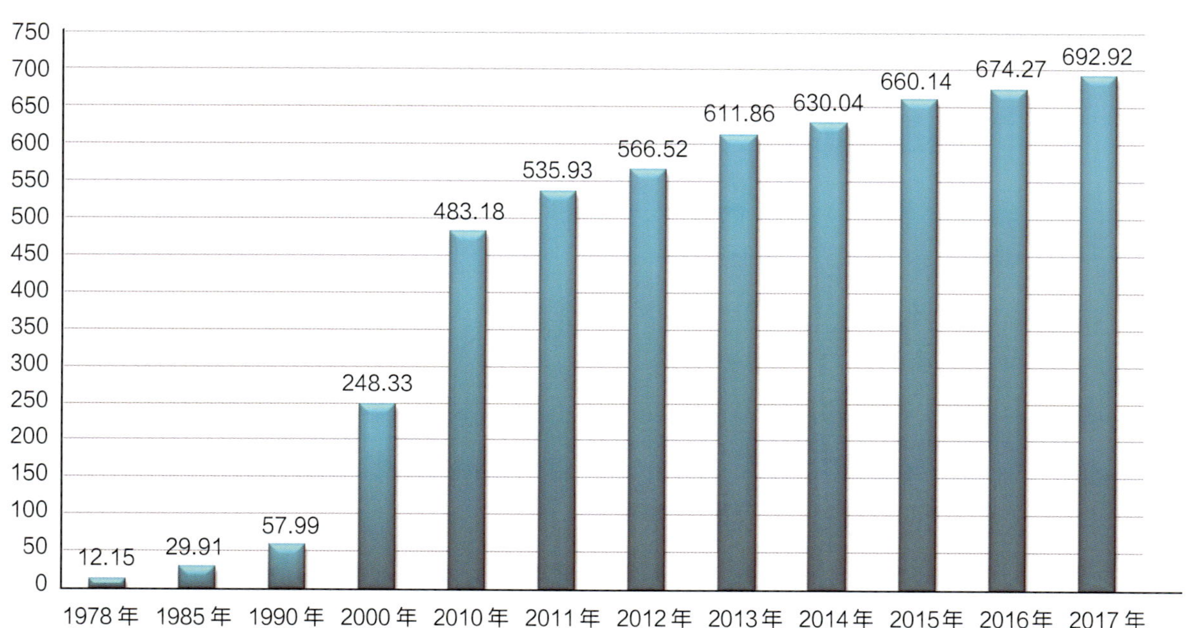

主要农产品产量（万吨）

Output Of Farm Products（10 000 tons）

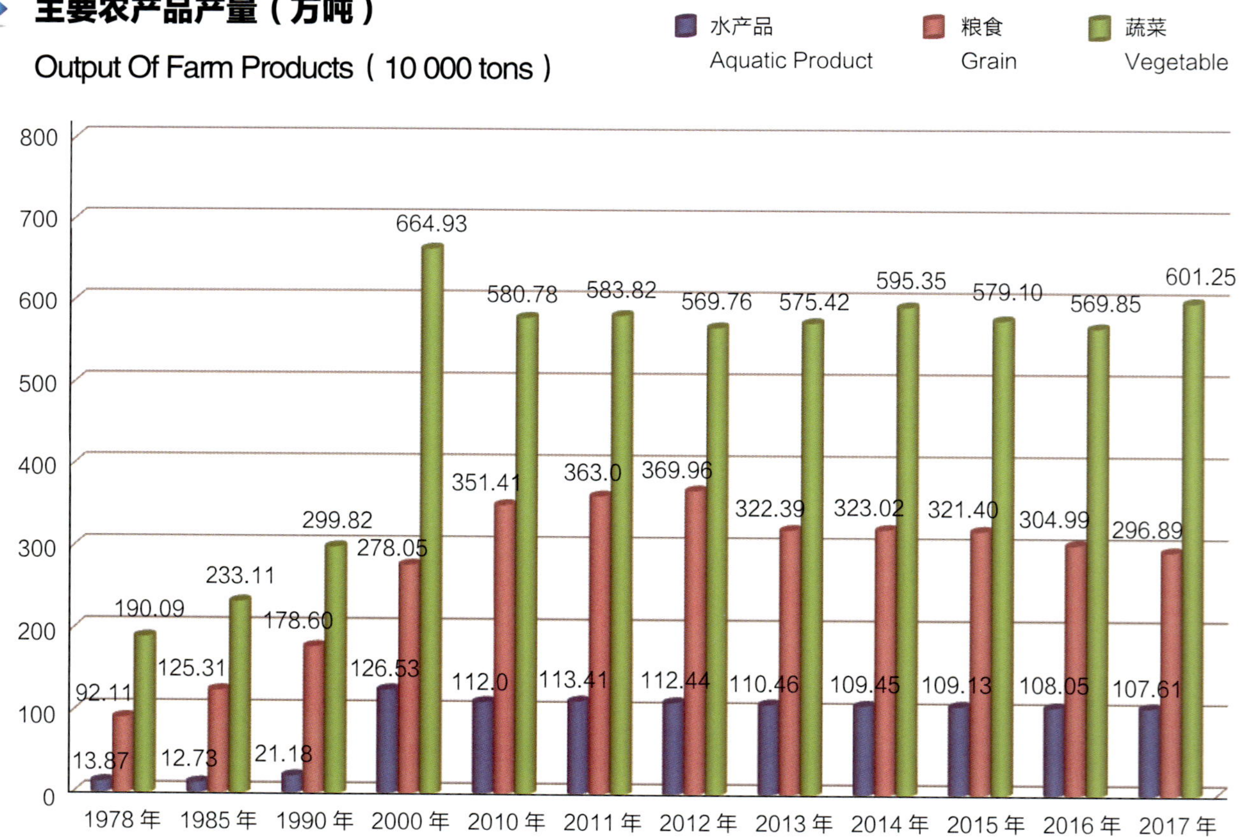

工业总产值（亿元）

Gross Industrial Output Value（100 million yuan）

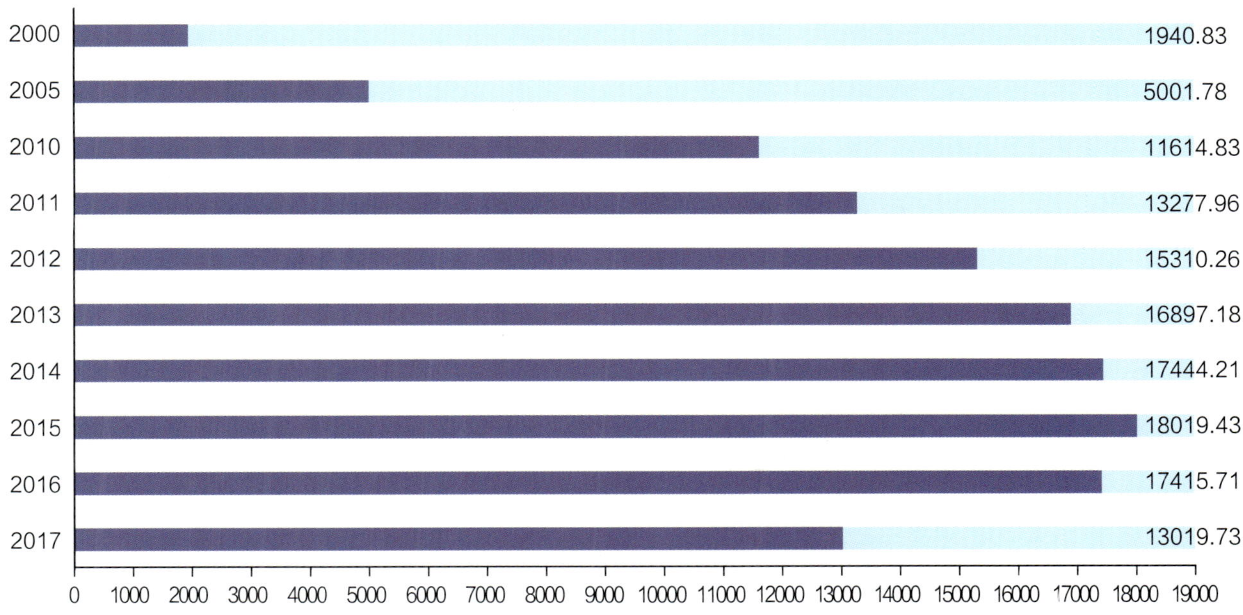

规模以上工业实现利润总额（亿元）

The Total Profits Made By The Industries Above The Designated Size（100 million yuan）

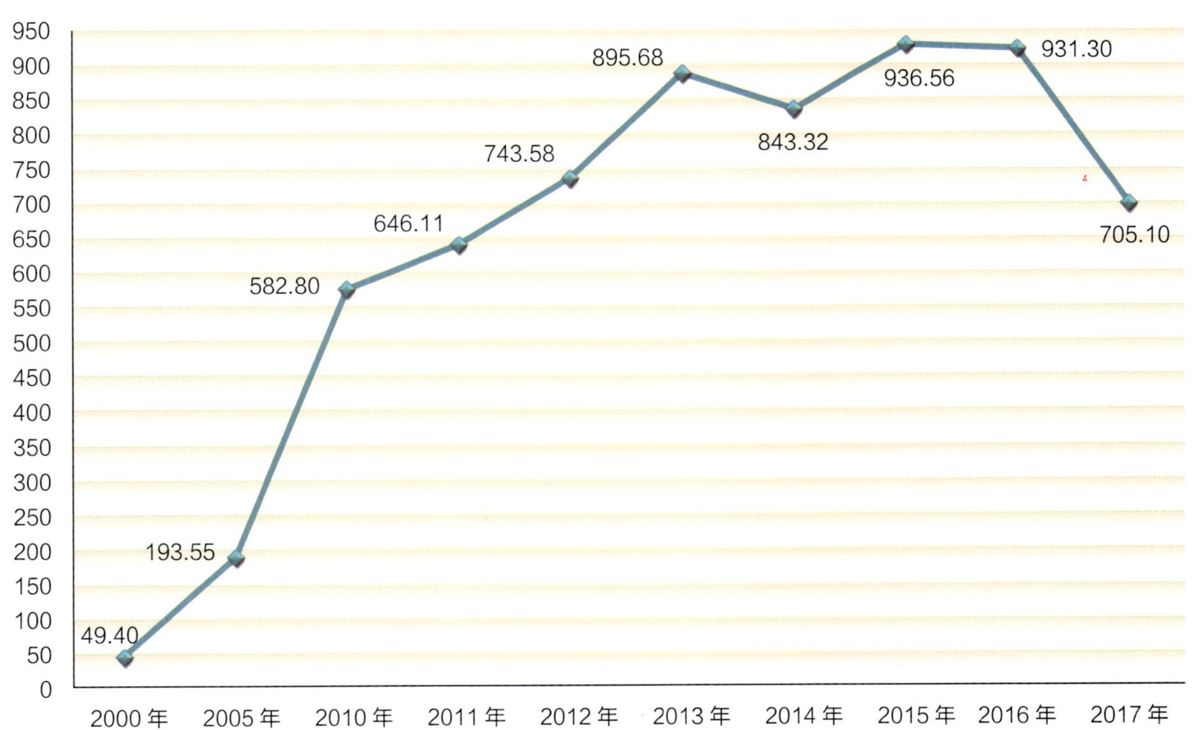

固定资产投资（亿元）

Investment In Fixed Assets（100 million yuan）

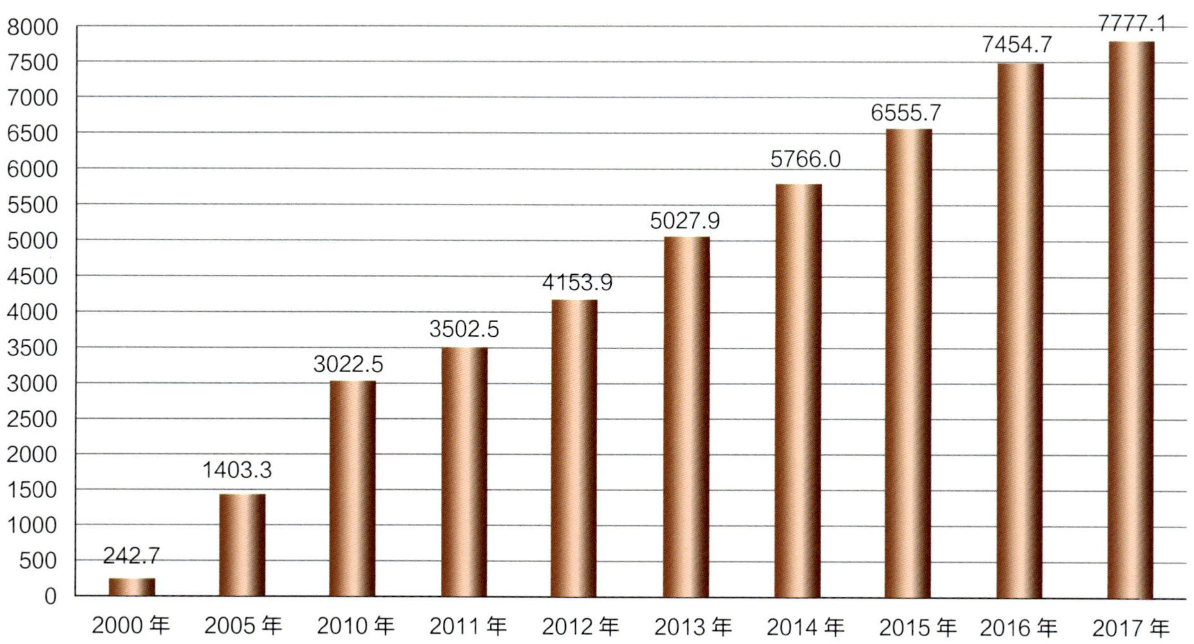

房地产开发投资（亿元）、房屋销售面积（万平方米）

Investrment In Real Estate Development（100 million yuan），Floor Space Of Commercial Buildings Sold（10 000 sq.m）

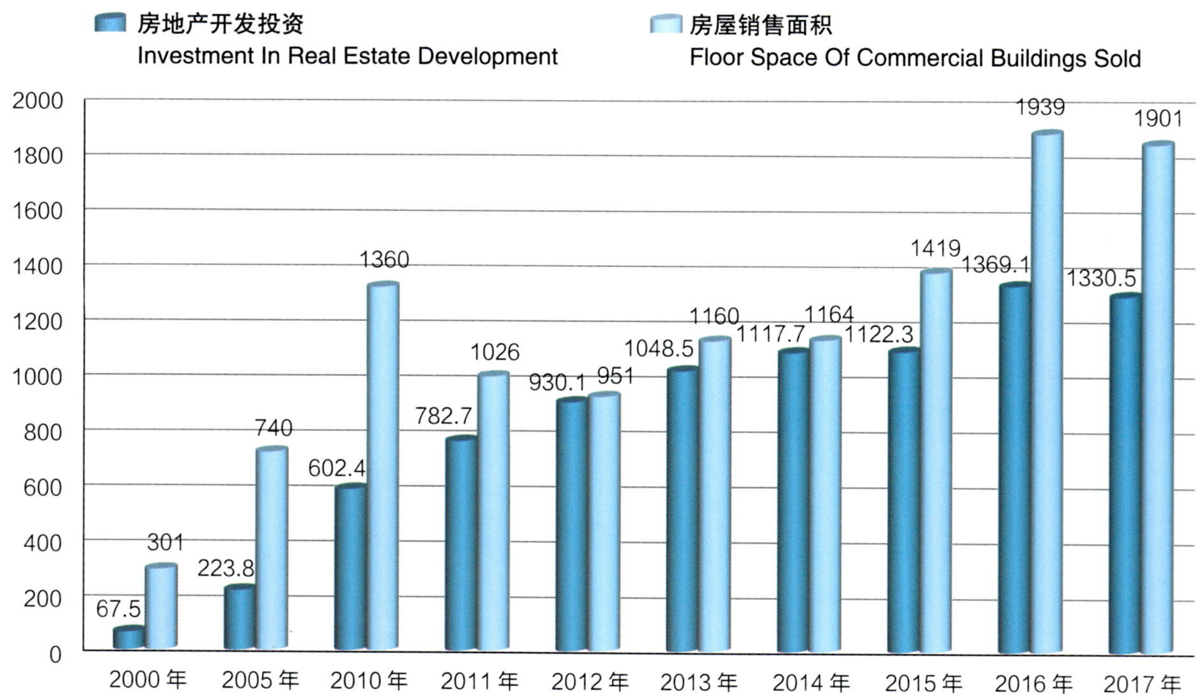

消费构成（%）（2017年）

2017 Composition Of Consumption（%）

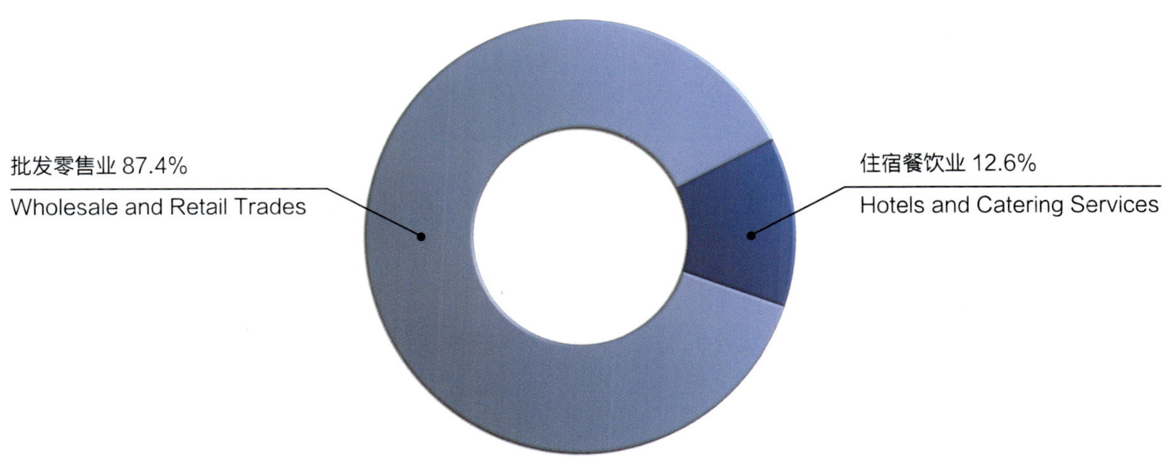

社会消费品零售总额（亿元）

Total Retail Sales Of Consumer Goods（100 million yuan）

旅游总人数（万人次）

Number Of Tourists（10 000 person-times）

入境旅游人数
Number Of Oversea Visitor Arrivals

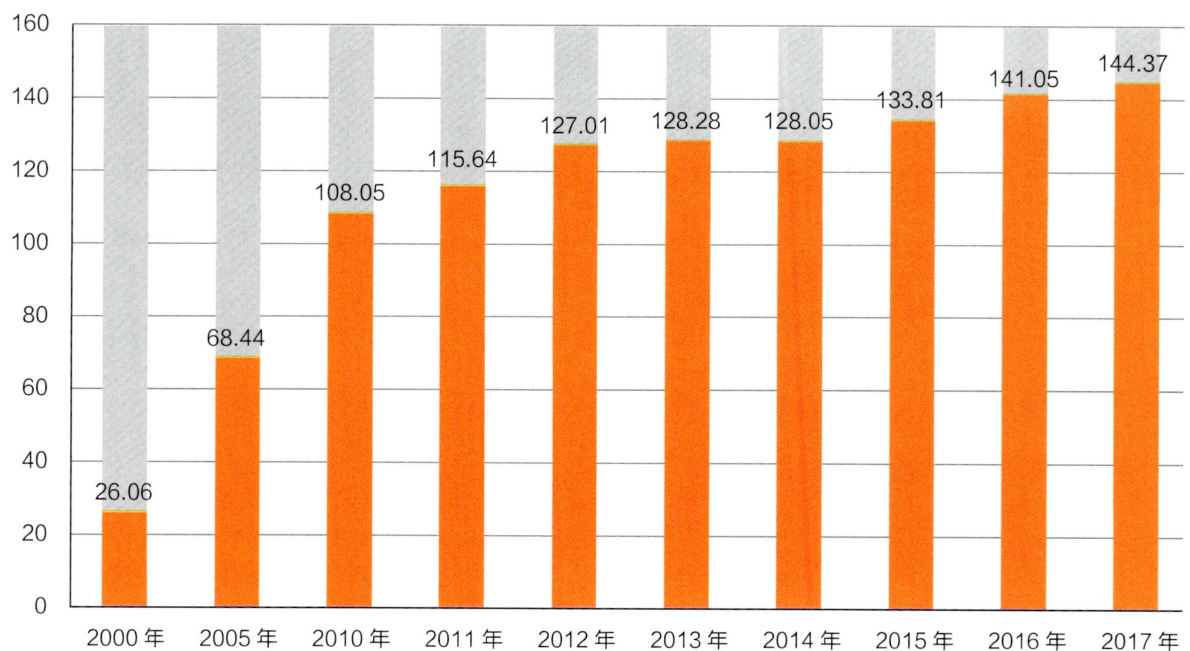

国内旅游人数
Number Of Domestic Tourists

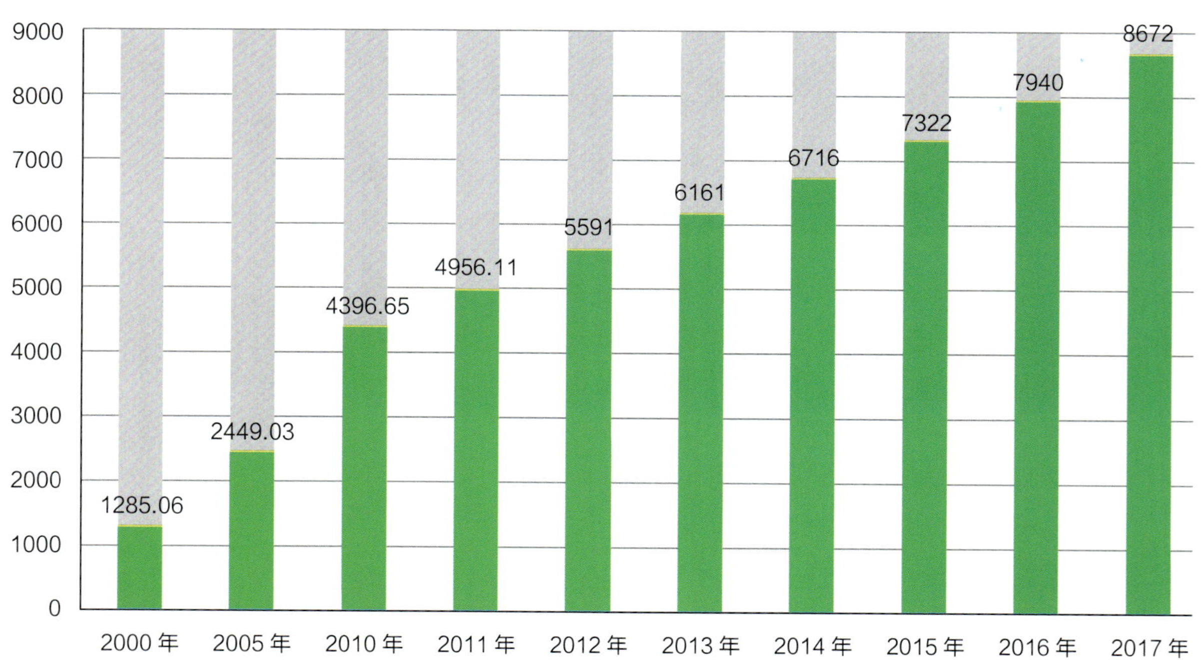

地方财政收入（亿元）

Revenue Of Local Government Finance（100 million yuan）

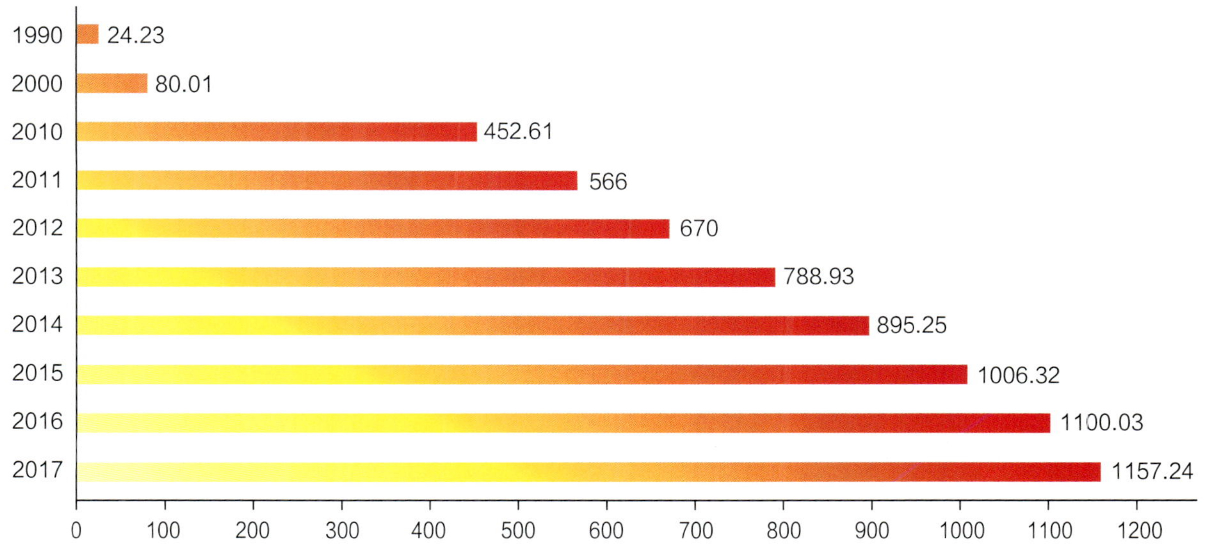

注：2002 年以后财政收入为一般预算收入数。

Note：Since 2002，revenue of government finance refers to general budgetary revenue.

金融机构年末人民币存贷款余额（亿元）

Year-end Savings Deposits And Loans Of Financial Institution（RMB）（100 million yuan）

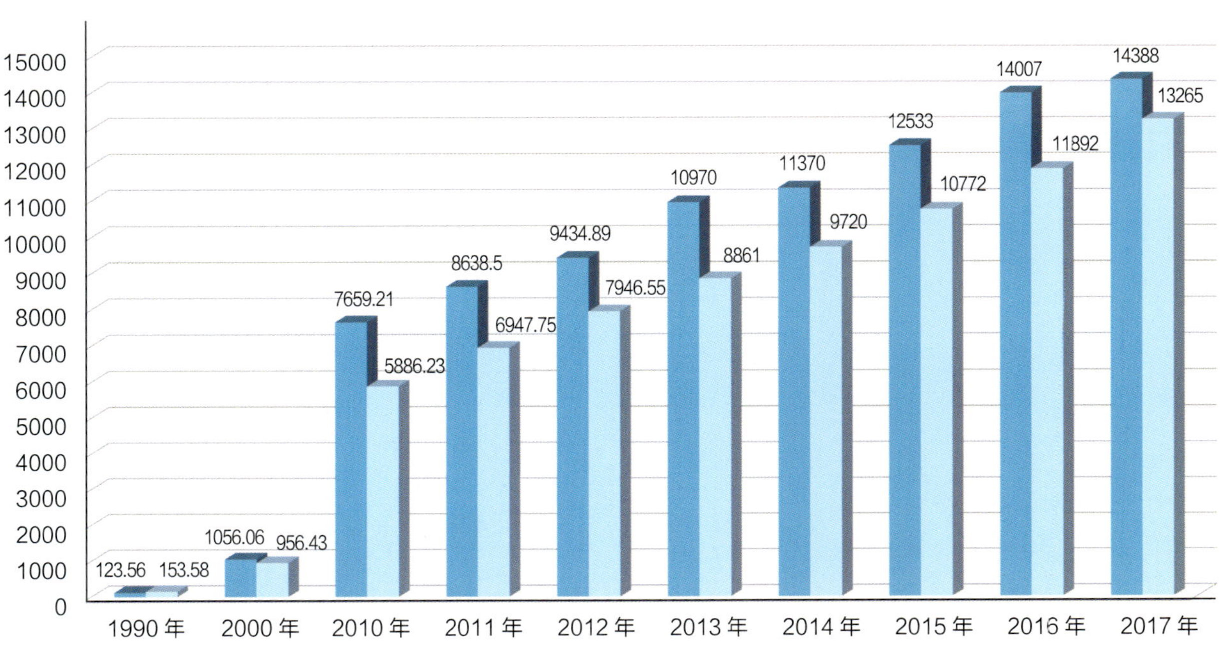

社会从业人数（万人）

Social Employment（10 000 persons）

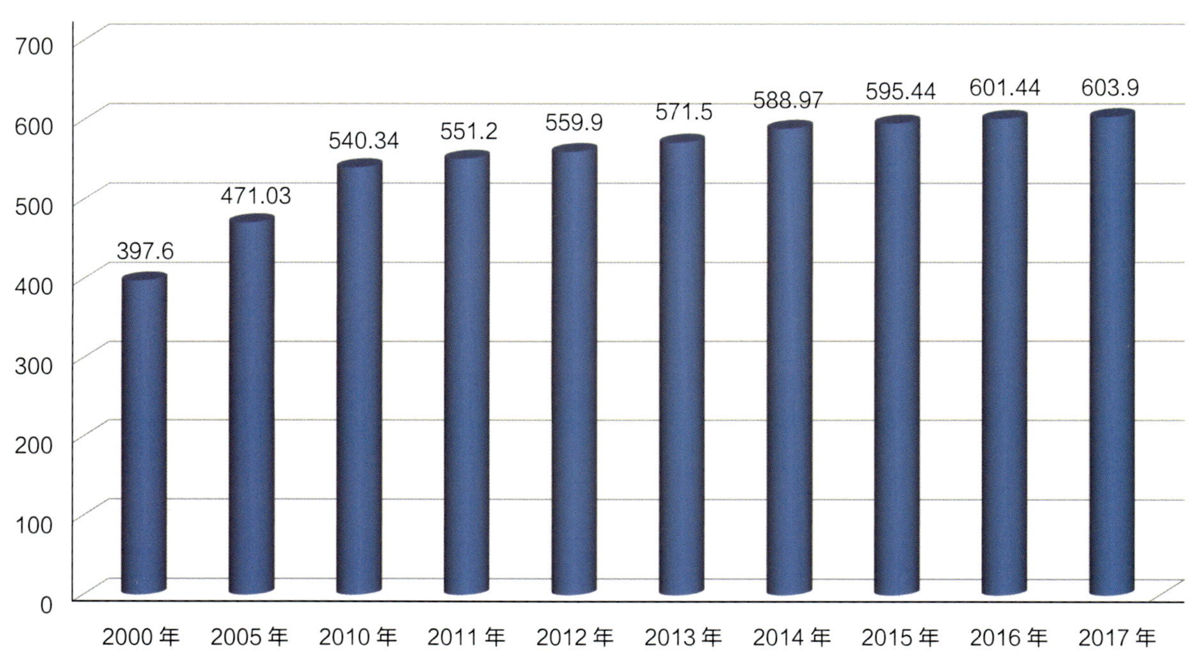

在岗职工平均工资（元）

Average Wage Of Employed Staff And Workers（yuan）

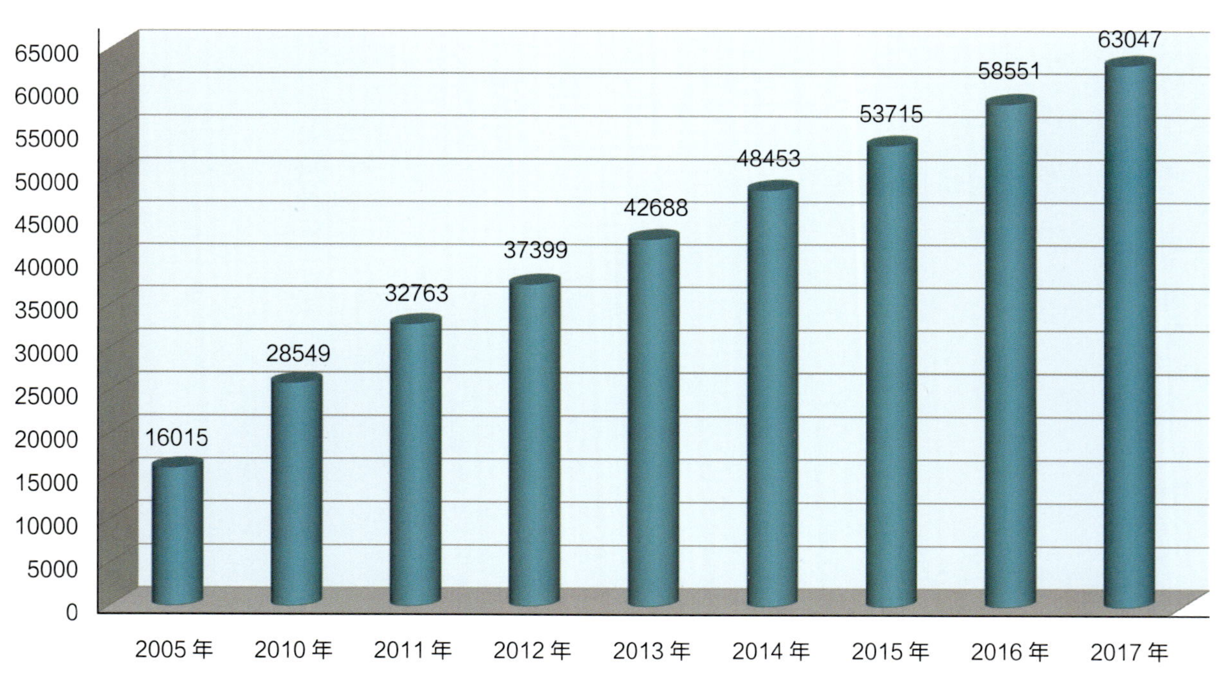

居民消费价格指数（上年＝100）

Consumer Price Indices（preceding year＝100）

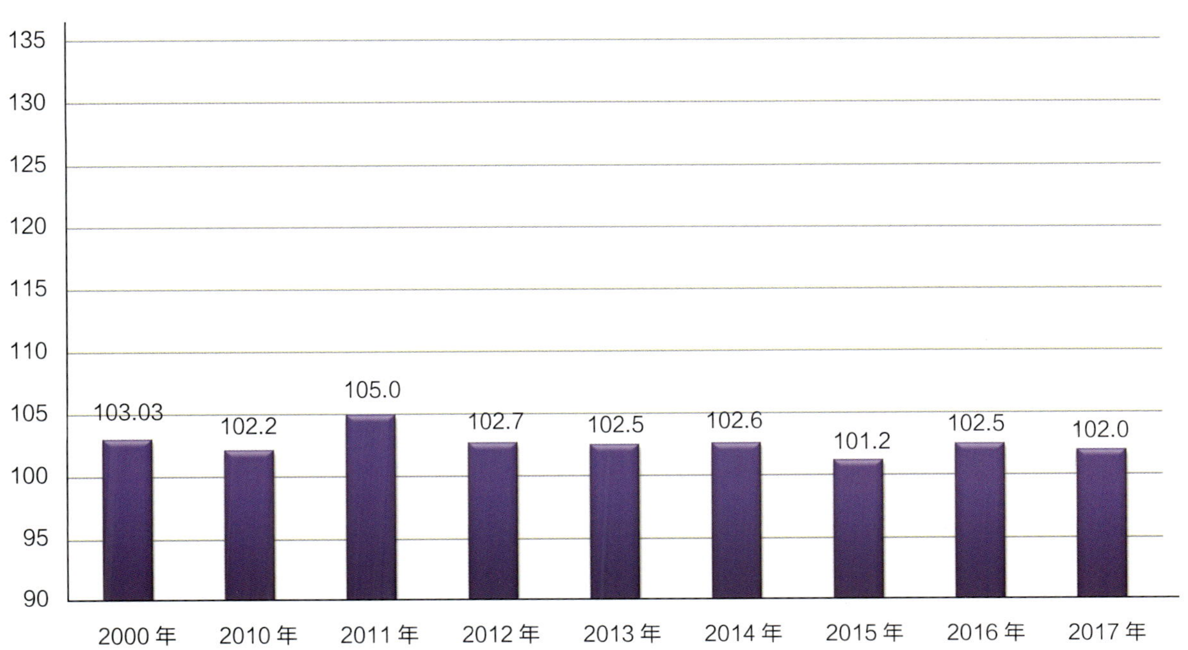

商品零售价格指数（上年＝100）

Retail Price Indices（preceding year＝100）

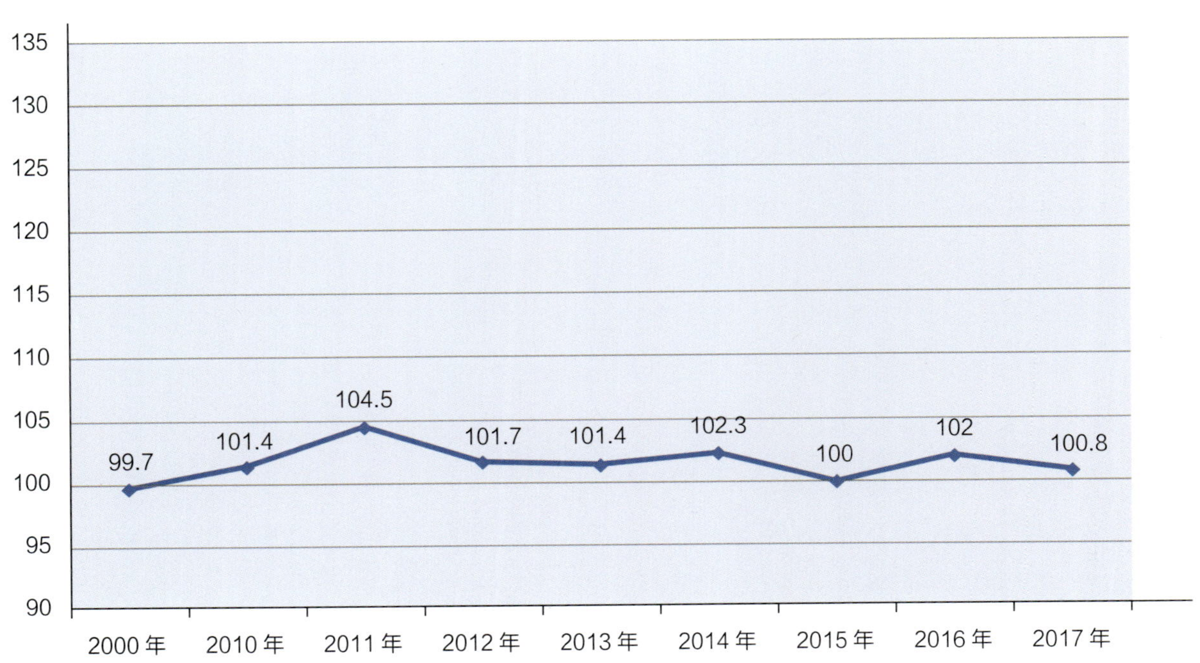

城市建成区面积、铺装道路面积

Developed Area Of the City And Area Of Roads

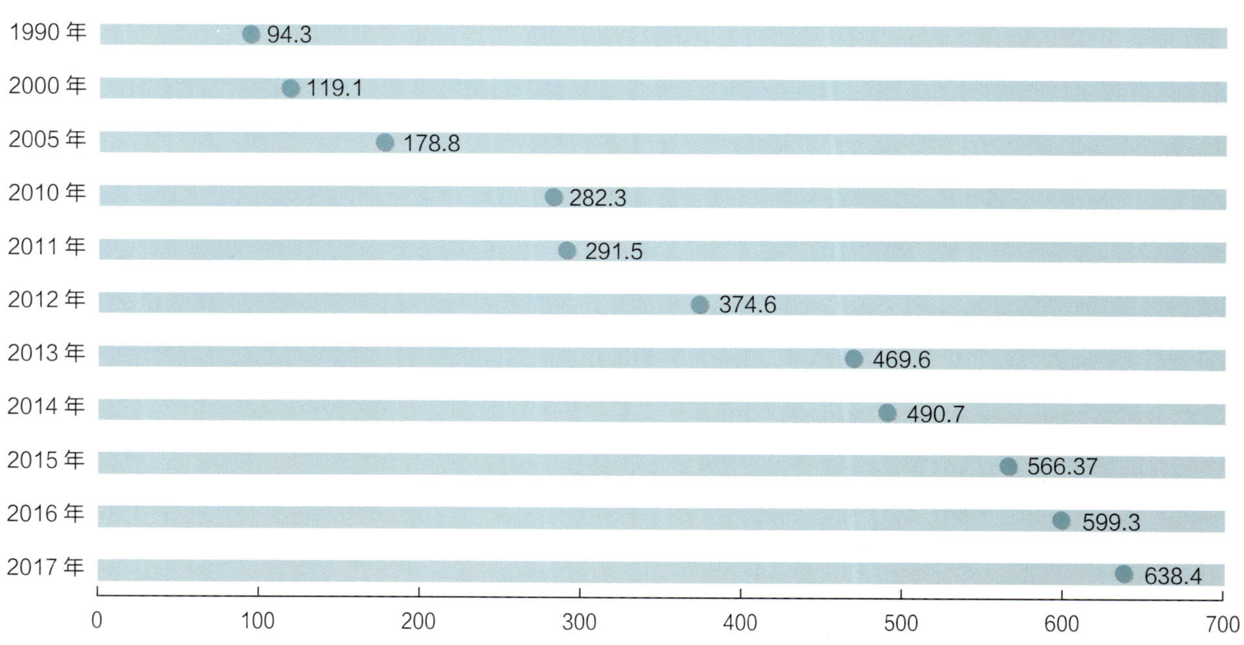

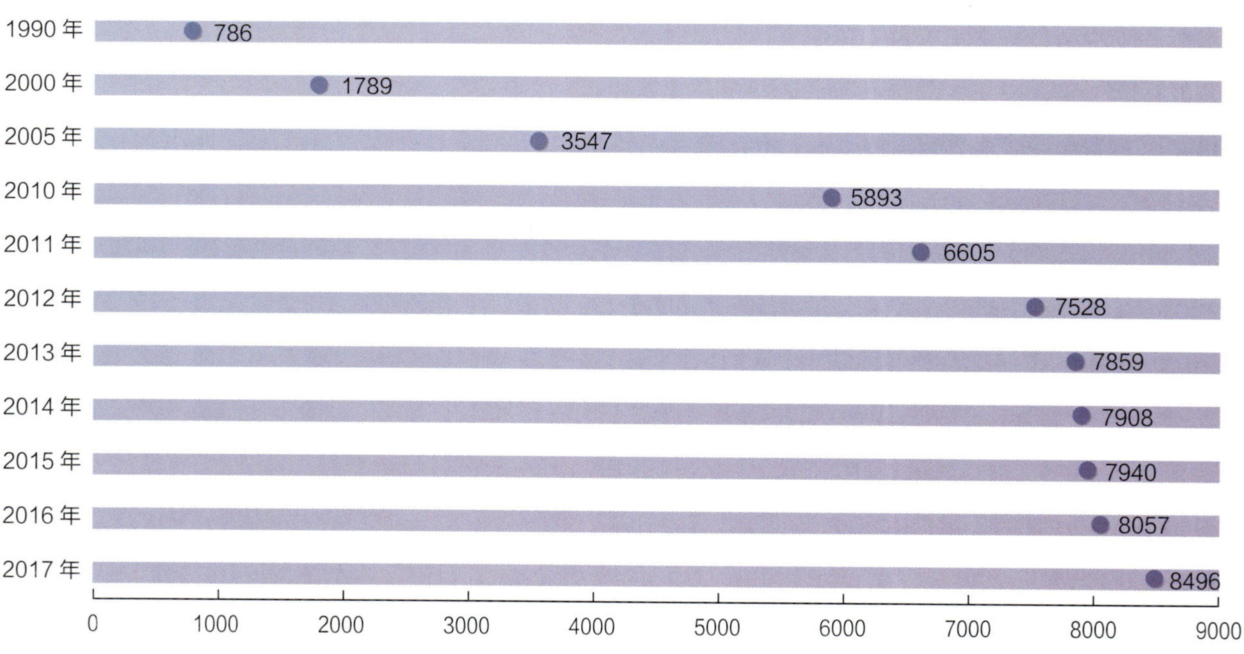

医疗卫生机构（个）

Health Care Institutions（unit）

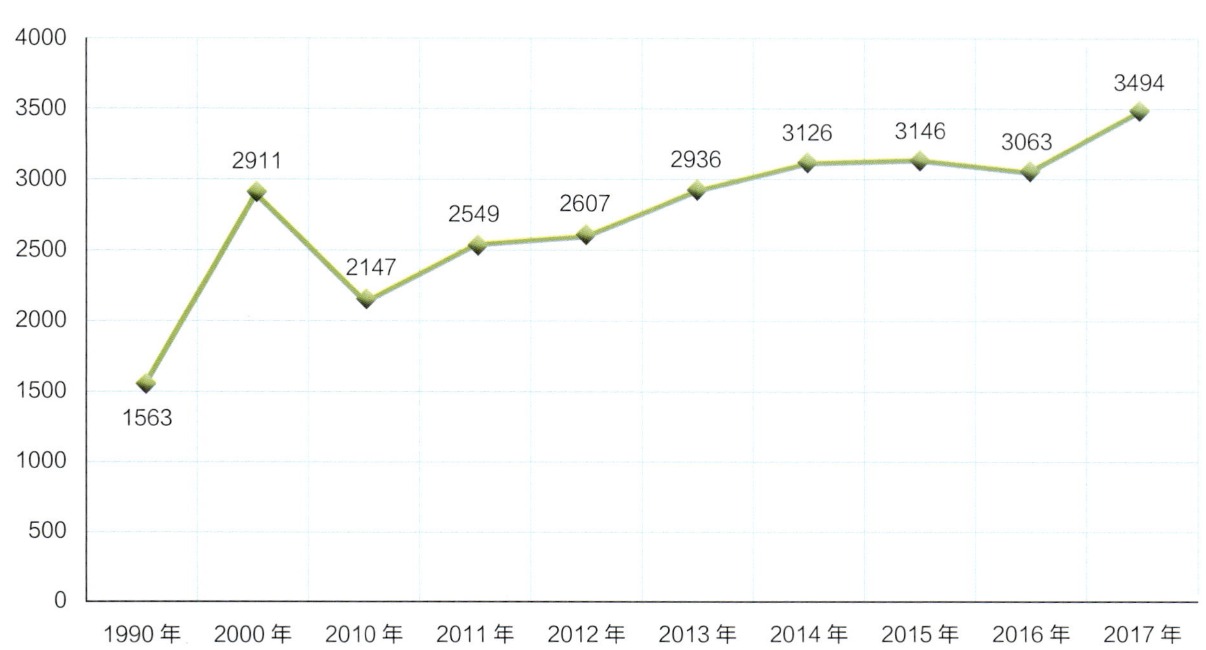

普通高校在校人数（万人）

Students Enrollment Of Regular Institutions Of Higher Education（10 000 persons）

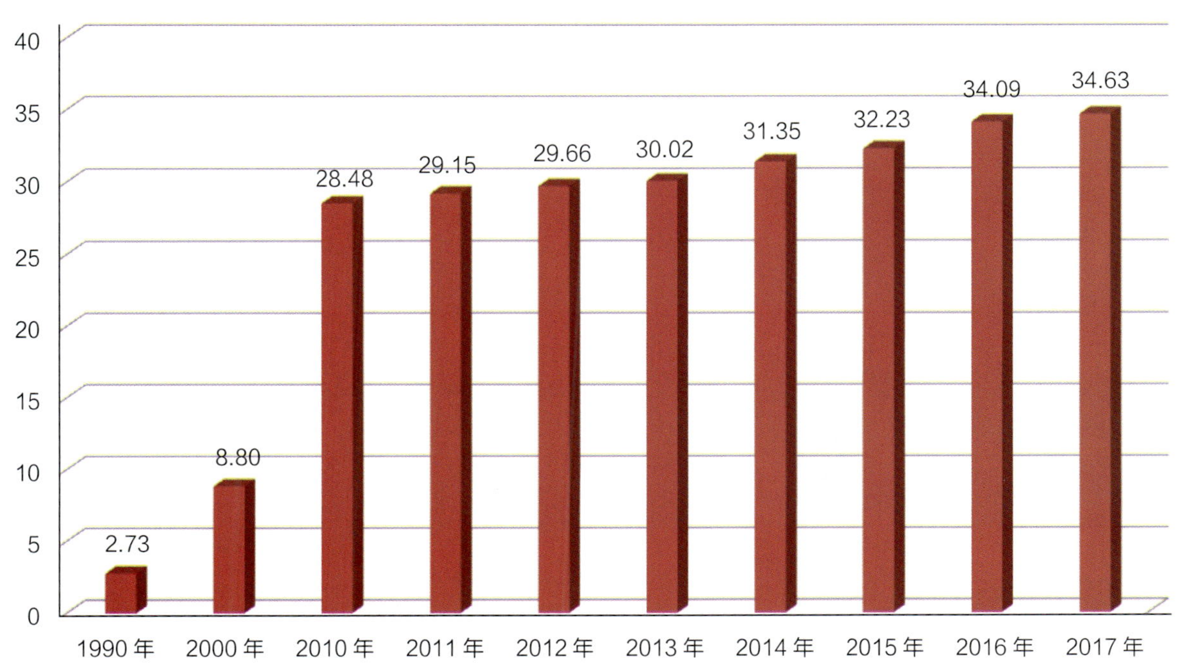

编辑委员会

EDITORIAL BOARD

编者说明

一、《青岛统计年鉴 -2018》是一部全面反映青岛市国民经济和社会发展情况、信息高度密集的资料工具书。

二、《青岛统计年鉴 -2018》共包括发展成果图、统计公报、统计表、附录四大部分。

统计表部分收录了 2017 年青岛市经济和社会等各方面的统计数据，以及建国以来重要年份和改革开放以来的主要统计数据，包括：综合，人口，从业人员及职工工资，固定资产投资，对外经济贸易，城市建设、环境保护，能源消耗，财政金融和保险业，价格指数，人民生活，农业，工业，建筑业，运输、邮电，批发和零售业，住宿、餐饮业和旅游，教育、科技和文化，体育、卫生和民政、司法。

为方便读者正确地使用年鉴资料，各篇章前设有《简要说明》，概括介绍各篇主要内容和资料来源；篇末还附有《主要统计指标解释》。

三、本《年鉴》部分历史数据已根据经济普查数据进行了调整，在此之前公布的数据凡与本年鉴数字不符的一律以本年鉴为准。

四、本年鉴中的符号说明：年鉴各表中的“空格”表示该项统计指标数据不足本表最小单位数、数据不详或无该项数据；“#”表示其中的主要项。

五、《青岛统计年鉴》自公开出版以来，受到社会各界的关心和支持，对于年鉴的内容和编辑工作提出了许多宝贵的意见，对此我们深表谢意。限于我们的水平，欢迎读者继续对年鉴的不足之处给予批评和指正，帮助我们进一步改进年鉴编辑工作，以期更好地为广大读者服务。

《青岛统计年鉴》编委会

2018 年 9 月

Editor's Note

Ⅰ. *Qingdao Statistical Yearbook 2018* is a very important reference book, which reflects various aspects of Qingdao's social and economic development and contains High-density information.

Ⅱ.The yearbook contains the following four parts: achievement graphs, statistic gazette, statistics and appendixes.

Statistics contains all kinds of data on Qingdao's social and economic development in 2017, and data in significant year or data since the beginning of reform and opening up, including: General Survey; Population; Employment and Wages; Investment in Fixed Assets; Foreign Trade; City Construction and Environment Protection ; Consumption of Energy; Government Finance ,Financial Intermediation and Insurance; Price; People's Living Conditions; Agriculture ; Industry ; Construction ; Transport, Postal and Telecommunication Services ; Wholesale and Retail Trades ; Hotels, Catering Services and Tourism ; Education, Science and Culture; Sports, Public Health and Civil Affairs, Judicial Affairs; Enterprises Survey.

In brief introduction at the beginning of each chapter, main coverage, data sources and statistical coverage are concerned. Meanwhile explanatory notes on major statistical indicators have been attached for readers to use the data correctly.

Ⅲ. All of the data in the book are in accordance with new administrative division.

Some of the data have been adjusted on the basis of statistics of economic census. In any case the data of this book shall be deemed as the authentic ones.

Ⅳ. Marks in this book:

"(blank)" indicates that the figure is not large enough to be measured with the smallest unit in the table, the data is not available, or the data is not available;

"#" indicates the major items of the total.

Ⅴ. Previous editions of Qingdao Statistical Yearbook have won wide acclaim among the readers. In order to excel, we welcome all candid comments and criticism from our readers.

Editorial Board

September, 2018

目　　录
CONTENTS

一、综　　合
Chapter 1.　GENERAL SURVEY

二、人　口
Chapter 2.　POPULATION

三、从业人员及职工工资
Chapter 3.　EMPLOYMENT AND WAGES

四、固定资产投资
Chapter 4.　INVESTMENT IN FIXED ASSETS

五、对外经济贸易
Chapter 5.　FOREIGN TRADE

六、城市建设、环境保护

Chapter 6.　COTY CONSTRUCTION AND ENVIRONMENT PROTECTION

七、能源消耗

Chapter 7. CONSUMPTION OF ENERGY

八、财政、金融和保险业

Chapter 8. GOVERNMENT FINANCE FINACIAL INTERMEDIATION AND INSURANCE

九、价格指数
Chapter 9. PRICE INDEXES

十、人民生活

Chapter 10.　PEOPLE'S LIVING CONDITIONS

十一、农 业
Chapter 11. AGRICULTURE

十二、工　　业
Chapter 12.　INDUSTRY

十三、建 筑 业
Chapter 13.　CONSTRUCTION

十四、运输、邮电
Chapter 14.　TRANSPORT，POSTAL AND TELECOMMUNICATION SERVICES

十五、批发和零售业
Chapter 15.　WHOLESALE AND RETAIL TRADES

十六、住宿、餐饮业和旅游
Chapter 16.　HOTELS，CATERING SERVICES AND TOURISM

十七、教育、科技和文化
Chapter 17.　EDUCATION SCIENCE & TECHNOLOY AND CULTURE

十八、体育、卫生和民政、司法

Chapter 18.　SPORTS，PUBLIC HEALTH AND CIVIL AFFAIRS，JUDICIAL AFFAIRS

附　录
APPENDIX

2017 年
青岛市国民经济和社会发展
统 计 公 报

青岛市统计局

国家统计局青岛调查队

（2018 年 3 月 16 日）

2017 年，全市以习近平新时代中国特色社会主义思想为指导，深入贯彻落实党的十九大精神，按照全市“创新 + 三个更加”目标要求和“一三三五”工作思路，在市委市政府的坚强领导下，坚持稳中求进工作总基调，以供给侧结构性改革为主线，加快实施新旧动能转换重大工程，经济保持持续健康发展，社会事业全面进步。

一、综 合

初步核算，2017 年全市生产总值 11037.28 亿元，按可比价格计算，增长 7.5%；其中，第一产业增加值 380.97 亿元，增长 3.2%；第二产业增加值 4546.21 亿元，增长 6.8%；第三产业增加值 6110.10 亿元，增长 8.4%。三次产业比例为 3.4:41.2:55.4。人均 GDP 达到 119357 元。

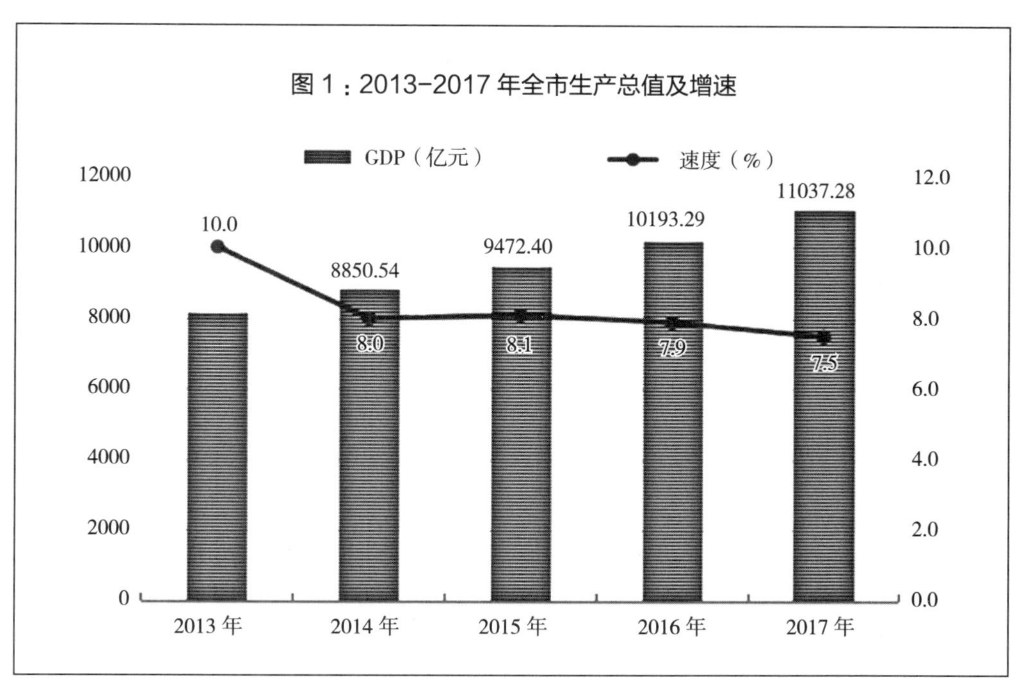

注：2013-2016 年全市生产总值及增速为研发支出计 DGP 入核算修订后数据。

表1：2017年全市分行业增加值及增速

行 业	总量（亿元）	增长(%)
全市生产总值	11037.28	7.5
农林牧渔业	403.36	3.6
工业	3952.87	6.7
建筑业	602.22	7.5
批发和零售业	1337.85	9.4
交通运输、仓储和邮政业	776.64	7.3
住宿和餐饮业	221.75	5.9
金融业	750.98	8.1
房地产业	587.36	1.1
其他服务业	2404.25	10.3

据初步测算，全年实现海洋生产总值2909亿元，增长15.7%（现价），占GDP比重为26.4%。全市现代服务业实现增加值3340.2亿元，增长8.4%，占GDP比重为30.3%。

年末全市常住总人口929.05万人，增长0.94%；其中，市区常住人口625.25万人，增长25.79%。

表2：2017年全市常住人口情况

区 市	年末数（万人）
全 市	929.05
市南区	58.53
市北区	109.32
李沧区	56.12
崂山区	43.87
西海岸新区	153.92
城阳区	70.93
即墨区	122.45
胶州市	89.33
平度市	138.05
莱西市	76.42
红岛经济区	10.11

全年财政总收入 3222 亿元，增长 13.4%。一般公共预算收入 1157.1 亿元，增长 7.1%；其中，税收收入 823.9 亿元，增长 11.4%；增值税 309 亿元，增长 31.7%；企业所得税 146.5 亿元，增长 18%；个人所得税 42.4 亿元，增长 16.4%；城市维护建设税 52.7 亿元，增长 4.7%。一般公共预算支出 1403 亿元，增长 3.4%；其中，一般公共服务支出 152.1 亿元，增长 7.9%；教育支出 253.8 亿元，增长 0.3%；科学技术支出 38.6 亿元，增长 59.8%；社会保障和就业支出 153.4 亿元，增长 14.7%；城乡社区事务支出 322.5 亿元，增长 9%。全年国税系统组织税收收入（含海关代征）1692 亿元，增长 24.8%；其中，国内税收 1017 亿元，增长 19.3%。地税各项收入 623.3 亿元，剔除"营改增"因素影响，同口径增长 17%。

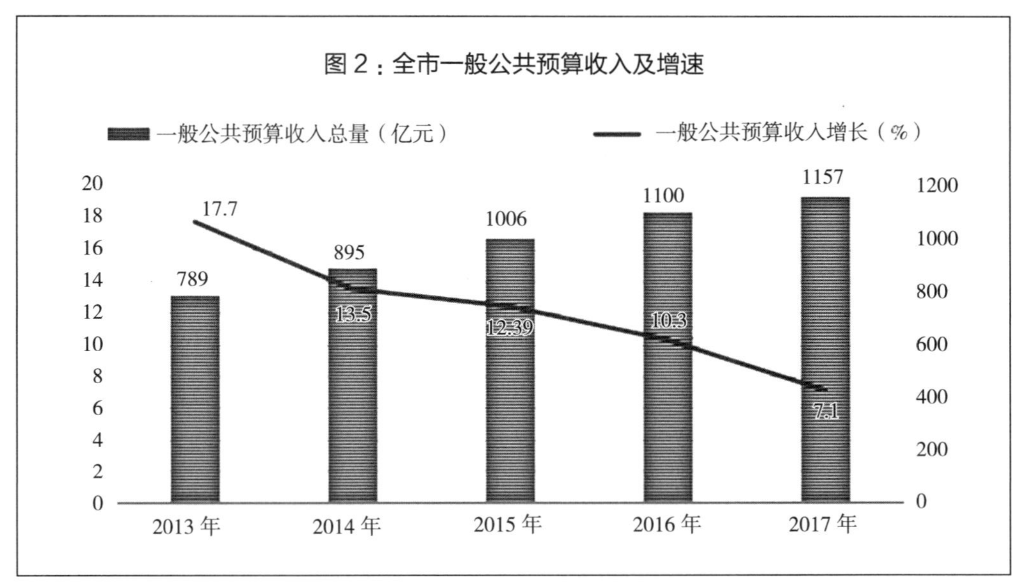

全年居民消费价格比上年上涨 2.0%，涨幅低于上年 0.5 个百分点；其中，食品价格下降 0.4%，非食品价格上涨 2.6%。

表3：2017年全市居民消费价格指数

指标名称	全年（上年同期=100）
居民消费价格总指数	102.0
非食品价格指数	102.6
服务价格指数	103.4
消费品价格指数	101.2
一、食品烟酒	100.9
食品	99.6
#粮食	104.8
鲜菜	94.5
猪肉	88.1
鸡蛋	98.3
二、衣着	100.5
三、居住	102.3
四、生活用品及服务	99.7
五、交通和通信	100.7
六、教育文化和娱乐	101.7
七、医疗保健	109.6
八、其他用品和服务	104.1

工业生产者出厂价格全年平均上涨4.4%,工业生产者购进价格全年平均上涨10.7%。

截止年末，全市实施贫困人口、贫（弱）村脱贫成效“双提升”工程，200个省定贫困村和310个市定经济薄弱村基本实现脱贫摘帽。

二、新动能与创新

全年全市高技术产业实现增加值579.5亿元，增长10.9%，占GDP比重为5.3%；其中，高技术制造业增加值290.1亿元，增长10.6%，占GDP比重为2.7%;高技术服务业增加值289.4亿元，增长11.2%，占GDP比重为2.6%。战略性新兴产业增加值1104.7亿元，增长10.9%，占GDP比重为10%;其中，战略性新兴产业工业增加值806.5亿元，增长11.7%，占GDP比重为7.3%；战略性新兴产业服务业增加值298.2亿元，增长9.1%，占GDP比重为2.7%。高附加值、高技术含量的产品快速增长：生产新能源汽车8.1万辆；智能电视1372万台；生产智能手机2062万部，增长20.3%；城市轨道车辆1276辆，增长80.2%。

全市规模以上服务业企业营业收入 1696.7 亿元，增长 15.1%；其中，体育服务业企业营业收入 2.9 亿元，增长 67.5%；广播、电视、电影和影视录音制作业营业收入 5.3 亿元，增长 27.9%；教育行业企业营业收入 13.1 亿元，增长 25.9%。

全年 134 家规模以上互联网和相关服务业及软件和信息技术服务业实现营业收入 132.3 亿元，增长 23.2%。全市 5 家电信运营商业务总量达 225 亿元，增长 72%，其中互联网相关业务总量占电信业务总量的 60% 以上。全市 70 家重点电子商务交易平台（电商企业或个人通过青岛本地电子商务交易平台实现的交易）实现交易额 10638 亿元，增长 31.7%。

全市技术合同交易额 126.66 亿元，增长 21.7%。涉海技术合同成交额 14.99 亿元，增长 21.8%。全年有效发明专利 21802 件，增长 19.2%。每万人有效发明专利拥有量 23.75 件，PCT 国际专利申请 761 件。国家知识产权示范企业 7 家，国家知识产权优势企业 52 家，国家技术创新示范企业 13 家，高新技术企业总数达到 2039 家。

截至年末，全市拥有世界名牌 2 个，山东省服务名牌 198 个；中国名牌产品 68 种，山东名牌产品 644 种，青岛名牌产品 773 种。

三、农　业

全年农林牧渔业分行业情况：种植业增加值 214.6 亿元，增长 4.5%；林业增加值 1.6 亿元，增长 5.1%；牧业增加值 77.9 亿元，增长 5.2%；渔业增加值 86.9 亿元，下降 1.0%。农林牧渔服务业增加值 22.4 亿元，增长 12%。

全年粮食播种面积 47.8 万公顷，蔬菜播种面积 10.8 万公顷，花生播种面积 8.2 万公顷。粮食总产量 296.9 万吨，受春旱影响，下降 2.7%；蔬菜及食用菌总产量 601.2 万吨，增长 5.5%；花生总产量 38.4 万吨，增长 3.9%；水果（含果用瓜）总产量 118.4 万吨，下降 1.7%。现代农业园区 889 个，新增 52 个；认证“三品一标”（无公害农产品、绿色食品、有机农产品和农产品地理标志）产品 926 个，其中国家地理标志保护产品 51 个。

全年新增造林 3.5 万亩，更新造林 1.1 万亩，修复退化林 5.7 万亩。

全年肉类总产量 54.3 万吨，下降 3.6%；禽蛋产量 17.7 万吨，下降 2.4%；奶类产量 30.9 万吨，下降 2.5%。

全年水产品产量（不包括远洋捕捞）107.6 万吨，下降 0.4%。海、淡水养殖面积 4.3 万公顷，下降 4.4%。远洋捕捞量 14.1 万吨，下降 0.4%。

农机总动力 728 万千瓦，增加 30 万千瓦。农作物生产综合机械化水平达到 87.2%。农田有效灌溉面积 33.0 万公顷，其中节水灌溉面积 17.8 万公顷。

表 4：2017 年主要种植业产品产量及增速

指　标	单位	产量	增长（%）
粮食	万吨	296.9	−2.7
夏粮	万吨	126.4	−12.8
秋粮	万吨	170.5	6.5
油料	万吨	38.8	5.1
蔬菜及食用菌	万吨	601.2	5.5
水果	万吨	118.4	−1.7
园林水果	万吨	75.2	2.8

四、工业与建筑业

全年全市规模以上工业增加值增长 7.5%。分经济类型看，国有控股企业增长 2.5%，集体企业增长 20.5%，股份制企业增长 6.9%，外商及港澳台商投资企业增长 8.1%，私营企业增长 10.7%。

分行业看，电气机械和器材制造业增长 14.2%，金属制品业增长 7.7%，农副食品加工业增长 11.7%，通用设备制造业增长 13.0%，石油加工、炼焦和核燃料加工业下降 8.2%，专用设备制造业增长 18.1%，铁路、船舶、航空航天和其他运输设备制造业增长 2.7%，汽车制造业增长 27.7%，非金属矿物制品业下降 2.1%，计算机、通信和其他电子设备制造业下降 7.2%，电力、热力生产和供应业增长 3.5%。装备制造业增加值增长 12.5%，占规模以上工业增加值的比重为 45.8%。

表 5：2017 年规模以上工业主要产品产量及增速

产品名称	单位	产量	增长（%）
彩色电视机	万台	1703.0	−19.4
其中：智能电视	万台	1371.7	−13.2
家用电冰箱	万台	818.7	−7.2
家用洗衣机	万台	603.4	−0.6
房间空气调节器	万台	1004.5	37.2
智能手机	万台	2062.1	20.3
啤酒	万千升	158.1	−2.6
橡胶轮胎外胎	万条	5452.9	8.3
平板玻璃	万重量箱	557.4	−3.2
粗钢	万吨	281.0	49.4
汽车	万辆	74.1	16.4
动车组	辆	1512	−24.6
城市轨道车辆	辆	1276	80.2
金属集装箱	万立方米	1272.6	11.5

规模以上工业利润增长 7.3%，其中，国有控股企业下降 0.4%，集体企业增长 23.5%，股份制企业增长 7.8%，外商及港澳台商投资企业下降 0.9%。

表6：2017年规模以上工业利润增速

指　标	增长(%)
规模以上工业利润	7.3
其中：国有控股	-0.4
集体企业	23.5
股份制企业	7.8
外商及港澳台投资企业	-0.9

全年建筑业实现增加值602.2亿元，增长7.5%。实现利税总额98.7亿元，增长9.1%。

五、固定资产投资

全市固定资产投资7777.1亿元，增长7.4%；其中，第一产业投资增长17.8%，第二产业投资下降9.3%，第三产业投资增长22.5%。战略性新兴产业投资增长5%，高技术投资增长15.5%。

全市亿元以上新开工项目（含房地产）701个，较上年增加102个，完成投资1984亿元，增长29%，占全市固定资产投资的比重为25.5%。

全年房地产开发完成投资1330.5亿元，下降2.8%；其中，住宅投资925.5亿元，下降3.2%。商品房销售面积1900.7万平方米，下降2%；其中，住宅销售面积1633.8万平方米，下降6.7%。商品房待售面积470万平方米，下降26.3%；其中，住宅待售面积210.1万平方米，下降41.6%。

表7：2017年全市房地产开发投资、商品房销售面积及增速

分　类	房地产开发投资（亿元）	增长（%）	商品房销售面积（万平方米）	增长（%）
总计	1330.5	-2.8	1900.7	-2.0
住宅	925.5	-3.2	1633.8	-6.7
办公楼	112.5	-5.7	97.9	76.3
商业营业用房	185.8	26.4	130.2	57.4
其他	106.7	-27.2	38.8	-20.6

全年保障性住房基本建成11569套，其中，公共租赁住房9111套，经济适用住房1503套，限价商品住房955套。截至年底，全市正在享受租赁补贴家庭共6557户，全年发放租赁补贴4628万元。

六、国内贸易

全年实现社会消费品零售额4541.0亿元，增长10.6%。按经营地统计，城镇消费品零售额3786.1亿元，增长

10.2%；乡村消费品零售额 754.9 亿元，增长 12.9%。分行业看，批发和零售业实现零售额 3967.0 亿元，增长 10.7%；住宿和餐饮业实现零售额 574.0 亿元，增长 10.2%。全年限额以上单位实现消费品零售额 1554.7 亿元，增长 12.8%。限额以上批发和零售业法人企业汽车类零售额 388.5 亿元，增长 9.1%；石油及制品类零售额 183.5 亿元，增长 11.2%；粮油、食品类零售额 145.6 亿元，增长 11.1%；日用品类零售额 58.5 亿元，增长 31.9%；化妆品类零售额 21.3 亿元，下降 8.8%。

七、对外经济

全市实现外贸货物进出口总额 5033.5 亿元，增长 15.7%；其中，出口额 3031.8 亿元，增长 7.5%；进口额 2001.7 亿元，增长 30.8%。对“一带一路”沿线国家市场进出口总额 2485.3 亿元，增长 11.2%；其中，出口 1601.1 亿元，增长 6.8%；进口 884.2 亿元，增长 20.1%。全市跨境电商进出口总额 241.3 亿元，增长 101.1%。

青岛口岸对外贸易进出口总额 11102.4 亿元，增长 16.9%；其中，出口额 6329.8 亿元，增长 12.0%；进口额 4772.6 亿元，增长 24.2%。

表 8：2017 年全市主要商品进出口情况

项　目	进出口		出　口		进　口	
	金额（亿元）	增长（%）	金额（亿元）	增长（%）	金额（亿元）	增长（%）
纺织服装	480.1	1.5	447.7	1.9	32.4	−3.2
农产品	713.8	13.3	357.5	9.0	356.3	18.0
机电产品	1765.1	10.1	1345.5	13.4	419.6	1.0
高新技术产品	499.7	6.9	300.8	11.6	198.9	0.6

表 9：2017 年对主要国家和地区货物进出口额及增速

国别（地区）	出口额（亿美元）	增长（%）	进口额（亿美元）	增长（%）
亚洲	189.9	2.6	121.4	17.6
香港	17.6	17.8	1.0	0.2
台湾	3.8	4.6	10.2	0.4
日本	52.8	5.8	17.9	−3.0
韩国	41.3	−0.2	30.4	−3.4
东盟	37.4	−4.1	44.4	80.9
南亚	13.9	−4.7	2.5	9.4
中东	21.5	7.9	7.4	−12.9

国别（地区）	出口额（亿美元）	增 长（%）	进口额（亿美元）	增 长（%）
非洲	16.9	−19.4	18.0	65.0
南非	4.0	18.7	2.2	11.9
欧洲	105.4	11.7	39.1	8.5
欧盟	82.3	12.9	24.3	−5.1
英国	13.0	−0.2	4.0	58.0
德国	14.7	4.2	6.8	−4.7
法国	8.6	24.1	3.3	−1.7
意大利	7.7	22.8	2.1	−25.5
独联体及东欧	21.6	8.8	12.0	47.0
俄罗斯	19.1	6.6	11.6	53.1
南美洲	29.4	10.4	54.4	56.0
巴西	4.2	29.1	24.4	30.3
北美洲	92.0	7.3	30.7	17.8
美国	82.9	6.3	25.7	15.3
加拿大	9.1	16.6	4.4	27.4
大洋洲	12.2	4.8	31.2	58.8
澳大利亚	10.1	4.1	27.1	56.1

注：本表非全口径。

全年全市实际到账外资金额 77.4 亿美元，增长 14.0%。引进青岛市以外国内资金 1887.2 亿元，增长 13.3%。全年新增备案对外投资项目 156 个，协议投资额 64.3 亿美元，新增实际投资额 10.2 亿美元，占全省 18.2%。全年对“一带一路”沿线国家和地区投资项目 68 个，协议投资额 21.9 亿美元。全市对外承包工程业务新承揽项目 120 个，新签合同额 44.1 亿美元，增长 18.3%，占全省 34%；完成营业额 38.2 亿美元，增长 4.9%，占全省 32.5%。全市对外劳务合作业务派出各类劳务人员 18294 人，占全省 25.6%。

八、交通运输、邮电和旅游业

全市港口吞吐量 5.1 亿吨，下降 0.3%；外贸吞吐量 3.7 亿吨，增长 7.9%；集装箱吞吐量 1831 万标准箱，增长 1.4%。

表 10：2017 年各种运输方式完成的运输量及增速

运输方式	单 位	运输量	增长 (%)
客运周转量	亿人公里	171.6	11.1
铁路	亿人公里	97.0	17.7
公路	亿人公里	74.4	3.6
水运	亿人公里	0.2	-6.6
货运周转量	亿吨公里	1507.0	10.3
铁路	亿吨公里	183.0	8.1
公路	亿吨公里	515.9	9.7
水运	亿吨公里	808.1	11.1

年末拥有国内航线 157 条，国际航线 27 条，港澳台地区航线 2 条，全年航空旅客吞吐量达到 2321.1 万人次，增长 13.2%；航空货邮吞吐量 23.2 万吨，增长 0.6%。全年完成邮电业务总量 327.5 亿元，增长 58.3%；其中，邮政业务总量 72.5 亿元，增长 23.7%；电信业务总量 255 亿元，增长 72%。快递业务量 3.11 亿件，增长 24.7%。固定宽带互联网用户 369.3 万户，增长 25.4%。全市移动电话 1410 万户，其中 3G 和 4G 用户 790.1 万户。

年末全市机动车保有量 261.45 万辆，增长 12.1%；其中，私人汽车 212.26 万辆，增长 11.4%。

地铁实现 3 号线安全运营和 2 号线东段顺利开通，2 条线运营总长度 44.8 公里，地铁车站总数 40 座。全年开行列车 11.9 万列次，总运营里程 291.9 万列公里，总客运量 6573.2 万人次。

全年全市社会物流总额 30198.5 亿元，增长 9.8%；物流产业增加值 987.1 亿元，增长 8.9%。

全年全市接待游客总人数 8816.5 万人次，增长 9.1%；实现旅游消费总额 1640.1 亿元，增长 14.0%。其中，接待入境游客 144.4 万人次，增长 2.4%；入境游客消费 10.2 亿美元，增长 4.1%。接待国内游客 8672.1 万人次，增长 9.2%；国内游客消费 1468.1 亿元，增长 14.4%。年末拥有 A 级旅游景区 123 处，其中，5A 级旅游景区 1 处，4A 级旅游景区 24 处 ,3A 级旅游景区 74 处。拥有星级酒店 104 个，其中，5 星级酒店 9 个，4 星级酒店 27 个，3 星级酒店 63 个。拥有旅行社 504 个，其中，经营出境旅游业务旅行社 52 个，经营入境和国内旅游业务旅行社 452 个。

九、金融业

年末金融机构本外币存款余额 15129 亿元，比年初增加 456.3 亿元；人民币存款余额 14387.8 亿元，比年初增加 381.7 亿元，其中，住户存款 5394.2 亿元，比年初增加 68.8 亿元。本外币贷款余额 14388.4 亿元，比年初增加 1436.7 亿元；人民币贷款余额 13264.8 亿元，比年初增加 1376.7 亿元。

保险业实现保费收入 396.7 亿元，增长 18.1%。其中，产险公司实现保费收入 110.6 亿元，增长 2%；寿险公司实现保费收入 286.1 亿元，增长 25.8%。

证券公司代理买卖证券交易金额 35263.4 亿元，增长 2.4%。年末私募基金机构 191 家，管理基金规模 489.4 亿元，增长 8.1%。境内外上市公司累计 43 家，比上年增加 5 家。“新三板”、蓝海股权交易中心挂牌企业分别为 114 家和 1124 家，分别比上年增加 22 家、570 家。

十、科技、创业孵化和人才

初步统计，全市共取得重要科技成果 588 项。获得国家级科技奖励 9 项，其中，技术发明奖 3 项，科技进步奖 6 项；获得省级科技奖励 52 项，其中，最高奖 1 项，自然科学奖 7 项，技术发明奖 3 项，科技进步奖 41 项。

全市国家级创业孵化载体达到 129 家，其中，国家备案众创空间 80 家，国家级星创天地 30 家，国家级孵化器 19 家。累计认定各级孵化器、众创空间 320 家，孵化器入驻企业 1.3 万家，毕业企业 740 家。

全市全年共引进各类人才 13.14 万人，增长 8.5%；其中，引进博士 1668 人，硕士 1.34 万人，本科学历 6.67 万人，专科及以下学历 4.96 万人。

十一、教育、卫生和体育

年末全市共有各类大专院校（含民办高校）25 所，其中，普通高校 23 所；全年研究生招生 1.4 万人，在学研究生 3.7 万人，毕业生 0.9 万人（不含驻青科研院所研究生）。普通本专科招生 9.9 万人，在校生 34.6 万人，毕业生 9.5 万人。中等职业教育招生 2.9 万人，在校生 8.8 万人，毕业生 2.5 万人。接受中等职业教育的学生占高中阶段在校生的 50.8%。普通高中招生 4 万人，在校生 11.7 万人，毕业生 3.7 万人。初中招生 9.3 万人，在校生 25.5 万人，毕业生 7.9 万人。普通小学招生 9.4 万人，在校生 55.1 万人，毕业生 9.3 万人。特殊教育招生 0.04 万人，在校生 0.3 万人，毕业生 0.05 万人。幼儿园在园幼儿 25.3 万人。

年末全市共有卫生机构（不含村卫生室）3494 处，其中，医院、卫生院 410 处，疾病预防控制中心 25 处，妇幼保健机构 12 处，门诊部（所）、诊所、卫生所、医务室 2670 处。年末各类卫生技术人员 7.6 万人，其中，医生 3.1 万人。全市拥有医疗床位 6.1 万张，其中，医院、卫生院床位 5.3 万张。

全市运动员在各项比赛中共获得金牌 1342 枚，银牌 805 枚，铜牌 874 枚。重点体校 2 所，学员 1061 人；业余体校 10 所，学员 1537 人。

十二、城市建设

年末全市常住人口城镇化率达到 72.57%，比上年提高 1.04 个百分点。全市建成区面积 638.4 平方公里。城市平均每天供水量 119.4 万吨，增长 1.2%。城市全年实际用水量 3.8 亿吨，其中生产用水和生活用水分别为 1.2 亿吨和 2.6 亿吨。

城市使用液化气、天然气的总户数达到 202.5 万户，全年供应液化气总量 3.7 万吨，供应天然气总量 9.2 亿立方米。城市气化率达到 100%。

全年新增供热面积 400 万平方米，年末供热面积达到 1.9 亿平方米。

年末市区公共汽、电车线路 477 条。共有营运的公交汽、电车 7208 辆。共有出租汽车 10055 辆。年末市区共有地铁线路 2 条，年客运量 6573.2 万人次，日均客运量 18 万人次。

全市共有公共厕所 660 座，三类以上的 660 座，新增 17 座，改建 62 座。

年末城市道路总长度 4697 公里，城市下水道总长度 7667 公里。

十三、能源、环境和安全生产

初步统计，全年全市规模以上工业综合能源消费量 1493 万吨标准煤，增长 3.3%；其中，煤炭消费量 1385 万吨，下降 4.1%；原油消费量 1524 万吨，增长 0.3%；天然气消费量 5.3 亿立方米，增长 22.2%。全社会用电量 401 亿千瓦时，增长 9.2%；其中，工业用电 232 亿千瓦时，增长 9.1%；城乡居民生活用电 75 亿千瓦时，增长 7.7%。

全年全市能源生产量 2775 万吨标准煤，下降 0.9%；其中，原油加工量 1523 万吨，增长 1%；汽油生产量 456 万吨，下降 0.9%；柴油生产量 408 万吨，下降 2.7%；发电量 182 亿千瓦时，增长 0.1%。新能源发电量 13.5 亿千瓦时，增长 29.9%；其中，风力发电量增长 28.7%，生物质发电量增长 24.1%。新能源发电量占全市发电总量比重为 7.5%，提高 1.7 个百分点。

全市年平均气温 13.9℃，平均年降水量为 687 毫米。“蓝天白云，繁星闪烁”天数为 342 天，较上年增加 24 天。主要污染物细颗粒物 (PM2.5)、二氧化硫、二氧化氮年均值分别为 37、14、33 微克 / 立方米，与上年相比 ,PM2.5 改善 17.8%, 二氧化硫改善 30%，二氧化氮增长 3.1%。全市近岸海域水质达到或好于二类海水水质标准的点位数占 90.6%，提升 6.2 个百分点。市区区域环境噪声平均值 57.3 分贝，市区交通干线噪声平均值 68.7 分贝。

全市七个行业（领域）发生各类生产安全事故 106 起，死亡 111 人，分别下降 54.7% 和 33.9%。亿元 GDP 生产安全事故死亡率 0.01，十万工矿商贸企业就业人员生产安全事故死亡率 1.05，道路交通事故万车死亡 1.24 人。

十四、人民生活和社会保障

全年全市居民人均可支配收入 38763 元，增长 8.6%。按常住地分，城镇居民人均可支配收入 47176 元，增长 8.2%；农村居民人均可支配收入 19364 元，增长 7.8%。全市居民人均可支配收入中位数 36285 元。全市居民人均消费支出 25232 元，增长 8.5%，恩格尔系数为 29.7%。按常住地分，城镇居民人均消费支出 30569 元，增长 8.1%；农村居民人均消费支出 12928 元，增长 7.7%。

表 11：2017 年城乡居民人均可支配收入构成情况

指标名称	全体居民		城镇居民		农村居民	
	绝对值（元）	增长（%）	绝对值（元）	增长（%）	绝对值（元）	增长（%）
可支配收入	38763	8.6	47176	8.2	19364	7.8
工资性收入	23514	8.4	28992	7.8	10882	8.0
经营净收入	7485	6.8	7299	6.6	7913	7.2
财产净收入	3082	10.8	4297	9.9	280	9.0
转移净收入	4682	11.8	6588	10.8	289	12.2

表 12：2017 年城乡居民人均消费支出情况

指标名称	全体居民		城镇居民		农村居民	
	绝对值（元）	增长（%）	绝对值（元）	增长（%）	绝对值（元）	增长（%）
消费支出	25232	8.5	30569	8.1	12928	7.7
食品烟酒	7489	7.2	9059	6.9	3869	6.0
衣着	2467	8.6	3117	8.1	971	7.3
居住	5454	8.7	6605	8.2	2801	8.3
生活用品及服务	1747	8.7	2121	8.1	885	8.8
交通和通信	3753	7.9	4399	7.6	2262	7.0
教育文化娱乐	2347	13.1	2875	12.6	1129	12.4
医疗保健	1350	9.5	1624	9.0	717	9.0
其他用品和服务	625	6.0	769	5.2	294	6.8

表 13：2017 年每百户居民家庭主要耐用消费品拥有量

指标名称	单 位	数 量		
		全体居民	城镇居民	农村居民
家用汽车	辆	57	60	48
摩托车	辆	31	15	70
电冰箱（柜）	台	98	95	106
洗衣机	台	93	91	98
热水器	台	93	94	90
空调	台	95	101	78
彩色电视机	台	103	100	110
计算机	台	72	80	52
中高档乐器	架	11	14	3
移动电话	部	211	205	223

据抽样调查，年末城镇居民人均现住房建筑面积 32.7 平方米，农村居民人均现住房建筑面积 34.8 平方米。

全年城镇新增就业 73 万人，增长 13.4%；其中，本市劳动者就业增长 8.9%，外来劳动者来青就业增长 19.3%。服务业吸纳就业 45.3 万人，增长 13.8%。民营经济吸纳就业 55.1 万人，增长 16.3%。

年末全市城镇居民最低生活保障人数达 24220 人，城镇居民最低生活保障资金 23815.6 万元；农村五保供养人数 4687 人，农村五保供养支出 6257 万元。

年末全市城镇职工基本养老保险参保缴费人数为 258.7 万人，参加失业保险人数为 210.3 万人，全年累计领取失业保险金的人数为 7.83 万人。全市城镇登记失业率为 3.12%，降低 0.05 个百分点。

注：

1、公报中统计数据均为初步统计数。

2、全市生产总值（GDP）及各产业增加值绝对数按现价计算，增长速度按可比价计算。根据《三次产业划分规定》（国统字〔2012〕108 号），农林牧渔业中的农林牧渔服务业，工业中的开采辅助活动以及金属制品、机械和设备修理业等三个行业划入第三产业。

3、常住人口包括：①住本户、户口在本乡镇街道的人（含户口在本户，外出不满半年的人）；②住本户半年以上，户口在外乡镇街道的人；③住本户不满半年，户口在外乡镇街道，离开户口登记地半年以上的人；④住本户，户口待定的人。

4、PCT（Patent Cooperation Treaty）是《专利合作条约》的英文缩写。PCT 国际专利是指我国专利申请人根据 PCT 规定，可以向中国专利局或向世界知识产权组织提交国际专利申请，是反映地区外向型经济发展水平和地区国际技术竞争能力的重要指标。

5、战略性新兴产业根据国家规划，现阶段主要包括节能环保、新一代信息技术、生物、高端装备制造、新能源、新材料、新能源汽车等七个产业领域。

6、规模以上工业企业为年主营业务收入 2000 万元及以上企业。限额以上贸易企业为批发业年主营业务收入在 2000 万元及以上、零售业 500 万元及以上、住宿和餐饮业 200 万元及以上的单位。固定资产投资项目统计的起点标准为计划总投资额500万元。规模以上服务业企业，一是指年营业收入1000万元及以上或年末从业人员50人及以上服务业法人单位。包括：交通运输、仓储和邮政业，信息传输、软件和信息技术服务业，租赁和商务服务业，科学研究和技术服务业，水利、环境和公共设施管理业，教育，卫生和社会工作；以及物业管理、房地产中介服务、自有房地产经营活动和其他房地产业等行业。二是指年营业收入500万元及以上或年末从业人员50人及以上服务业法人单位。包括：居民服务、修理和其他服务业，文化、体育和娱乐业。

7、各类生产安全事故起数、死亡人数统计范围包括生产经营性道路交通、水上交通、铁路交通、民航飞行、农业机械、渔业船舶和工矿商贸七个行业（领域）发生的事故，不再包括森林火灾、火灾事故和非生产经营性道路交通。

8、建成区面积、供水、用水、供气、供热、道路、厕所、下水道等有关数据暂不含即墨区。

9、资料来源：本公报中财政数据来自市财政局；人才、登记失业率、社会保障数据来自市人力资源社会保障局；银行数据来自人民银行青岛市中心支行；证券数据来自青岛证监局；保险数据来自青岛保监局；水产品数据来自市海洋与渔业局；林业数据来自市林业局；“三品一标”、农机等数据来自市农委；灌溉面积数据来自市水利局；交通运输数据来自市交通运输委；邮政数据来自市邮政管理局；固定电话、宽带、移动电话等数据来自市通信管理局；建成区面积、供水、供气、供热、道路、下水道等数据来自市城乡建设委；进出口、外资、对外承包工程、对外劳务合作、跨境电商等数据来自市商务局；旅游数据来自市旅游发展委；教育数据来自市教育局；科技、专利数据来自市科技局；体育数据来自市体育局；卫生数据来自市卫生计生委；环境数据来自市环保局；气象数据来自市气象局；安全生产数据来自市安全监管局；扶贫数据来自市扶贫协作办；汽车保有量来自市公安局；居民收支、价格、城乡居民住房面积等数据来自国家统计局青岛调查队；其他数据来自市统计局。

STATISTICS COMMUNIQUE
QINGDAO'S ECONOMIC AND SOCIAL DEVELOPMENT IN THE YEAR OF 2017

Qingdao Statistics Bureau
NBS Qingdao Survey Office

(March 16, 2018)

In 2017, the City takes Xi Jinping's new era of socialism with Chinese characteristics as a guide and deeply implements the 19–th spirit of the Party. In accordance with the "Innovation + three more" 's objectives and the working ideas of the "One–third and three–five" , under the strong leadership of the municipal government of the Communist Party of China, the overall tone of the work is maintained. Take the supply side structural reform as the main line, accelerate the implementation of the new and old kinetic energy conversion major projects, the economy keeps the healthy development, the social cause all–round progress.

I. General

According to the preliminary accounting, annual gross domestic product 1.103728 trillion yuan in 2017, calculated at the comparable price, with an increase of 7.5%. Therein, the 38.097 billion yuan of added value of the first industry increased by 3.2 percent. The value–added 454.621 billion yuan of the second industry increased by 6.8%. The value–added 611.01 billion yuan of the tertiary industry increased by 8.4%.The proportion of three industries is 3.4: 41.2: 55.4.GDP per capita reached 119357 yuan.

Figure 1 : Qingdao GDP and Growth Rate from 2013 to 2017

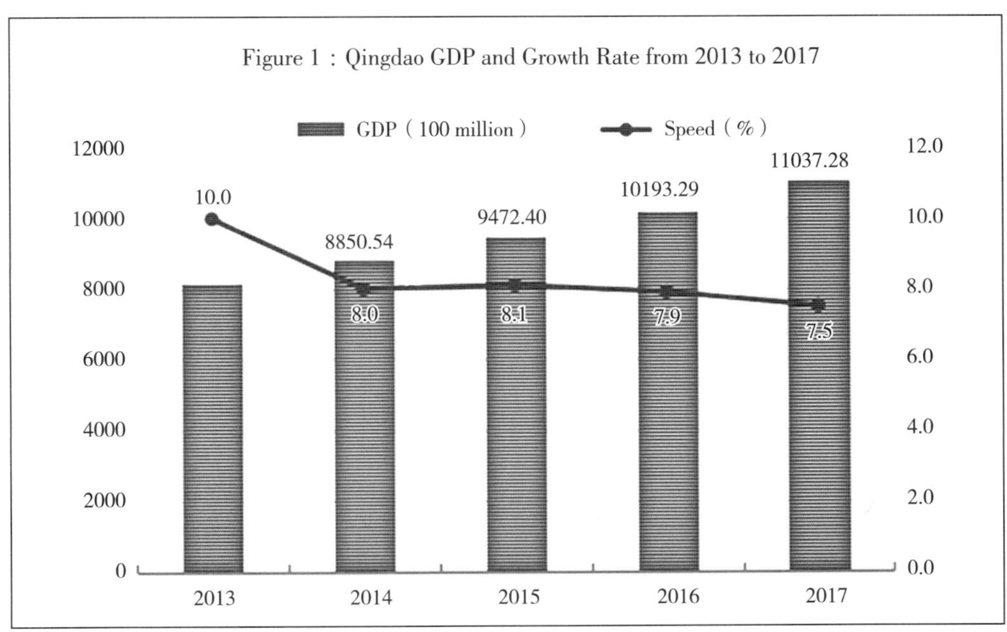

Note: The gross domestic product (GDP) and the growth rate in 2013–2016 are the revised data of DGP input accounting for R & D expenditures.

Table 1: Added value and growth rate of the whole city in 2017

Industry Classification	Total Amount (100 million yuan)	Growth (%)
GDP	11037.28	7.5
Farming, Forestry, Animal Husbandry and Fishery	403.36	3.6
Industry	3952.87	6.7
Construction	602.22	7.5
Wholesale and Retail Sales	1337.85	9.4
Transport, Storage and Post	776.64	7.3
Accommodation and Catering Services	221.75	5.9
Finance	750.98	8.1
Real Estate	587.36	1.1
Other Services	2404.25	10.3

According to the preliminary estimate, the annual gross domestic product (GDP) 290.9 billion yuan grew by 15.7% (current price) , accounting for 26.4% of GDP.The value-added 334.02 billion yuan of modern service industry in the whole city increased by 8.4%, accounting for 30.3% of GDP.

At the end of the year, the total population of the city is 929.05 million, with an increase of 0.94%. Therein, the urban resident population is 625.25 million, with an increase of 25.79%.

Table 2 : City resident population in 2017

Region	Number of end-of-year (10 000 persons)
Total	929.05
Shinan District	58.53
Shibei District	109.32
LIcang District	56.12
Laoshan District	43.87
West Coast New Area	153.92
Chengyang District	70.93
JImo District	122.45
Jiaozhou	89.33
Pingdu	138.05
Laixi	76.42
Qingdao National High-tech Industrial Development Zone	10.11

The total annual financial income is 322.2 billion yuan, increased by 13.4%. The general public budget income 115.71 billion yuan rises by 7.1%. Therein the total price is RMB 3.9 billion Yuan, with an increase of 11.4%. The VAT accounting to 30.9 billion yuan increased by 31.7%. The enterprise income tax accounts to 14.65 billion yuan, with an increase of 18%. The individual income tax accounts to 4.24 billion yuan, increased by 16.4%. The urban maintenance and construction tax, accounting to 5.27 billion yuan, increased by 4.7%. The 140.3 billion yuan of general public budget expenditures increased by 3.4%. Of these, general public service expenditure 15.21 billion yuan rises by 7.9%. Educational expenditure accounts to 25.38 billion yuan, with an increase of 0.3%. The 3.86 billion yuan of scientific and technological expenditure increased by 59.8%. The 15.34 billion yuan of social security and employment expenditure increased by 14.7%. The 32.25 billion yuan of urban and rural community affairs expenditure increased by 9%.The annual national tax system organization revenue, including customs collected as as an agency, accounts 169.2 billion yuan, increased by 24.8%. Therein, the domestic tax revenue accounts to 101.7 billion yuan, increased by 19.3%.The various local taxation revenues accounts to 62.33 billion yuan, with a same caliber growth of 17%.

Figure 2 : General Public Budget Income and Speed-increasing in the City

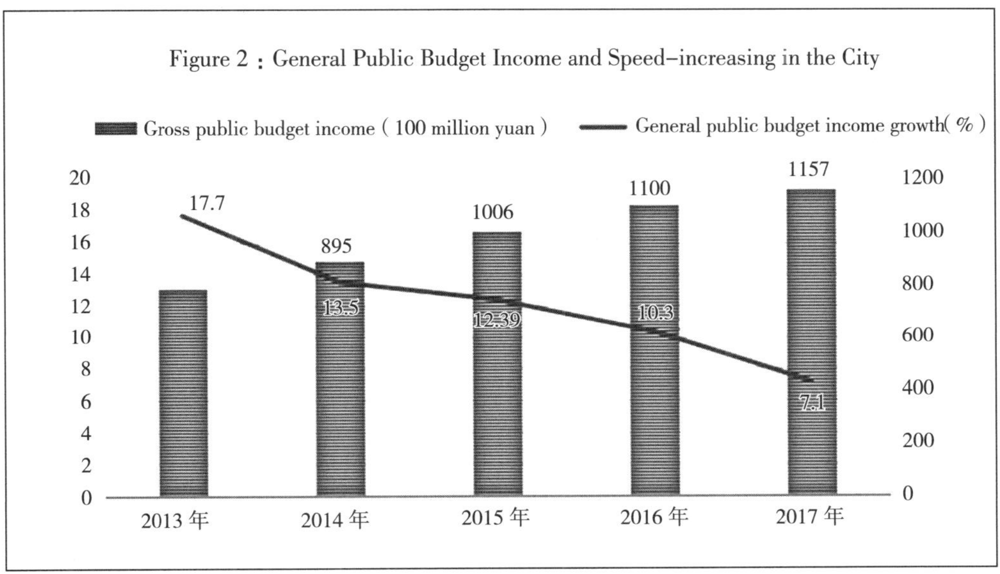

In the year, the consumer's consumption price is up 2.0% from the previous year, with the increase of 0.5 percentage points over the previous year. Food prices fell by 0.4%, and non-food prices rises 2.6%.

Table 3 : Consumer Price Index of the City in 2017

Name	Annual (the same period of last year = 100)
General Consumer Price Index	102.0
Non-Food Price Index	102.6
Service Price Index	103.4
Consumer Price Index	101.2
1. Food, Tobacco and Liquor	100.9
Food	99.6
#Grain	104.8
Vegetables	94.5
Pork	88.1
Egg	98.3
2. Clothing	100.5
3. Residence	102.3
4. Supplies and Services	99.7
5. Transportation and Communication	100.7
6. Education, Culture and Recreation	101.7
7. Medical Care	109.6
8. Others	104.1

Industrial producers factory-exiting prices have risen by 4.4% throughout the year, and industrial producers purchase-in price rises by 10.7% on average throughout the year.

By the end of the year, the whole city has implemented dual-lifting projects for poverty alleviation, poor (weak) village poverty alleviation, with 200 poverty-stricken villages and 310 weak villages in the city are included.

Ⅱ. New Kinetic Energy and Innovation

In the whole year, the value-added 57.95 billion yuan of high-tech industry in the whole city increased 10.9%, accounting for 5.3% of GDP. Therein, the added value of high-tech manufacturing is 290.1 billion yuan, with an increase of 10.6%, accounting for 2.7% of GDP. The added value of high-tech service industry is 289.40 billion yuan, with an increase of 11.2%, accounting for 2.6% of GDP. The added value for the strategic emerging industry accounts to 110.47 billion yuan, with an increase of 10.9%, accounting for 10% of GDP. Among them, the industrial added value of strategic emerging industry is80.65 billion yuan, increased by 11.7%, accounting for 7.3% of

GDP. The added value of strategic emerging industry service sector is 298.2 billion yuan, with an increase of 9.1%, accounting for 2.7 percent of GDP. The high-value-added and high-tech products increasing rapidly: 81,000 new energy automobiles are produced.13.72 million sets of intelligent televisions. 20.62 sets of intelligent phones are produced, increasing by 20.3%. 1276 urban tracked vehicles, with an increase of 80.2%.

The business revenue for the above-scale service enterprises of the city stands at 169.67 billion yuan, increased by 15.1%. Therein, the sports service enterprises maintain a business revenue of 290 million yuan, increased by 67.5%. The business revenue for broadcasting, television, films and sound recording industries stands at 530 million yuan, increased by 27.9%. The business revenue of the education industry stands at 1310 million yuan, increased by 25.9%.

Throughout the year, 134 above-scale internet and related industry and software and information technology service industry realized a business revenue of 13.23 billion yuan, increased by 23.2%. The gross business volume for 5 telecommunication operators in the city reached 22.5 billion, increased by 72%. Therein, the total volume of internet-related business accounts for above 60% in the gross volume of telecommunication business. 70 key e-commerce platforms (transactions realized by e-commerce enterprises or individuals through the local e-commerce platforms in Qingdao) through the city realized a transaction volume of 1063.8 billion yuan, increased by 31.7%.

The technical contracts transaction amount within the entire city valued 12.666 billion yuan, increased by 21.7%. The maritime-involved technical contracts transaction amount within the entire city valued. 1.499 billion yuan, increased by 21.8%. The effective innovation patents throughout the year amounts to 21802 pieces, increased by 19.2%.23.75 pieces of effective innovation patents are owned by each ten thousand persons. The PCT international patent application amounts to 761 pieces. There are 7 national intellectual property demonstration enterprises, 52 national intellectual property right enterprises, 13 national technological innovation demonstration enterprises, and 2039 high-tech enterprises.

By the end of the year, there are 2 famous brands in the world owned by the city and 198 service brands in Shandong. There are 68 famous products in China, 644 kinds of famous products in Shandong and 773 famous products in Qingdao.

Ⅲ. Agriculture

Within the entire year, the farming, forestry, husbandry and fishing industries distribution status: the added value for the planting industry amounted to 21.46 billion yuan, increased by 4.5%. The added value for forestry amounted to 160 million yuan, increased by 5.1%. The added value for the husbandry amounted to 7.79 billion yuan, increased by 5.2%. The added value for the fishing industry amounted to 8.69 billion, declined by 1.0%.The added value for the service industry for farming, forestry, husbandry and fishing stands at 2.24 billion yuan, increased by 12%.

The grain sowing area stands at 478,000 acres throughout the year. The vegetables sowing area stands at 108,000 acres. And peanuts sowing area stands at 82,000 acres.The total output of grain stands at 2,969,000 tons, which declined by 2.7% for the spring draught reason. The total output of vegetables and edible fungi stands at 6,012,000 tons, increased by 5.5%. The total output of peanuts stands at 384,000 tons, increased by 3.9%. The total output of fruits (including the fruits-purpose melons) stands at 1,184,000 tons, declined by 1.7%. The modern agricultural parks amount to 889, increased by 52. Those certified with ′three products and one mark (pollution-free agricultural products, green food, organic agricultural products and agricultural products geographical indication) amounts to 926, including 51 national geographic mark protected products.

Throughout the year, 35,000 mu of new trees are planted. 11,000 mu forests are refreshed. And 57,000 mu of forests are recovered.

The total meat output is 543,000 tons in the whole year, decreased by 3.6%. The output of poultry eggs weighs 177,000 tons, decreased by 2.4%. The output of diary stands at 309,000 tons, decreased by 2.5%.

Annual aquatic product yield (excluding far ocean fishing) stands at 1.076 million tons, decreased by 0.4%. The ocean and fresh water cultivation area stands at 43,000 acres, decreased by 4.4%.The ocean fishing volume stands at 141,000 tons, decreased by 0.4%.

The total power of agricultural machinery is 7.28 million kW, increasing by 300,000 kW. The mechanization level of crop production reached 87.2%.The effective irrigation area of the farmland stands at 330,000 hectares, of which the water-saving irrigation area stands at 178,000 hectares.

Table 4 : Table 4: Production and Growth of Major Plantation Products in 2017

Indicators	Unit	Yield	Growth (%)
Grain	10 000 tons	296.9	-2.7
Summer grain	10 000 tons	126.4	-12.8
Autumn grain	10 000 tons	170.5	6.5
Oilseed	10 000 tons	38.8	5.1
Vegetable and edible fungi	10 000 tons	601.2	5.5
Fruit	10 000 tons	118.4	-1.7
Garden fruit	10 000 tons	75.2	2.8

Ⅳ. Industry and Construction

Over the whole year, the industrial added value of the whole city increased by 7.5%.According to the economic types, state-controlled enterprises grew by 2.5 %. The collective enterprises grew by 20.5%. Shareholding enterprises grew by 6.9%. The foreign and Hong Kong, Macao and Taiwan business investment enterprises grew by 8.1%. And private enterprises grew by 10.7%.

According to the industry, the manufacturing of electrical machinery and equipment increased by 14.2%, metalwork industry increased 7.7%, agro-staple food processing industry increased by 11.7%, general equipment manufacturing increased by 13.0%, petroleum processing, coking and nuclear fuel processing industry declined by 8.2%, manufacturing of special equipment increased by 18.1%, railway, Manufacturing of ships, aerospace and other transportation equipment increased by 2.7%, Automobile manufacturing increased by 27.7%, and the commodity production industry declined by 2.1%, and manufacturing of computers, communications and other electronic equipment declined by 7.2%, and electricity, thermal production and the supply industry rises by 3.5%.The added value of equipment manufacturing increased by 12.5%, accounting for 45.8% of the industrial added value above the scale.

Table 5 : The Output and Growth Rate of the Main Products of Industries above Designated Size in 2017

Description	Unit	Output	Growth (%)
Color TV	10 000 sets	1703.0	-19.4
Of which: Smart TV	10 000 sets	1371.7	-13.2
Household refrigerators	10 000 sets	818.7	-7.2
Household washing machine	10 000 sets	603.4	-0.6

Room air conditioners	10 000 sets	1004.5	37.2
Smartphone	10 000 sets	2062.1	20.3
Beer	10 000 kiloliters	158.1	-2.6
Tire casing	10 000 pieces	5452.9	8.3
Sheet glass	10 000 weight cases	557.4	-3.2
Raw steel	10 000 tons	281.0	49.4
Automobile	10 000 vehicle	74.1	16.4
Motor train units	vehicle	1512	-24.6
urban rail vehicle	vehicle	1276	80.2
Metal shipping containers	10 000 m^3	1272.6	11.5

The above-scale industrial profits rises by 7.3%, therein, the state-owned holding enterprises fell by 0.4%, the collective enterprises increased by 23.5%, the shareholding enterprises increased by 7.8%, the foreign merchants and Hong Kong, Macao and Taiwan merchants decreased by 0.9%.

Table 6 : Above-scale industrial profit growth in 2017

Indicators	Growth(%)
Industrial profits above the scale	7.3
Of which : State-owned holding	-0.4
Collective businesses	23.5
Shareholder businesses	7.8
Businesses invested by foreigner or by compatriots from Hong Kong, Macao and Taiwan	-0.9

The construction industry realized an added value of 60.22 billion yuan, increased by 7.5%. The total amount of profits and taxes stands at 9.87 billion, increased by 9.1%.

V. Fixed Investment

The fixed-assets investment stands at 777.71 billion yuan, increased by 7.4%. Therein, the growth for the first industry is 17.8%, 9.3% for the secondary industry and 22.5% for. the tertiary industry.The strategic emerging industry investment increased by 5%, and the high-tech investment increased 15.5%.

The newly–established projects (real estate included) with a value of above 100 million yuan amounted to 701, increased by 102 than the previous year. An investment valuing 198.4 billion yuan is accomplished, increased by 29%. The proportion taken in the fixed assets investment within the entire city stands at 25.5%.

An investment of 133.05 billion yuan has been accomplished for the real estate development, decreased by 2.8%. Therein, the residential investment stands at 92.55 billion yuan, decreased by 3.2%. The sales area of the Commodity House is 19.007 million square meters, decreased by 2%. Therein, residential sales area stands at 16.338 million square meters, decreased by 6.7%.The area for sales of commercial house stands at 4.7 million square meters, decreased by 26.3%. Therein, the residential area for sale stands at 2.101 million square meters, decreased by 41.6%.

Table 7 : Real Estate Development Investment, Commodity Housing Sales Area and Speed Increase in 2017

Category	Real Estate Development Investment (100 million yuan)	Growth (%)	Sales Area of Commodity House (10 000 m^2)	Growth (%)
Total	1330.5	–2.8	1900.7	–2.0
Residential	925.5	–3.2	1633.8	–6.7
Office building	112.5	–5.7	97.9	76.3
Commercial operation house	185.8	26.4	130.2	57.4
Other	106.7	–27.2	38.8	–20.6

Throughout the year, the guaranteed housing basically established stands at 11,569 sets, including 9,111 sets of public rental housing, 1,503 sets of affordable housing and 955 sets of commodity housing. By the end of the year, 6,557 families are enjoying the rental subsidy, and the rental subsidy 46.28 million yuan is distributed throughout the year.

Ⅵ. Domestic Trade

454.1 billion yuan of retail sales of consumer goods is achieved in the whole year, with an increase of 10.6%. According to the statistics, the retail sales amount of consumer goods in town stands at 3786.1 billion yuan, with an increase of 10.2%. Retail sales of consumer goods in rural areas stands at 75.49 billion yuan, with an increase of 12.9%.According to the industry, retail sales of wholesale and retail sales amounted to 396.07 billion, with an increase of 10.7%. The retail sales of accommodation and catering industry realized 57.4 billion yuan, increased by 10.2%.The retail sales of consumer goods above designated size reached 155.47 billion yuan, increased by 12.8%.The retail sales of wholesales and retails enterprise automobile above designated size reached 33.85 billion yuan, increased by 9.1%. 18.35 billion yuan for petroleum and its products, increased by 11.2%. 14.56 billion yuan for grain, oil and food, increased by 11.1%. 5.85 billion yuan for the daily–use commodities, increased by 31.9%. 2.13 billion yuan for cosmetics, decreased by 8.8%.

Ⅶ. Foreign Trabe

The total imports and exports sales throughout the city stands at 503. 35 billion yuan, increased by 15.7%. Therein, the exports valued 303.18 billion yuan, increased by 7.5%. The imports valued 200.17 billion yuan, increased by 30.8%.The total imports and exports to the countries along the 'Belt and Road' stands at 248.53 billion yuan, increased by 11.2%. Therein, the exports stands at

160.11 billion, increased by 6.8%. The imports stands at 88.42 billion, increased by 20.1%.The total import and export of cross-border E-commerce in the whole city stands at 24.13 billion yuan, increasedby 101.1%.

The total of import and export of foreign trade in Qingdao port stands at 1.11024 trillion yuan, increased by 17.8%. Among them, the exports stands at 632.98 billion yuan, increased by 12.0%. The imports stands at477.26 billion yuan, increased by 17.8%.

Table 8：Import & Export of Main Commodities to/from Qingdao in 2017

Unit：100 million，%

Category	Import & Export		Export		Import	
	Amount	GrowthRate	Amount	GrowthRate	Amount	GrowthRate
Textiles and garments	480.1	1.5	447.7	1.9	32.4	-3.2
Agricultural products	713.8	13.3	357.5	9.0	356.3	18.0
Elextrical and mechanical	1765.1	10.1	1345.5	13.4	419.6	1.0
High-tech products	499.7	6.9	300.8	11.6	198.9	0.6

Table 9：Import and Export Volume and Growth Ratefrom/to Major Countries and Regions in 2017

Unit：USB 100 million，%

Country（Region）	ExportAmount	Growth	Import Amount	Growth
Asia	189.9	2.6	121.4	17.6
Hong Kong	17.6	17.8	1.0	0.2
Taiwan	3.8	4.6	10.2	0.4
Japan	52.8	5.8	17.9	-3.0
Korea	41.3	-0.2	30.4	-3.4
ASEAN	37.4	-4.1	44.4	80.9
South Asia	13.9	-4.7	2.5	9.4
Middle East	21.5	7.9	7.4	-12.9
Africa	16.9	-19.4	18.0	65.0
South Africa	4.0	18.7	2.2	11.9
Europe	105.4	11.7	39.1	8.5
EU	82.3	12.9	24.3	-5.1

Country (Region)	ExportAmount	Growth	Import Amount	Growth
U.K.	13.0	-0.2	4.0	58.0
Germany	14.7	4.2	6.8	-4.7
France	8.6	24.1	3.3	-1.7
Italy	7.7	22.8	2.1	-25.5
CIS and Eastern Europe	21.6	8.8	12.0	47.0
Russia	19.1	6.6	11.6	53.1
South America	29.4	10.4	54.4	56.0
Brazil	4.2	29.1	24.4	30.3
North America	92.0	7.3	30.7	17.8
U.S.A.	82.9	6.3	25.7	15.3
Canada	9.1	16.6	4.4	27.4
Oceania	12.2	4.8	31.2	58.8
Australia	10.1	4.1	27.1	56.1

Note : This table is not full caliber.

The foreign capital entering the accounts within the city for the year amounted to USD 7.74 billion, with an increase of 14.0%. A domestic capital amounting to 188.72 billion yuan is introduced from other places outside Qingdao, with an increase of 13.3%.In the year, 156 foreign investment projects have been added. The agreed investment amount amounted to USD 6. 43 billion. The actual investment amount newly increased amounted to USD 1.02 billion, taking 18.2% within the province. Throughout the year, there are 68 investment projects to the countries and regions along the 'Belt and Road', with an agreed investment amount of USD 2.19 billion. Of the 120 newly contracted projects in the whole city, the new contract amount is 44.1 billion US dollars, an increase of 18.3%, accounting for 34% of the whole province. The turnover $3.82 billion is completed by 4.9%, accounting for 32.5% of the province. In the city's foreign labor service cooperation service, 18,294 people are sent, accounting for 25.6% of the province.

Ⅷ. Transportation, Post, Telecommunications and Tourism

The throughput of the port in the city is 5.1 billion tons, down 0.3%.The throughput of the city's foreign trade is 3.7 billion tons, an increase of 7.9%.The container throughput of the city is 18 million 310 thousand standard boxes, an increase of 1.4%.

Table 10 : Volume and Growth Rate Completed by transportation in 2017

Transportation	Unit	Traffic volume	Growth (%)
Passenger volume	100 billion person-km	171.6	11.1
Railways	100 billion person-km	97.0	17.7
Highways	100 billion person-km	74.4	3.6
Waterways	100 billion person-km	0.2	-6.6
Cargo volumes	100 billion ton-km	1507.0	10.3
Railways	100 billion ton-km	183.0	8.1
Highways	100 billion ton-km	515.9	9.7
Waterways	100 billion ton-km	808.1	11.1

At the end of the year, there are 157 domestic airlines, 27 international airlines and 2 airlines from Hong Kong, Macao and Taiwan, with an annual total aviation passenger throughput of 2,321.1 million and an increase of 13.2%. The throughput of air cargo is 232000 tons, an increase of 0.6%. The total 32.75 billion yuan of the total business completed in the whole year increased by 58.3%. Among them, the total postal service 7.25 billion yuan increased by 23.7%. The total 25.5 billion yuan of telecommunication services increased by 72%.Express business volume amounted to 311 million, increased by 24.7%.Fixed broadband Internet users amounted to 3.693 million households, with an increase of 25.4%.The city′s mobile phone users amounted to 14.1 million households, of which 3G and 4G user 7.901 million households.

At the end of the year, there are 2.6145 million of motor vehicles in the city, with a 12.1% increase. Therein, private automobiles amounted to 2.1226 million, increased by 11.4%.

Metro Line 3 operating safely and the east section of Line 2 are opened smoothly. The total length of the two lines is 44.8 km, and the total number of metro stations is 40.In the year, the total train number is 119,000, with a total operation mileage of 29.19 million kilometers, and the total passenger capacity is 6,572,000 person times.

In the whole year, the total social logistics amounted to 3.01985 trillion yuan in the city, increased by 9.8%. The added value of logistics industry stands at 98.71 billion yuan, increased by 8.9%.

In the whole year, the total number of tourists received by the city is 88,165,000 million person times, with an increase of 9.1%. The total tourism consumption stands at164.01 billion yuan, increased by 14.0%. Among them, 144.4 million inbound visitors are received, with an increase of 2.4%. The consumption made by the inbound tourists stands at USD 1.02 billion, increased by 4.1%. 86.721 million of domestic tourists is received, with an increase of 9.2%. Domestic tourists made a consumption of 146.81 billion yuan, with an increase of 14.4%.At the end of the year, there are 123 scenic spots at level A, including 1 5A-level scenic spot, 24 4A-grade tourism scenic spots, and 74 3A-level tourism scenic spots. It owns 104 star hotels, 9 for 5 star hotels, 27 for 4 star hotels and 63 for 3 star hotels. There are 504 travel agencies, including 52 travel agencies operating outbound tourism business, 452 travel agencies operating inbound tourism business and tourism business within China.

Ⅸ. Science, Technology and Education

The foreign currency deposit balance of financial institution at year end stands at 1,512.9 billion yuan, increased by 45.63 billion yuan than the beginning of the year. The RMB deposit balance stands at 1,438.78 billion yuan, increased by 38.17 billion yuan than the beginning of the year. Therein, the residents savings amounts to 539.42 billion yuan, increased by 6.88 billion yuan than the beginning of the year. The foreign currency loan balance stands at 1.43884 trillion yuan, increased by 143.67 billion yuan than the beginning of the year. The RMB loan balance stands at 1.32648 trillion yuan, increased by 137.67 billion yuan than the beginning of the year.

The insurance industry realized the 39.67 billion yuan of premium income, increased by 18.1%.Among them, the insurance company realized the 11.06 billion yuan of premium income, increased by 2%. Life insurance company realized the 28.61 billion yuan of premium income, with an increase of 25.8%.

The securities company's securities trading volume stands at 3.52634 trillion yuan, increased by 2.4%. There are 191 private funds collection institutions at the end of the year. The scale of the management fund stands at 48.94 billion yuan, increased by 8.1%. There are 43 listed companies in China and abroad, 5 more than the previous year.114 and 1124 enterprises are listed in the "new three-plate" and Blue-sea Equity Transaction Center respectively, 22 and 570 more respectively compared with the previous year.

X. Science and Technology, Business Incubation and Talents

Preliminary statistics show that there are 588 key scientific and technological achievements in the city. There are 9 state-level scientific and technological awards, including 3 innovation awards, 6 awards for science and technology progress. There are 52 provincial scientific and technological awards, including 1 highest award, 7 natural science awards, 3 technical awards and 41 awards for scientific and technological progress.

There are 129 national undertaking hatching carriers in the whole city, of which 80 are registered in the state, 30 at the national level and 19 in national incubator.320 enterprises are recognized to enter the incubators of different levels and Zhongchuang Space. 13,000 enterprises enter the incubators and 740 are graduated.

During the whole year, all kinds of talents amounting to 131,400 persons are introduced in the whole city, with an increase of 8.5%. Among them, there are 1668 doctors, 1,340 graduates, 6,670 undergraduates and 4,960 persons with the education degree below the junior college (included) .

XI. Education, health and sport

At the end of the year, there are 25 colleges and universities (including private universities) within the city, including 23 universities. 14,000 post-graduate student enrollment in the entire year, 37,000 on-duty postgraduates and 9,000 graduates (excluding the postgraduates stationed in Qingdao Research Institute).99,000 students enrolled by the General Higher Education Institutes, 346,000 students in school and 95,000 graduated.29,000 persons for vocational education enrollment , 88,000 for in-school students, and 25,000 graduated. The students who received secondary vocational education accounted for 50.8% of the secondary vocational education.40,000 persons for senior high school enrollment , 117,000 for in-school students, and 37,000 graduated.40,000 persons for junior high school enrollment , 255,000 for in-school students, and 7,9000 graduated.94,000 persons for general primary school enrollment , 551,000 for in-school students, and 93,000 graduated.40 persons for special education enrollment , 300 for in-school students, and 50 graduated. There are 253,000 kids in the kindergartens.

At the end of the year, there are 3494 healthcare institutes (excluding the clinics in villages), 410 hospitals and health centers, 25 disease prevention and control centers, 12 maternal and child health institutions, 2670 clinics and Medical Rooms. At the end of the year, there are 76,000 various health technicians, among them, the doctors amounted to 31,000 persons. There are 61,000 of medical beds in the city, of which there are 53,000 beds in hospitals and health centers.

The city athletes won 1,342 gold medals, 805 silver medals and 874 bronze medals in the competitions. There are 2 key sports universities with 1061 students. The amateur sports schools amounted to 10, with 1537 students.

XII. Urban construction

At the end of the year, the urbanization rate of the city′s permanent residents reached 72.57%, increasing by 1.04 percentage points over the previous year. The built-up area of the whole city is 638.4 square kilometers. The daily water supply for the city is 119,400 tons, increased by 1.2%.The actual water consumption of the city is 380 million tons in the whole year, in which the production water and living water accounts to 120 million tons and 260 million tons, respectively.

The total household number of liquefied gas and natural gas in cities reaches 2.025 million households, and the total amount of liquefied gas is 37000 tons in the whole year, and the total amount of natural gas is 920 million cubic meters. And the gasification rate of the city reaches 100 percent.

In the year, the heating area is 4 million square meters, and the heating area at the end of the year reaches 190 million square meters.

At the end of the year, there are 477 bus routes and tram lines. There are 7208 buses running in public. There are 1,055 Taxis. At the end of the year, there are 2 metro lines, with 65.732 million of annual passenger capacity and 180000 of daily average passenger capacity.

There are 660 public toilets in the city, 660 above Category III, 17 newly-added toilets and 62 alterations.

At the end of the year, the total length of urban road is 4697 kilometers, and the total length of urban sewer is 7667 kilometers.

XIII. Energy, Environment and Work Safety

Preliminary statistics show that the total industrial comprehensive energy consumption of the whole city in the whole year is 14.93 million tons of standard coal, increasing by 3.3 percent. Of these, coal consumption is 13.85 million tons, down by 4.1%. The consumption of crude oil is 15.24 million tons, increased by 0.3%. The natural gas consumption is 530 million cubic meters, with an increase of 22.2%.The total power consumption of the whole society is 40.1 billion KWh, with an increase of 9.2%. Among them, the industrial electrical consumption amounted to 23.2 billion kilowatt-hour, increased by 9.1%. The living consumption of urban and rural residents amounts to 7.5 billion kilowatt-hours, with an increase of 7.7%.

In the year, the city′s energy production stands at 27.75 million tons of standard coal, falling by 0.9%. Among them, the processing capacity of crude oil is 15.23 million tons, with an increase of 1%. The production of gasoline is 4.56 million tons, with a decline of 0.9%. The production of diesel oil is 4.08 million tons and the drop of diesel oil is 2.7%. The power generating capacity is 18.2 billion kWh, increased by 0.1%.The output of new energy is1.35 billion, increased by 29.9%. The wind power generation increased by 28.7%, and the biomass power generation increased by 24.1%.The power generation of new energy accounts for 7.5% of the total power generation of the city, and increased by 1.7 percentage points.

The annual average temperature of the whole city is 13.9 ℃ , and the average annual precipitation is 687 millimeters. "The blue sky, white cloud and the twinkling stars" of days amounts to 342 days, with an increase of 24 days over the previous year. The major pollutants as the particulate matter (PM2.5), sulfur dioxide and nitrogen dioxide are 37, 14 and 33 micrograms per cubic meter, respectively. Compared with the previous year, 25.5% improved for PM2.5, 30% for sulfur dioxide and 3.1% for nitrogen dioxide .In the whole city, the water with quality up to or better than that of Category II sea water accounts for 90.6%, increased by 6.2 percentage points. The average value of environmental noise in urban area is 57.3 decibels, and the average noise of urban traffic trunk line is 68.7 decibels.

There are 106 production safety accidents in seven industries (domains) in the city, including 111 deaths, decreased by 54.7% and 33.9% respectively. The death rate of 100 million GDP production safety accident rate is 0.01. The death rate of the production safety accident of the employment personnel of the trade and commerce enterprise is 1.05. The death toll of the road traffic accidents is 12,400.

XIV. Living Conditions and Social Security

In the whole year, the per capita disposable income of the city residents stands at 38763 yuan, increased by 8.6%. Categorizing according to the permanent residential place, the per capita disposable income of urban residents stands at 47176 yuan, increased by 8.2%. The per capita disposable income of rural residents stands at19,364 yuan, increased by 7.8%. The median of disposable income per person in the city is 36,285 yuan. The per capita consumption expenditure, which stands at 25, 232 yuan, in the whole city increased by 8.5 percent, and the Engel coefficient is 29.7 percent. Categorizing according to the permanent residential place, the per capita consumption expenditure of urban residents stands at 30,569 yuan, increased by 8.1%. the per capita consumption expenditure of rural residents stands at 12,928 yuan, increased by 7.7%.

Table 11 : Per Capita Disposable Income of Urban and Rural Residents in 2017

Description of inducators	Residents		Urban Residents		Rural Residents	
	Absolute Value (yuan)	Growth Rate (%)	Absolute Value (yuan)	Growth Rate (%)	Absolute Value (yuan)	Growth Rate (%)
Disposable income	38763	8.6	47176	8.2	19364	7.8
Salary income	23514	8.4	28992	7.8	10882	8.0
Operating net income	7485	6.8	7299	6.6	7913	7.2
Propetry net income	3082	10.8	4297	9.9	280	9.0
Transfer net income	4682	11.8	6588	10.8	289	12.2

Table 12 : Per Capita Disposable Expense of Urban and Rural Residents in 2017

Description of inducators	Residents		Urban Residents		Rural Residents	
	Absolute Value (yuan)	Growth Rate (%)	Absolute Value (yuan)	Growth Rate (%)	Absolute Value (yuan)	Growth Rate (%)
Consumption expense	25232	8.5	30569	8.1	12928	7.7
Food, tobacco and liquor	7489	7.2	9059	6.9	3869	6.0
Chothing	2467	8.6	3117	8.1	971	7.3
Housing	5454	8.7	6605	8.2	2801	8.3
Living product and services	1747	8.7	2121	8.1	885	8.8
Transportation and communication	3753	7.9	4399	7.6	2262	7.0
Education, culture and entertainment	2347	13.1	2875	12.6	1129	12.4
Medical and health care	1350	9.5	1624	9.0	717	9.0
Other product and services	625	6.0	769	5.2	294	6.8

Table 13 : Amount of Major Consumer Durable Owned by every 100 Households in 2017

Description of inducators	Unit	Quantity		
		Residents	Urban Residents	Rural Residents
Household automobile	vehicle	57	60	48
Motorcycles	vehicle	31	15	70
Refrigerators	set	98	95	106
Washing machines	set	93	91	98
Water heaters	set	93	94	90
Air-conditioners	set	95	101	78
Color TV	set	103	100	110
computers	set	72	80	52
Midium and high quality musical instruments	set	11	14	3
Mobile telephones	set	211	205	223

According to the sample survey, the per capita housing construction area of urban residents at the end of the year is 32.7 square meters, and the per capita housing construction area of rural residents is 34.8 square meters.

In the whole year, the newly-increased urban residents employment number stands at 730,000 person, increased by 13.4%. Therein, the employment of workers in the city increased by 8.9%, and the employment of foreign workers increased by 19.3%.The service sector absorbed an employment of 453,000 persons, with an increase of 13.8%.The private economy absorbed an employment of 551,000 persons, with an increase of 16.3%.

At the end of the year, the minimum life guarantee number of urban residents in the city reached 24,220. The minimum living security fund for urban residents stands at 238.156 million yuan. There are a total of 4, 687 people in the rural five-guarantee support, and the rural five-guarantee support expenditure amounts to 62.57 million yuan.

At the end of the year, the number of insured persons in the basic old-age insurance for workers in the whole city is 2.587 million. The number of unemployed insurance is 2.103 million persons. The number of unemployed insurance contributions received in the whole year is 78,300 persons. The urban registered unemployment rate in the whole city is 3.12%, which decreased by 0.05 percentage points.

Note :

1. Figures reported herein are preliminary statistics.

2. The absolute figures of gross domestic product (GDP) and added value of each industry are calculated according to the current price, and the growth rate is calculated according to the current price. According to "three industry division regulations" (Guo Tong Zi[2012] No. 108), three industries, such as agro-forestry, fishing services, industry, auxiliary activities in industry, metalwork, machinery and equipment repair, are classified into the tertiary industry.

3. The resident population includes: (1) the person who lives in the household and the household registration in the township of this Town (including the person whose household registration is in the household and who has been out for less than half a year). (2) the person who has lived in the household for more than half a year, the household registration is in the street outside the township. (3) The household registration is in the street of the foreign township, and the person who has left the household registration for more than half a year. (4) who lives in the household and

whose household registration is pending.

4. PCT is an English abbreviation for "Patent Cooperation Treaty". The PCT international patent refers to Chinese patent application person can submit international patent application to the China Patent Office or to the World Intellectual Property Organization according to the PCT regulations, and is an important index to reflect the development level of export-oriented economic development in the region and the competitiveness of international technology in the region.

5. The strategic emerging industry, according to the national planning, mainly includes seven industrial fields such as energy conservation, environmental protection, new generation of information technology, biology, high-end equipment manufacturing, new energy, new materials and new energy Automobile.

6. The industrial enterprises above the scale are the annual main business income 20 million yuan and the above enterprises. Trade enterprises above designated size are units with a main business income of 20 million yuan or more in the wholesale industry, 5 million yuan or more in the retail industry, and 2 million yuan and above in the accommodation and catering industry. The starting point standard of the fixed asset investment project statistics is the planned total investment 5 million yuan. For service enterprises above designated size, the first refers to service companies with an annual business income of 10 million yuan or more or 50 or more employees at the end of the year. including transport, storage and postal services, information transmission, software and information technology services, rental and business services, scientific research and technology services, water resources, environmental and public facilities management, education, health and social work. As well as property management, real estate brokerage services, self-owned real estate business activities and other real estate industry. Second, it refers to a service legal entity with an annual operating income of 5 million yuan or more or 50 or more employees at the end of the year. Including: resident services, repairs and other services, cultures, sports and recreation.

7. The statistics range of the number of production safety accidents and the number of deaths include the accidents that occur in the seven industries (areas) of production and business road traffic, water transportation, railway transportation, civil aviation flight, agricultural machinery, fishery ship and maritime trade and commerce, and no longer includes forest fire, Real-time and non-production operational road traffic.

8. The area of built-up area, water supply, water use, gas supply, heat supply, roads, toilets, sewers and other relevant data excludes Jimo District for now.

9. Source: The financial data in this bulletin comes from the Municipal Finance Bureau. the talents, registered unemployment rate, and social security data come from the Municipal Human Resources and Social Security Bureau. the bank data comes from the Qingdao Central Branch of the People's Bank of China. the securities data comes from the Qingdao Securities Regulatory Bureau. the insurance data comes from Qingdao Insurance Regulatory Bureau. aquatic product data from the Municipal Ocean and Fisheries Bureau. forestry data from the Municipal Forestry Bureau. “three products and one standard” , agricultural machinery and other data from the Municipal Agricultural Commission. irrigated area data from the Municipal Water Resources Bureau. transportation data from the city traffic Transportation Committee. postal data from the Municipal Postal Administration. fixed telephone, broadband, mobile phone and other data from the Municipal Communications Administration. built-up area, water supply, gas supply, heating, roads, sewers and other data from the Municipal Urban and Rural Construction Committee. Export, foreign investment, foreign contracted projects, foreign labor cooperation, cross-border e-commerce and other data from the Municipal Bureau of Commerce. tourism data from the Municipal Tourism Development Committee. education data from the Municipal Education Bureau. technology, patent data from the Municipal Science and Technology Bureau. sports data from Municipal Sports Bureau. health data from the Municipal Health and Family Planning Commission. environmental data From the Municipal Environmental Protection Bureau. meteorological data from the Municipal Meteorological Bureau. safety production data from the Municipal Safety Supervision Bureau. poverty alleviation data from the Municipal Poverty Alleviation Cooperation Office. car ownership from the Municipal Public Security Bureau. household income and expenditure, prices, urban and rural residential housing area and other data from Qingdao Bureau of Investigation, National Bureau of Statistics. other data from the Municipal Bureau of Statistics.

综 合 1

GENERAL SURVEY

简要说明

一、本篇资料的主要内容

本篇资料是对我市行政区划、气象情况、分行业法人单位数、各部门机构数和国民经济、社会发展的综合反映，主要包括行政区划、气象情况、分行业法人单位数、各部门机构数、国民经济主要比例关系、国民经济和社会发展主要指标占全国全省比重、国民经济和社会发展主要指标及其增长速度等资料。

二、本篇资料的来源

1、"行政区划"主要包括2017年底各区（市）街道办事处（乡镇）、社区居委会（村民委员会）区划资料，数据来源于市民政局。

2、"气象情况"包括分区市、市区分月气象资料，数据来源于市气象局。

3、"全市生产总值"来源于国民经济核算统计报表，由市统计局国民经济核算处整理提供。

4、国民经济和社会发展综合部分来源于本年鉴各篇章中的资料，由市统计局国民经济综合统计处加工整理。

Brief Introduction

Ⅰ. Main Content

Data in this chapter cover the main indicators on divisions of administrative areas，meteorology，corporate units，number of grass-roots units and national economy and social development，including divisions of administrative areas，meteorology，number of corporate units，number of grass-roots units，average daily social and economic activities，ratio，and percentage of main indicators of Qingdao to the whole nation and the whole province and growth rate of main indicators.

Ⅱ. Source of Data

（1）Data on divisions of administrative areas are mainly including the information on sub-district offices（villages and towns）and community neighborhood committees（villagers residents' committees）at the end of 2017. The data are provided by Qingdao Municipal Bureau of Civil Affairs.

（2）Data on meteorology are provided by Qingdao Municipal Meteorological Bureau.

（3）Data on gross national product are prepared according to the data of national accounts and compiled by the Division of National Accounts of Qingdao Municipal Bureau of Statistics.

（4）Data on general survey of economy and society are based on those of different chapters? and compiled by the Division of Comprehensive Statistics of Qingdao Municipal Bureau of Statistics.

1-1 行政区划(2017 年底)
ADMINISTRATIVE DIVISION (END OF 2017)

单位：个(unit)

市区名称	Region	街道办事处 Subdistrict Offices	社区居委会 Community Residents' Committees	镇 Town	村民委员会 Villagers' Committees
全　市	**Whole Municipality**	**102**	**1168**	**43**	**5444**
市南区	Shinan District	14	65		
市北区	Shibei District	30	135		
李沧区	Licang District	11	117		
崂山区	Laoshan District	5	161		
黄岛区	Huangdao District	12	257	10	962
城阳区	Chengyang District	8	245		1
即墨区	Jimo District	8	57	7	1028
胶州市	Jiaozhou	6	51	6	811
平度市	Pingdu	5	51	12	1781
莱西市	Laixi	3	29	8	861

1-2　气象情况(2017年)
METEOROLOGY (2017)

市区名称	Region	平均气温（摄氏度）Average Temperature（℃）	极端气温 Extreme Temperature（centigrade）最高（摄氏度）Maximum（℃）	最低（摄氏度）Minimum（℃）	降水量（毫米/年）Precipitation（millimeter/year）	日照时数（小时/年）Sunshine Hours（hour/year）	平均气压（百帕）Average Atmospheric Pressure（100 pa）
市　区	Urban Area	14.1	36.9	-6.2	729.1	2314.0	1008.3
崂山区	Laoshan District	14.0	36.6	-7.5	690.1	2514.6	1011.0
黄岛区	Huangdao District	14.3	37.6	-8.1	785.2	2417.7	1016.4
即墨区	Jimo District	14.0	36.7	-10.1	636.2	2422.2	1011.8
胶州市	Jiaozhou	14.0	37.7	-8.5	612.1	2305.7	1007.4
平度市	Pingdu	13.7	37.2	-13.7	589.1	2449.0	1010.1
莱西市	Laixi	13.1	37.9	-14.8	768.7	2633.6	1008.2

注：以上为7个国家基准站或基本站
Note：These are 7 national reference or base stations.

1-3　市区分月气象情况(2017年)
MONTHLY METEOROLOGY OF URBAN AREA (2017)

月　份	Month	平均气温（摄氏度）Average Temperature（℃）	降水量（毫米）Precipitation（millimeter）	日照时数（小时）Sunshine Hours（hour）
一月	Jan.	1.6	44.6	140.5
二月	Feb.	2.8	11.1	167.1
三月	Mar.	7.0	9.7	197.4
四月	Apr.	14.0	12.6	256.9
五月	May.	18.4	35.6	248.1
六月	Jun.	21.6	40.7	228.3
七月	Jul.	26.5	228.7	166.2
八月	Aug.	26.4	204.4	177.4
九月	Sep.	23.2	82.5	214.0
十月	Oct.	15.9	58.8	150.7
十一月	Nov.	9.3	0.4	189.8
十二月	Dec.	3.0	0.0	177.6
全　年	Annual Total	14.1	729.1	2314.0

1-4 各部门机构数(2017 年底)

GRASS-ROOTS UNITS IN VARIOUS SECTORS (END OF 2017)

项目	Item	单位	Unit	机构数 Grass-roots Units
农村基层单位	**Rural Grass-roots Units**			
镇政府	Town Governments	个	unit	43
乡村户数	Number of Rural Households	万户	10 000 households	140.4
工业企业单位	**Industrial Enterprises**	**个**	**unit**	**32543**
规模以上工业	Above Designated Size	个	unit	3569
#国有企业	State-owned Enterprises	个	unit	131
集体企业	Collective-owned Enterprises	个	unit	5
外商及港澳台商投资企业	Enterprises with Funds from Hong Kong, Macao, Taiwan and Foreign Conutries	个	unit	1037
规模以下工业	Above Designated Size	个	unit	28974
交通运输业	**Transportation**			
铁路	Railway	个	unit	
公路	Highway	个	unit	151
水运	Waterway	个	unit	22
邮电业	**Rostal and Telecommunication Services**			
邮电局所	Post Offices	处	unit	454
建筑业企业	**Construction Enterprises**	**个**	**unit**	**679**
国有企业	State-owned Enterprises	个	unit	22
集体企业	Collective-owned Enterprises	个	unit	8
其他	Others	个	unit	649
批发和零售业、住宿和餐饮业	**Wholesale & Retail Trades, Hotels and Catering Services**			
限额以上批发业	Wholesale Trade above Designated Size	个	unit	1140
限额以上零售业	Retail Trade above Designated Size	个	unit	721
限额以上住宿业	Hotel above Designated Size	个	unit	173
限额以上餐饮业	Catering Service above Designated Size	个	unit	184

1-4 续表
Continued

项目	Item	单位	Unit	机构数 Grass-roots Units
教育事业	**Education**			
普通高等学校	Regular Institutions of Higher Education	所	unit	25
中等专业学校	Specialized Secondary Schools	所	unit	6
普通中学	Regular Secondary Schools	所	unit	311
普通小学	Regular Primary Schools	所	unit	722
幼儿园	Kindergartens	所	unit	2097
科研机构	**Science and Technology Institutions**			
中央属	Central Level	个	unit	22
地方属	Local	个	unit	35
文化及相关产业	**Culture and Related Industry**			
公共图书馆	Public Libraries	个	unit	12
影剧院	Cinemas	个	unit	52
卫生事业	**Public Health**			
#医院	Hospitals	个	unit	410
民政行政单位	**Civil Affairs Departments**			
#社会福利事业	Institutions of Social Welfare	个	unit	296

1-5　按行业分法人单位数
NUMBER OF CORPORATE UNITS BY SECTOR

单位：个（unit）

行　业	Sector	2017
总　计	Total	318797
农、林、牧、渔业	Agriculture Forestry Animal Husbandry and Fishery	9475
采矿业	Mining	155
制造业	Manufacturing	55001
电力、热力、燃气及水生产和供应业	Electricity, heat, gas, water production and supply industry	513
建筑业	Construction	20120
批发和零售业	Wholesale and Retail Trades	114155
交通运输、仓储和邮政业	Transport Storage and Post	11304
住宿和餐饮业	Hotels and Catering Services	4330
信息传输、软件和信息技术服务业	Information Transmission Computer Services and Software	9858
金融业	Financial Intermediation	2069
房地产业	Real Estate	7226
租赁和商务服务业	Leasing and Business Services	38830
科学研究和技术服务业	Scientific Research and Technical Services	16764
水利、环境和公共设施管理业	Management of Water Conservancy Environment and Public Facilities	1467
居民服务、修理和其他服务业	Services to Households and Other Services	6087
教育	Education	4629
卫生和社会工作	Health Social Security and Social Welfare	2037
文化、体育和娱乐业	Culture Sports and Entertainment	4094
公共管理、社会保障和社会组织	Public Management and Social Organizations	10683

1-6 国民经济主要平均指标
AVERAGE INDICATORS ON NATIONAL ECONOMY

指　标	Indicator	单位	Unit	2000 年	2005 年
人口密度	Density of Population	人 / 平方公里	person/sq.km	664	695
每户年平均人口	Average Household Size	人	person	3.14	3.12
城镇非私营单位在岗职工年平均工资	The Average Annual Wage of Staff and Workers in the Post in Non-Private Units in Towns and Cities	元	yuan	10 072	19086
城市居民人均年可支配收入	Annual Per Capita Net Income of Rural Households	元	yuan	8 016	12920
农民人均年纯收入	Annual Per Capita Net Income of Rural Households	元	yuan	3 637	5806
每一播亩平均粮食产量	Output of Grain Per Mu of Sowing Area	千克	kg	411	421
每亩蔬菜平均产量	Average Output of Vegetables Per Mu	千克	kg	2 735	2985
每亩茶叶平均产量	Average Output of Tea Per Mu	千克	kg	8.1	16.5
每亩花生平均产量	Average Output of Peanut Per Mu	千克	kg	298	327
每亩棉花平均产量	Average Output of Cotton Per Mu	千克	kg	83	74
每台拖拉机负担耕地面积	Cultivated Area Ploughed by Per Tractor	亩 / 台	mu/unit	56	39
每亩耕地施用化肥量（折纯）	Chemical Fertilizer Consumption Per Mu (convert to pure amount)	千克	kg	45	52
每人平均消费品零售额	Per Capita Retail Sales of Consumer Goods	元	yuan	6077	11822
城市每天平均生活用水量	Daily Residential Consumption of Water	万吨	10 000 tons	33.33	34.35
城市每人平均公园绿地面积	Per Capita Public Green Areas	平方米	sq.m	8.50	11.82
每万人拥有医疗床位	Number of Hospital Beds Per 10000 Population	张	bed	34.5	41.3
每万人拥有医生数	Number of Doctors per 10000 Population	人	person	21.0	20.3
每万人中高等学校学生数	Students Enrollment of Institutions of Higher Education per 10000 Population	人	person	65	324
每万人中中等学校学生数	Students Enrollment of Secondary Schools per 10000 Population	人	person	704	768
每万人中小学学生数	Students Enrollment of primary Schools per 10000 Population	人	person	757	648

注：自 2015 年开始，全市城乡住户调查统一使用一体化改革后的数据，与原数据相比，城乡居民收支指标的调查范围和口径均存较大变化。原“城市居民人均可支配收入”调整为“城镇居民人均可支配收入”；原“农民人均纯收入”调整为“农村居民人均可支配收入”。

Note : Since 2015, the urban and rural households investigation unified the data after the integrated reform, compared with the original data, the investigation scope and the caliber of urban and rural residents' income and expenditure indicators have changed greatly. The original “per capita disposable income of urban residents” is adjusted to be a “per capita disposable income of urban residents” . The original “per capita net income of farmers” is adjusted to “per capita disposable income of rural residents” .

2006 年	2008 年	2009 年	2010 年	2011 年	2012 年	2013 年	2014 年	2015 年	2016 年	2017 年
703	715	676	677	679	682					
3.13	3.13	3.12	3.10	3.09	3.09					
22575	29404	32507	37501	43077	49052	55363	62104	69465	76616	83539
15328	20464	22368	24998	28567	32145	35227	38294	40370	43598	47176
6546	8509	9249	10550	12370	13990	15731	17461	16730	17969	19364
407	436	446	437	444	456	430	435	435	423	414
3078	3511	3562	3606	3759	3756	3802	3786	3694	3552	3700
18.0	28.0	28	30	30	33	29	30	32	49	71
309	315	312	303	313	321	309	299	281	287	311
76	78	79	78	87	105	100	111	104	104	108
36	36	35	32	31			38	38	37	36
52	50	48	47	47			37	36	36	36
13640	19640	22699	25694	30043	34248	38606	43064	47423	51765	56452
29.27	30.96	33.56	34.31	27.53	33.21	32.50	40.60	42.10	67.60	50.3
11.80	14.53	14.50	14.58	14.58	14.60	14.60	14.60	14.60	18.60	17.4
38.3	42.5	43.0	47.2	52.2	61.4	58.0	60.3	62.0	63.9	69.4
20.6	21.4	21.9	23.2	23.9	28.1	31.2	32.0	33.5	34.9	38.4
347	354	361	373	380	386	388	402	411.0	430.0	431.0
740	765	740	701	659	635	626	614	596.0	593.0	611.0
646	627	610	606	626	630	642	662	685.0	690.0	685.3

1-7　主要年份社会经济主要指标
MAJOR YEAR'S INDICATORS ON SOCIETY AND ECONOMY

指标	Indicator	单位	Unit	2000年	2005年
人口	**Population**				
总人口（年末）	Population at Year-end	万人	10 000 persons	706.65	740.91
男性人口	Male	万人	10 000 persons	357.74	374.03
女性人口	Female	万人	10 000 persons	348.91	366.87
市区人口	Urban Area	万人	10 000 persons	234.60	265.43
就业	**Employment**				
社会从业人员	Employment	万人	10 000 persons	397.6	471.0
#单位从业人员	Employed Persons in Units	万人	10 000 persons	118.3	224.3
经济总量	**Gross Economic Amount**				
全市生产总值（当年价）	GDP（at current price）	亿元	100 million yuan	1191.25	2687.46
第一产业增加值	Primary Industry	亿元	100 million yuan	140.85	178.33
第二产业增加值	Secondary Industry	亿元	100 million yuan	555.21	1392.02
第三产业增加值	Tertiary Industry	亿元	100 million yuan	495.19	1117.10
人均生产总值	Per Capita GDP	元	yuan	16009	33085
农林牧渔业总产值（当年价）	Gross Output Value of Farming，Forestry，Animal Husbandry and Fishery（at current price）	亿元	100 million yuan	248.33	320.51
工业总产值（当年价）	Gross Industrial Output Value（at current price）	亿元	100 million yuan	1940.83	5001.78

注：1. 单位从业人员2004年以前为职工人数(不含私营企业)。
2. 规模以上固定资产投资数据2003年以前为城镇以上统计范围。
3. 2002年以前地方财政一般预算收支数据为地方财政收支口径。

Note：1.Before 2004，the data of employed persons in units refers to the number of staff and workers（excluding private enterprises）.
2.Before 2003，the data of investment in fixed assets above designated size refers to urban investment.
3.Before 2002，the data of general budgetaty revenue and expenditure of local government finance refers to revenue and expenditure of local government finance.

2006年	2008年	2009年	2010年	2011年	2012年	2013年	2014年	2015年	2016年	2017年
749.38	761.56	762.92	763.64	766.36	769.56					
377.99	382.46	382.35	381.92	382.69	383.82					
371.39	379.10	380.56	381.72	383.67	385.74					
270.99	276.25	275.47	275.50	277.09	279.57					
490.1	513.8	525.7	540.3	551.2	559.9	571.5	589.0	595.4	601.4	603.9
243.2	254.1	260.5	269.4	275.9	283.2	293.7	303.0	309.2	315.6	321.4
3183.18	4401.56	4853.87	5749.02	6725.76	7424.32	8147.32	8850.54	9472.40	10193.29	11037.28
183.95	223.40	230.25	276.99	306.38	324.41	340.50	349.62	363.98	371.01	380.97
1666.96	2234.83	2420.14	2823.43	3236.92	3496.46	3745.12	4014.99	4168.11	4309.65	4546.21
1332.28	1943.33	2203.48	2648.60	3182.46	3603.45	4061.70	4485.93	4940.31	5512.63	6110.1
38608	52266	57251	65827	76804	84063	91376	98283	104418	111396	119357
339.61	400.85	408.61	483.18	535.93	566.52	611.86	630.04	660.14	674.27	692.92
5918.81	8946.73	10255.62	11614.83	13277.96	15306.32	16897.18	17444.21	18019.43	17416.71	13019.73

1-7 续表 1
Contiuned

指　标	Indicator	单位	Unit	2000 年	2005 年
财政	**Government Finance**				
公共财政预算收入	Public Budget Revenue	亿元	100 million yuan	80.01	176.34
公共财政预算支出	Public Budget Expenditure	亿元	100 million yuan	87.87	203.06
规模以上固定资产投资额	**Investment in Fixed Assets above Designated Size**	亿元	**100 million yuan**	**242.68**	**1403.30**
社会消费品零售额	**Total Retail Sales of Consumer Goods**	亿元	**100 million yuan**	**428.29**	**870.11**
港口吞吐量	**Volume of Freight Handled in Ports**	万吨	**10 000 tons**	**8661**	**18727**
集装箱吞吐量	**Volume of Containers Handled**	万标箱	**Ten Thousand TEUs**	**212.0**	**630.7**
民航货物吞吐量	**Volume of Freight and Mail Handled in Covil Aviation**	万吨	**10 000 tons**	**4.84**	**8.91**
对外贸易	**Foreign Trade**				
外贸进出口总额	Imports and Exports（excluding central and provincial companies）	亿美元	100 million USD	108.31	304.55
#出口总额	Exports	亿美元	100 million USD	61.14	175.88
教育、卫生、文化	**Education Public Health，Culture**				
小学在校学生数	Students Enrollment in Primary Schools	万人	10 000 persons	53.49	47.98
普通中学在校学生	Students Enorllment in Regular Secorndary Schools	万人	10 000 persons	39.85	39.11

2006年	2008年	2009年	2010年	2011年	2012年	2013年	2014年	2015年	2016年	2017年
225.77	342.44	376.99	452.61	566.14	670.18	788.93	895.25	1006.26	1100.03	1157.24
236.79	369.41	433.58	532.39	658.06	765.98	1014.23	1074.71	1222.87	1352.85	1403.03
1485.69	**2019.01**	**2458.89**	**3022.48**	**3502.54**	**4153.91**	**5027.86**	**5766.03**	**6555.70**	**7454.70**	**7777.09**
1016.35	**1492.22**	**1730.22**	**1961.13**	**2302.37**	**2635.62**	**2986.81**	**3361.72**	**3713.69**	**4104.93**	**4541.01**
22438	**30029**	**31668**	**35012**	**37971**	**41465**	**45782**	**47701**	**49749**	**51463**	**51314**
770.0	**1037.7**	**1027.7**	**1201**	**1302**	**1450**	**1552**	**1658**	**1743**	**1805**	**1831**
10.10	**13.05**	**13.54**	**16.37**	**16.65**	**17.19**	**18.62**	**20.44**	**20.80**	**23.07**	**23.00**
365.57	521.59	439.86	561.49	712.63	732.08	779.12	798.88	702.22	4350.67（亿元）	5033.50（亿元）
216.45	314.62	269.22	333.51	400.56	408.20	419.86	457.77	453.50	2821.91（亿元）	3031.81（亿元）
48.39	47.72	46.50	46.27	47.95	49.50	49.63	51.65	53.65	54.72	55.05
36.52	37.39	37.74	38.00	37.32	36.96	36.51	36.26	35.54	35.61	37.22

1-7　续表 2
Contiuned

指标	Indicator	单位	Unit	2000 年	2005 年
高等学校在校学生	Students Enrollment in Instutions of Higher Education	万人	10 000 persons	4.61	23.98
小学专任教师	Full-time Teachers in Primary Schools	万人	10 000 persons	3.17	3.17
普通中学专任教师	Full-time Teachers in Regular Secorndary Schools	万人	10 000 persons	2.63	2.97
医生总数	Doctors	万人	10 000 persons	1.49	1.50
医院床位数	Hospital Beds	万张	10 000 beds	2.01	2.86
人民生活	**People's Living Conditions**				
就业人员工资总额	Total wages of Employed Persons	亿元	100 million yuan	120.40	359.5
城市居民人均可支配收入	Per Capita Disposable Income of Urban Households	元	yuan	8 016	12920
农民人均纯收入	Per Capita Net Income of Rural Households	元	yuan	3 637	5806
城乡人民币储蓄存款余额	Savings Deposit of Urban and Rural Households	亿元	100 million yuan	535.32	1343.10
物价指数	**Price Indexes**				
商品零售价格指数（以 1950 年价格为 100）	Retail Price Index（1950=100）	%	%	520.5	495.0
居民消费价格指数（以 1950 年价格为 100）	Consumer Price Index（1950=100）	%	%	711.9	753.1
#食品价格指数（以 1950 年价格为 100）	Food Price Index（1950=100）	%	%	800.1	871.8

注：1. 2005 年及以前为在岗职工工资总额，在岗职工工资总额 2005 年前统计范围为全部职工不含私营企业；
2. 2015 年“城乡人民币储蓄存款余额”改为“住户存款”。

Note：1. Total wages for staff and workers in 2005 and before，The total wages of the workers on duty were before 2005. The statistics ranged from all employees to private enterprises.
2. In 2015，“balance of RMB deposits in urban and rural areas” changed to “household deposits.”

2006 年	2008 年	2009 年	2010 年	2011 年	2012 年	2013 年	2014 年	2015 年	2016 年	2017 年
26.03	26.93	27.52	28.49	29.15	29.66	30.02	31.35	32.23	34.09	34.62
3.22	3.24	3.22	3.2	3.16	3.17	3.28	3.22	3.45	3.42	3.47
2.92	2.99	3.06	3.08	3.14	3.20	3.18	3.2	3.29	3.39	3.47
1.55	1.63	1.67	1.77	1.83	2.16	2.41	2.5	2.63	2.76	3.09
2.67	2.99	3.05	3.34	3.56	4.12	3.97	4.3	4.51	4.73	4.63
445.6	578.7	638.1	738.0	877.5	1044.3	1251.7	1456.0	1644.4	1852.7	2034.7
15328	20464	22368	24998	28567	32145	35227	38294	40370	43598	47176
6546	8509	9249	10550	12370	13990	15731	17461	16730	17969	19364
1567.62	2123.36	2527.88	2912.33	3198.51	3757.60	4141	4436	5024	5326	5394
493.5	526.6	519.2	526.5	550.2	559.6	567.4	580.5	580.5	592.1	596.8
759.9	831.4	835.6	854.0	896.7	920.9	943.9	968.4	980.0	1004.5	1024.6
886.6	1105.3	1123.0	1194.9	1327.5	1384.6	1458.0	1522.2	1548.1	1625.5	1619.0

1-8 国民经济主要结构指标
COMPOSITION INDICATORS ON NATIONAL ECONOMY

指　标	Indicator	2000年	2005年	2006年	2008年
社会从业人员	**Employment**				
产业结构	Industrial Composition				
第一产业	Primary Industry	36.4	22.2	21.0	19.9
第二产业	Secondary Industry	33.9	41.8	42.8	43.0
第三产业	Tertiary Industry	29.7	36.0	36.2	37.1
全市生产总值	**GDP**				
产业结构	Industrial Composition				
第一产业	Primary Industry	11.8	6.6	5.8	5.1
第二产业	Secondary Industry	46.6	51.8	52.4	50.8
第三产业	Tertiary Industry	41.6	41.6	41.8	44.1
农业	**Agriculture**				
农林牧渔业产值结构	Composition of Farming, Forestry, Animal Husbandry and Fishery				
#农业	Farming	45.0	39.5	40.1	44.4
林业	Forestry	0.8	0.8	0.7	0.6
牧业	Animal Husbandry	27.9	33.4	31.7	30.3
渔业	Fishery	26.4	26.3	25.2	21.4
工业	**Industy**				
轻重工业产值结构	Composition of Output Value of Light and Heavy Industry				
轻工业	Light Industry	64.1	49.4	48.5	42.3
重工业	Heavy Industry	35.9	50.6	51.5	57.7
固定资产投资	**Investment in Fixed Assets**				
投资结构	Composition of Investment				
生产性	Productive	54.0	65.4	62.0	61.6
非生产性	Non-productive	46.0	34.6	38.0	38.4

2009 年	2010 年	2011 年	2012 年	2013 年	2014 年	2015 年	2016 年	2017 年
20.1	19.5	19.2	18.8	18.8	18.4	18.1	17.8	16.9
41.9	41.4	41.2	41.0	40.6	39.0	38.5	38.0	37.8
38.0	39.1	39.6	40.2	40.6	42.6	43.3	44.2	45.3
4.7	4.8	4.6	4.4	4.2	3.9	3.8	3.6	3.4
49.9	49.1	48.1	47.1	46	45.4	44.0	42.3	41.2
45.4	46.1	47.3	48.5	49.8	50.7	52.2	54.1	55.4
45.4	48.4	44.1	44.0	46.4	47.6	51.1	49.3	50.2
0.5	0.4	0.4	0.4	0.4	0.4	0.4	0.4	0.4
28.4	26.2	29.1	27.9	26.8	26.3	24.6	26.0	24.2
22.0	21.8	23.0	24.2	22.8	21.8	19.7	19.7	20.1
41.7	38.7	38.3	39.5	39.5	38.8	39.5	39.4	37.6
58.3	61.3	61.7	60.5	60.5	61.2	60.5	60.6	62.4
56.3	53.6	53.2	58.4	61.65	57.08	63.16	59.81	53.64
43.7	46.4	46.8	41.6	38.35	42.92	36.84	40.19	46.36

1-9 平均每天主要社会经济活动
SELECTED INDICATORS ON AVERAGE DAILY SOCLAL AND ECONOMIC ACTIVITIES

指　标	Indicator	单位	Unit	2000 年	2005 年
全市生产总值	GDP	万元	10 000 yuan	32637	73629
工业总产值	Gross Industrial Output Value	万元	10 000 yuan	53174	137035
农林牧渔业总产值	Gross Output Value of Farming, Forestry, Animal Husbandry and Fishery	万元	10 000 yuan	6803	8781
主要工业产品产量	Output of Major Industrial Products				
发电量	Electricity	万千瓦时	10 000 kW · h	2489	2701
钢材	Rolled-steel	吨	ton	2558	9049
纱	Yarn	吨	ton	191	198
布	Cloth	万米	10 000 m	114	141
家用电冰箱	Refrigerator	台	unit	8523	24899
彩色电视机	Color TV set	台	unit	10395	36282
社会消费品零售总额	Total Retail Sales of Consumer Goods	万元	10 000 yuan	11734	23839
固定资产投资	Investment in Fixed Assets above Designated Size	万元	10 000 yuan	6649	38446
外贸进出口总额	Imports and Exports	万美元	10 000 USB	3707	9047
港口吞吐量	Volume of Freight Handled in Ports	万吨	10 000 tons	23.73	51.31

注：固定资产投资包括城镇、农村 500 万元以上投资项目。
Note: Investment in fixed assets includes construction projects involving an urban or rural investment of 5, 000, 00 yuan and over.

2006年	2008年	2009年	2010年	2011年	2012年	2013年	2014年	2015年	2016年	2017年
87210	120591	132983	157507	184267	203406	223214	242481	259518	279268	302391
162159	245116	280976	318215	363780	419351	462936	477924	493683	477143	356705
9304	10982	11195	13238	14683	15521	16763	17261	18086	18473	18984
3412	4509	4730	4984	4759	4787	4935	4885	4754	4805	4981
10288	9593	9579	9136	9101	7525	6312	5830	3853	5243	7996
154	118	106	97	53	53	92	89	76	92	73
151	133	85	48	120	134	141	122	77	68	65
35342	19813	22663	21951	19686	15754	14366	16714	23893	24170	22429
33030	22922	29170	30444	31622	39452	41426	46984	37704	57855	46658
27845	40883	47403	52130	63079	72209	81831	92102	101745	112464	124411
40704	55315	67367	82808	95960	113806	137751	157973	179608	204238	213071
12527	14695	12288	15633	19768	20057	21346	21887	19239	119196 （万元）	137904 （万元）
61.47	82.27	86.76	96	104	114	125	131	136	141	141

1-10 主要指标占全国全省比重（2017年）

PERCENTAGE OF MAIN INDICATORS TO CHINA AND SHANDONG（2017）

指 标	Indicator	单位	Unit
一、生产总值	GDP	亿元	100 million yuan
第一产业	Primary Industry	亿元	100 million yuan
第二产业	Secondary Industry	亿元	100 million yuan
第三产业	Tertiary Industry	亿元	100 million yuan
二、年末总人口（常住人口）	The Total Population（Resident Population）at the End of the Year	万人	10 000 persons
三、主要工业产品产量	Output of Major Industrial Products		
纱	Yarn	万吨	10 000 tons
布	Cloth	亿米	100 million m
家用电冰箱	Refrigerator	万台	10 000 units
彩色电视机	Color TV Set	万台	10 000 units
发电量	Electricity	亿千瓦小时	100 million kW·h
钢材	Rolled-steel	万吨	10 000 tons
水泥	Cement	万吨	10 000 tons
四、主要农产品产量	Output of Major Farm Products		
粮食	Grain	万吨	10 000 tons
油料	Oil Plants	万吨	10 000 tons
肉类产量	Meat	万吨	10 000 tons
水产品	Aquatic Products	万吨	10 000 tons
五、固定资产投资额	Investment in Fixed Assets	亿元	100 million yuan
六、社会消费品零售总额	Total Retail Sales of Consumer Goods	亿元	100 million yuan
七、高等学校在校学生	Students Enrollment of Institutions of Higher Education	万人	10 000 persons

注：1. 本表全国、全省均为公报数。
2. 青岛市主要工业产品产量数据为本地口径。

Note：1. The number of the country and province in the table are obtained from the statistical report.
2. The output of main industrial products of qingdao are at local calibre.

全国 China	全省 Shandong	青岛市 Qingdao	青岛市占全国比重（%） Qingdao/China	青岛市占全省比重（%） Qingdao/Shandong
827122	72678.2	11037.28	1.33	15.19
65468	4876.7	380.97	0.58	7.81
334623	32925.1	4546.21	1.36	13.81
427032	34876.3	6110.10	1.43	17.52
139008	10005.83	929.05	0.67	9.29
4050.0	876.8	2.65	0.07	0.30
868.1	121.1	2.36	0.27	1.95
8548.4	821.4	818.7	9.58	99.67
15755.9	1704.4	1703.0	10.81	99.92
64951.4	4979.6	181.8	0.28	3.65
104958.8	9209.8	291.9	0.28	3.17
234000	15300	525.4	0.22	3.43
61791	4723	297	0.48	6.29
3732	328	39	1.05	11.90
8431	772	54	0.64	7.03
6938	881	108	1.56	12.26
641238	54236	7777.1	1.21	14.34
366262	33649	4541	1.24	13.50
2753.6	201.5	34.6	1.26	17.17

1-11　主要年份全市生产总值（按当年价格计算）
MAJOR YEAR'S GROSS DOMESTIC PRODUCT（AT CURRENT PRICE）

单位：亿元（100 million yuan）

年 份 Year	全市生产总值 GDP	第一产业 Primary Industry	第二产业 Secondary Industry	#工 业 Industry	第三产业 Tertiary Industry	人均生产总值（元） Per Capita GDP（yuan）
1949	2.87	1.19	1.10		0.58	71
1952	6.74	1.76	3.25	2.95	1.73	163
1957	10.82	2.00	5.76	5.39	3.06	239
1962	9.69	1.11	4.68	4.27	3.90	205
1965	15.50	1.80	8.96	8.48	4.74	325
1970	23.23	3.15	14.46	13.86	5.62	451
1975	29.07	6.93	15.39	14.67	6.75	522
1978	38.43	8.73	20.25	19.15	9.45	663
1980	48.65	10.19	26.27	24.28	12.19	819
1985	82.28	21.29	37.55	34.03	23.44	1311
1988	142.87	32.72	70.32	63.42	39.83	2199
1990	180.77	39.26	86.76	78.94	54.75	2714
1991	205.65	43.04	98.94	89.64	63.67	3053
1992	261.35	43.92	130.27	117.61	87.16	3856
1993	371.90	62.20	183.35	164.35	126.35	5455
1994	510.81	85.12	244.30	218.87	181.39	7436
1995	631.45	112.53	294.43	263.98	224.49	9089
1996	713.60	133.27	322.33	289.87	258.00	10130
1997	802.59	117.47	378.25	342.80	306.87	11235
1998	901.19	140.66	409.60	369.89	350.93	12443
1999	1018.97	138.19	468.67	424.15	412.11	13884
2000	1191.25	140.85	555.21	504.44	495.19	16009

1-11 续表 1
Continued

单位：亿元（100 million yuan）

年 份 Year	全市生产总值 GDP	第一产业 Primary Industry	第二产业 SecondaryIndustry	#工 业 Industry	第三产业 Tertiary Industry	人均生产总值（元） Per Capita GDP（yuan）
2001	1368.55	144.35	643.44	582.99	580.76	18128
2002	1583.51	147.21	758.33	686.55	677.97	20655
2003	1869.44	148.92	923.76	832.31	796.76	23986
2004	2270.16	163.49	1149.94	1032.50	956.73	28540
2005	2687.46	178.33	1392.02	1259.06	1117.10	33085
2006	3183.18	183.95	1666.96	1517.28	1332.28	38608
2007	3750.16	203.59	1934.52	1766.28	1612.05	44964
2008	4401.56	223.40	2234.83	2034.25	1943.33	52266
2009	4853.87	230.25	2420.14	2174.43	2203.48	57251
2010	5749.02	276.99	2823.43	2519.00	2648.60	65827
2011	6725.76	306.38	3236.92	2880.76	3182.46	76804
2012	7424.32	324.41	3496.46	3135.54	3603.45	84063
2013	8147.32	340.50	3745.12	3356.16	4061.70	91376
2014	8850.54	349.62	4014.99	3559.81	4485.93	98283
2015	9472.40	363.98	4168.11	3689.57	4940.31	104418
2016	10193.29	371.01	4309.65	3802.65	5512.63	111396
2017	11037.28	380.97	4546.21	3952.87	6110.10	119357

注：1. 人均生产总值按常住人口计算。
2. 自 2005 年起三次产业分类采用《国民经济行业分类》（GB/T4754-2002）标准，自 2013 年起，根据《国民经济行业分类》（GB/T4754－2011）和《三次产业划分规定》（国统字［2012］108 号），将农林牧渔业中的农林牧渔服务业以及工业中的开采辅助活动和金属制品、机械和设备修理业归入第三产业。
3. 实施研发支出核算方法改革后，对各年度 GDP 数据进行了系统修订（以下相关表同）。

Note：1. Per capita GDP are calculated at permanent population.
2. Three Industries are grouped by "Classification and Code of the Sectors of the National Economy"（GB/T4754-2002）since 2005，from 2013 on，According to the Industrial Classification for National Economic Activities（GB/T4754-2011）and the Rules for Classification of Three Industries（NBS No.［2012］108），the service industries of Agriculture，Forestry，Animal Husbandry and Fishery and mining auxiliary activities and metal products，machinery and equipment repair industries in the Industry are classified into the tertiary industry.
3. After implementing the reform of R&D expenditure accounting method, the annual GDP data were systematically revised（the same as the following tables）。

1-12　主要年份全市生产总值构成（以全市生产总值为100）
COMPOSITION OF MAJOR YRAR'S GROSS DOMESTIC PRODUCT（GROSS DOMESTIC PRODUCT=100）

单位：%

年份 Year	全市生产总值 GDP	第一产业 Primary Industry	第二产业 Secondary Industry	#工业 Industry	第三产业 Tertiary Industry
1952	100	26.1	48.2	43.8	25.7
1957	100	18.5	53.3	49.8	28.2
1962	100	11.4	48.3	44.1	40.3
1965	100	11.6	57.8	54.7	30.6
1970	100	13.6	62.2	59.7	24.2
1975	100	23.9	52.9	50.5	23.2
1978	100	22.7	52.7	49.8	24.6
1980	100	21.0	54.0	49.9	25.1
1985	100	25.9	45.6	41.4	28.5
1988	100	22.9	49.2	44.4	27.9
1990	100	21.7	48.0	43.7	30.3
1991	100	20.9	48.1	43.6	31.0
1992	100	16.8	49.8	45.0	33.4
1993	100	16.7	49.3	44.2	34.0
1994	100	16.7	47.8	42.8	35.5
1995	100	17.8	46.6	41.8	35.6
1996	100	18.7	45.2	40.6	36.2
1997	100	14.6	47.1	42.7	38.2
1998	100	15.6	45.5	41.0	38.9
1999	100	13.6	46.0	41.6	40.4
2000	100	11.8	46.6	42.3	41.6
2001	100	10.5	47.0	42.6	42.4
2002	100	9.3	47.9	43.4	42.8
2003	100	8.0	49.4	44.5	42.6
2004	100	7.2	50.7	45.5	42.1
2005	100	6.6	51.8	46.8	41.6
2006	100	5.8	52.4	47.7	41.8
2007	100	5.4	51.6	47.1	43.0
2008	100	5.1	50.8	46.2	44.1
2009	100	4.7	49.9	44.8	45.4
2010	100	4.8	49.1	43.8	46.1
2011	100	4.6	48.1	42.8	47.3
2012	100	4.4	47.1	42.2	48.5
2013	100	4.2	46.0	41.2	49.8
2014	100	3.9	45.4	40.2	50.7
2015	100	3.8	44.0	39.0	52.2
2016	100	3.6	42.3	37.3	54.1
2017	100	3.4	41.2	35.8	55.4

1-13 主要年份全市生产总值增长速度(以上年为100)

GROWTH RATE OF MAJOR YEAR'S GROSS DOMESTIC PRODUCT (PRECEDING YEAR=100)

单位：%

年份 Year	全市生产总值 GDP	第一产业 Primary Industry	第二产业 Secondary Industry	第三产业 Tertiary Industry	人均生产总值(元) Per Capita GDP (yuan)
1979	12.0	10.6	12.9	11.4	10.4
1980	10.4	4.3	13.1	10.3	9.4
1981	-2.0	-9.1	-2.4	4.7	-3.2
1982	4.1	5.5	-0.2	11.9	2.6
1983	16.9	42.8	9.3	12.7	15.3
1984	13.0	18.9	11.5	10.3	12.0
1985	9.9	5.4	5.8	21.3	9.3
1986	9.2	2.6	12.1	10.0	8.3
1987	12.0	3.6	16.0	12.0	10.6
1988	13.8	-0.3	21.5	11.2	12.1
1990	9.3	9.8	7.3	12.2	8.0
1991	10.6	9.9	11.0	10.5	9.4
1992	18.1	2.7	23.5	20.7	17.4
1993	22.4	20.5	21.1	25.6	21.7
1994	14.4	3.6	14.7	20.2	13.5
1995	12.0	10.9	12.1	12.4	10.8
1996	7.2	7.7	7.6	6.4	5.7
1997	11.5	-10.6	16.8	14.6	9.9
1998	12.9	17.6	11.3	13.4	11.3
1999	13.9	4.1	15.5	15.3	12.4
2000	15.2	6.5	16.4	16.4	13.6
2001	13.7	2.3	16.3	14.2	12.1
2002	14.5	3.2	16.9	14.6	12.7

1-13 续表 1
Continued

单位：%

年 份 Year	全市生产总值 GDP	第一产业 Primary Industry	第二产业 Secondary Industry	第三产业 Tertiary Industry	人均生产总值 （元） Per Capita GDP （yuan）
2003	16.3	2.5	20.1	14.9	14.4
2004	16.7	2.7	20.3	15.2	14.3
2005	16.6	0.4	19.6	15.7	14.1
2006	15.3	0.9	16.8	15.8	13.6
2007	15.5	-2.6	15.3	18.3	14.2
2008	13.2	1.4	11.1	17.1	12.1
2009	12.2	3.0	12.8	12.5	11.4
2010	12.9	1.4	12.6	14.4	11.2
2011	11.8	5.0	11.9	12.5	11.5
2012	10.6	3.2	11.3	10.5	9.6
2013	10.0	2.0	10.1	10.6	9.0
2014	8.0	3.8	8.3	8.1	7.0
2015	8.1	3.2	7.3	9.3	7.3
2016	7.9	2.9	6.7	9.2	6.9
2017	7.5	3.2	6.8	8.4	6.4
1978-2010 平均每年增长 1978-2010 Average Increase Rate	12.4	5.3	13.1	13.9	11.0
1991-2010 平均每年增长 1991-2010 Average Increase Rate	14.2	4.2	15.5	15.3	12.8
1996-2010 平均每年增长 1996-2010 Average Increase Rate	13.8	2.5	15.2	14.5	13.0
2001-2010 平均每年增长 2001-2010 Average Increase Rate	14.7	1.5	16.1	15.2	13.0
2006-2010 平均每年增长 2006-2010 Average Increase Rate	13.8	0.8	13.7	15.6	12.5
2010-2015 平均每年增长 2010-2015 Average Increase Rate	9.7	2.8	9.8	10.3	8.9

1-14 分市、区生产总值（2017 年）
GROSS DOMESTIC PRODUCT BY REGION (2017)

单位：亿元（100 million yuan）

市、区名称	Region	地区生产总值 GDP	第一产业 Primary Industry	第二产业 Secondary Industry	第三产业 Tertiary Industry
市南区	Shinan District	1095.21		100.77	994.44
市北区	Shibei District	756.57		153.37	603.20
李沧区	Licang District	400.63		122.22	278.41
崂山区	Laoshan District	623.13	6.48	280.16	336.49
黄岛区	Huangdao District	3092.11	67.45	1440.36	1584.30
城阳区	Chengyang District	1009.60	3.60	517.36	488.64
即墨区	Jimo District	1310.61	64.32	711.76	534.53
胶州市	Jiaozhou	1137.02	51.30	587.47	498.25
平度市	Pingdu	875.19	109.61	447.41	318.17
莱西市	Laixi	595.72	66.28	288.03	241.41
红岛经济区	Qingdao National High-tech Industrial Development Zone	90.67	11.93	42.35	36.39
保税港区	Qingdao Free Trade Port Area of China	120.60		33.97	86.63

1-15 按支出法计算的全市生产总值(2017年)

GROSS DOMESTIC PRODUCT BY EXPENDITURE APPROACH (2017)

单位：亿元(100 million yuan)

项　目	Item	2017年	2016年	2017年为2016年% 2017/2016(%)
支出法计算的全市生产总值	**Gross Domestic Product by Expenditure Approach**	**11037.27**	**10193.29**	**107.5**
(一)最终消费	Final Consumption Expenditures	3922.08	3615.16	107.8
1. 居民消费	Household Consumption Expenditures	2832.30	2574.17	108.1
农村居民	Rural Household	482.11	443.76	106.9
城镇居民	Urban Household	2350.19	2130.41	108.4
2. 政府消费	Government Consumption Expenditures	1089.77	1040.99	107.0
(二)资本形成总额	Gross Capital Formation	6878.26	6381.46	106.3
1. 固定资产形成总额	Gross Fixed Capital Formation	6642.94	6140.60	106.7
2. 存货增加	Change in Inventories	235.33	240.86	94.1
(三)货物和服务净流出	Net Exports of Goods and Services	236.93	196.67	132.7

注：绝对额按当年价格计算，速度按可比价格计算。
Note：The absolute numbers are calculated at current price，their growth are calculated at constant price.

1-16　全市生产总值构成(2017 年)
COMPOSITION OF GROSS DOMESTIC PRODUCT（2017）

指　　标	Indicator	增加值（亿元）Added Value（100 million yuan）	2017 年为 2016 年 % 2017/2016（%）
地区生产总值	**GDP**	**11037.28**	**107.5**
农、林、牧、渔业	Farming，Forestry，Animal Husbandry and Fishery	403.36	103.6
农、林、牧、渔服务业	Agriculture，Forestry，Animal Husbandry and Fishery Service Industry	22.39	112.0
工业	Industry	3952.87	106.7
#开采辅助活动	#Mining Auxiliary Activities		
#金属制品、机械和设备修理业	#Metal Products，Machinery and Equipment Pepair Industries	8.88	106.6
建筑业	Construction	602.22	107.5
批发和零售业	Wholesale and Retail Trade	1318.89	108.9
交通运输、仓储和邮政业	Transport，Storage and Post	777.96	108.9
住宿和餐饮业	Hotels and Catering Services	244.55	117.8
信息传输、软件和信息技术服务业	Information Transmission Computer Services and Softwar	261.90	119.7
金融业	Financial Intermediation	730.98	105.2
房地产业	Real Extate	620.32	107.0
租赁和商务服务业	Leasing and Business Services	554.05	129.3
科学研究和技术服务业	Scientific Research and Technical Services	264.52	132.7
水利、环境和公共设施管理业	Management of Water Conservancy Environment and Public Facilities	50.24	81.0
居民服务、修理和其他服务业	Services to Households and Other Services	276.89	113.5
教育	Education	310.36	80.7
卫生和社会工作	Health Social Security and Social Welfare	212.68	98.3
文化、体育和娱乐业	Culture Sports and Entertainment	78.22	92.5
公共管理、社会保障和社会组织	Public Management and Social Organizations	377.29	103.3
第一产业	Primary Industry	380.97	103.2
第二产业	Secondary Industry	4546.21	106.8
第三产业	Tertiary Industry	6110.10	108.4

主要统计指标解释

国内生产总值（GDP） 指按市场价格计算的一个国家（或地区）所有常住单位在一定时期内生产活动的最终成果。国内生产总值有三种表现形态，即价值形态、收入形态和产品形态。从价值形态看，它是所有常住单位在一定时期内生产的全部货物和服务价值超过同期中间投入的全部非固定资产货物和服务价值的差额，即所有常住单位的增加值之和；从收入形态看，它是所有常住单位在一定时期内创造并分配给常住单位和非常住单位的初次收入分配之和；从产品形态看，它是所有常住单位在一定时期内最终使用的货物和服务价值与货物和服务净出口价值之和。在实际核算中，国内生产总值有三种计算方法，即生产法、收入法和支出法。三种方法分别从不同的方面反映国内生产总值及其构成。对于一个地区来说，称为地区生产总值或地区 GDP。

人均 GDP 人均 GDP 是一定时期内 GDP 与同期人口平均数的比值。按照国际标准，人口平均数应该是同期平均常住人口。我国在核算制度中也规定，无论是国家还是地区，人口数都采用常住人口。国家统计局规定从 2004 年开始，过去采用户籍人口计算人均 GDP 的地区，作为过渡性措施，可在两年内同时计算两种口径的人均 GDP（数据后面必须注明是什么口径），两年后取消按户籍人口计算的人均 GDP。我市采用常住人口计算人均 GDP。

三次产业 是根据社会生产活动历史发展的顺序对产业结构的划分，产品直接取自自然界的部门称为第一产业，对初级产品进行再加工的部门称为第二产业，为生产和消费提供各种服务的部门称为第三产业。它是世界上通用的产业结构分类，但各国的划分不尽一致。我国的三次产业划分是：

第一产业：是指农业、林业、畜牧业、渔业和农林牧渔服务业。

第二产业：是指采矿业，制造业，电力、燃气及水的生产和供应业；建筑业。

第三产业：除第一、第二产业以外的其他行业。

支出法国内生产总值 是从最终使用角度反映一个国家（或地区）一定时期内生产活动最终成果的一种方法，包括最终消费支出，资本形成总额及货物和服务净出口三部分。对于地区，名称为“支出法地区生产总值”。

最终消费指常住单位为满足物质、文化和精神生活的需要，从本国经济领土和国外购买的货物和服务的支出；不包括非常住单位在本国经济领土内的消费支出。最终消费分为居民消费和政府消费。

居民消费 指常住住户在一定时期内对货物和服务的全部最终消费支出。居民消费支出除了直接以货币形式购买货物和服务的消费之外，还包括以其他方式获得的货物和服务的消费支出，即所谓的虚拟消费支出。居民虚拟消费支出包括以下几种类型：单位以实物报酬及实物转移的形式提供给劳动者的货物和服务；住户生产并由本住户消费了的货物和服务，其中的服务仅指住户的自有住房服务和付酬的家庭雇员提供的家庭和个人服务；金融机构提供的金融媒介服务。

政府消费 指政府部门为全社会提供公共服务的消费支出和免费或以较低价格向居民住户提供的货物和服务的净支出。前者等于政府服务的产出价值减去政府单位所获得的经营收入的价值；后者等于政府部门免费或以较低价格向居民住户提供的货物和服务的市场价值减去向住户收取的价值。

资本形成总额 指常住单位在一定时期内获得的减去处置的固定资产和存货的净额，包括固定资本形成总额和存货增加。

固定资本形成总额 指常住单位在一定时期内获得的固定资产减处置的固定资产的价值总额。固定资产是通过生产活动生产出来的，且使用年限在一年以上、单位价值在规定标准以上的资产，不包括自然资产。分有形固定资产形成总额和无形固定资产形成总额。有形固定资产形成总额包括一定时期内完成的建筑工程、安装工程和设备工器具购置（减处置）价值，以及土地改良、新增役、种、奶、毛、娱乐用牲畜和新增经济林木价值。无形固定资产形成总额包括矿藏的勘探、计算机软件等获得减处置。

存货增加 指常住单位在一定时期内存货实物量变动的市场价值，即期末价值减期初价值的差额，再扣除当期由于价格变动而产生的持有收益。存货增加可以是正值，也可以是负值；正值表示存货上升，负值表示存货下降。它包括生产单位购进的原材料、燃料和储备物资等存货，以及生产单位生产的产成品、在制品和半成品等存货。

货物和服务净出口　指货物和服务出口减货物和服务进口的差额。出口包括常住单位向非常住单位出售或无偿转让的各种货物和服务的价值；进口包括常住单位从非常住单位购买或无偿得到的各种货物和服务的价值。由于服务活动的提供与使用同时发生，一般把常住单位从国外得到的服务作为进口，非常住单位从本国得到的服务作为出口。货物的出口和进口都按离岸价格计算。

气候　指地球与大气之间长期能量交换与质量交换所形成的一种自然环境状态，它是多种因素综合作用的结果。气候既是人类生活和生产的环境要素之一，又是供给人类生活和生产的重要资源。气温、降水、湿度等气象要素的多年平均值是用来描述一个地区气候状况的主要参数，而各种气象要素某年、某月的平均值（或总量）则可以反映出该时期天气气候状况的重要特征。

气温　指空气的温度，我国一般以摄氏度（℃）为单位表示。气象观测的温度表是放在离地面约 1.5 米处通风良好的百叶箱里测量的，因此，通常说的气温指的是离地 1.5 米处百叶箱中的温度。其统计计算方法为：月平均气温是将全月各日的平均气温相加，除以该月的天数而得。

年平均气温　是将 12 个月的月平均气温累加后除以 12 而得。

降水量　指从天空降落到地面的液态或固态（经融化后）水，未经蒸发、渗透、流失而在地面上积聚的深度。其统计计算方法为：月降水量是将全月各日的降水量累加而得。年降水量是将 12 个月的月降水量累加而得。

Explanatory Notes on Main Statistical Indicators

Gross Domestic Product（GDP）　refers to the final products at market prices producted by all resident units in a country（or a region）during a certain period of time. Gross domestic product is expressed in three different persperctives，namely value，income，and products respectively. GDP in its value perspective refers to the total value of all goods and services produced by all resident units during a certain period of time，minus the total value of input of goods and services of the nature of non-fixed assets；in other words，it is the sum of the value-added of all resident units. GDP from the perspective of products refers to the value of all goods and services for final consumption by all resident units minus the net exports of goods and services during a given period of time. In the practice of national accounting，gross domestic product is calculated from three approaches，namely produciton approach，income approach and expenditure approach，which reflect gross domestic product and its composition from different angles. For a certain region，it refers region gross product or region GDP.

Per Capita GDP　refers to the ratio of GDP in a certain term and average population in the same term. According to the international standard，average population should be average permanent population in the same term. In the account regulation，population of both the country and the region should be permanent population. In the after two yers since 2004，per capita GDP can be calculated at two coverage. i. e. at permanent oppulation and household registered population（the note of coverage should follow the data.）The per capita GDP calculated with household registered population will be abolished after two years. Per capita GDP of Qingdao is calculated at permanent population.

Three Strata of Industries　has been classfied according to the historical sequence of development. Primary industry refers to extraction of natural resources；secondary industry involves processing of primary products；and tertiary industry provides services of various kinds for production and consumption. The above classification is universal although it varies to some extent form country to country. In China economic activities are categorized into the following three strata of industry：

Primary industry refers to farming，forestry，animal husbandryand fishery and services in support of these industries.

Secondary industry refers to mining and quarrying，manufacturing，production and supply of electricity，water and gas，and construction.

Tertiary industry refers to all other economic activities not included in primary or secondary industries.

GDP by Expenditure Approach refers to the method of measuring the final results of production activities of a country (region) during a given period from the perspective of final use. It includes final consumption, total capital formation and net export of goods and services. It reflects use and composition of gross domestic product. For a certain region, it refers region gross product by expenditure approach.

Final Consumption refers to the total expenditure of resident units for purchases of goods and services from both the domestic economic territory and abroad to meet the needs of material, cultural and spiritual life. It does not include the expenditure of non-resident units on consumption in the economic territory of the country. The final consumption is broken down into household consumption and government consumption.

Household Consumption refers to the total expenditure of resident households on the final consumption of goods and services. In addition to the consumption of goods and services bought by the households directly with money, the household consumption also includes expenditure on goods and services obtained by the households in other ways, i. e. the so-called imputed consumption, which includes the following : (a) the goods and services provided to households by employers in the form of payment in kind and transfer in kind ; (b) goods and services produced and consumed by the households themselves, in which the services refer to the owner-occupied housing and services offered by payed family employees ; (c) financial intermediate services provided by financial institution.

Government Consumption refers to the consumption expenditure spent for the provision of public services provided by the government to the whole country and the net expenditure on the goods and services provided by the government to households free of charge or at reduced prices. The former equals to the output value of the government services minus the value of operating income obtained by the government departments. The latter equals to the market value of the goods and services provided by the government free of charge or at reduced prices to the households minus the value received by the government from the households.

Gross Capital Formation refers to the fixed assets acquired less disposal and the net value of inventory, thus including the gross fixed capital formation and charges in inventories.

Gross Fixed Capital Formation refers to the value of acquisitions less those disposals of fixed assets during a given period. Fixed assets are the assets produced through production activities with unit value above a specified amount and which could be used for over one year. Natural assets are not included. Gross fixed capital formation can be categorized into total tangible fixed capital formation and total intangible fixed capital formation. Total tangible fixed capital formation includes the value of the construction projects and installation projects completed and the equipment, apparatus and instruments purchased (less those disposed) as well as the value of land improved, the value of draught animals, breeding stock and animals for milk, for wool and for recreational purposes and the newly increased forest with economic value. Total intangible fixed capital formation includes the prospecting of minerals and the acquisition of computer software minus the disposal of them.

Charges in Inventories refers to the market value of the change in the physical volume of inventory of resident units during a given period, i. e. the difference between the values at the beginning and at the end of the period minus the gains due to the change in prices. The changes in inventories can have a positive or a negative value. A positive value indicates an increase in inventory while a negative value indicates a decrease in inventory. The inventory includes raw materials, fuels and reserve materials purchased by the production units as well as the inventory of finished products, semi-finished products and work-in-progress.

Net Export of Goods and Services refers to the exports of goods and services subtracting the imports of goods and services. Exports include the value of various goods and services sold or gratuitously transferred by resident units to non-resident units. Imports include the value of various goods and services purchased or gratuitously acquired resident units from non-resident units. Because the provision of services and the use of them happen simultaneously, the acquisition of services by resident units from abroad is usually treated as import while the acquisition of services by non-resident units in this country is usually treated as export. The exports and imports of goods are calculated at FOB.

Climate refers to the natural environmental status formed by the long-term exchange of energy and mass between the earth and the air, and is the results of interaction of many factors. Climate is both one of the environment factors and the important resources for the living and production activities of the human being. The average values across several years of meteorological factors such as temperature, rainfall and humidity are used as important parameters to describe the climate of a region, while the average values (or total values) of a given year or month of meteorological factors reflect the key characteristics of climate for that period of time.

Temperature refers to the air temperature. China uses centigrade as the unit. The thermometry used for weather observation is put in a breezy shutter, which is 1.5 meters high from the ground. Therefore, the commonly used temperature refers to the temperature in the breezy shutter 1.5 meters away from the ground. The calculation method is as follows :

Monthly average temperature is the summation of average daily temperature of one month divided by the actual days of that particular month.

Annual average temperature is the summation of monthly average of a year divided by 12 months.

Volume of Precipitation refers to the deepness of liquid state or solid state (thawed) water falling from the sky to the ground that has not been evaporated, infiltrated or run off. The calculation method is as follows :

Monthly precipitation is the summation of daily precipitation of a month.

Annual precipitation is the summation of 12 months precipitation of a year.

人 口 2

POPULATION

简要说明

一、本篇资料的主要内容

本篇资料主要反映了全市人口方面的基本情况，包括全市主要年份和区（市）的户数、人口数、人口密度、土地面积数据、人口出生率、死亡率、自然增长率、计划生育等数据。另外还对建国以来开展的六次人口普查主要数据进行了比较。

二、本篇资料的来源

本篇资料分别来源于国家开展的人口普查、人口抽样调查和市公安局的户籍登记资料，由市统计局人口和社会科技统计处整理提供。

Brief Introduction

Ⅰ. Main Content

Data in this chapter show the basic condition of population, such as the basic condition of districts and county-level cities, household, population, density of population, birth rate, death rate, natural growth rate and family planning situation. Furthermore, relevant figures obtained from the six national population censuses have been compared.

Ⅱ. Source of Data

Data in this chapter are from national population censuses, national sample survey. Some are derived from household registration provided by Qingdao Municipal Bureau of Public Security. The data are compiled by the Division of Population and Science & Technology of Qingdao Municipal Bureau of Statistics.

2-1 主要年份全市户籍人口数
MAJOR YEAR'S TOTAL REGISTERED POPULATION

单位：人（person）

年 份 Year	总人口 Total Population	按性别分 Grouped by Sex		平均人口 Average Population
		男 Male	女 Female	
1949	4056550	1997293	2059257	4054431
1952	4233586	2125392	2108194	4203428
1957	4822756	2424729	2398027	4773862
1962	4627432	2319658	2307774	4578313
1965	4901670	2461629	2440041	4859712
1970	5391852	2720633	2671219	5337282
1975	5742206	2904347	2837859	5717456
1978	5853321	2959800	2893521	5841638
1980	5961129	3015357	2945772	5937187
1985	6267223	3185409	3081814	6253157
1988	6516920	3319534	3197386	6474541
1989	6571597	3348454	3223143	6544259
1990	6666482	3392253	3274229	6619040
1991	6709277	3411776	3297501	6687880
1992	6731072	3420886	3310186	6720175
1993	6753497	3431149	3322348	6742285
1994	6785291	3446019	3339272	6769394
1995	6846346	3476300	3370046	6815819
1996	6902677	3502600	3400077	6874512
1997	6954391	3527588	3426803	6928534
1998	6995666	3545403	3450263	6975029
1999	7029707	3561061	3468646	7012687
2000	7066481	3577367	3489114	7048094
2001	7104875	3595652	3509223	7085678
2002	7156537	3619778	3536759	7130706
2003	7206806	3644032	3562774	7181672
2004	7311228	3692991	3618237	7259017
2005	7409052	3740309	3668743	7360140
2006	7493812	3779891	3713921	7451432
2007	7579910	3816620	3763290	7536861
2008	7615647	3824665	3790982	7597779
2009	7629161	3823534	3805627	7622404
2010	7636392	3819240	3817152	7632777
2011	7663612	3826931	3836681	7650002
2012	7695585	3838205	3857380	7679599

注：截止出书前，未获得公安部门青岛市 2013 年—2017 年户籍人口信息。
Note：Data come from the Qingdao Nunicipal Public Security Bureau，and the Data of 2013—2017 are absent.

2-2　主要年份全市户数、人口数、人口密度（户籍）

MAJOR YEAR'S HOUSEHOLDS, POPULATION AND DENSITY OF POPULATION（WITH PERMANENT RESIDENCE）

年份 Year	总户数（万户） Total Households （10000 households）		总人口（万人） Total Population （10000 persons）		平均每户人口（人） Average Persons Per Household（person）		人口密度（人/平方公里） Density of Population （person/sq.km）	
	全市 Whole Municipality	市区 Urban Area	全市 Whole Municepality	市区 Urban Area	全市 Whole Municepality	市区 Urban Area	全市 Whole Municepality	市区 Urban Area
1949	90.64	21.68	405.66	103.69	4.48	4.78	381	941
1952	93.96	22.70	423.36	107.62	4.51	4.74	397	977
1957	102.56	27.41	482.28	134.76	4.70	4.92	453	1223
1962	106.11	29.29	462.74	137.86	4.36	4.71	434	1251
1965	105.31	29.64	490.17	146.74	4.65	4.95	460	1332
1970	113.07	32.14	539.19	150.81	4.77	4.69	506	1369
1975	123.18	36.56	574.22	161.13	4.66	4.41	539	1462
1978	131.27	40.08	585.33	168.00	4.46	4.19	549	1525
1980	138.44	43.03	596.11	175.27	4.31	4.07	560	1591
1985	157.06	53.43	626.72	190.87	3.99	3.57	588	1732
1988	169.72	58.95	651.69	201.38	3.84	3.42	612	1827
1989	177.47	61.57	657.16	203.63	3.70	3.31	617	1848
1990	186.79	63.94	666.65	205.78	3.57	3.22	626	1867
1991	192.46	67.15	670.93	207.22	3.49	3.09	630	1880
1992	199.08	68.94	673.11	209.28	3.38	3.04	632	1899
1993	201.36	70.13	675.35	212.06	3.35	3.02	634	1924
1994	204.05	71.24	678.53	214.97	3.33	3.02	637	1951
1995	208.13	72.53	684.63	218.38	3.29	3.01	643	1982
1996	212.40	75.11	690.27	223.86	3.25	2.98	648	2032
1997	215.12	76.39	695.44	227.22	3.23	2.97	653	2062
1998	218.59	77.90	699.57	229.58	3.20	2.95	657	2084
1999	222.61	79.27	702.97	231.94	3.16	2.93	660	2105
2000	224.73	80.46	706.65	234.60	3.14	2.92	664	2129
2001	227.43	81.41	710.49	237.60	3.12	2.92	667	2156
2002	229.67	82.85	715.65	241.74	3.12	2.92	672	2194
2003	232.26	84.15	720.68	246.77	3.10	2.93	677	2240
2004	235.29	86.93	731.12	258.40	3.11	2.97	686	2229
2005	237.35	87.99	740.91	265.43	3.12	3.02	695	2290
2006	239.33	89.12	749.38	271	3.13	3.04	703	2338
2007	241.55	90.21	757.99	275.55	3.14	3.05	711	2377
2008	243.18	91.22	761.56	276.25	3.13	3.03	715	2384
2009	244.74	92.15	762.92	275.47	3.12	2.99	676	1873
2010	246.11	93.30	763.64	275.50	3.10	2.95	677	1873
2011	247.94	94.69	766.36	277.09	3.09	2.93	679	1884
2012	249.27	95.87	769.56	279.57	3.09	2.92	682	1901

2-3　主要年份全市常住人口数
MAJOR YEAR' S TOTAL RESIDENT POPULATION

单位：万人（10 000 persons）

年　份 Year	总人口 Total Population
2005	819.55
2006	829.42
2007	838.67
2008	845.61
2009	850.03
2010	871.51
2011	879.51
2012	886.85
2013	896.41
2014	904.62
2015	909.70
2016	920.40
2017	929.05

2-4　青岛市常住人口
TOTAL RESIDENT POPULATION

单位：万人（10 000 persons）

市、区名称	Region	2017 年	2016 年	2017 年比 2016 年 ±% 2017/2016（±%）
全市	**Whole Municipality**	**929.05**	**920.40**	**0.94**
市南区	Shinan District	58.53	58.03	0.86
市北区	Shibei District	109.32	108.37	0.88
李沧区	Licang District	56.12	55.33	1.43
崂山区	Laoshan District	43.87	43.55	0.73
黄岛区	Huangdao District	153.92	151.59	1.54
城阳区	Chengyang District	70.93	70.23	1.00
即墨区	Jimo District	122.45	121.45	0.82
胶州市	Jiaozhou	89.33	88.52	0.92
平度市	Pingdu	138.05	137.26	0.58
莱西市	Laixi	76.42	76.10	0.42
红岛经济区	Qingdao National High-tech Industrial Development Zone	10.11	9.97	1.40

注：黄岛区含保税港区数据。
Note：The Huangdao District contains the data of the bonded harbor area.

2-5　分市、区土地面积（2017 年底）
LAND AREA（END OF 2017）

市、区名称	Region	土地面积（平方公里） Land Area（aq.km）
全　市	**Whole Municipality**	**11293.36**
市南区	Shinan District	32.21
市北区	Shibei District	65.85
李沧区	Licang District	99.10
崂山区	Laoshan District	395.79
黄岛区	Huangdao District	2128.31
城阳区	Chengyang District	583.68
即墨区	Jimo	1920.90
胶州市	Jiaozhou	1323.65
平度市	Pingdu	3175.65
莱西市	Laixi	1568.22

注：2017 年度土地变更调查结果
Note：Survey results of land quality change in 2017.

2-6 第一、二、三、四、五、六次人口普查主要数据
MAIN DATA FROM THE SIX NATIONAL POPULATION CENSUSES

项　目	Item	第一次人口普查 1st National Population Census	第二次人口普查 2nd National Population Census	第三次人口普查 3rd National Population Census	第四次人口普查 4th National Population Census	第五次人口普查 5th National Population Census	第六次人口普查 6th National Population Census
一、总人口（万人）	**Total Population （10000 persons）**	**91.68**	**138.34**	**422.76**	**666.40**	**749.42**	**871.51**
按性别分	By Sex						
男（万人）	Male（10000 persons）	48.44	69.64	214.09	338.86	375.74	439.18
女（万人）	Female（10000 persons）	43.24	68.71	208.67	327.54	373.68	432.33
二、总户数（万户）	**Total Household （10000 households）**	**19.27**	**28.01**	**101.41**	**186.61**	**241.62**	**296.64**
家庭户（万户）	Family Household （10000 households）			101.09	185.56	232.70	282.43
平均家庭户规模（人）	Average Family Household Size（person）			4.07	3.49	2.97	2.79
三、民　族	**Ethnicity**						
民族个数（个）	Number of Ethnic groups （unit）	14	16	25	41	51	53
汉族人口（万人）	Populaiton of Han （10000 persons）	91.33	137.76	422.09	665.58	746.12	863.84
少数民族人口（万人）	Populaiton of Ethnic Minorities（10000 persons）	0.36	0.58	0.67	0.82	3.30	7.67
四、各种文化程度人口	**Popution with Various Education Attainments**						
大　学（万人）	College（10000 persons）		1.51	3.62	12.39	41.64	129.54
高　中（万人）	Senior Secondary School （10000 persons）		4.86	34.82	68.42	111.40	150.82
初　中（万人）	Junior Secondary School （10000 persons）		13.72	102.28	195.10	281.91	334.22
小　学（万人）	Premary School （10000 persons）		51.25	144.52	236.34	206.91	170.77

2-7 计划生育情况（1978-2017 年）
FAMILY PLANNING SITUATION（1978－2017）

年 份 Year	已婚有生育能力的人数（人） Married and Fertile Persons（person）	节育人数（人） Persons under Birth Control（person）	节育率（%） Contraceptive Prevalence Rate（%）	四项手术人数（人） Persons Performed Four-operation（person）	#放环人数 Persons Set Rings
1978	694292	571077	82.25	125913	68475
1980	763226	673069	88.19	180979	70927
1985	1017649	929284	91.32	146742	67234
1990	1258232	1165216	92.61	149327	70964
1991	1319722	1219795	92.43	153970	77406
1992	1348503	1256271	93.16	90107	56226
1993	1380717	1271884	92.12	76783	45492
1994	1400425	1268378	90.57	73169	41482
1995	1427442	1285264	90.04	84099	52716
1996	1459465	1316516	90.21	84370	57648
1997	1482204	1340399	90.43	76579	55285
1998	1505499	1367648	90.84	74199	50526
1999	1523471	1378131	90.46	73663	44976
2000	1521331	1371447	90.15	74285	45999
2001	1514274	1360543	89.85	70205	43601
2002	1541855	1400145	90.81	50575	45453
2003	1518448	1354917	89.23	57458	47953
2004	1540706	1357703	88.04	52934	42859
2005	1590476	1417755	89.14	58097	49716
2006	1604665	1427785	88.98	51864	42457
2007	1595390	1426787	89.43	50074	41198
2008	1587344	1410426	88.85	120539	93291
2009	1623969	1418178	87.33	111084	100193
2010	1591103	1377726	86.59	78721	51794
2011	1581231	1355808	85.74	70823	48210
2012	1575996	1349572	85.63	62880	43021
2013	1527731	1293810	84.69	53252	30851
2014	1506274	1275142	84.66	34008	12827
2015	1475887	1226439	83.10	34879	9108
2016	1456953	1183221	81.21	36449	4474
2017	1439008	1188307	82.58	20905	4669

2-8 分市、区计划生育情况（2017年）
FAMILY PLANNING SITUATION BY REGION（2017）

市、区名称	Region	计划生育率（%）Fertility Rate（%）	计划内（人）Birth within the Plan（person）		计划外出生（人）Birth without the Plan（person）		多胎（人）Third Birth and Above（person）
			一胎 First Birth	二胎 Second Birth	一胎 First Birth	二胎 Second Birth	
全市	**Whole Municipality**	**98.59**	**40545**	**71844**	**206**	**115**	**2973**
市南区	Shinan District	99.50	3613	2858	2	7	95
市北区	Shibei District	99.81	5330	4878	4	10	94
李沧区	Licang District	99.62	2611	3637	1	5	66
崂山区	Laoshan District	99.72	1719	2208		1	41
黄岛区	Huangdao District	98.65	6858	14411	42	22	557
城阳区	Chengyang District	99.42	2990	5134	2	3	149
即墨区	Jimo District	98.39	4915	11174	23	9	493
胶州市	Jiaozhou	97.54	3814	8986	44	20	496
平度市	Pingdu	97.65	5595	12546	53	19	686
莱西市	Laixi	98.27	3100	6012	35	19	296

注：黄岛区含保税港区数据；城阳区含红岛经济区数据。
Note：The Huangdao area contains the data of the bonded harbor area. Chengyang District contains red island economic zone data.

主要统计指标解释

人口数　指一定时点、一定地区范围内有生命的个人总和。

出生率（又称粗出生率）　指在一定时期内（通常为一年）一定地区的出生人数与同期内平均人数（或期中人数）之比，用千分率表示。本资料中的出生率指年出生率，其计算公式为：

$$出生率=\frac{年出生人数}{年平均人数}\times 1000‰$$

式中：出生人数指活产婴儿，即胎儿脱离母体时（不管怀孕月数），有过呼吸或其他生命现象。

死亡率（又称粗死亡率）　指在一定时期内（通常为一年）一定地区的死亡人数与同期内平均人数（或期中人数）之比，用千分率表示。本资料中的死亡率指年死亡率，其计算公式为：

$$死亡率=\frac{年死亡人数}{年平均人数}\times 1000‰$$

人口自然增长率　指在一定时期内（通常为一年）人口自然增加数（出生人数减死亡人数）与该时期内平均人数（或期中人数）之比，用千分率表示。计算公式为：

$$人口自然增长率=\frac{本年出生人数-本年死亡人数}{年平均人数}\times 1000‰$$

$$=人口出生率-人口死亡率$$

Explanatory Notes on Main Statistical Indicators

Total Population　refers to the total number of people alive at a certain point of time within a given area.

Birth Rate (or Crude Birth Rate)　refers to the ratio of the number of births to the average population (or mid-period population) during a certain period of time (usually a year), expressed in ‰. Binth rate in the chapter refers to annual birth rate. The following formula is used :

Birth Rate = (Number of Births/Average Number of Population) × 1000‰

Number of births in the formula refers to live births, i. e. when a baby has breathed or showed any vital phenomena regardless of the longth of pregnancy.

Annual averagc number of population is the average of the number of population at the beginning of the year and that at the end of the year. Sometimes it is substituted by the mid-year population.

Death Rate (or Crnde Death Rate)　refers to the ratio of the number of deaths to the average population (or mid-period population) during a certain period of time (usually a year), expressed in‰. Death rate in the chapter refers to annual death rate. The following formula is used :

Death Rate =(Number of Deaths/Annual Average Number of population) × 1000‰

Natural Growth Rate of Population　refers to the ratio of natural increase in populatlon (number of births minus number of deaths) in a certain period of time (usually a year) to the average population (or mid-period population) of the same period, expressed in ‰. The following formula is applied :

Natural Crowth Rate of Population =[(Number of Births−Number of Deaths)/Average Number of Population] × 1000‰

Natural Crowth Rate of Population = Birth Rate−Death Rate

从业人员及职工工资 3

EMPLOYMENT AND WAGES

简要说明

一、本篇资料的主要内容

本篇资料主要反映了全市从业人员和职工工资方面的基本情况，主要包括全市社会从业人数及各区（市）单位从业人数、在岗职工工资总额和平均工资等方面的资料。

二、本篇资料的来源

单位从业人员和职工工资来源于劳动统计年报，全市从业人员根据劳动统计年报、农村年报和市工商行政管理局、市人力资源和社会保障局、市交通委相关资料测算。由市统计局人口和社会科技统计处整理提供。

Brief Introduction

Ⅰ. Main Content

Data in this chapter show the basic conditions of Qingdao's employment and wages, including the main data on labor statistics of employment, number of employment of the whole city and 12 district and county-level cities, total wage bill and average wage of staff and workers, etc.

Ⅱ. Source of Data

Data on employment and wages are prepared according to the annual reports of labor statistics. Data on social employment are measured according to the annual reports of labor statistics, countryside statistics and related information from Industry & Commerce Administration Bureau, Human Resources & Social Security Bureau and Transportation Commision.

Data in this chapter are compiled by the Division of Population and Science & Technology of Qingdao Municipal Bureau of Statistics.

3-1 社会就业人数（1978-2017 年）
SOCIAL EMPLOYMENT（1978-2017）

单位：万人（10 000 persons）

年份 Year	合计 Total	第一产业 Primary Industry	第二产业 Secondary Industry	第三产业 Tertiary Industry
1978	256.70	157.40	65.60	33.70
1979	265.60	156.10	72.20	37.30
1980	270.10	153.60	82.10	43.20
1981	278.90	153.60	82.10	43.20
1982	282.70	151.10	86.20	45.40
1983	289.60	156.40	85.00	48.10
1984	304.20	149.20	97.70	57.40
1985	315.30	149.20	104.50	61.70
1986	326.40	149.60	112.10	64.60
1987	334.80	149.90	120.20	64.70
1988	336.50	147.60	123.20	65.70
1989	344.20	152.50	122.10	69.60
1990	352.80	156.50	123.30	73.10
1991	361.20	161.90	124.30	74.90
1992	370.30	161.70	127.80	80.80
1993	365.70	160.50	128.80	76.40
1994	367.60	157.10	129.40	81.20
1995	374.20	155.40	132.40	86.40
1996	381.50	152.20	137.10	92.20
1997	388.70	155.20	138.10	95.30
1998	393.10	154.80	138.60	99.70
1999	396.10	150.30	142.00	103.80
2000	397.60	144.70	134.91	117.99
2001	400.50	133.90	142.30	124.30
2002	413.31	121.38	153.85	138.08
2003	438.96	119.91	163.93	155.12
2004	458.81	113.98	180.63	164.20
2005	471.03	104.48	196.80	169.75
2006	490.10	102.97	209.83	177.30
2007	505.80	102.30	217.80	185.70
2008	513.80	102.40	220.80	190.60
2009	525.71	105.65	220.33	199.73
2010	540.34	105.16	223.85	211.33
2011	551.18	106.02	227.08	218.08
2012	559.88	104.95	229.79	225.14
2013	571.47	107.59	232.17	231.71
2014	588.97	108.45	229.91	250.61
2015	595.44	107.92	229.51	258.01
2016	601.44	107.30	228.44	265.70
2017	603.90	101.86	228.14	273.90

3-2 主要年份全市单位就业人员人数
MAJOR YEAR' S NUMBER OF EMPLOYED PERSONS IN ALL UNITS OF THE CITY

单位：万人（10 000 persons）

年份 Year	合计 Total	#市区 Urban Area	#国有单位 State-owned Units	#集体单位 Collective-owned Units	其他所有制单位 Other Ownership Units
1949	14.8	13.4	9.3	5.5	
1952	23.4	20.1	18.3	5.1	
1957	29.7	24.5	24.1	5.6	
1962	32.3	26.8	24.5	7.8	
1965	36.7	30.6	26.8	9.9	
1970	45.6	37.4	32.2	13.4	
1975	53.4	43.5	38.0	15.4	
1978	70.7	54.5	49.2	21.5	
1980	79.2	61.5	55.0	24.2	
1985	88.8	66.7	59.8	28.9	0.1
1988	98.2	70.0	66.7	31.2	0.3
1990	103.2	70.6	69.5	32.9	0.8
1991	105.4	78.4	71.5	32.5	1.4
1992	108.2	80.4	73.6	32.8	1.8
1993	109.4	80.8	75.3	29.5	4.6
1994	110.1	80.2	72.4	28.3	9.4
1995	111.6	80.2	72.4	27.5	11.7
1996	118.4	81.1	71.6	26.0	20.8
1997	117.1	78.1	69.0	22.6	25.5
1998	116.2	75.6	64.2	19.0	33.0
1999	119.0	78.3	60.4	16.6	42.0
2000	118.3	76.6	57.6	14.2	46.5
2001	117.5	75.1	53.2	12.2	52.1
2002	119.1	75.2	49.5	10.3	59.3
2003	118.0	74.3	47.2	8.9	61.9
2004	207.1	111.1	43.7	18.0	145.4
2005	224.3	122.3	43.9	18.2	162.2
2006	243.2	133.7	41.7	16.2	185.3
2007	249.8	137.3	45.1	17.9	186.8
2008	254.1	140.9	44.4	15.4	194.3
2009	260.5	145.6	44.4	14.6	201.5
2010	269.4	151.1	44.6	15.1	209.7
2011	275.9	156.5	44.3	14.7	216.9
2012	283.2	162.1	44.0	13.8	225.4
2013	293.7	184.1	37.8	5.4	250.5
2014	303.0	191.4	36.7	4.9	261.4
2015	309.2	192.4	35.8	4.6	268.8
2016	315.6	196.4	35.5	4.7	275.4
2017	321.4	249.1	35.1	4.6	281.7

注：1. 2004 年以前为城镇单位职工人数。
2. 2013 年统计口径变化，国有单位、集体单位数据与上年不可比。

Note：1. Before 2004，the data refer to number of staff and workers in urban units.
2. Because of the adjustment about the statistics system，the data of State-owned Units and Collective-owned Units since 2013are not fully comparable with historical statistics.

3-3 全市单位国民经济各行业就业人员人数（2017 年）

NUMBER OF EMPLOYED PERSONS IN ALL UNITS OF THE CITY BY SECTOR（2017）

单位：万人（10 000 persons）

		2017 年		2016 年	
		合计 Total	女性 Female	合计 Total	女性 Female
总计	**Total**	**321.4**	**125.7**	**315.6**	**123.8**
1. 农、林、牧、渔业	Farming，Forestry，Animal Husbandry and Fishery	1.2	0.5	1.2	0.4
2. 采矿业	Mining	0.1		0.3	
3. 制造业	Manufacturing	139.4	52.9	146.9	57.0
4. 电力、热力、燃气及水生产和供应业	The Electricity，Heat，Gas and Water Production and Supply Industry	2.6	0.6	2.8	0.7
5. 建筑业	Construction	29.4	4.7	26.3	4.4
6. 批发和零售业	Wholesale and Retail Trade	48.8	23.7	45.5	21.7
7. 交通运输、仓储和邮政业	Transport，Storage and Post	12.8	4.1	12.9	4.0
8. 住宿和餐饮业	Hotels and Catering Services	6.9	3.6	6.0	3.2
9. 信息传输、软件和信息技术服务业	Information Transmission Computer Services and Software	4.2	1.6	3.7	1.4
10. 金融业	Financial Intermediation	6.4	3.5	6.4	3.4
11. 房地产业	Real Estate	8.1	3.0	7.8	2.8
12. 租赁和商务服务业	Leasing and Business Services	14.7	5.7	11.5	4.5
13. 科学研究和技术服务业	Scientific Research and Technical Services	6.7	2.1	6.1	2.1
14. 水利、环境和公共设施管理业	Management of Water Conservancy，Environment and Public Facilities	3.3	1.0	3.4	1.1
15. 居民服务、修理和其他服务业	Residents Service，RePair and Other Services	2.6	1.0	2.4	1.0
16. 教育	Education	14.4	8.4	13.4	7.5
17. 卫生和社会工作	Health and Social Welfare	7.7	5.3	7.1	4.8
18. 文化、体育和娱乐业	Culture，Sports and Entertainment	1.9	0.8	1.8	0.7
19. 公共管理、社会保障和社会组织	Public Management，Social Security and Social Organization	10.2	3.2	10.1	3.1

3-4 全市单位分市、区国民经济各部门就业人员人数（2017年）

NUMBER OF EMPLOYED PERSONS IN ALL UNTTS OF THE CITY BY REGION AND SECTOR（2017）

市、区名称	Region	合计 Total	农林牧渔业 Farming, Forestry, Animal Husbandry and Fishery	采矿业 Mining	制造业 Manufacturing	电力热力燃气及水生产和供应业 The Electricity, Heat, Gas and Water Production and Supply Industry
全市	**Whole Municipality**	**321.4**	**1.2**	**0.1**	**139.4**	**2.6**
市南区	Shiman District	39.1			2.8	0.2
市北区	Shibei District	26.7			2.7	0.5
李沧区	Licang District	14.5			3.7	0.1
崂山区	Laoshan District	22.2	0.1		5.5	0.1
黄岛区	Huangdao District	66.7	0.4		28.0	0.5
城阳区	Chengyang District	37.7			26.1	0.2
即墨区	Jimo District	35.9	0.1		23.6	0.3
胶州市	Jiaozhou	33.9			20.4	0.4
平度市	Pingdu	18.0	0.3	0.1	10.7	0.2
莱西市	Laixi	20.4	0.3		11.7	0.1
红岛经济区	Qingdao National High-tech Industrial Development Zone	3.7			2.3	
保税港区	Qingdao Free Trade Port Area of China	2.6			1.9	

单位：万人（10 000 persons）

建筑业 Construction	批发和零售业 Wholesale and Retail Trade	交通运输仓储和邮政业 Transport，Storage and Post	住宿和餐饮业 Hotels and Catering Services	信息传输软件和信息技术服务业 Information Transmission Computer Services and Software
29.4	**48.8**	**12.8**	**6.9**	**4.2**
2.7	8.8	2.5	2.6	1.7
2.8	7.8	2.5	0.5	0.4
0.7	3.7	0.5	0.6	0.1
4.2	2.2	0.8	0.6	1.5
8.3	12.2	3.2	1.3	0.4
1.8	2.5	1.5	0.4	0.1
1.7	4.5	0.4	0.5	
2.6	4.1	0.8	0.2	
1.0	0.8	0.1	0.1	
3.4	1.4	0.2		
0.2	0.3	0.1	0.1	
	0.5	0.2		

3-4 续表
Continued

市、区名称	Region	金融业 Financial Intermediation	房地产业 Real Estate	租赁和商务服务业 Leasing and Business Services	科学研究和技术服务业 Scientific Research and Technical Services	水利环境和公共设施管理业 Management of Water Conservancy，Environment and Public Facilities
全市	**Whole Municipality**	**6.4**	**8.1**	**14.7**	**6.7**	**3.3**
市南区	Shiman District	4.8	1.5	4.2	1.2	0.4
市北区	Shibei District	0.1	1.5	2.6	0.7	0.3
李沧区	Licang District		0.4	2.0	0.5	0.1
崂山区	Laoshan District	0.3	0.7	0.7	2.0	0.6
黄岛区	Huangdao District	0.3	1.3	2.9	1.0	0.5
城阳区	Chengyang District	0.1	0.6	1.3	0.4	0.2
即墨区	Jimo District	0.3	0.7	0.1	0.1	0.3
胶州市	Jiaozhou	0.2	0.7	0.5	0.4	0.1
平度市	Pingdu	0.2	0.4	0.2	0.2	0.5
莱西市	Laixi	0.1	0.2		0.1	0.3
红岛经济区	Qingdao National High-tech Industrial Development Zone		0.1	0.2	0.1	
保税港区	Qingdao Free Trade Port Area of China					

单位：万人（10 000 persons）

居民服务修理和其他服务业 Services to Households and Other Services	教育 Education	卫生和社会工作 Health and Social Welfare	文化体育和娱乐业 Culture，Sports and Entertainment	公共管理社会保障和社会组织 Public Management, Social Security and Social Organization	国际组织 International Organization
2.6	**14.4**	**7.7**	**1.9**	**10.2**	
0.4	1.9	1.4	0.4	1.6	
0.1	1.5	1.7	0.1	0.9	
0.2	0.7	0.5	0.2	0.5	
0.6	1.0	0.3	0.3	0.7	
0.4	2.8	0.9	0.5	1.8	
0.4	0.9	0.5	0.1	0.6	
0.2	1.3	0.6	0.1	1.1	
0.1	1.5	0.8	0.1	1.0	
0.2	1.5	0.5		1.0	
	1.2	0.5		0.9	
	0.1		0.1	0.1	

3-5 全市单位分市、区全部就业人员人数（2017 年底）

NUMBER OF EMPLOYED PERSONS IN ALL UNITS OF THE CITY BY REGION（END OF 2017）

单位：万人（10 000 persons）

市、区名称	Region	年末人数 Year-end Population	国有单位 State-owned Units	集体单位 Collective-owned Units	其他经济类型单位 Units in Other Types of Economy
全市	**Whole Municipality**	**321.4**	**35.1**	**4.6**	**281.7**
市南区	Shiman District	39.1	6.8	0.3	32.0
市北区	Shibei District	26.7	5.1	0.2	21.4
李沧区	Licang District	14.5	1.8	0.1	12.6
崂山区	Laoshan District	22.2	2.9	2.3	17.0
黄岛区	Huangdao District	66.7	5.5	0.4	60.8
城阳区	Chengyang District	37.7	2.0	0.1	35.6
即墨区	Jimo District	35.9	2.6	0.7	32.6
胶州市	Jiaozhou	33.9	3.0	0.2	30.7
平度市	Pingdu	18.0	2.9	0.2	14.9
莱西市	Laixi	20.4	2.2	0.1	18.1
红岛经济区	Qingdao National High-tech Industrial Development Zone	3.7	0.2		3.5
保税港区	Qingdao Free Trade Port Area of China	2.6	0.1		2.5

3-6 全市就业人员工资总额、平均工资（1978-2017 年）

TOTAL WAGES AND AVERAGE WAGE OF CITYWIDE FULL-TIME EMPLOYEES（1978-2017）

年份 Year	工资总额（亿元） Total Wage Bill（100 million yuan）		平均工资（元） Avergae Wage（yuan）	
	全社会单位 All Units	其中：非私营单位 of which：Non-private Units	全社会单位 All Units	其中：非私营单位 of which：Non-private Units
1978		4.0		584
1979		4.8		662
1980		6.0		782
1981		6.3		778
1982		6.6		785
1983		6.9		809
1984		9.0		1041
1985		9.6		1103
1986		11.8		1311
1987		14.2		1519
1988		18.0		1862
1989		20.7		2120
1990		24.4		2400
1991		26.4		2553
1992		31.8		2970
1993		40.4		3694
1994		59.5		5455
1995		68.3		6164
1996		78.2		6640
1997		82.5		7030
1998		87.2		7518
1999		100.1		8405
2000		120.4		10072
2001		135.8		11426
2002		153.8		12839
2003	225.6	160.3	12597	15335
2004	280.5	193.4	13932	17190
2005	359.5	242.8	16015	20022
2006	445.6	292.0	18574	23457
2007	518.1	338.6	21419	27083
2008	578.7	371.9	23296	30233
2009	638.1	393.2	25396	33258
2010	738.0	446.8	28549	37805
2011	877.5	522.0	32763	43077
2012	1044.3	613.1	37399	49052
2013	1251.7	785.7	42688	55363
2014	1456.0	890.5	48453	62104
2015	1644.4	993.0	53715	69465
2016	1852.7	1088.5	58551	75803
2017	2034.7	1193.6	63047	82177

注：1. 2003 年以前为职工工资总额、平均工资。
　　2. 2015 年以前为在岗职工工资总额、平均工资。

Note：1. The data before 2003 refer to the total wage bill and average wage of stall and workers.
　　2. It was the total salary and average salart of the on -spot staff before 2015.

3-7 全市就业人员工资总额、平均工资指数（1978-2017 年）
INDEXES OF TOTAL WAGES AND AVERAGE WAGE OF CITYWIDE FULL-TIME EMPLOYEES（1978-2017）

年份 Year	工资总额指数 Total Wage Bill Indexed		平均工资指数 Avergae Wage Indexes	
	全社会单位 All Units	其中：非私营单位 of which：Non-private Units	全社会单位 All Units	其中：非私营单位 of which：Non-private Units
1978		120.80		104.66
1979		119.53		113.36
1980		123.95		118.13
1981		106.71		99.49
1982		103.80		100.90
1983		104.14		103.06
1984		130.64		128.68
1985		107.11		105.96
1986		123.22		118.86
1987		120.10		115.87
1988		126.48		122.58
1989		115.29		113.86
1990		117.66		113.21
1991		108.28		106.38
1992		120.26		116.33
1993		127.09		124.38
1994		147.46		147.67
1995		114.76		113.00
1996		114.54		107.72
1997		105.50		105.87
1998		105.64		106.94
1999		114.81		111.80
2000		120.29		119.83
2001		112.77		113.44
2002		113.31		112.37
2003		108.84		110.30
2004	124.34	120.65	110.60	112.10
2005	128.16	125.54	114.95	116.47
2006	123.95	120.26	115.98	117.16
2007	116.27	115.96	115.32	115.46
2008	111.70	109.83	108.76	111.63
2009	110.26	105.73	109.01	110.01
2010	115.66	113.63	112.42	113.67
2011	118.90	116.83	114.76	113.95
2012	119.01	117.45	114.15	113.87
2013	119.86	128.15	114.14	112.87
2014	116.32	113.34	113.50	112.18
2015	112.94	111.51	110.86	111.85
2016	110.25	106.49	109.71	110.33
2017	109.82	109.66	107.68	108.41

注：1. 2004 年以前为职工工资总额、平均工资指数。
2. 2015 年以前为在岗职工工资总额、平均工资。

Note：1. The data before 2004 refer to the indexes of total wage of stall and workers.
2. It was the total salary and average salart of the on -spot staff before 2015.

3-8 分行业就业人员平均工资（2017 年）
AVERAGE WAGE OF FULL-TIME EMPLOYEES BY INDUSTRY（2017）

行业	Sector	全部单位（元）All Units（yuan）	非私营单位（元）Non-private Units（yuan）	私营单位（元）Private Units（yuan）
总计	**Total**	**63047**	**82177**	**48497**
（一）农、林、牧、渔业	Farming，Forestry，Animal Husbandry	40678	52127	39519
（二）采矿业	Mining	50099	49807	50361
（三）制造业	Manufacturing	55211	65571	47609
（四）电力、热力、燃气及水生产和供应业	The Electricity，Heat，Gas and Water Production and Supply Industry	69979	76668	46438
（五）建筑业	Construction	57813	67739	48211
（六）批发和零售业	Wholesale and Retail Trade	50219	62621	47736
（七）交通运输、仓储和邮政业	Transport，Storage and Post	71899	84826	55162
（八）住宿和餐饮业	Hotels and Catering Services	44817	51023	40668
（九）信息传输、软件和信息技术服务业	Information Transmission Computer Services and Software	92031	109770	79498
（十）金融业	Financial Intermediation	130074	133891	61821
（十一）房地产业	Real Estate	64069	83058	47253
（十二）租赁和商务服务业	Leasing and Business Services	56876	74356	50818
（十三）科学研究和技术服务业	Scientific Research and Technical Services	78966	104804	55524
（十四）水利、环境和公共设施管理业	Management of Water Conservancy，Environment and Public Facilities	56846	69308	40369
（十五）居民服务、修理和其他服务业	Residents Service，RePair and Other Services	44988	53700	40773
（十六）教育	Education	112906	118403	39316
（十七）卫生和社会工作	Health and Social Welfare	104502	113564	45736
（十八）文化、体育和娱乐业	Culture，Sports and Entertainment	86603	86812	86237
（十九）公共管理、社会保障和社会组织	Public Management，Social Security and Social Organization	121194	121194	

3-9 分市、区就业人员工资总额（2017 年）
TOTAL WAGES OF FULL-TIME EMPLOYEES BY CITY OR DISTRICT（2017）

单位：亿元（100 million yuan）

市、区名称	Region	合计 Total	国有单位 State-owned Units	集体单位 Collective-owned Units	其他经济类型单位 Other Owership Units
全市	**Whole Municipality**	**2034.7**	**405.6**	**41.3**	**1587.8**
市南区	Shiman District	318.3	90.2	2.9	225.2
市北区	Shibei District	182.1	58.9	0.6	122.6
李沧区	Licang District	85.5	20.6	0.6	64.3
崂山区	Laoshan District	171.1	35.0	20.7	115.4
黄岛区	Huangdao District	407.7	63.1	3.5	341.1
城阳区	Chengyang District	232.2	28.2	1.4	202.6
即墨区	Jimo District	197.1	26.3	7.5	163.3
胶州市	Jiaozhou	185.9	28.5	1.6	155.8
平度市	Pingdu	95.3	30.3	1.5	63.5
莱西市	Laixi	117.2	22.2	1.0	94.0
红岛经济区	Qingdao National High-tech Industrial Development Zone	24.7	1.5		23.2
保税港区	Qingdao Free Trade Port Area of China	17.6	0.8		16.8

3-10 分市、区就业人员平均工资（2017年）
AVERAGE WAGE OF FULL-TIME EMPLOYEES BY CITY OR DISTRICT (2017)

单位：元/年（yuan/yuar）

市、区名称	Region	合计 Total	国有单位 State-owned Units	集体单位 Collective-owned Units	其他经济类型单位 Other Owership Units
全市	**Whole Municipality**	**63047**	**116950**	**92939**	**56798**
市南区	Shiman District	83635	135243	89645	72489
市北区	Shibei District	69393	117358	43999	58152
李沧区	Licang District	57764	114505	51015	49900
崂山区	Laoshan District	77378	123217	95400	67482
黄岛区	Huangdao District	62082	114790	97614	57021
城阳区	Chengyang District	62229	140515	96691	57632
即墨区	Jimo District	54454	102655	113473	49535
胶州市	Jiaozhou	55729	96705	77641	51584
平度市	Pingdu	54354	105445	68844	43979
莱西市	Laixi	55408	100331	99943	49883
红岛经济区	Qingdao National High-tech Industrial Development Zone	68119	77552	81308	67566
保税港区	Qingdao Free Trade Port Area of China	67271	132271		65692

主要统计指标解释

单位从业人员 指报告期末最后一日24时在本单位中工作，并取得工资或其他形式劳动报酬的人员数。该指标为时点指标，不包括最后一日当天及以前已经与单位解除劳动合同关系的人员，是在岗职工、劳务派遣人员及其他就业人员之和。就业人员不包括：

（1）离开本单位仍保留劳动关系，并定期领取生活费的人员；

（2）利用课余时间打工的学生及在本单位实习的各类在校学生；

（3）本单位因劳务外包而使用的人员。

在岗职工 指在本单位工作且与本单位签订劳动合同，并由单位支付各项工资和社会保险、住房公积金的人员，以及上述人员中由于学习、病伤、产假等原因暂未工作仍由单位支付工资的人员。在岗职工还包括：

（1）应订立劳动合同而未订立劳动合同人员（如使用的农村户籍人员）；

（2）处于试用期人员；

（3）编制外招用的人员；

（4）派往外单位工作，但工资仍由本单位发放的人员（如挂职锻炼、外派工作等情况）。

工资总额 指根据《关于工资总额组成的规定》（1990年1月1日国家统计局发布的一号令）进行修订，在报告期内（季度或年度）直接支付给本单位全部就业人员的劳动报酬总额。包括计时工资、计件工资、奖金、津贴和补贴、加班加点工资、特殊情况下支付的工资，是在岗职工工资总额、劳务派遣人员工资总额和其他就业人员工资总额之和。

工资总额是税前工资，包括单位从个人工资中直接为其代扣或代缴的房费、水费、电费、住房公积金和社会保险基金个人缴纳部分等。

工资总额不论是计入成本的还是不计入成本的，不论是以货币形式支付的还是以实物形式支付的，均应列入工资总额的计算范围。

平均工资 指单位就业人员在一定时期内平均每人所得的工资额。它表明一定时期工资收入的高低程度，是反映就业人员工资水平的主要指标。

Explanatory Notes on Main Statistical Indicators

Jobholders refers to the number of employees who works in the institution or company and gets salary or other form of labor reward at 24：00 of the last day of the report period. This is a time-point indicator which is the total of on-spot staff，labor dispatched personnel and other employees，excluding persons that have released the employment contract with the institution or company on the last day or bedore. The following are not deemed as Jobholders：

（1）Persons that keep the employment relations and get regular living expenst after leaving the institution or company；

（2）Various students who work part time or as internship；

（3）Personnel that uses by the institution or company in labour outsourcing.

On-spot staff refers to the employees that works for and signs the employment contract with the institution or company，and relevant salary，social insurance and house funding are paid by the institution or company，and the persons of the previous employees that are not working but still gets salary from the institution or company due to the reason of learning，injury，maternity leave，etc. It also includes the following：

（1）Employees who shall sign the employment contract with institution or company but not signed（for example，employees of rural household registration）.

（2）Employees that are still in probation period；

（3）Employees that are recruited outside the authorized size；

（4）Employees that are sent to other institution or company but the salaries are still paid by the institution or company（such as onsite training and labour dispatching）.

Total salary refers to total payment for labour made directly to all jobholders of the institution or company within the report period（quarterly or annually）revised according to Regulations on Constitution of Total Salary，Order No. 1 released by National Bureau of Statistics on January 1，1990，including hourly wage，piece wage，bonus，allowance and subsidy，overtime wage，and wages paid under special situations. It is also the total volume of on-spot staff，labour dispatching staff and other employment.

Total salary is the pre-tax salary，including the expenses of housing，water，power and the personal part of house funding and social insurance funds，which has been withheld and paid by the institution or company from personal salaries.

No matter it is credited into cost or not，no matter it is paid in currency or in kind，all total salary shall be categorized as total salary.

Average salary refers to the total salary per capita of employees of the institution or company within the certain period，which is the major indicator of the salary level of employees and the level of salary income of the certain salary.

固定资产投资 4

INVESTMENT IN FIXED ASSETS

简要说明

一、本篇资料的主要内容

本篇资料主要反映了全市固定资产投资及房地产开发方面的情况，主要包括固定资产投资的规模、结构、资金来源和房地产开发投资、施竣工及销售情况等方面的资料。

二、本篇资料的来源

本篇资料来源于固定资产投资及房地产开发投资统计年报，由市统计局固定资产投资统计处整理提供。

Brief Introduction

Ⅰ. Main Content

Data in this chapter show the basic conditions of investment in fixed assets and real estate development of the whole city, mainly including the total investment in fixed assets, the structure of investment, the resources of investment and investment in real estate development, construction, completion, sales, etc.

Ⅱ. Source of Data

Data in this chapter are based on the annual report on investment in fixed assets and real estate development, and provided by the Division of Investment and Construction Statistics of Qingdao Municipal Bureau of Statistics.

4-1 主要年份固定资产投资

MAJOP YEAP' S INVESTMENT IN FIXED ASSETS

单位：万元（10 000 yuan）

年 份 Year	规模以上固定资产投资总额 Investment in Fixed Assets above Designated Size	按用途分 Crouped by Use		
		生产性投资 Productive Investment	非生产性投资 Non-Productive Investment	#住宅投资 Investment in Residential Buildings
1949	16	12	4	3
1952	3097	1368	1729	1007
1957	5923	3947	1976	1151
1962	2747	2049	698	192
1965	5481	4155	1326	375
1970	6100	5813	287	154
1975	15839	13548	2381	1064
1978	29660	23499	6161	3203
1980	47499	33865	13634	9335
1985	107421	60643	73424	19058
1990	284576	210453	74123	38898
1991	349031	256633	92398	51898
1992	583068	420748	162320	83844
1993	953274	511684	441590	162419
1994	1329716	728532	601184	324094
1995	1648281	925194	723087	390206
1996	1610562	972398	638164	285412
1997	1611902	932207	679695	278951
1998	1909711	1125821	783890	316999

4-1 续表 1
Continued

单位：万元（10 000 yuan）

年 份 Year	规模以上固定资产投资总额 Investment in Fixed Assets above Designated Size	按用途分 Crouped by Use 生产性投资 Productive Investment	非生产性投资 Non-Productive Investment	#住宅投资 Investment in Residential Buildings
1999	2205891	1246328	959563	421151
2000	2426820	1311538	1115282	470963
2001	2934728	1487762	1446966	729181
2002	3683623	1962588	1721035	765030
2003	5475526	3023930	2451596	1038304
2004	9845646	6336279	3509367	1608738
2005	14032960	9172206	4860754	1841644
2006	14856894	9214578	5642316	2222733
2007	16353636	10231673	6121963	2720970
2008	20190098	12443179	7746919	3315538
2009	24588889	13852653	10736236	3831976
2010	30224785	16207885	14016900	5609189
2011	35025382	18622819	16402563	5707625
2012	41539146	24246803	17292343	6689114
2013	50278649	30996768	19281881	7220432
2014	57660308	32913906	24746402	7311090
2015	65556685	41402714	24153971	7569123
2016	74547006	44588200	29958806	9561782
2017	77770902	41719893	36051009	9255095

注：1. 规模以上固定资产投资数据 2003 年以前为城镇以上统计范围。
2. 因 2004 年以来数据有调整，故表中数据不可比。

Note：1. The data of investment above designated size refer to investment above city and town level before 2003.
2. The data since 2004 are not comparable with other data because of the adjustment.

4-1 续表 2
Continued

单位：万元（10 000 yuan）

年 份 Year	按构成分 Gouped by Composition of Funds			按资金来源分 Grouped by Sources of Funds			
	建筑安装工程 Constrection and Installation	设备工器具购置 Purchase of Equipment and Instruments	其他费用 Others	国家投资 State Investment	国内贷款 Domestic Loans	利用外资 Foreign Investment	自筹及其他 Self-raising Fund and Others
1949	11	3	2	16			
1952	2146	870	81	1512			1585
1957	2853	2773	297	3816			2107
1962	1631	984	132	2205			542
1965	3346	1859	276	4451			1030
1970	3136	2835	129	2721			3379
1975	7489	8133	217	9378	1362		5099
1978	19968	9124	568	16828	1601		11231
1980	30993	15541	965	10371	12925	1420	22783
1985	64665	35100	7656	17377	35888	1136	53020
1990	167731	91305	25540	24687	91895	23688	144306
1991	196212	108929	43890	22615	131676	38325	156415
1992	304060	208384	70624	22660	213217	89130	258061
1993	600011	225555	127708	23736	208672	94469	626397
1994	842809	272126	214781	26062	318334	221265	764055
1995	1020484	385934	241863	25683	379198	328124	915276
1996	929735	458284	222543	35639	444443	310722	819758
1997	875057	485122	251723	27928	297089	363789	923096
1998	1034500	574852	300359	67762	491812	170709	1179428

4-1 续表 3
Continued

单位：万元（10 000 yuan）

年　份 Year	按构成分 Gouped by Composition of Funds			按资金来源分 Grouped by Sources of Funds			
	建筑安装工程 Constrection and Installation	设备工器具购置 Purchase of Equipment and Instruments	其他费用 Others	国家投资 State Investment	国内贷款 Domestic Loans	利用外资 Foreign Investment	自筹及其他 Self-raising Fund and Others
1999	1456473	459596	289822	128603	584120	145589	1347579
2000	1476397	652640	297783	75978	489697	164175	1806238
2001	1781235	744549	408944	93491	620562	217526	2157787
2002	2328492	796685	558446	78775	719677	411704	2831288
2003	3544790	1133333	797403	127861	989178	722644	4237643
2004	6413046	2312139	1120461	85549	1100297	1016145	8245272
2005	8949231	3141732	1941997	136632	1250343	1850921	11540604
2006	8818614	3668191	2370089	391315	2126523	1662897	11856506
2007	9981666	4171878	2200092	215649	2427031	1788056	13109824
2008	11795435	5907195	2487468	322484	3309471	1951468	15855082
2009	14911874	5869214	3807801	778090	4217265	1593287	21555685
2010	18725922	6362880	5135983	1305737	5881886	2135736	27898294
2011	22865421	7521441	4638520	1640702	5871709	1766278	33579182
2012	26080239	8601282	6857625	1324159	5484459	1561597	37356847
2013	33237368	9969777	7071504	1959340	8154829	1528585	49552883
2014	39006113	11640126	7014069	1404667	7452983	1181541	55024776
2015	42893643	15972153	6690889	2067396	7249574	1098178	62458544
2016	45915827	16425993	8789790	1788103	14203650	903773	66069945
2017	55647641	10977494	11145767	2257927	14569701	641216	65055089

4-2 主要年份固定资产投资构成(以投资总额为100)

COMPOSITION OF MAJOR YEAR'S INVESTMENT IN FIXED ASSETS (TOTAL INVESTMENT=100)

年 份 Year	按用途分 Grouped by Use		
	生产性投资 Productive Investment	非生产性投资 Non-Productive Investment	#住宅投资占非生产性比重 Percentage of Investment in Residential Buildings to Non-Productive Investment
1949	75.00	25.00	75.00
1952	44.17	55.83	58.24
1957	66.64	33.36	58.25
1962	74.59	25.41	27.51
1965	75.81	24.19	28.28
1970	95.30	4.70	53.66
1975	84.97	15.03	44.69
1978	79.23	20.77	51.99
1980	71.30	28.70	68.47
1985	56.45	43.55	40.74
1990	73.95	26.05	52.50
1991	73.53	26.47	56.17
1992	72.16	27.84	51.65
1993	53.68	46.32	36.78
1994	54.79	45.21	53.91
1995	56.10	43.90	54.00
1996	60.40	39.60	44.70
1997	57.80	42.20	41.00
1998	59.00	41.00	16.60

4-2 续表 1
Continued

年 份 Year	按用途分 Grouped by Use		
	生产性投资 Productive Investment	非生产性投资 Non-Productive Investment	#住宅投资占非生产性比重 Percentage of Investment in Residential Buildings to Non-Productive Investment
1999	56.50	43.50	19.10
2000	54.00	46.00	19.40
2001	50.70	49.30	50.40
2002	53.30	46.70	44.50
2003	55.20	44.80	42.40
2004	64.40	35.60	45.80
2005	65.40	34.60	37.90
2006	62.00	38.00	39.40
2007	62.60	37.40	44.40
2008	61.60	38.40	42.80
2009	56.30	43.70	35.70
2010	53.62	46.38	40.02
2011	53.17	46.83	34.80
2012	58.37	41.63	38.68
2013	61.65	38.35	37.45
2014	57.08	42.92	29.54
2015	63.16	36.84	31.34
2016	59.81	40.19	31.92
2017	53.6	46.4	25.7

4-2 续表 2
Continued

年 份 Year	按构成分 Grouped by Composition of Funds			按资金来源分 Grouped by Sources of Funds			
	建筑安装工程 Construction and Installation	设备工器具购置 Purchase of Equipment and Instruction	其他费用 Others	国家投资 State Investment	国内贷款 Domestic Loans	利用外资 Foreign Investment	自筹及其他 Self-raising Fund and Others
1949	68.75	18.75	12.5	100			
1952	69.29	28.09	2.62	48.82			51.18
1957	48.17	46.82	5.01	64.43			35.57
1962	59.37	35.82	4.81	80.27			19.73
1965	61.05	33.92	5.03	81.21			18.79
1970	51.41	46.48	2.11	44.61			55.39
1975	47.28	51.35	1.37	59.21	8.60		32.19
1978	67.32	30.76	1.92	56.74	5.40		37.86
1980	65.25	32.72	2.03	21.83	27.21	2.99	47.97
1985	60.2	32.68	7.12	16.18	33.41	1.06	49.35
1990	58.94	32.08	8.98	8.68	32.29	8.32	50.71
1991	56.22	31.21	12.57	6.48	37.73	10.98	44.81
1992	52.15	35.74	12.11	3.89	36.56	15.29	44.26
1993	62.94	23.66	13.4	2.49	21.89	9.91	65.71
1994	63.38	20.46	16.16	1.96	23.94	16.64	57.46
1995	61.9	23.4	14.7	1.6	23.0	19.9	55.5
1996	57.7	28.5	13.8	2.2	27.6	19.3	50.9
1997	54.3	30.1	15.6	1.7	18.4	22.6	57.3
1998	54.2	20.8	15.7	3.5	25.8	8.9	61.8

4-2 续表 3
Continued

年 份 Year	按构成分 Grouped by Composition of Funds			按资金来源分 Grouped by Sources of Funds			
	建筑安装工程 Construction and Installation	设备工器具购置 Purchase of Equipment and Instruction	其他费用 Others	国家投资 State Investment	国内贷款 Domestic Loans	利用外资 Foreign Investment	自筹及其他 Self-raising Fund and Others
1999	66.0	20.8	13.2	5.8	26.5	6.6	61.1
2000	60.8	26.9	12.3	3.1	20.2	6.8	74.4
2001	60.7	25.4	13.9	3.0	20.1	7.0	69.9
2002	63.2	21.6	15.2	1.9	17.8	10.2	70.1
2003	64.7	20.7	14.6	2.1	16.3	11.9	69.7
2004	65.1	23.5	11.4	0.8	10.6	9.7	78.9
2005	63.8	22.4	13.8	0.9	8.5	12.5	78.1
2006	59.4	24.7	15.9	2.4	13.3	10.4	73.9
2007	61.0	25.5	13.5	1.2	13.8	10.2	74.8
2008	58.4	29.3	12.3	1.5	15.4	9.1	74.0
2009	60.6	23.9	15.5	2.8	15.0	5.6	76.6
2010	62.0	21.0	17.0	3.5	15.8	5.7	75.0
2011	65.3	21.5	13.3	3.8	13.7	4.1	78.4
2012	62.8	20.7	16.5	2.9	12.0	3.4	81.7
2013	66.1	19.8	14.1	3.2	13.3	2.5	81.0
2014	67.6	20.2	12.2	2.2	11.5	1.8	84.6
2015	65.4	24.4	10.2	2.8	10.0	1.5	85.7
2016	61.6	22.0	11.8	2.2	17.1	1.1	79.6
2017	71.6	14.1	14.3	2.7	17.7	0.8	78.8

4-3 按三次产业分规模以上固定资产投资(2017 年)
INVESTMENT IN FIXED ASSETS ABOVE DESIGNATED SIZE BY THREE STRATA OF INDUSTRY (2017)

单位:万元(10 000 yuan)

指　标	Indicator	2017 年
总　计	**Total**	**77770902**
第一产业	Primary Industry	1287821
第二产业	Secondary Industry	31063560
# 工业	Industry	30803907
第三产业	Tertiary Industry	45419521

4-4 分市、区固定资产投资额(2017 年)
INVESTMENT IN FIXED ASSETS BY REGION (2017)

单位:万元(10 000 yuan)

市、区名称	Region	规模以上固定资产投资额 Investment in Fixed Assets above Designated Size	# 房地产开发 Investment in Real Estate Development
全　市	**Whole Municipality**	**77770902**	**13305432**
市南区	Shinan District	1062723	873534
市北区	shibei District	1520384	1415691
李沧区	Licang District	5389113	2038408
崂山区	Laoshan District	1833427	1343718
黄岛区	Huangdao District	22559979	2755388
城阳区	Chengyang District	7177432	1738029
即墨区	Jimo District	10445551	1052299
胶州市	Jiaozhao	10053178	541617
平度市	Pingdu	7701362	580282
莱西市	Laixi	5271036	241553
红岛经济区	Qingdao National High-tech Industrial Development Zone	2275028	724543
保税港区	Qingdao Free Trade Port Area of China	60121	370

4-5 规模以上固定资产投资(2017年)
INVESTMENT IN FIXED ASSETS ABOVE DESIGNATED SIZE (2017)

单位：万元（10 000 yuan）

项 目	Item	合计 Total	#房地产开发 Investment in Real Estate Development
一、本年施工项目(个)	**Projects Under Consruction This Year（unit）**	**7084**	
#本年新开工(个)	of which：Newly Started（unit）	5343	
二、本年建成投产项目(个)	**Projects Completed and Put into Use This Year（unit）**	**5856**	
三、本年完成投资	**Investment Completed This Year**	**77770902**	**13305432**
1. 按构成分	Grouped by Composition		
#建筑工程	Construction Projects	48176979	8388327
安装工程	Installation Projects	7470662	1573844
设备工器具购置	Purchase of Equipment and Instruments	10977494	166687
2. 按建设性质分	Grouped by Type of Construction		
#新建	New Construction	40172537	
扩建	Expansion	12892549	
改建	Reconstruction	10293863	
3. 按隶属关系分	Grouped by Subordination Relation		
中央单位	Central Units	3044615	239146
地方单位	Local Units	74726287	13066286
4. 按国民经济行业分	Grouped by Economic Sector		
（1）农、林、牧、渔业	Farming, Forestry, Animal Husbandry and Fishery	1287821	
农业	Farming	680640	
林业	Forestry	60025	
畜牧业	Animal Husbandry	138740	
渔业	Fishery	316549	
农、林、牧、渔服务业	Farming, Forestry, Animal Husbandry and Fishery Services	91867	
（2）采矿业	Mining	42195	
煤炭开采和洗选业	Mining and Washing of Coal		
石油和天然气开采业	Extraction of Petroleum and Natural Gas		
黑色金属矿采选业	Mining of Ferrous Metal Ores	1129	
有色金属矿采选业	Mining of Non-ferrous Metal Ores	27616	
非金属矿采选业	Mining and Processing of Nonmetal Ores	9753	
开采辅助活动	Auxiliary Activities of Mining	3697	
其他采矿业	Mining of Other Ores		

4-5 续表 1
Continued

单位：万元（10 000 yuan）

项　目	Item	合计 Total	#房地产开发 Investment in Real Estate Development
（3）制造业	Manufacturing	29337299	
农副食品加工业	Processing of Food from Agricultural Products	1733089	
食品制造业	Manufacture of Foods	716374	
酒、饮料和精制茶制造业	Manufacture of Liquor，Beverage and Refind Tea	201404	
烟草制品业	Manufacture of Tobacco		
纺织业	Manufacture of Textile	812285	
纺织服装、服饰业	Manufacture of Textile Wearing Apparel	1360364	
皮革、毛皮、羽毛及其制品和制鞋业	Manufacture of Leather，Fur，Feather & Its Products Footwear	460791	
木材加工和木、竹、藤、棕、草制品业	Processing of Timbers，Manufacture of Wood，Bamboo，Rattan，Palm and Straw Products	443029	
家具制造业	Manudacture of Furniture	854872	
造纸和纸制品业	Manufacture of Paper and Paper Products	361231	
印刷和记录媒介复制业	Printing，Reproduction of Recording Media	387806	
文教、工美、体育和娱乐用品制造业	Manufacture of Articles for Culture，Arts & Crafts，Sports and Entertainment	991613	
石油加工、炼焦和核燃料加工业	Processing of Petroleum，Coking，Processing of Nucleus Fuel	458852	
化学原料和化学制品制造业	Manufacture of Chemical Raw Material and Chemical Products	1313528	
医药制造业	Manufacture of Medicines	414638	
化学纤维制造业	Manufacture of Chemical Fiber	19647	
橡胶和塑料制品业	Manufacture of Rubber and Plastic	1725166	
非金属矿物制品业	Manufacture of Non-metallic Mineral Products	1896510	
黑色金属冶炼和压延加工业	Smelting and Pressing of Ferrous Metals	517850	
有色金属冶炼和压延加工业	Smelting and Pressing of Non-ferrous Metals	122756	
金属制品业	Manufacture of Metal Products	2380226	
通用设备制造业	Manufacture of General Purpose Machinery	3756269	
专用设备制造业	Manufacture of Special Purpose Machinery	2534683	
汽车制造业	Manufacture of Vehicle	2169745	
铁路、船舶、航空航天和其他运输设备制造业	Manufacture of Transport Equipement for Railway，Shipping，Aerospace and other uses	515248	
电气机械和器材制造业	Manufacture of Electrical Machinery & Equipment	1729604	
计算机、通信和其他电子设备制造业	Namufacture of Computer，Communication Equipment and Other Electronic Equipment	897416	
仪器仪表制造业	Manufacture of Measuring Instrument	238400	
其他制造业	Manufacture of Other Products	191926	
废弃资源综合利用业	Recycling and Disposal of Waste Resources	27760	
金属制品、机械和设备修理业	Maintenance of Metal Products，Machinery and Equipment	104217	

4-5 续表 2
Continued

单位：万元（10 000 yuan）

项　目	Item	合计 Total	#房地产开发 Investment in Real Estate Development
（4）电力、燃气及水的生产和供应业	Production and Supply of Electricity Gas and Water	1424413	
电力、热力的生产和供应业	Production and Supply of Electric Power and Heat Power	969189	
燃气生产和供应业	Production and Supply of Gas	73550	
水的生产和供应业	Production and Supply of Water	381674	
（5）建筑业	Construction	259653	
（6）交通运输、仓储及邮政业	Transport Storage and Post	9365129	
铁路运输业	Railway Transport	1672967	
道路运输业	Road Transport	4150332	
水上运输业	Water Transport	334552	
航空运输业	Air Transport	1674409	
管道运输业	Pipeline Transport	307116	
装卸搬运和运输代理业	Handing，Corrying and Transportation Agent	254883	
仓储业	Ware houses and Storage	956150	
邮政业	Post	14720	
（7）信息传输、软件和信息技术服务业	Information Transmission Computer Services and Software	568605	
（8）批发和零售业	Wholesale and Retail Trade	1581434	
（9）住宿和餐饮业	Hotels and Catering Services	482626	
（10）金融业	Financial Intermediation	192760	
（11）房地产业	Financial Intermediation	16100128	13305432

4-5 续表 3
Continued

单位：万元（10 000 yuan）

项　　目	Item	合计 Total	#房地产开发 Investment in Real Estate Development
（12）租赁和商务服务业	Leasing and Business Services	5240610	
（13）科学研究和技术服务业	Scientific Research，Technical Service and Geologic Prospecting	2040178	
（14）水利、环境和公共设施管理业	Management of Water Conservancy，Environment and Pubic Facilities	4529624	
水利管理业	Management of Water Conservancy	440113	
环境管理业	Environmental Management	42279	
公共设施管理业	Management of Public Facilities	4047232	
（15）居民服务和其他服务业	Services to Households and Other Services	77210	
居民服务业	Serviced to Households	38265	
机动车、电子产品和日用产品修理业	Maintenance of Vehicle，Electronic Products and Daily Articles	15240	
其他服务业	Other Services	23705	
（16）教育	Educatilon	1696441	
（17）卫生和社会工作	Health and Social Work	636123	
卫生	Health	466502	
（18）文化、体育和娱乐业	Culture，Sports and Entertainment	2239981	
新闻出版业	Journalism and Publishing Activities	62763	
广播、电视、体育和音像业	Broadcasting，Movies，Televisions and Audiovisual Activities	1197092	
文化艺术业	Cultural and Art Activities	420812	
体育	Sports Activities	360104	
娱乐业	Entertainment	199210	
（19）公共管理、社会保障和社会组织	Public Management，Social Security and Social Organzation	668672	
中国共产党机关	Communist Party of China	4624	
国家机构	Govenment Agencies	523864	
人民政协、民主党派	People's Political Consultatioe Conference，Democratic Party		
社会保障	Social Security	8040	
群众团体、社会团体和其他成员组织	Non-Governmental Institutions，Social Organizations and Other Organizations		
基层群众自治组织	Local People Self-government Organization	132144	
（20）国际组织	International Organization		

4-5 续表 4
Continued

单位：万元（10 000 yuan）

项　目	Item	合计 Total	#房地产开发 Investment in Real Estate Development
四、本年新增固定资产	**Newly Increased Fixed Assets This Year**	**45059633**	**5343419**
（1）农、林、牧、渔业	Farming, Forestry, Animal Husbandry and Fishery	865950	
（2）采矿业	Mining	46510	
（3）制造业	Manufacturing	20843266	
（4）电力、燃气及水的生产和供应业	Production and Supply of Electricty, Gas and Water	1221043	
（5）建筑业	Construction	190957	
（6）交通运输、仓储和邮政业	Transport, Storage and Post	1532370	
（7）信息传输、计算机服务和软件业	Information Transmission, Computer Services and Software	3333342	
（8）批发和零售业	Wholesale and Retail Trade	201377	
（9）住宿和餐饮业	Hotels and Catering Services	194080	
（10）金融业	Financial Intermediation	53105	
（11）房地产业	Real Estate	6794345	5343419
（12）租赁和商务服务业	Leasing and Business Services	3112536	
（13）科学研究、技术服务业	Scientific Research and Technical Services	961334	
（14）水利、环境和公共设施管理业	Management of Water Conservancy, Environmeng and Public Facilities	2445601	
（15）居民服务、修理和其他服务业	Services to Households, Repair and Other Services	59444	
（16）教育	Education	812195	
（17）卫生和社会工作	Health and Social Work	167923	
（18）文化、体育和娱乐业	Culture, Sports and Entertainment	1822425	
（19）公共管理、社会保障和社会组织	Public Management, Social Sevurity and Social Organization	401830	
（20）国际组织	International Organization		
五、本年资金来源合计	**Total Funds This Year**	**91529897**	**31087496**
上年末结余资金	Balance of Last Year	9005964	8359922
本年资金来源小计	Sub-total Funds This Year	82523933	22727574
国家预算内资金	State Budget	2257927	
国内贷款	Domestic Loans	14569701	4973191
债券	State Treasury Bond		
利用外资	Foreign Investment	641216	16654
自筹资金	Self-raising Funds	50937654	6127893
其他资金来源	Others	14117435	11609836

4-6 主要年份房地产开发投资
MAJOR YEAR'S INVESTMENT IN REAL ESTATE DEVELOPMENT

单位：万元、万平方米（10 000 yuan，10 000 sq.m）

年份 Year	房地产开发投资额 Investment in Real Estate Development	房屋施工面积 Floor Space Under Construction	房屋竣工面积 Floor Space Completed	房屋实际销售面积 Floor Space of Buildings Sold	房屋实际销售额 Sale of Buildings
1995	562861	1008	240	103	185384
1996	455765	748	203	80	125150
1997	426570	675	237	113	216311
1998	438059	742	259	178	351805
1999	629717	900	474	240	430123
2000	675142	1047	352	301	550401
2001	925153	1374	532	406	802364
2002	1036476	1417	537	427	933031
2003	1277969	1765	552	469	1121885
2004	1626965	2101	635	516	1530964
2005	2238370	2363	811	740	2666 738
2006	2683631	2751	654	719	3054907
2007	3223547	3224	641	833	4333566
2008	3805652	3773	672	770	3924175
2009	4594829	4310	814	1262	7036744
2010	6024387	5058	1020	1360	8952942
2011	7827193	5693	925	1026	7702379
2012	9301099	6474	1212	951	7660684
2013	10485229	7073	957	1160	9786176
2014	11177297	8171	1136	1164	9708984
2015	11223458	8971	1523	1419	12628568
2016	13691425	9101	1426	1939	17899532
2017	13305432	9533	1487	1901	19992012

4-7 房地产开发投资情况(2017年)
INVESTMENT IN REAL ESTATE DEVELOPMENT (2017)

单位：万元(10 000 yuan)

指标名称	Indicator	合计 Total	按经济类型分 Grouped by Economic Types		
			国有经济 State-owned	集体经济 Collective-owned	其他经济 Others
本年完成投资额	**Investment Completed This Year**	**13305432**	**1017008**	**2486**	**12285938**
1. 住宅	Residential Buildings	9255095	509174	2108	8743813
2. 办公楼	Office Buildings	1124854	196184		928670
3. 商业营业用房	Houses for Business Use	1857834	110775	360	1746699
4. 其他	Others	1067649	200875	18	866756

4-7 续表
Continued

单位：万元(10 000 yuan)

指标名称	Indicator	按资质等级分 Grouped by Qualification Criteria					
		一级 First Grade	二级 Second Grade	三级 Third Grade	四级 Fourth Grade	暂定 Provistonal	其他 Others
本年完成投资额	**Investment Completed This Year**	**260587**	**586138**	**526685**	**256441**	**9873644**	**1801937**
1. 住宅	Residential Buildings	152814	489642	353687	184108	7086425	988419
2. 办公楼	Office Buildings	49500	7801	57555	34832	668537	306629
3. 商业营业用房	Houses for Business Use	5589	44240	92763	14885	1368991	331366
4. 其他	Others	52684	44455	22680	22616	749691	175523

4-8 房地产施工、竣工面积及竣工价值(2017 年)
FLOOR SPACE UNDER CONSTRUCTION AND COMPLETED AND COMPLETED VALUE OF REAL ESTATE (2017)

单位：万平方米（10 000 sq.m）

施工、竣工房屋面积及竣工价值	Indicator	施工面积 Floor Space Under Construction	#新开工 Newly Started	竣工房屋 Floor Space Completed	竣工房屋价值（万元）Completed Value（10 000 yuan）
房屋建筑面积总计	**Floor Space of Buildings**	**9533**	**2031**	**1487**	**3975018**
住宅	Residential Buildings	6256	1424	969	2470770
办公楼	Office Buildings	647	95	90	296843
商业营业用房	Houses for Business Use	1086	224	227	674042
其他	Others	1544	288	201	533363

4-9 商品房屋销售情况(2017 年)
BASIC STATISTICS ON SALES OF COMMERCIALIZED BUILBINGS (2017)

单位：万平方米（10 000 sq.m）

商品房屋销售情况	Sales and Rental of Commercialized Buildings	实际销售 Actual Sales	实际销售额（万元）Actual Sales Volume（10 000 yuan）	待售面积 Area for Sale
房屋面积总计	**Floor Space of Buildings**	**1901**	**19992012**	**470**
住宅	Residential Buildings	1634	16422765	210
办公楼	Office Buildings	98	1399596	71
商业营业用房	Houses for Business Use	130	1944320	155
其他	Others	39	225331	34

主要统计指标解释

固定资产投资 是以货币形式表现的在一定时期内建造和购置固定资产的工作量以及与此有关的费用的总称。

房地产开发投资 指各种登记注册类型的房地产开发法人单位统一开发的住宅、厂房、仓库、饭店、宾馆、度假村、写字楼、办公楼等房屋建筑物，配套的服务设施，土地开发工程（如道路、给水、排水、供电、供热、通讯、平整场地等基础设施工程）和土地购置的投资；不包括单纯的土地开发和交易活动。

固定资产投资的资金来源 根据固定资产投资的资金来源不同，分为国家预算资金、国内贷款、利用外资、自筹资金和其他资金。

固定资产投资 按建设性质分建设项目的性质一般分为新建、扩建、改建和技术改造、单纯建造生活设施、迁建、恢复、单纯购置。

固定资产投资 按构成分固定资产投资活动按其工作内容和实现方式分为建筑安装工程，设备、工具、器具购置，其他费用三个部分。

新增生产能力（或工程效益） 指建成投产项目或工程新增生产能力（或工程效益）的名称。

房屋施工面积 是指报告期内施工的全部房屋建筑面积。包括本期新开工的面积和上期开工跨入本期继续施工的房屋面积，以及上期已停缓建在本期恢复施工的房屋面积。本期竣工和本期施工后又停缓建的房屋，其建筑面积仍计入本期房屋施工面积中。

房屋竣工面积 是指在报告期内房屋建筑按照设计要求全部完工，达到住人和使用条件，经验收鉴定合格（或达到竣工验收标准），正式移交使用单位的各栋房屋建筑面积的总和。

本年新增固定资产 指在报告期已经完成建造和购置过程，并已交付生产或使用单位的固定资产的价值，包括已经建成投入生产或交付使用的工程投资和达到固定资产标准的设备、工具、器具的投资及有关应摊入的费用。

Explanatory Notes on Main Statistical Indicators

Fixed investment is a generic term of quantity of work from building and acquiring of fixed assets over a period of time and any relevant expenses incurred thereby in the form of currency.

Real estate development investment means investments in all kinds of registered housing & building, including residences, plants, warehouses, restaurants, hotels, resorts, office buildings and administrative buildings which are developed uniformly by real estate development corporation, supporting sevice facilities and land development projects (such as road, water supply & drainage, power supply, heat supply, telecommunication and ground leveling and other infrastructure projects) and land acquisition; excludes simple land development and transaction activities.

Source of funds for fixed-asset investment can be divided into national budget funds, domestic loans, utilization of foreign capital, self-raised funds and other funds in accordance with the different sources.

Construction items of fixed-asset investment can be divided into new construction, extension, reconstruction, technical reform, simply-constructed living facilities, relocation, restoration and simple acquisition by property of construction.

Fixed - asset investment activities can be divided into three parts, namely construction and installation project, acquisition of equipement, tools and appliances and other expenses by working content and method of achieving.

New productive capacity (or project benefit) means the completed projects or new productive capacity (or projevt benefit) of projects.

Construction area neans total areas of all buildings which are under construction in the ruport period, including the area which is newly constructed in this period and the areas of buildings which commence in the last period and carry forward to this period for continuing construction. and the areas of buildings which stop constructing in the last period and resume to be constructed in this period. The areas of the buildings which are completed in this period and stop constructing after this period' s construction are still reckoned in floor space under construction in this period.

Completed ares means the wum total of areas of housings & buildings which are completed according to design requirements in the report period, reach conditions of living and using and are transferred to building users formally after checked and accepted (or reach the standards of completion and acceptance) .

New fixed assets in this year means the value of fixed assets which are completed and acquired in the report period and delivered for production or use, including investment in constructions which are put into production or service, investment in equipment, tools and appliances which reach the standards of fixed asset, and the expenses which should be added into fixed assets.

对外经济贸易 5

FOREIGN TRADE

简要说明

一、本篇资料的主要内容

本篇资料主要反映了全市外经外贸和外资企业的基本情况，主要包括外贸进出口、利用外资、对外投资与经济合作等方面的资料。

二、本篇资料的来源

1、口岸进出口数据来源于青岛市海关。

2、进出口、利用外资、对外投资与经济合作等资料来源于市商务局。

本篇资料由市统计局外经贸易统计处整理提供。

Brief Introduction

Ⅰ. Main Content

Data in this article mainly reflects the general condition about foreign economy and trade as well as foreign-funded enterprises in this city, including data about import and export of foreign trade, use of foreign capital, foreign investment and economic cooperation.

Ⅱ. Source of Data

1. Data of import and export in port comes from China Customs of Qingdao.

2. Date including import and export, foreign investment by using foreign capital and economic cooperation is taken from Bureau of Commerce of the coty.

Data in this article is cleared up and provided by Department of Statistics for Foreign Trade and Economy affiliated to Municipal Statistics Bureau.

5-1 青岛口岸进出口总额(1985-2017 年)
TOTAL VALUE OF IMPORTS AND EXPORTS OF QINGDAO PORT（1985-2017）

单位：万美元（10 000 USD）、万元（10 000 yuan）

年份 Year	青岛口岸进出口总额 Total Value of Imports and Exports Oing dao Port	出口 Exports	进口 Imports
1985	414448	234652	179796
1986	382840	191926	190914
1987	445090	259458	185632
1988	474516	259176	215340
1989	506152	268397	237755
1990	477117	304011	173106
1991	519273	332949	186324
1992	581495	350163	231332
1993	678013	360297	317716
1994	888574	510760	377814
1995	1307508	705245	602263
1996	1391323	760566	629757
1997	1542284	936142	609142
1998	1463718	933392	530326
1999	1696514	1063768	632746
2000	2520420	1423266	1097154
2001	2797085	1636888	1160197
2002	3128048	1889612	1238436
2003	4088096	2366046	1722050
2004	5677570	3197697	2479873
2005	6932944	3959947	2972997
2006	8019198	4495731	3523467
2007	9257099	5263539	3993560
2008	11558079	5953501	5604578
2009	9049699	4694832	4354867
2010	11912702	5988254	5924448
2011	15095088	7294226	7800862
2012	14888716	7120813	7767903
2013	15662732	7696141	7966591
2014	16489966	8736358	7753608
2015	14448349	8776286	5672063
2016	94927180	56513317	38413863
2017	111024375	63298062	47726314

注：2016 年起，统计单位为人民币万元。
Note：Statistic unit is RMB ten thousand Yuan as from 2016.

5-2 进出口总额(1988-2017 年)
TOTAL VALUE OF IMPORTS AND EXPORTS(1988-2017)

单位：万美元(10 000 USD)、万元(10 000 yuan)

年份 Year	进出口总额(含中央、省驻青公司) Total Value of Imports and Exports (including central and provincial companies)	出口 Exports	进口 Imports	进出口总额(不含中央、省驻青公司) Total Value of Imports and Exports (including central and provincial companies)	出口 Exports	进口 Imports
1988				28097	21731	6366
1989				39327	27797	11530
1990				41649	33529	8120
1991				54624	44746	9878
1992				88600	66291	22309
1993	517643	346288	171355	139048	100201	38847
1994	633213	434102	199111	234978	164135	70843
1995	858560	536386	322174	376372	245072	131300
1996	863521	516317	347204	461950	287123	174827
1997	916269	579261	377008	521967	338535	183432
1998	882042	573020	309022	595826	382657	213169
1999	1009885	631072	378813	775565	446260	329305
2000	1353222	826891	526331	1083133	611426	471707
2001	1541564	950160	591404	1235781	712024	523757
2002	1692567	1057141	635426	1409598	850420	559178
2003	2065912	1239199	826713	1784556	1035528	749028
2004	2698781	1578167	1120614	2433188	1391171	1042017
2005	3302230	1942242	1359988	3045542	1758834	1286708
2006	3911543	2346552	1564991	3655737	2164541	1491196
2007	4572534	2831004	1741530	4360499	2677596	1682903
2008	5363659	3262476	2101183	5215886	3146246	2069640
2009	4485115	2729865	1755250	4398639	2692197	1706442
2010	5705963	3391560	2314403	5614928	3335141	2279787
2011	7215217	4061309	3153908	7126310	4005572	3120738
2012				7320781	4081968	3238813
2013				7791217	4198605	3592612
2014				7988833	4577696	3411137
2015				7022243	4535015	2487228
2016				43506659	28219059	15287600
2017				50334973	30318103	20016870

注：1. 2012 年起，中央、省驻青公司外贸统计划归青岛，取消含中央、省驻青公司统计口径；
2. 2016 年起，统计单位为人民币万元。

Note：1. Since 2012, the statistical calibre including central and provincoal companies has been cancled.
2. Statistic unit is RMB ten thousand Yuan as from 2016.

5-3 分国别外贸出口总额
TOTAL VALUE OF EXPORTS BY COUNTRIES OR REGIONS

单位：万美元（10 000 USD）

国别（地区）	Country（Region）	2017 年	2017 年比 2016 年 ±% 2017/2016（±%）	占比 % Ratio（%）
亚洲	Aioa	1898618	2.6	42.6
香港	Hong Kong	175885	17.8	3.9
日本	Japan	527724	5.8	11.8
韩国	Korea	412729	–0.2	9.3
东盟	ASEAN	373923	–4.1	8.4
非洲	Africa	168941	–19.4	3.8
南非	South Africa	40000	18.7	0.9
欧洲	Europe	1054059	11.7	23.6
欧盟	EU	822555	12.9	18.4
南美洲	South America	294020	10.4	6.6
北美洲	North America	920285	7.3	20.6
美国	United States	828640	6.3	18.6
大洋洲	Oceanica	122498	4.8	2.7
澳大利亚	Australia	101345	4.1	2.3

5-4 外贸出口商品分类
EXPORT COMMODITIES BY CATEGORY

单位：万元（10 000 yuan）

项　目	Item	2017年	2017年比2016年 ±% 2017/2016（±%）	占比% Ratio（%）
合　计	**Total**	**30318103**	**7.5**	**100.0**
按企业性质划分	By Enterprises Nature			
国有企业	State-owned Enterprises	3742190	6.0	12.3
外商投资企业	Foreign Funded Enterprises	9920467	6.3	32.7
其他企业	Other Enerprises	16655446	8.5	54.9
#集体企业	#Collective-owned Enterprises	986368	-7.7	3.3
私营企业	Private Enterprises	15657776	9.8	51.6
按贸易方式划分	By Customs Regime			
一般贸易	Ordinary Trade	19402081	7.7	64.0
加工贸易	Processing Trade	9745919	7.9	32.1
其他贸易	Others	1170103	1.1	3.9
按大类商品划分	By Category of Commodities			
纺织服装	Textile Garments	4477029	1.9	14.8
农产品	Agricultural Products	3574814	9.0	11.8
机电产品	Mechanical and Electrical Products	13454563	13.4	44.5
高新技术产品	High-tech Products	3008057	11.6	10.0

5-5 外贸进口商品分类
IMPORT COMMODITIES BY CATEGORY

单位：万元（10 000 yuan）

项目	Item	2017年	2017年比2016年 ±% 2017/2016（±%）	占比% Ratio（%）
合计	**Total**	**20016870**	**30.8**	**100.0**
按企业性质划分	By Enterprises Nature			
国有企业	State-owned Enterprises	4613367	21.6	23.0
外商投资企业	Foreign Funded Enterprises	5537091	13.7	27.7
其他企业	Other Enerprises	9866412	48.7	49.3
#集体企业	#Collective-owned Enterprises	176856	49.1	0.9
私营企业	Private Enterprises	9617706	48.3	48.0
按贸易方式划分	By Customs Regine			
一般贸易	Ordinary Trade	10854370	30.4	54.2
加工贸易	Processing Trade	3146364	–5.6	15.7
其他贸易	Others	6016136	65.3	30.1
按大类商品划分	By Category of Commodities			
纺织服装	Textile Garments	324062	–3.2	1.6
农产品	Agricultural Products	3562825	18.0	17.8
机电产品	Mechanical and Electrical Products	4196281	1.0	21.0
高新技术产品	High-tech Products	1988992	0.6	9.9

5-6 二十大出口商品出口情况
INFORMATION ON THE EXPORTATION OF TOP 20 PRODUCTS

单位：万美元（10 000 USD）

商品名称	Name	2017 年	2017 年比 2016 年 ±% 2017/2016（±%）	占比 % Ratio（%）
合　计	**Total**	**3919926**	**6.8**	**100.0**
机械设备	Machinery and Equipment	727241	7.4	18.6
电器及电子类产品	Electric Appliance and Electronic Products	546234	11.7	13.9
服装	Garments	429854	-3.2	11.0
计算机与通信技术	Computer and Communication Technology	359864	10.6	9.2
运输工具	Transport Tools	357687	24.8	9.1
纺织品	Textile Products	230638	3.8	5.9
金属制品	Metal Products	217453	0.2	5.5
轮胎	Tyre	140697	0.6	3.6
电话机	Telephone Sets	130834	12.4	3.3
水海产品	Aquatic and Seawater Products	125765	0.7	3.2
蔬菜	Vegetables	115863	10.7	3.0
家具及其零件	Furniture	100783	2.1	2.6
钢材	Rolled Steel	99806	4.7	2.5
鞋类	Shoes	88721	-2.5	2.3
塑料制品	Plastic Articles	74759	0.2	1.9
箱包	Luggage and Bags	69174	-8.6	1.8
汽车零件	Parts of Motor Vehicles	57401	5.1	1.5
空调	Air Conditioner	47123	42.2	1.2
游戏机	Game Console	29	-77.2	
铁合金	Ferroalloy			

5-7 二十大进口商品进口情况
INFORMATION ON THE IMPORTATION OF TOP 20 PRODUCTS

单位：万美元（10 000 USD）

商品名称	Name	2017年	2017年比2016年±% 2017/2016（±%）	占比% Ratio（%）
合　计	**Total**	**1843126**	**18.1**	**100.0**
铁矿砂	Machinery and Equipment	337517	38.7	18.3
电器及电子产品	Electric Appliance and Electronic Products	252531	1.5	13.7
机械设备	Machinery and Equipment	172284	5.5	9.3
粮食	Grain	153878	37.0	8.3
合成橡胶	Synthetic Rubber	130122	107.5	7.1
天然橡胶	Natural Rubber	128020	88.2	6.9
仪器仪表	Instruments and Meters	114028	-10.5	6.2
集成电路	Integrated Circuits	104730	12.4	5.7
塑料原料	Plastic Raw Materials	97076	27.8	5.3
冻鱼	Frozen Fish	90960	1.7	4.9
液晶显示板	Liquid Crystal DIsplay	52465	-18.1	2.8
棉花	Cotton	49684	42.0	2.7
纺织品	Textile Products	44467	-8.1	2.4
运输工具	Means of Conveyance	41888	-22.9	2.3
钢材	Rolled Steel	38583	1.4	2.1
塑料制品	Plastic Articles	10546	1.2	0.6
铝锭及铝材	Aluminum Ingots and Aluminum Products	8864	6.3	0.5
成品油	Refined Petroleum Products	7849	-27.2	0.4
氧化铝	Alumina	4439	307.4	0.2
钻石	Diamonds	3194	-39.5	0.2

5-8 利用外资情况（2000-2017年）
UTILIZATION OF FOREIGN CAPITAL（2000-2017）

项 目	Item	单位	Unit	2000年	2005年
批准企业（项目）个数	**Number of Enterprises（Projects）Approved**	**个**	**unit**	**1132**	**2530**
一、外商直接投资	Foreign Direct Investments	个	unit	1128	2530
中外合资企业	Sino-foreign Joint Ventures	个	unit	303	274
中外合作企业	Sino-foreign Cooperative Enterprises	个	unit	57	18
外商独资企业	Foreign-owned Enterprises	个	unit	76	2236
其它	Others	个	unit	1	2
二、外商其他投资	Other Foreign Investments	个	unit	4	
合同外资金额	**Total Amount of Contracted Foreign Investment**	**万美元**	**10000 USD**	**269081**	**954486**
一、外商直接投资	Foreign Direct Investments	万美元	10000 USD	266221	954486
中外合资企业	Sino-foreign Joint Ventures	万美元	10000 USD	69889	112777
中外合作企业	Sino-foreign Cooperative Enterprises	万美元	10000 USD	26835	17588
外商独资企业	Foreign-owned Enterprises	万美元	10000 USD	169370	813485
其它	Others	万美元	10000 USD	127	10636
二、外商其他投资	Other Foreign Investments	万美元	10000 USD	2860	
实际利用外资金额	**Total Amount of Foreign Investment Actually Utilized**	**万美元**	**10000 USD**	**128171**	**365625**
一、外商直接投资	Foreign Direct Investments	万美元	10000 USD	126132	365625
中外合资企业	Sino-foreign Joint Ventures	万美元	10000 USD	39224	77636
中外合作企业	Sino-foreign Cooperative Enterprises	万美元	10000 USD	3886	5654
外商独资企业	Foreign-owned Enterprises	万美元	10000 USD	82992	280130
其它	Others	万美元	10000 USD	30	2205
二、外商其他投资	Other Foreign Investments	万美元	10000 USD	2039	

单位：万美元（10 000 USD）

2006 年	2008 年	2009 年	2010 年	2011 年	2012 年	2013 年	2014 年	2015 年	2016 年	2017 年
1397	**640**	**647**	**731**	**707**	**553**	**645**	**619**	**763**	**680**	**650**
1397	640	647	731	707	553	645	619	763	680	650
267	99	99	153	158	113	165	140	162	154	188
13	4	2	4	4	2	2	1	2		1
1117	537	545	574	544	438	478	475	597	523	457
		1		1			3	2	3	4
311697	**304505**	**271504**	**475723**	**528501**	**600231**	**758063**	**638637**	**827357**	**769101**	**909629**
311697	304505	271504	475723	528501	600231	758063	638637	827357	769101	909629
31368	81796	61734	124148	142535	102252	191172	126878	116013	207933	246280
6883	367	4531	9179	15173	122	4765	−849	1731	28	327
273446	221759	204187	341977	369425	490764	562208	506271	706172	554073	655377
	583	1052	419	1368	7093	−82	6337	3441	7067	7645
365815	**264295**	**186397**	**284281**	**363350**	**460027**	**552227**	**608100**	**669062**	**700273**	**773500**
365815	264295	186397	284281	363350	460027	552227	608100	669062	700273	773500
49240	43810	46856	84920	100699	169469	159424	172180	135671	171051	195189
7123	2945	3971	3567	2759	6262	2355	128	1570	251	220
309452	217540	135026	194500	255763	275579	390210	435102	531544	520052	569461
		544	1294	4129	8717	238	690	277	8918	8325

5-9 当年外商直接投资项目数和投资额（2017年）
NUMBER OF PROJECTS AND TOTAL AMOUNT OF FOREIGN DIRECT INVESTMENT （2017）

项　目	Item	批准企业项目数（个）Number of Projects Approved（unit）	合同外资金额（万美元）Total Amount of Contracted Foreign Investment（10000 USD）	实际利用外资金额（万美元）Total Amount of Foreign Investment Aetually Utilized（10000 USD）
外商直接投资	**Foreign Direct Investments**	**650**	**909629**	**773500**
一、按投资方式分	**Grouped by Investment Form**			
#中外合资企业	Sino-foreign Joint Ventures	188	246280	195189
中外合作企业	Sino-foreign Cooperative Enterprises	1	327	220
外商独资企业	Foreign-owned Enterprises	457	655377	569461
二、按主要行业分	**Grouped by Sector**			
#农、林、牧、渔业	Farming，Foresty，Animal Hus-bandry and Fishery	2	161	4041
制造业	Manufacturing	192	399112	411755
电力、燃气及水的生产和供应业	Production and Supply of Electricity，Gas and Water	6	17379	22063
建筑业	Construction	10	11870	7614
信息传输、计算机服务和软件业	Information transmission, computer services and software industry	41	73438	66592
批发和零售业	Wholesale and Retail Trades	188	104995	44425
房地产业	Real estate industry	34	98267	101599
租赁和商务服务业	Leasing and Business Services	62	46343	10946
科学研究、技术服务和地质勘查业	Scientific Research，Technical Service and Geological Survey	31	33316	46799
三、按主要国别（地区）分	**Grouped by Countries（Regions）**			
#香港	Hong Kong	196	422500	358488
韩国	Korea	208	154235	106604
美国	United States	30	4565	34059
日本	Japan	25	15657	29838
德国	Germany	13	75722	79402
澳大利亚	Australia	12	7570	4507
新加坡	Singapore	11	24485	38030

5-10 对外投资与经济合作
OUTBOUND INVESTMENT AND INTERNATIONAL ECONOMIC COOPERATION

名　称	Name	单位	Unit	2017 年	2017 年比 2016 年 ±% 2017/2016（±%）
对外投资项目数	Number of Outbound Investment Projects	个	unit	156	-17.9
对外投资中方投资额	The Amount of Investment by Chinese Sides in Outbound Investment	万美元	10000 USD	643001	-49.3
对外承包工程新签合同额	The Amount of New Contracts for Foreign Contracted Projects	万美元	10000 USD	440525	18.3
对外承包工程完成营业额	The Completed Turnover of Foreign Contracted Projects	万美元	10000 USD	382220	4.9
对外劳务合作	Number of Persons Sent Overseas for International Labor Srevice Cooperation	人	Person	18294	3.2

5-11 对外投资分国别（地区）情况表（2017 年）
INFORMATION ON OUTBOUND INVESTMENT BY COUNTRY/REGION FOR（2017）

国别（地区）	Country（Region）	项目数量（个） Number of Projects （unit）	2017 年比 2016 年 ±% 2017/2016 （±%）	中方投资额（万美元） Amount of Investment by Chinese Sides （10000 USD）	2017 年比 2016 年 ±% 2017/2016 （±%）
总　计	**Total**	**156**	**-17.9**	**643001**	**-49.3**
亚洲	Asia	87	-8.4	221450	11.1
中国香港	Hong Kong，China	25	-16.7	19713	-61.7
越南	Victnam	13	116.7	19354	-19.3
韩国	Korea	13	62.5	14838	322.2
日本	Japan	9	50.0	12368	3092.9
新加坡	Singapore	6	200.0	5383	-17.2
马来西亚	Malaysia	5	-37.5	73908	2102.8
柬埔寨	Cambodia	4	-33.3	13150	-49.9
印度	India	2	100.0	3700	270.0
印度尼西亚	Indonesia	2		30600	26.8
台湾省	Taiwan	2		1350	
泰国	Thailand	2	-50.0	6779	180.9
缅甸	Myanmar	1	-66.7	500	-97.7

5-11 续表
continued

国别（地区）	Country（Region）	项目数量（个）Number of Projects（unit）	2017年比2016年 ±% 2017/2016（±%）	中方投资额（万美元）Amount of Investment by Chinese Sides（10000 USD）	2017年比2016年 ±% 2017/2016（±%）
老挝	Laos	1		13669	2937.4
巴基斯坦	Pakistan	1	-80.0	121	-99.1
巴林	Bahrain	1		6000	
中国澳门	Macao，China	增资	-100.0	18	-30.5
非洲	Africa	10	-37.5	33240	-64.4
乌干达	Uganda	2		89	
毛里塔尼亚	Mauritania	2		20001	-64.6
几内亚	Guinea	1			
加纳	Ghana	1		2400	
坦桑尼亚	Tanzania	1		350	
南非	South Africa	1		9900	-20.8
尼日利亚	Nigeria	1		500	
欧洲	Europe	10	-37.5	15368	-23.8
德国	Germany	5	25.0	2745	-21.0
英国	U.K.	3	-25.0	6394	275.6
俄罗斯联邦	Russian Federation	2		6210	23.8
荷兰	Holland	增资	-100.0	20	-7.8
拉丁美洲	Latin America	6	20.0	297716	3955.8
英属维尔京群岛	British Virgin Islands	2		6405	141.0
秘鲁	Peru	2		291292	
厄瓜多尔	Ecuador	1		3	
巴西	Brazil	增资		16	303.9
北美洲	North America	37	-22.9	73360	-92.1
美国	United States	33	-23.3	44730	-94.8
加拿大	Canada	4	-20.0	28630	-61.9
大洋洲	Oceanica	6	-40.0	1866	-90.6
澳大利亚	Australia	5	-50.0	1322	-93.3
新西兰	New Zealand	1		544	

主要统计指标解释

批准企业（项目）个数 是指外商直接投资中批准设立的外商投资企业个数、批准的合作开发项目个数。

合同外资金额 是指批准外商投资企业的合同、章程中规定的外国投资者认缴的出资额和企业投资总额内的应由外方投资者以自己的境外自有资金直接向企业提供的贷款。包括新批准企业合同外资和原有企业的增资减资，增资减资不对企业（项目）个数进行调整。

实际使用外资金额 是指合同外资金额的实际执行金额。

外商直接投资 是指外国企业和经济组织或个人（包括华侨、港澳台胞以及我国在境外注册的企业）按我国有关政策、法规，用现汇、实物、技术等在我国境内开办外商独资企业、与我国境内的企业或经济组织共同举办中外合资经营企业、合作经营企业或合作开发资源的投资（包括外商投资收益的再投资）以及经政府有关部门批准的项目投资总额内，企业从境外借入的资金。

外商其它投资 是指除外商直接投资以外其他方式吸收的外资。

进出口总额 指实际进出我国国境的货物总金额。包括对外贸易实际进出口货物，来料加工装配进出口货物，国家间、联合国及国际组织无偿援助物资和赠送品，华侨、港澳台同胞和外籍华人捐赠品，租赁期满归承租人所有的租赁货物，进料加工进出口货物，边境地方贸易及边境地区小额贸易进出口货物（边民互市贸易除外），中外合资企业、中外合作经营企业、外商独资经营企业进出口货物和公用物品，到、离岸价格在规定限额以上的进出口货样和广告品（无商业价值、无使用价值和免费提供出口的除外），从保税仓库提取在中国境内销售的进口货物，以及其他进出口货。

Explanatory Notes on Main Statistical Indicators

Enterprises（Projects）Permitted refers to number of foreign invested enterprises and developed projects under cooperation through the permission.

Contracted Foreign Investment refers to expenditure promised by the foreign investor and loan stemed from broad innate fund of the foreign investor, according to the contract and regulation approved of enterprise invested by foreigner.

Actual Utilization of Foreign Investment refers to actual usage of contracted foreign investment, including cash, investment in kind and incorporeal agreed by the both sides as part of the investment, such as services and technology.

Foreign Direct Investment refers to the investments by foreign enterprises and economic organizations or individuals（including overseas Chinese, compatriots from Hong dong, Macao and Taiwan, and Chinese enterprises registered abroad）, following the relevant policies and laws of China, for the establishment of ventures and cooperative enterprises or cooperative exploration of resources with enterprises or economic organizations in China, It includes the reinvestment of the foreign entrepreneurs with the profits gained from the investment and the funds that enterprises borrow from aboard in the total invesment of projects which are approved by the relevant department of the government.

Other Investment by Foreign Entrepreneurs refers to all forms of utilization of foreign capitals other than foreign direct investment.

Total Imports and Exports refers to the real value of commodities imported into and exported from the boundary of China. They include the actual imports and exports through foreign trade, imported and exported goods under the processing and assembling trades and materials, supplies and gifts as aid given gratis between governments and by the United Nations and other international organizations, and contributions donated by overseas Chninese, compatriots in Hong Kong and Macao and Chinese with foreign citizenship, leasing commodities owned by tenant at the expiration of leasing period, the imported and exported commodities processed with imported materials, commodities trading in border areas (excluding mutual exchange goods), the imported and exported commodities and articles for public use of the Sino-foreign joint ventures, cooperative enterprises and ventures exclusively with foreign own invesment. Also included are import or export of samples and advertising goods for whose CIF or FOB value are beyond the permitted ceiling (excluding goods of no trading or use value and free commodities for export), imported goods sold in China from bonded warehouses and other imported or exported goods.

城市建设、环境保护

COTY CONSTRUCTION AND
ENVIRONMENT PROTECTION

简要说明

一、本篇资料的主要内容

本篇资料主要反映了全市城市基础设施基本情况，包括市政设施、供水、供电、公共交通、园林绿化、燃气供热、城市环卫、环境保护及工业“三废”排放情况等方面的资料。

二、本篇资料的来源

1、本篇资料中市政设施、供水、公共交通、园林绿化、燃气供热、城市环卫相关资料来源于市建设委员会的城市建设统计年报，由市统计局固定资产投资统计处整理提供。

2、本篇资料中供电资料来源于青岛供电公司，由市统计局能源统计处整理提供。

3、本篇资料中环境保护、环境质量及工业“三废”排放情况来源于市环境保护局，由市统计局能源统计处整理提供。

Brief Introduction

Ⅰ. Main Content

Data in this chapter show the basic conditions of public facilities of the whole city, including urban construction and infrastructure, water supply, electricity supply, public communications, urban greenery, gas and heating, urban sanitation, environmental protection and discharge conditions of industrial waste water, waste gas and solid waste, etc.

Ⅱ. Source of Data

(1) Data on conditions of urban construction and infrastructure, water supply, public communications, urban greenery, gas and heating, urban sanitation are based on the annual report of city construction provided by Qingdao Municipal Construction Commission, and compiled by the Division of Investment and Construction Statistics of Qingdao Municipal Bureau of Statistics.

(2) Date on electricity supply are provided by Qingdao Power Corporation, and compiled by the Division of Energy Statistics of Qingdao Municipal Bureau of Statistics.

(3) Data on environmental protection, environmental conditions and discharge conditions of industrial waste water, waste gas and solid waste are provided by Qingdao Municipal Bureau of Environmental Protection, and compiled by the Division of Energy Statistics of Qingdao Municipal Bureau of Statistics.

6-1 主要年份城市建设和公用事业
MAJOR YEAR'S CITY CONSTRUCTION AND PUBLIC UTILITIES

年 份 Year	建成区面积 （平方公里） Developed Areas （sq.km）	年末道路长度 （公里） Length of Roads at Year-end（km）	年末道路面积 （万平方米） Area of Roads at Year-end（10 000 sq.m）	公共汽车、电车线路网长度 （公里） Network Length of Bus and Trolley Bus（km）
1949	27	243	206	26.4
1952	29	245	213	124.4
1957	36	248	217	232.3
1962	55	266	235	252.8
1965	57	266	235	308.1
1970	59	374	346	358.5
1975	63	392	355	389.3
1978	66	408	368	422.1
1980	72	408	377	474.1
1985	79	462	464	611.3
1990	94.3	667	786	777
1991	94.7	673	826	922
1992	95.4	683	840	988
1993	99.9	764	944	1094
1994	103.9	811	985	1372
1995	106	936	1177	1101
1996	110	991	1339	1211
1997	112	1047	1436	1492
1998	114	1106	1436	1859
1999	116	1171	1698	2339
2000	119.1	1192	1789	2711
2001	123	1248	2169	2521
2002	133	1426	2594	896
2003	145.9	1595	2816	973
2004	154.8	1755	3254	1185
2005	178.8	1862	3547	1159
2006	227.5	3160	5218	1362
2007	250.7	3288	5411	1480
2008	267.1	3318	5596	1470
2009	272.9	3402	5763	1216
2010	282.3	3409	5893	1383
2011	291.5	3705	6605	1719
2012	374.6	4281	7528	1978
2013	469.6	4334	7859	2002
2014	490.7	4393	7908	2023
2015	566.4	4375	7940	2106
2016	599.3	4484	8057	2116
2017	638.4	4865	8496	2220

6-1 续表 1
Continued

年份 Year	自来水供水管道长度（公里）Length of Tap Water Pipelines (km)	全年供水总量（万立方米）Annual Volume of Tap Water Supply (10 000 cu.m)	#全年售水量（万立方米）Annual Volume of Tap Water Sale (10 000 cu.m)	#居民家庭用水 of which: Consumption for Residential Use	用水普及率（%）Coverage Rate of Population with Access to Tap Water (%)	排水管道长度（公里）Length of Sewage Pipes (km)	全年用电量（亿千瓦时）Annual Volume of Electricity Supply (100 million kW·h)	#居民生活用电 of which Consumption for Residential Use
1949	308	721	456	331	89	200	0.88	0.14
1952	341	778	612	310	90	227	1.85	0.14
1957	412	1392	1 296	606	93	273	2.61	0.26
1962	483	2700	2 512	937	98	290	3.77	0.57
1965	500	3220	2 979	929	98	295	5.92	0.68
1970	521	4503	4106	1085	99	350	9.83	1.02
1975	564	6726	6302	1950	99	361	12.41	1.43
1978	572	5334	4975	1314	99	382	16.34	1.62
1980	588	8224	7874	2577	99	394	21.48	2.78
1985	685	7557	7038	2628	99.9	505	26.39	2.87
1990	873	11896	10211	4270	96.9	645	41.08	4.32
1991	908	13865	11760	4990	96.6	649	44.51	5.34
1992	1035	16385	13070	5931	96.5	672	51.78	6.84
1993	1123	16137	14027	6124	99.1	734	55.02	7.66
1994	1124	17367	14716	6405	100	811	60.74	8.78
1995	1046	22513	15810	7050	100	990	67.23	10.16
1996	1182	23277	16566	7731	100	1051	72.87	12.23
1997	1266	24130	17215	8787	100	1167	77.82	13.73
1998	1390	23845	17271	9115	100	1210	79.65	14.28
1999	1471	23849	18558	10032	100	1301	88.12	15.31
2000	1524	25414	20642	11405	100	1460	106.80	16
2001	1665	22225	18556	10555	100	1539	116.10	17.62
2002	1781	27662	21684	10129	100	1641	131.44	18.31
2003	2060	27594	21483	10142	100	1884	147.68	19.88
2004	2566	30877	23864	11695	100	2002	167.95	23.63
2005	2876	33265	25874	12536	100	2309	193.81	33.76
2006	3984	30524	25572	10682	100	3994	215.35	34.87
2007	4187	31533	26454	11408	100	4079	236.42	37.40
2008	4642	32675	27396	11301	100	4229	250.07	40.31
2009	4767	33490	28274	12250	100	4555	259.42	43.29
2010	4926	34909	29617	12524	100	4708	292.97	49.50
2011	5121	34109	28837	10049	100	5187	313.44	50.13
2012	5243	38945	33039	12121	100	6814	318.36	51.64
2013	5522	38331	32418	11851	100	6536	339.27	57.52
2014	6177	46649	40612	14834	100	6840	337.82	59.95
2015	6142	46203	40202	15381	100	6993	342.29	64.71
2016	6132	43033	36748	14430	100	7146	367.26	69.52
2017	6498	45991	38963	17439	100	7367	401.06	74.84

6-1 续表 2
Continued

年 份 Year	公共汽车、电车营运车辆（辆） Number of Bus and Trolley Bus under Operation（unit）	全年客运量（万人次） Annual Passenger Traffic（10 000 person-times）	出租汽车（辆） Number of Taxi（unit）	使用液化气、煤气、天然气人数（万人） Population with Access to Gas（10 000 persons）	液化气 Liquefied Petroleum	煤气 Coal Gas	天然气 Natural Gas	液化气供气量（吨） Volume of Liquefied Petroleum Supply（ton）
1949	32	298						
1952	76	932						
1957	112	4110						
1962	127	4747						
1965	173	6092						
1970	224	13002						
1975	324	14426		2	2			184.9
1978	409	27351		17	17			3246
1980	485	38981	48	24	24			4345
1985	621	48852	219	42.1	42.1			10619
1990	801	63495	832	75.0	57.4	17.6		17512
1991	1372	67552	1070	76.2	57.4	18.8		17963
1992	1470	73529	1828	82.8	62.0	20.8		19565
1993	1875	72427	4874	88.4	64.6	23.8		22224
1994	1850	78231	5806	103.6	77.4	26.2		24684
1995	1891	71867	5887	116.2	82.9	33.3		32443
1996	2012	49077	6660	126.0	88.0	38.0		4065
1997	2148	55642	6861	133.6	92.9	40.7		38717
1998	2184	51042	7469	146.8	97.8	49.0		45381
1999	2470	55414	7839	154.9	98.3	56.6		40537
2000	3141	59879	7933	164.1	93.3	70.8		46951
2001	3453	60167	8110	168.8	87.5	81.3		45295
2002	3681	61713	8376	224.2	133.8	90.4		60123
2003	3648	58792	8109	246.7	138.3	93.1	15.3	67803
2004	3848	66463	8144	258.4	140.6	78.8	39.0	58548
2005	4039	68776	8121	265.0	132.6	45.7	86.7	78000
2006	4167	73726	8146	271.0	112.5	49.5	109.0	97343
2007	4524	78702	8221	275.6	104.1	12.1	159.4	79715
2008	4701	82460	9241	276.3	91.9	10.5	173.9	81987
2009	4288	81768	9316	276.1	59.8	12.3	204.0	96721
2010	4664	85251	9539	276.3	36.7	12.6	227.0	80073
2011	5419	89614	9683	277.1	25.8	12.6	238.7	79812
2012	5640	97922	9693	313.7	36.7	13.1	263.9	54341
2013	6179	101108	9826	318.9	33.0	0.0	285.9	41302
2014	6515	105592	9720	325.4	33.0	0.0	292.4	39255
2015	6748	102402	10033	338.3	28.9	0.0	309.4	35255
2016	7210	99596	10048	441.6	29.0	0.0	412.6	32291
2017	7420	104898	10875	445.8	26.2	0.0	419.6	28309

注：1990 年以前公共营运车辆不包括系统外及个体。
Note：Vehicles not belonging to system and individual vehicles are not contained in public operating vehicles before 1990.

6-1 续表 3
Continued

年份 Year	煤气供气量（万立方米）Volume of Coal Gas Supply（10 000 cu.m）	天然气供气量（万立方米）Volume of Natural Gas Supply（10 000 cu.m）	燃气普及率(%) Coverage Rate of Population with Access to Gas（%）	绿地面积（公顷）Area of Green Areas（Hectate）	公园绿地面积（公顷）Park Green Areas（hectare）	人均公园绿地面积(平方米) Per Capita Park Green Areas（sq.m）	建成区绿化覆盖率（%）Green Coverage Rate of Developed Areas（%）	公园(个) Number of Parks and Zoos（unit）	公园面积（公顷）Area of Parks and zoos（hectare）
1949				133	42	0.7	4.9	3	43
1952				134	43	0.7	4.4	4	45
1957				245	132	1.7	6.9	10	122
1962				771	184	2.2	14.0	12	174
1965				777	184	2.1	13.7	12	174
1970				772	184	2.1	13.0	6	117
1975			2.3	465	162	1.8	7.6	5	134
1978			18.6	469	162	1.7	7.6	6	165
1980			24.5	625	206	2.1	10.4	6	152
1985			36.3	1072	255	2.3	17.3	7	153
1990	3073		56.2	2120	492	3.7	22.8	26	404
1991	3439		56.5	2318	500	3.7	24.4	28	443
1992	3824		60.0	2471	515	3.7	25.9	28	417
1993	4215		63.1	2488	543	3.9	26.5	31	453
1994	4116		63.1	2866	572	4.0	27.9	31	463
1995	4734		79.2	4547	771	5.3	30.1	33	675
1996	5447		83.9	4679	836	5.6	30.4	33	675
1997	5920		87.3	4717	924	6.0	31.3	34	730
1998	5959		92.5	6812	1047	6.6	35.0	35	775
1999	7319		96.0	7007	1186	7.4	35.9	36	791
2000	9567		98.0	7439	1423	8.5	37.0	37	790
2001	11814		99.0	7688	1588	9.3	37.5	39	832
2002	13500		99.5	7967	1791	8.1	36.4	43	926
2003	14826	1181	100	8829	2305	9.3	37.5	45	1034
2004	15503	2710	100	10047	2842	11.0	38.0	48	1421
2005	16573	7456	100	11137	3132	11.8	38.8	47	1110
2006	9821	13876	100	11756	3198	11.8	39.2	47	1188
2007	9516	18103	100	15369	3661	13.3	37.8	73	1268
2008	8691	21780	100	15630	4014	14.5	41.5	77	1815
2009	7523	26948	100	16003	4003	14.5	43.4	71	1897
2010	9153	35681	100	16619	4027	14.6	43.38	72	1917
2011	9137	46147	100	18013	4041	14.6	44.69	74	1931
2012	8148	68397	100	21471	4573	14.6	44.7	78	2112
2013	0	70918	100	28007	4649	14.6	44.7	87	2698
2014	0	74823	100	28805	4741	14.6	44.7	91	2988
2015	0	70311	100	29117	4802	14.6	44.7	87	3163
2016	0	70586	100	34851	8194	18.6	38.6	151	4460
2017	0	91572	100	36209	7763	17.4	39.1	175	4727

注：1. 自 2002 年起人均公共绿地面积按辖区内全部人口计算。
2. 2005 年以前所用园林绿地面积；公共绿地面积；人均公共绿地面积；公园、动物园个数；公园、动物园面积指标分别改为现在的绿地面积；公共绿地面积；人均公园绿地面积；公园个数；公园面积。

Note：1. Per capita public green areas is calculated at total population in the area under jurisdiction since 2002.
2. Before 2005，the corresponding indicators of greenbelt atea，public greenbelt area，public greenbelt area，ber capita public greenbelt area，coverage rate of green，number of parks and zoos，area of parks and zoos.

6-2 全年供电(2017 年)
ANNUAL ELECTRICITY SUPPLY (2017)

全年供电项目	Item	单位	Unit	2017 年
发电设备总容量	Total Capacity of Generation Equipment	万千瓦	10 000 kW	365.36
#青岛电厂	Qingdao Power Plant	万千瓦	10 000 kW	127.00
黄岛电厂	Huangdao Power Plant	万千瓦	10 000 kW	156.50
全年发电量	Annual Electricity Generation	亿千瓦时	100 million kw · h	167.10
#青岛电厂	Qingdao Power Plant	亿千瓦时	100 million kw · h	62.37
黄岛电厂	Huangdao Power Plant	亿千瓦时	100 million kw · h	77.05
全年实际用电量	Annual Electricity Consumption	亿千瓦时	100 million kw · h	401.10
#工业	Industrial Consumption	亿千瓦时	100 million kw · h	231.80
农业	Agricultural Consumption	亿千瓦时	100 million kw · h	3.40
生活	Residential Consumption	亿千瓦时	100 million kw · h	74.80
平均每日用电量	Average Daily Consumption	万千瓦时	100 million kw · h	10988

6-3 分行业用电(2017年)
ELECTRICTTY CONSUMPTION BY SECTOR (2017)

单位：万千瓦时(10 000 kW·h)

行 业	Sector	2017年	2017年比2016年增长(%) Growth Rate in 2017 over 2016(%)
全社会用电总计	**Total Electricity Consumption**	**4010565**	**9.20**
一、农、林、牧、渔业	Tarming, Forestry, Animal Husbandryand Fishery	82217	16.57
二、工业	Industry	2318315	9.07
三、建筑业	Construction	69096	1.91
四、交通运输、仓储和邮政业	Transport, Storage and Post	135121	10.89
五、信息传输、计算机服务和软件业	Information Transmission, Computer Services and Software	53009	11.01
六、商业、住宿和餐饮业	Trade, Hotels and Catering Services	203318	8.74
七、金融、房地产、商务及居民服务业	Financial Intermediation, Real Estate and Business Services	218960	14.19
八、公共事业及管理组织	Public Management and Social Organization	182172	10.32
九、城乡居民生活用电	Household Consumption	748356	7.65
城镇居民	Urban Area	492441	22.38
乡村居民	Rural Area	255915	-12.61

6-4 城市供水（2017 年）
URBAN WATER SUPPLY（2017）

项　目	Item	单位	Unit	2017 年
自来水供水管道长度	Length of Tap Water Pipelines	公里	km	6498
综合生产能力	Synthesis Producton Capacity	万立方米 / 日	10 000 cu.m/day	181.67
全年供水总量	Annual Volume of Tap Water Supply	万立方米	10 000 cu.m	45991
#售水量	of which：Volume of Tap Water Supply	万立方米	10 000 cu.m	38963
#生产运营用水	of which：Consumption for Production Use	万立方米	10 000 cu.m	13546
公共服务用水	Consumption for Public Services Use	万立方米	10 000 cu.m	7354
居民家庭用水	Consumption for Residential Use	万立方米	10 000 cu.m	17439
其他用水	Consumption for Other Uses	万立方米	10 000 cu.m	624
平均每日供水量	Daily Volume of Tap Water Supply	万立方米	10 000 cu.m	106.7
#生产用	of which：Consumption for Production Use	万立方米	10 000 cu.m	37.1
生活用	Consumption for Residential Use	万立方米	10 000 cu.m	50.3
用水户数	Households with Access to Water	户	household	1602023
用水人口	Population with Access to water	万人	10 000 persons	434
工业用水量重复利用率	Recycle Rate of water for Industrial Use	%	%	89.15

6-5 城市公共交通（2017 年）
URBAN PUBLIC TRAFFIC（2017）

项　目	Itme	单位	Unit	2017 年
公共汽车、电车线路网长度	Network Length of Bus and Trolley Bus	公里	km	2220
公共汽车、电车营运车辆	Number of Bus and Trolley Bus under Operation	辆	unit	7420
#汽车	Bus	辆	unit	5870
电车	Trolley Bus	辆	unit	1550
公共汽车、电车全年客运量	Annual Passenger Traffic of Bus and Trolley Bus	万人次	10 000 person-times	104898
公共汽车、电车平均每日客运量	Daily Passenger Traffic of Bus and Trolley Bus	万人	10 000 persons	287
出租汽车数	Number of Taxi	辆	unit	10875
轮渡运营船数	Number of Ferry Boat under Operation	艘	ship	4
轮渡客运总量	Passenger Traffic of Ferry Boat	万人次	10 000 person-times	50.4
轮渡平均每日客运量	Daily Passenger Traffic of Ferry Boat	万人	10 000 persons	0.14

6-6 城市供气(2017年)
URBAN GAS SUPPLY (2017)

项 目	Item	单位	Unit	2017年
煤气供应总量	Volume of Coal Gas Supply	万立方米	10 000 cu.m	0
#家庭用量	Household Consumption	万立方米	10 000 cu.m	0
煤气用气户数	Households with Access to Coal Gas	户	household	0
#家庭用户	Household Users	户	household	0
液化石油气供应总量	Volume of Liquefied Petroleum Supply	吨	ton	28309
#家庭用量	Household Consumption	吨	ton	14585
液化石油气用气户数	Households with Access to Liquefied Petroleum	户	household	112579
#家庭用户	Household Users	户	household	110989
天然气供应总量	Volume of Natural Gas Supply	万立方米	10 000 cu.m	91572
#家庭用量	Household Consumption	万立方米	10 000 cu.m	22123
天然气用气户数	Households with Access to Natural Gas	户	household	1699398
#家庭用户	Household Users	户	household	1687925
燃气普及率	Coverage Rate of Population with Access to Gas	%	%	100

6-7 城市环境卫生(2017年)
URBAN ENVIRONMENTAL SANITATION (2017)

项　目	Item	单位	Unit	2017年
市容环卫专用车辆总数	Number of Special Vehicles for Environmental Sanitation	辆	unit	7236
生活垃圾清运量	Volume of Garbage Disposal	万吨	10 000 ton	208
生活垃圾无害化处理厂（场）数	Number of Bio-safety Disposal Plant of Garbage	座	unit	4
生活垃圾无害化处理能力	Bio-safety Disposal Capacity of Garbage	吨/日	ton/dan	5900
生活垃圾无害化处理量	Bio-safety Disposal Volume of Garbage	万吨	10 000 ton	208
道路清扫保洁面积	Area under Cleaning Program	万平方米	10 000 sq.m	7064
#机械化	of which：Mechanization	万平方米	10 000 sq.m	3402
公共厕所	Public Toilets	个	unit	597

6-8 城市道路、下水道及绿化(2017年)
URBAN ROAD, SEWAGE AND GREEN (2017)

项 目	Item	单位	Unit	2017年
道路	**Road**			
年末道路长度	Length of Roads at Year-end	公里	km	4865
年末道路面积	Area of Roads at Year-end	万平方米	10 000 sq.m	8496
#人行道面积	of which：Area of Pavements	万平方米	10 000 sq.m	1880
排水管道长度	Length of Sewage Pipes	公里	km	7367
园林绿化	**Greening**			
绿化覆盖面积	Area of Green Coverage Areas	公顷	hectare	38631.44
绿地面积	Area of Green Areas	公顷	hectare	36208.52
公园绿地面积	Area of Park Green Areas	公顷	hectare	7763.33
公园数	Number of Parks and Zoos	个	unit	175
公园面积	Area of Parks and Zoos	公顷	hectare	4726.93
城市每人平均公园绿地面积	Per Capita Park Green Area	平方米	sq.m	17.4
建成区绿化覆盖率	Green Coverage Rate of Developed Areas	%	%	39.05

6-9 环境保护基本情况(2017 年)
BASIC CONDITIONS OF ENVIRONMENTAL PROTECTION（2017）

项　目	Item	单位	Unit	2017 年	2016 年	2017 年比 2016 年增（+）减（-）% 2017 Compared to 2016（+/-）
二氧化硫排放总量	Sulphur Dioxide Emission	吨	ton	15540.54	23319.64	-33.36
氮氧化物排放总量	Discharge Amount of Nitrogenoxides	吨	ton	16673.86	58686.98	-71.59
烟（粉）尘排放总量	Soot（Dust）Emission	吨	ton	15404.52	24386.9	-36.83
工业固体废物排放总量	Industrial Solid Wastes Discharged	吨	ton	0	0	
化学需氧量排放总量	Discharge Amount of Chemical Oxygen Demand	吨	ton	27615.18	29094.68	-5.09
氨氮排放总量	Discharge Amount of Ammonia and Nitrogen	吨	ton	2796.91	3538.84	-20.97
废水排放总量	Waste Water Discharged	万吨	10 000 tons	53421.38	51536.05	3.66

6-10 环境质量状况(2017 年)
ENVIRONMENT CONDITION（2017）

项　目	Item	单位	Unit	2017 年	2016 年	2017 年比 2016 年增（+）减（-）% 2017 Compared to 2016（+/-）
一、二类海水水质点位比例	Point Location Proportion of Sea Water Quality of Category 2	%	%	90.6	84.4	7.35
市区区域环境噪声平均等效声级	The Average Equivalent Sound Level of the Urban Regional Environmental Noise	分贝（A）	db（A）	57.3	56.9	0.70
市区道路交通噪声平均等效声级	The Average Equivalent Sound Level of the Urban Road Traffic Noise	分贝（A）	db（A）	68.7	68.2	0.73

6-11 工业“三废”排放情况(2017年)
DISCHARGE CONDITIONS OF INDUSTRIAL WASTE WSTER, WASTE GAS AND SOLID WASTE (2017)

项 目	Item	单位	Unit	2017年	2016年	2017年比2016年增(+)减(-)% 2017 Compared to 2016(+/-)
工业废水排放总量	Industrial Waste Water Discharged	万吨	10 000 tons	5613.22	6865	-18.23
废水治理设施数	Number of Facilities for Treatment of Wsate water	套	set	391	346	13.01
废水治理设施处理能力	Capacity of Facilities for Treatment of Waste Water	万吨/日	10 000 tons/day	40.02	37.48	6.78
进入城市污水处理厂量	Volume Handled by Sewage Treatment Plant	万吨	10 000 tons	5195.84	6195.57	-16.14
化学需氧量排放量	Discharge Amount of Chemical Oxygen Demand	吨	ton	2184.05	2335.22	-6.47
氨氮排放量	Discharge Amount of Ammonia and Nitrogen	吨	ton	115.17	127.11	-9.39
工业废气排放总量	Industrial Waste Air Discharged	万标立方米	10 000 cu.m	28818474	27626957	4.31
废气治理设施数	Number of Facilities for Treatment of Waste Air	套	set	1704	1050	62.29
其中：脱硫设施数	of which：Desulphurization Facilities	套	set	270	260	3.85
废气治理设施处理能力	Capacity of Facilities for Treatment of Waste Air	万标立方米/时	10 000 cu.m/hr	10377.1	8622.7	20.35
二氧化硫去除量	Sulphur Dioxide Removed	吨	ton	225677.97	216132.87	4.42
二氧化硫排放量	Sulphur Dioxide Emission	吨	ton	5136.54	12907.7	-60.21
烟(粉)尘排放量	Soot (Dust) Emission	吨	ton	7244.52	13348.02	-45.73
工业固体废物产生量	Industrial Solid Wastes Producted	万吨	10 000 tons	769.55	755.43	1.87
其中：危险废物	of which：Hazardous Wastes	吨	ton	114589	68925	66.25
工业固体废物综合利用量	Industrial Solid Wastes Comprehensive Utilized	万吨	10 000 tons	707.17	721.84	-2.03
工业固体废物排放量	Industrial Solid Wastes Discharged	万吨	10 000 tons	0	0	
其中：危险废物	of whick：Hazardous Wastes	吨	ton	0	0	
污染治理项目完成投资	Investment in Treatment Projects of Pollution	万元	10 000 yuan	61194.7	47411.2	29.07
污染治理项目数	Number of Treatment Projects of Pollution	个	item	62	40	55.00
当年竣工治理项目数	Number of Completed Treatment Projects in the Year	个	item	48	34	41.18

主要统计指标解释

供水综合生产能力　指按供水设施取水、净化、送水、出厂输水干管等环节设计能力计算的综合生产能力。

年末供水管道长度　指从送水泵至用户水表之间所有管道的长度。不包括新安装尚未使用的管道。

用水普及率　指城市用水人口数与城市人口总数的比率。计算公式：

$$用水普及率=\frac{城市用水人口数}{城市人口总数}\times 100\%$$

全年供水总量　指报告期供水企业（单位）供出的全部水量。包括有效供水量和漏损水量。

全年供气总量　指全年燃气企业（单位）向用户供应的燃气数量。包括销售量和损失量。

用气普及率　指报告期末使用燃气的城市人口数与城市人口总数的比率。计算公式为：

$$用气普及率=\frac{城市用气人口数}{城市人口总数}\times 100\%$$

年末道路长度　指年末道路长度和与道路相通的广场、桥梁、隧道的长度，按车行道中心线计算。在统计时只统计路面宽度在 3.5 米（含 3.5 米）以上的各种铺装道路，包括开放型工业区和住宅区道路在内。

工业废气排放量　指报告期内企业厂区内燃料燃烧和生产工艺过程中产生的各种排入大气的含有污染物的气体的总量，以标准状态（273K，101325Pa）计算。

工业废水排放量　指经过企业厂区所有排放口排到企业外部的工业废水量。包括生产废水、外排的直接冷却水、超标排放的矿井地下水和与工业废水混排的厂区生活污水，不包括外排的间接冷却水（清污不分流的间接冷却水应计算在内）。

工业废水排放达标量　指各项指标都达到国家或地方排放标准的外排工业废水量，包括未经处理外排达标的和经过处理后外排达标的和两部分。国家排放标准见 GB8978–88。

工业固体废物产生量　指企业在生产过程中产生的固体状、半固体状和高浓度液体状废弃物的总量，包括危险废物、冶炼废渣、粉煤灰、炉渣、煤矸渣、尾矿、放射性废物和其他废物等；不包括矿山开采的剥离废石和掘进废石（煤矸石和呈酸性或碱性的废石除外）酸性或碱性废石是指采掘的废石其流经水、雨淋水的 pH 值小于 4 或 pH 值大于 10.5 者。

工业粉尘排放量　指企业在生产工艺过程中排放的能在空气中悬浮一定时间的固体颗粒物排放量。如钢铁企业的耐火材料粉尘、焦化企业的筛焦系统粉尘、烧结机的粉尘、石灰窑的粉尘、建材企业的水泥粉尘等。不包括电厂排入大气的烟尘。

化学需氧量（COD）　测量有机和无机物质化学分解所消耗氧的质量浓度的水污染指数。

Explanatory Notes on Main Statistical Indicators

Production Capacity of Water Supply　refers to the designed comprehensive production capacity of water facilities, covering the 4 links of water collection, purification, conveyance, and outflow through trunk pipelines.

Length of Water Supply Pipelines at the Yeay-end　refers to the total length of all the pipelines between the water pumps and the user water meters, excluding pipelines newly installed but not used yet.

Coverage Rate of Urban Population with Access to Tap Water refers to the ratio of the urban population with access to tap water to the total urban population. The formula is :

Coverage rate of urban population with access to tap water = (Urban population with access to tap water) / (Urban population) × 100%

Annual Volume of Water Supply refers to the total volume of water supplied by water-works (units) during the reference period, including both the effective water supply and loss during the water supply.

Annual Volume of Gas Supply refers to the total volume of gas provided to users by gas-producing enterprises (units) in a year, including the volume sold and the volume lost.

Coverage Rate of Urban population with Access to Gas refers to the tatio of the urban population with access to gas to the total urban population at the end of the reference period. The formula is :

Coverage rate of urban population with access to gas = (Urban population with access to gas/Urban population) × 100%

Length of Paved Roads at the Year-end tefers to the length of roads with paved surface including squares bridges and tunnels connected with roads by the end of the year. Length of the roads is measured by the central lines for vehicles for paved roads with a width of 3.5 meters and over, including roads in open-ended factory compounds and residential quarters.

Industrial Waste Air Emission refers to discharge into atmosphere of waste air containing pollutants generated from fuel burning and production process in enterprises within a given period of time. It is calculated at standard status (273K, 101325Pa) .

Waste Water Discharged by Industry refers to the volume of waste water discharged by industrial enterprises through all their outlets, including waste water from production process, directly cooled water, groundwater from mining wells which does not meet discharge standards and sewage from households mixed with waste water produced by industrial activities, but excluding indirectly cooled water discharged (It shoudl be included if the discharge is not separated with waste water) .

Industrial Waste Water Meeting Discharge Standards refers to volume of industrial waste water discharge which, with or without treatment, reaches national or local standards with regard to all pollutants. National Discharge standards see GB8978-88.

Industrial Solid Wastes Produced refers to total volume of solid, semi-solid and high concentration liquid residues produced by industrial enterprises from production process in a given period of time, including hazardous wastes, soag, coal ash, gangue, tailings, radioactive residues and other wastes, but excluding stones stripped or dug out in mining (gangue and acid or alkaline stones not included), A stone is acid or alkaline depending on the pH value of the water below 4 or above 10.5 when the stone is in, or soaked by, the water.

Industrial Dust Emission refers to volume of dust emitted by production process of enterprises and suspended in the air for a given period of time, including dust from refractoyr material of iron and steel works, dust from cohe-screening systems and sintering machines of coke plants, dust from lime kilns and dust from cement production in building material enterprises, but excluding soot and dust emitted from power plants.

Chemical Oxygen Demand (COD) refers to index of water pollution measuring the mass concentration of oxygen consumed by the chemical breakdown of organic and inorganic matter.

7 能源消耗

CONSUMPTION OF ENERGY

简要说明

一、本篇资料的主要内容

本篇资料主要反映了全市规模以上工业主要能源消费与库存情况，主要包括规模以上工业主要能源消费与库存、规模以上工业主要能源分行业消费量、重点耗能工业企业能源加工转换、规模以上工业主要能源工业消费量等方面的资料。

二、本篇资料的来源

本篇资料来源于规模以上工业能源统计年报，由市统计局能源统计处整理提供。

Brief Introduction

Ⅰ. Main Content

Data in this chapter show the consumption and stock of major energy of industry above designated size，including consumption and stock of major energy of industry above designated size，major energy consumption of industry above designated size grouped by sector，energy conversion of major energy-consumimg industrial enterprises and major energy consumption of industry above designated size，etc.

Ⅱ. Source of Data

Data in this chapter are based on the annual report of energy consumed by industrial enterprises above designated size. The data are provided by the Division of Energy Statistics of Qingdao Municipal Bureau of Statistics.

7-1 规模以上工业主要能源消费与库存（2017年）
CONSUMPTION AND STOCK OF MAJOR ENERGY OF INDUSTRY ABOVE DESIGNATED SIZE（2017）

名 称	Name	计算单位	Unit	年初库存 Stock at Year-beginning	本年消费 Consumption in the Yeat	#工 业 Industry	非工业 Non-industry	年末库存 Stock at Year-end
原 煤	Raw Coal	吨	ton	1459644.48	11792729.79	11759710.28	33019.51	1592597.01
焦 炭	Coke	吨	ton	74.42	1336795.40	1336793.77	1.63	23.00
焦炉煤气	Coking Gas	万立方米	10 000 cu.m		30126.70	30126.70		
高炉煤气	Blast Furnace Gas	万立方米	10 000 cu.m		144943.20	144943.20		
原 油	Grude Oil	吨	ton	395444.36	15243030.76	15243030.76		391907.36
汽 油	Petrol	吨	ton	240.00	114383.30	97048.24	17335.06	260.59
煤 油	Kerosene	吨	ton	1.17	391.54	283.10	108.44	
柴 油	Diesel Oil	吨	ton	1612.45	115475.20	98402.87	17072.33	1306.72
燃料油	Fuel Oil	吨	ton	8447.31	135386.40	135378.21	8.19	8416.97
液化石油气	Liquefied Petroleum Gas	吨	ton	371.10	98722.87	98691.25	31.62	
炼厂干气	Refinery Dry Gas	吨	ton		556164.00	556164.00		
热 力	Heat	百万千焦	million kJ		18165596.03	17739794.05	425801.98	
电 力	Electricity	万千瓦时	10 000 kW · h		2200270.04	2177187.24	23082.80	

补充资料：2017年综合能源消费量1492.62万吨标准煤。
Nole：In 2017，comprehensive energy consumption is 1492.62 million rons SCE.

7-2 规模以上工业主要能源分行业消费量(2017 年)
MAJOR ENERGY CONSUMPTION OF INDUSTRY ABOVE DESIGNATED SIZE BY SECTOR(2017)

名 称	Name	原煤(吨) Raw Coal (ton)	焦炭(吨) Coke (ton)	焦炉煤气(万立方米) Coking Cas (10 000 cu.m)	原油(吨) Crude Oil (ton)	汽油(吨) Petrol (ton)
总 计	**Total**	**11792730**	**1336795**	**30127**	**15243031**	**114383**
采掘业	Mining	102				158
制造业	Manufacturing	2105335	1336795		15243031	112144
电力煤气及水生产供应业	Production and Supply of Electricity, Gas and Water	9687294		30127		2082

7-2 续表
Continued

名 称	Name	煤油(吨) Kerosene (ton)	柴油(吨) Diesel Oil (ton)	燃料油(吨) Fuel Oil (ton)	液化石油气(吨) Liquefied Petroleum Gsa (ton)	热 力(百万千焦) Heat (millon kJ)	电 力(万千瓦时) Electricity (10 000 kW·h)
总 计	**Total**	**392**	**115475**	**135386**	**98723**	**18165596**	**2200270**
采掘业	Mining		526				5832
制造业	Manufacturing	392	112192	134394	98720	17236186	1829227
电力煤气及水生产供应业	Production and Supply of Electricity, Gas and Water		2757	993	3	929410	365210

7-3 重点耗能工业企业能源加工转换（2017年）

ENERGY CONVERSION OF MAJOR ENERGY-CONSUMING INDUSTRIAL ENTERPRISES（2017）

名称	Name	单位	Unit	能源消费合计 Total Energy Constumption	#加工转换投入 Conversion Input	火电 Thermal Power	供热 Leating	炼油 Petrolume Refining	制气 Gas Production	能源加工转换产出 Conversion Output of Energy
原煤	Raw Coal	吨	ton	10300794.18	9814467.18	6035648.80	3778818.38			
洗精煤	Dressing Coal	吨	ton	1960854.00	1960854.00					
煤制品	Coal Products	吨	ton	22571.38	22571.38		22571.38			
焦炭	Coke	吨	ton	1317821.00						1470459.00
其他焦化产品	Other Coking Products	吨	ton	80277.82						70855.00
焦炉煤气	Coking Gas	万立方米	10 000 cu.m	30126.70	30126.70	28913.38	1213.32			31257.00
高炉煤气	Blast Furnace GAS	万立方米	10 000 cu.m	134818.40	134818.40	129388.75	5429.65			
原油	Raw Oil	吨	ton	15243003.00	15228681.00			15228681.00		
汽油	Petrol	吨	ton	75.79						4560744.00
煤油	Kerosene	吨	ton							1864391.00
柴油	Diesel Oil	吨	ton	3744.48	280.00	280.00				4080806.00
燃料油	Fule Oil	吨	ton	75257.60	75145.00	746.00	134.00	74265.00		120842.00
液化石油气	Liquefied Petroleum Gas	吨	ton							1061967.00
炼厂干气	Refinery Dry Gas	吨	ton	556164.00	4674.00	467.00	4207.00			556164.00
其他石油制品	Other Petroleum Products	吨	ton	654976.73	233271.00			233271.00		1274346.00
热力	Heat	百万千焦	million kJ	1119139.00						70352967.77
电力	Electricity	万千瓦时	10 000 kW·h	459169.50						1727888.52
其他燃料	Other Fuel	吨标准煤	ton SCE							
能源合计	**Total**	**吨标准煤**	**ton SCE**	**35950378.89**	**32150464.77**	**5117806.88**	**3060167.34**	**22109679.25**		**27723841.27**

7-4 规模以上工业主要能源工业消费量(2017年)

MAJOR ENERGY CONSUMPTION Of INDUSTRY ABOVE DESIGNATED SIZE（2017）

行　业	Sector
总　计	**Total**
煤炭开采和洗选业	Mining and Washing of Coal
石油和天然气开采业	Extraction of Petroleum and Natural Gas
黑色金属矿采选业	Mining of Ferrous Metal Ores
有色金属矿采选业	Mining of Non-ferrous Metal Ores
非金属矿采选业	Mining and Processing of Nonmetal Ores
开采辅助活动	Auxiliary Activities of Mining
其他采矿业	Mining of Other Ores
农副食品加工业	Processing of Food from Agricultural Products
食品制造业	Manufacture of Foods
酒、饮料和精制茶制造业	Manufacture of Liquor，Beverage and Refind Tea
烟草制品业	Manufacture of Tobacco
纺织业	Manufacture of Textile
纺织服装、服饰业	Manufacture of Textil Wearing Apparel
皮革、毛皮、羽毛及其制品和制鞋业	Manufacture of Leather，Fur，Feathre&Its Products Footwear
木材加工和木、竹、藤、棕、草制品业	Processing of Timbers，Manufacture of Wood，Bamboo，Rattan，Palm and Straw Products
家具制造业	Manufacture of Furniture
造纸和纸制品业	Manufacture of Paper and Paper Products
印刷和记录媒介复制业	Printing，Reproduction of Recording Media
文教、工美、体育和娱乐用品制造业	Manufacture of Articles for Culture，Arts&Crafts，Sports and Entertainment
石油加工、炼焦和核燃料加工业	Processing of Petroleum，Coking，Processing of Nucleus Fuel
化学原料和化学制品制造业	Manufacture of Chemical Raw Material and Chemical Products
医药制造业	Manufacture of Medicines
化学纤维制造业	Manufacture of Chemical Fiber
橡胶和塑料制品业	Manufacture of Rubber and Plastic
非金属矿物制品业	Manufacture of Non-metallic Mineral Products
黑色金属冶炼和压延加工业	Smelting and Pressing of Ferrous Metals
有色金属冶炼和压延加工业	Smelting and Pressing of Non-ferrous Metals
金属制品业	Manufacture of Metal Products
通用设备制造业	Manufacture of General Purpose Machinery
专用设备制造业	Manufacture of Special Purpose Machinery
汽车制造业	Manufacture of Vehicle
铁路、船舶、航空航天和其他运输设备制造业	Manufacture of Transport Equipment for Railway，Shipping，Aerospace and other uses
电气机械和器材制造业	Manufacture of Electrical Machinery&Equipment
计算机、通信和其他电子设备制造业	Manufacture of Computer，Communication Equipment and Other Electronic Equipment
仪器仪表制造业	Manufacture of Measuring Imstrument
其他制造业	Manufacture of Other Products
废弃资源综合利用业	Recycling and Disposal of Waste Resources
金属制品、机械和设备修理业	Manufacture of Metal Products，Machinery and Equipment
电力、热力生产和供应业	Production and Supply of Electric Power and Heat Power
燃气生产和供应业	Production and Supply of Gas
水的生产和供应业	Production and Supply of Water

原煤 （吨） Raw Coal （ton）	洗精煤 （吨） Dressing Coal （ton）	其他洗煤 （吨） Other Dressing Coal （ton）	煤制品 （吨） Coal Products （ton）	焦炭 （吨） Coke （ton）
11792730	**1960854**	**65926**	**26958**	**1336795**
102				
93030		9837	1062	68
11040				
39043				
24187			6	
85405		3009		
27835				
1242				
11962				
86815			185	
70289				
50129				2
242791		53080		1
3542			1880	
313593				
225920				
501727	1960854			1317990
2731				
150741				15879
55839				692
25336			1233	2163
14034				
7648				
44158				
11687			20	
1100				
1200				
2309				
9686350			22571	
943				

7-4 续表 1
Continued

行　业	Sector
总　计	**Total**
煤炭开采和洗选业	Mining and Washing of Coal
石油和天然气开采业	Extraction of Petroleum and Natural Gas
黑色金属矿采选业	Mining of Ferrous Metal Ores
有色金属矿采选业	Mining of Non-ferrous Metal Ores
非金属矿采选业	Mining and Processing of Nonmetal Ores
开采辅助活动	Auxiliary Activities of Mining
其他采矿业	Mining of Other Ores
农副食品加工业	Processing of Food from Agricultural Products
食品制造业	Manufacture of Foods
酒、饮料和精制茶制造业	Manufacture of Liquor, Beverage and Refind Tea
烟草制品业	Manufacture of Tobacco
纺织业	Manufacture of Textile
纺织服装、服饰业	Manufacture of Textil Wearing Apparel
皮革、毛皮、羽毛及其制品和制鞋业	Manufacture of Leather, Fur, Feathre&Its Products Footwear
木材加工和木、竹、藤、棕、草制品业	Processing of Timbers, Manufacture of Wood, Bamboo, Rattan, Palm and Straw Products
家具制造业	Manufacture of Furniture
造纸和纸制品业	Manufacture of Paper and Paper Products
印刷和记录媒介复制业	Printing, Reproduction of Recording Media
文教、工美、体育和娱乐用品制造业	Manufacture of Articles for Culture, Arts&Crafts, Sports and Entertainment
石油加工、炼焦和核燃料加工业	Processing of Petroleum, Coking, Processing of Nucleus Fuel
化学原料和化学制品制造业	Manufacture of Chemical Raw Material and Chemical Products
医药制造业	Manufacture of Medicines
化学纤维制造业	Manufacture of Chemical Fiber
橡胶和塑料制品业	Manufacture of Rubber and Plastic
非金属矿物制品业	Manufacture of Non-metallic Mineral Products
黑色金属冶炼和压延加工业	Smelting and Pressing of Ferrous Metals
有色金属冶炼和压延加工业	Smelting and Pressing of Non-ferrous Metals
金属制品业	Manufacture of Metal Products
通用设备制造业	Manufacture of General Purpose Machinery
专用设备制造业	Manufacture of Special Purpose Machinery
汽车制造业	Manufacture of Vehicle
铁路、船舶、航空航天和其他运输设备制造业	Manufacture of Transport Equipment for Railway, Shipping, Aerospace and other uses
电气机械和器材制造业	Manufacture of Electrical Machinery&Equipment
计算机、通信和其他电子设备制造业	Manufacture of Computer, Communication Equipment and Other Electronic Equipment
仪器仪表制造业	Manufacture of Measuring Imstrument
其他制造业	Manufacture of Other Products
废弃资源综合利用业	Recycling and Disposal of Waste Resources
金属制品、机械和设备修理业	Manufacture of Metal Products, Machinery and Equipment
电力、热力生产和供应业	Production and Supply of Electric Power and Heat Power
燃气生产和供应业	Production and Supply of Gas
水的生产和供应业	Production and Supply of Water

焦炉煤气（万立方米）Coking Gas（10 000 cu.m）	高炉煤气（万立方米）Blast Furnace Gas（10 000 cu.m）	原油（吨）Crude Oil（ton）	汽油（吨）Petrol（ton）	煤油（吨）Kerosene（ton）
30127	**144943**	**15243031**	**114383**	**392**
			8	
			150	
			10487	101
			1395	
			1496	4
			3202	
			9556	5
			1145	
			467	
			1570	
			1235	
			5963	25
		25	10223	
		15243003	61	
			3108	
			1109	
			4	
			6600	
	10125		5605	
			1162	
			1566	
			15772	48
		3	9001	76
			6841	
			4479	
			2244	132
			4187	
			1845	
			381	
			186	
			123	
			1131	
30127	134818		865	
			597	
			619	

7-4 续表 2
Continued

行　业	Sector
总　计	**Total**
煤炭开采和洗选业	Mining and Washing of Coal
石油和天然气开采业	Extraction of Petroleum and Natural Gas
黑色金属矿采选业	Mining of Ferrous Metal Ores
有色金属矿采选业	Mining of Non-ferrous Metal Ores
非金属矿采选业	Mining and Processing of Nonmetal Ores
开采辅助活动	Auxiliary Activities of Mining
其他采矿业	Mining of Other Ores
农副食品加工业	Processing of Food from Agricultural Products
食品制造业	Manufacture of Foods
酒、饮料和精制茶制造业	Manufacture of Liquor, Beverage and Refind Tea
烟草制品业	Manufacture of Tobacco
纺织业	Manufacture of Textile
纺织服装、服饰业	Manufacture of Textil Wearing Apparel
皮革、毛皮、羽毛及其制品和制鞋业	Manufacture of Leather, Fur, Feathre&Its Products Footwear
木材加工和木、竹、藤、棕、草制品业	Processing of Timbers, Manufacture of Wood, Bamboo, Rattan, Palm and Straw Products
家具制造业	Manufacture of Furniture
造纸和纸制品业	Manufacture of Paper and Paper Products
印刷和记录媒介复制业	Printing, Reproduction of Recording Media
文教、工美、体育和娱乐用品制造业	Manufacture of Articles for Culture, Arts&Crafts, Sports and Entertainment
石油加工、炼焦和核燃料加工业	Processing of Petroleum, Coking, Processing of Nucleus Fuel
化学原料和化学制品制造业	Manufacture of Chemical Raw Material and Chemical Products
医药制造业	Manufacture of Medicines
化学纤维制造业	Manufacture of Chemical Fiber
橡胶和塑料制品业	Manufacture of Rubber and Plastic
非金属矿物制品业	Manufacture of Non-metallic Mineral Products
黑色金属冶炼和压延加工业	Smelting and Pressing of Ferrous Metals
有色金属冶炼和压延加工业	Smelting and Pressing of Non-ferrous Metals
金属制品业	Manufacture of Metal Products
通用设备制造业	Manufacture of General Purpose Machinery
专用设备制造业	Manufacture of Special Purpose Machinery
汽车制造业	Manufacture of Vehicle
铁路、船舶、航空航天和其他运输设备制造业	Manufacture of Transport Equipment for Railway, Shipping, Aerospace and other uses
电气机械和器材制造业	Manufacture of Electrical Machinery&Equipment
计算机、通信和其他电子设备制造业	Manufacture of Computer, Communication Equipment and Other Electronic Equipment
仪器仪表制造业	Manufacture of Measuring Imstrument
其他制造业	Manufacture of Other Products
废弃资源综合利用业	Recycling and Disposal of Waste Resources
金属制品、机械和设备修理业	Manufacture of Metal Products, Machinery and Equipment
电力、热力生产和供应业	Production and Supply of Electric Power and Heat Power
燃气生产和供应业	Production and Supply of Gas
水的生产和供应业	Production and Supply of Water

柴油 （吨） Diesel Oil （ton）	燃料油 （吨） Fuel Oil （ton）	液化石油气 （吨） Liquefied Petroleum Gas （ton）	炼厂干气 （吨） Refinery Dry Gas （ton）
115475	**135386**	**98723**	**556164**
526			
7663	849	17	
1270			
1981		296	
2379	1264	6	
6810			
631	200		
336			
644			
1055			
2993			
5028	878		
1938	74265	365	556164
4669	228	97460	
1643			
5238	3096	2	
27692	53563		
2281			
1182			
9419	51	144	
8232			
5995		3	
3029		316	
3877			
2998		89	
1688		21	
611			
180			
111			
619			
1555	993	3	
49			
1152			

7-4 续表 3
Continued

行　业	Sector
总　计	**Total**
煤炭开采和洗选业	Mining and Washing of Coal
石油和天然气开采业	Extraction of Petroleum and Natural Gas
黑色金属矿采选业	Mining of Ferrous Metal Ores
有色金属矿采选业	Mining of Non-ferrous Metal Ores
非金属矿采选业	Mining and Processing of Nonmetal Ores
开采辅助活动	Auxiliary Activities of Mining
其他采矿业	Mining of Other Ores
农副食品加工业	Processing of Food from Agricultural Products
食品制造业	Manufacture of Foods
酒、饮料和精制茶制造业	Manufacture of Liquor，Beverage and Refind Tea
烟草制品业	Manufacture of Tobacco
纺织业	Manufacture of Textile
纺织服装、服饰业	Manufacture of Textil Wearing Apparel
皮革、毛皮、羽毛及其制品和制鞋业	Manufacture of Leather，Fur，Feathre&Its Products Footwear
木材加工和木、竹、藤、棕、草制品业	Processing of Timbers，Manufacture of Wood，Bamboo，Rattan，Palm and Straw Products
家具制造业	Manufacture of Furniture
造纸和纸制品业	Manufacture of Paper and Paper Products
印刷和记录媒介复制业	Printing，Reproduction of Recording Media
文教、工美、体育和娱乐用品制造业	Manufacture of Articles for Culture，Arts&Crafts，Sports and Entertainment
石油加工、炼焦和核燃料加工业	Processing of Petroleum，Coking，Processing of Nucleus Fuel
化学原料和化学制品制造业	Manufacture of Chemical Raw Material and Chemical Products
医药制造业	Manufacture of Medicines
化学纤维制造业	Manufacture of Chemical Fiber
橡胶和塑料制品业	Manufacture of Rubber and Plastic
非金属矿物制品业	Manufacture of Non-metallic Mineral Products
黑色金属冶炼和压延加工业	Smelting and Pressing of Ferrous Metals
有色金属冶炼和压延加工业	Smelting and Pressing of Non-ferrous Metals
金属制品业	Manufacture of Metal Products
通用设备制造业	Manufacture of General Purpose Machinery
专用设备制造业	Manufacture of Special Purpose Machinery
汽车制造业	Manufacture of Vehicle
铁路、船舶、航空航天和其他运输设备制造业	Manufacture of Transport Equipment for Railway，Shipping，Aerospace and other uses
电气机械和器材制造业	Manufacture of Electrical Machinery&Equipment
计算机、通信和其他电子设备制造业	Manufacture of Computer，Communication Equipment and Other Electronic Equipment
仪器仪表制造业	Manufacture of Measuring Imstrument
其他制造业	Manufacture of Other Products
废弃资源综合利用业	Recycling and Disposal of Waste Resources
金属制品、机械和设备修理业	Manufacture of Metal Products，Machinery and Equipment
电力、热力生产和供应业	Production and Supply of Electric Power and Heat Power
燃气生产和供应业	Production and Supply of Gas
水的生产和供应业	Production and Supply of Water

其他油制品（吨）Other Petoleum Products（ton）	热 力（百万千焦）Heat（million kJ）	电 力（万千瓦时）Electricity（10 000 kW・h）	其他燃料（吨标准煤）Other Fuel（ton SCE）
658519	**18165596**	**2200270**	**2515**
		17	
		5815	
	837260	116601	26
	373670	24085	1950
	2256759	21616	
	1019828	25592	288
	1698170	48565	
	101311	16909	
		5106	
	942	14533	
	843180	20870	
	14160	34834	
	21711	48234	
622468		127491	
36028	5039724	213943	
	503055	15305	87
	2564	5108	
	945561	147855	
	66401	123885	
	130009	204991	
	49511	21277	
14	489857	106395	
	54885	91740	
	9043	52322	
	771298	100542	
10	921797	60455	
	643144	91897	164
	346603	64099	
		6964	
	95742	15263	
		320	
		2432	
	913535	335045	
	15875	8079	
		22087	

主要统计指标解释

工业企业能源消费量 工业企业能源消费包括工业企业在生产过程中作为燃料、动力、原料、辅助材料使用的能源以及工艺用能、非生产用能；作为能源加工转换企业，还要包括能源加工转换的投入量。工业企业能源消费量具体包括：

（1）用于本企业产品生产、工业性作业和其他生产性活动的能源。

（2）用于技术更新改造措施、新技术研究和新产品试制以及科学试验等方面的能源。

（3）用于经营维修、建筑及设备大修理、机电设备和交通运输工具等方面的能源。

（4）用于劳动保护的能源。

（5）其他非生产消费的能源。

不包括：

（1）由仓库发到车间，但在报告期最后一天没有消费的能源。这部分能源应在办理假退料手续后计入库存量。

（2）拨到外单位，委托外单位加工用的能源。

（3）调出本单位或借给外单位的能源。

工业生产能源消费 是指工业企业为进行工业生产活动所使用的能源。主要包括：

1. 用于本企业产品生产、工业性作业的能源，包括用作原料、材料、燃料、动力；作为能源加工转换企业，还包括用作加工转换的能源。

2. 产品生产过程中作为辅助材料使用的能源。

3. 生产工艺过程使用的能源。

4. 新技术研究、新产品试制、科学试验使用的能源。

5. 为了工业生产活动而在进行的各种修理过程中使用的能源。

6. 生产区内的劳动保护用能等。

Explanatory Notes on Main Statistical Indicators

Energy Consumption of Industrial Enterprises include emergy in the production process as fuel, power, raw materials, supplementary materials, and for use of technology and non-production. As energy processing and conversion enterprises, also include energy processing and conversion of inputs. These specifically include：(1) Energy for the enterprise product, industrial production operations and other activities. (2) Energy for technical upgrading measures and new technology research and new product production and scientific experiments. (3) Energy for operation maintenance, construction and equipment overhaul, electrical and mechanical equipment and transport, and other aspects. (4) Energy for the protection of labor. (5) Enorgy for Other non-production and consumption. And these exclude：(1) Energy from the warehouse to the workshop, but out of consumption on the last day of the reporting period. This part of the energy shoudl leave retreat materials handling procedures included stock. (2) Energy transferred to other units, entrusted with the processing. (3) Energy transferred out of the unit or loans to other units.

Energy Consumption for Industrial Production refers to energy for industrial enterprises in industrial production activities. These mainly include：1. Energy for the enterprise products, industrial operations, including energy as raw materials, materials, fuels, and Power. As energy processing and conversion enterprises, also include energy for processing and conversion. 2. Energy as supplementary material in product process. 3. Energy used in production process. 4. Energy for new technologies, new product production, and scientific experiment. 5. Energy in process of repairing for industrial production activities. 6. Energy for labor protection in production areas and so on.

财政、金融和保险业

GOVERNMENT FINANCE FINACIAL INTERMEDIATION AND INSURANCE

简要说明

一、本篇资料的主要内容

本篇资料主要反映了全市财政收支、金融和保险方面的情况，主要包括财政收入、财政支出、金融机构存贷款、保险业务开展等方面的资料。

二、本篇资料的来源

1、财政部分的资料来源于市财政局。

2、金融方面的资料来源于中国人民银行青岛市中心支行。

3、保险方面的资料来源于中国保险监督管理委员会青岛监管局。

本篇资料由市统计局国民经济核算处整理提供。

Brief Introduction

Ⅰ. Main Content

Data in this chapter show the conditions of local government budgetary finance, banking and insurance, and securities, including government revenue and expenditrue, deposits and loans of financial institutions and statistics on insurance companies.

Ⅱ. Source of Data

(1) Data on local government finance are provided by Qingdao Municipal Finance Bureau.

(2) Data on banking are provided by Qingdao Branch of the People's Bank of China.

(3) Data on insurance are provide by China Insurance Regulatory Commission of Qingdao Bureau.

Data in this chapter are prepared and compiled by the Division of National Accounts of Qingdao Municipal Bureau of Statistics.

8-1 主要年份地方财政收支

MAFOR YEAR'S REVENUE AND EXPENDRRURE OF LOCAL GOVERNMENT FINANCE

单位：万元（10 000 yuan）

年份 Year	财政收入 Revenue of Government Finance	财政支出 Expenditure of Government Finance
1949	1527	306
1952	19809	2226
1957	29875	3556
1962	32869	4327
1965	47682	6280
1970	95778	7825
1975	90220	11966
1978	130749	19427
1980	124835	20064
1985	165155	41996
1988	201206	93931
1990	242303	133875
1991	259377	137716
1992	275589	155696
1993	182348	211938
1994	227490	277331
1995	294771	376982
1996	379674	469569
1997	476804	564787
1998	580434	678575
1999	680089	740937
2000	800120	878702
2001	987080	1097848
2002	1006616	1243880
2003	1201398	1471747
2004	1305136	1646214
2005	1763412	2030622
2006	2257663	2367875
2007	2925798	3211777
2008	3424359	3694111
2009	3769896	4335754
2010	4526138	5323888
2011	5661400	6580605
2012	6701820	7659801
2013	7889313	10142273
2014	8952450	10747138
2015	10063220	12228664
2016	11000303	13528516
2017	11572389	14030252

注：1. 1993 年以后实行新制度，财政收入数与历年不可比。
　　2. 2002 年以后，财政收入、支出为一般预算数。

Note：1. Since 1993，new regulations have been adopted in calculating revenue of government finance，the figutrs are not comparable with those over the years.
　　2. Since 2002，revenue of government finance and expenditure of government finance refer to general budgetary revenue and expenditure.

8-2 分市、区公共财政预算收入（2017 年）
PULBIC FINANCE BUDGET REVENUE BY CITY AND DISTRICL（2017）

单位：万元（10 000 yuan）

市、区名称	Region	公共财政预算收入 Public Finance Bodget Revenue	增值税 Value-added Tax	营业税 Business Tax	企业所得税 Enterprise Income Tax
全市	**Whole Municipality**	**11572389**	**3090488**	**11779**	**1466509**
市南区	Shiman District	1000817	312165	1831	158193
市北区	Shiben District	1069126	314798	1348	166416
李沧区	Licang District	801617	186337	1057	49908
崂山区	Laoshan District	1418065	352667	568	325240
黄岛区	Huangdao District	2312895	749449	815	311106
保税港区	Qingdao Free Trade Port Area of China	123916	36095	189	45881
城阳区	Chengyang District	1046715	410646	979	136167
即墨区	Jimo District	1043467	246546	1162	52446
胶州市	Jiaozhou	965177	193703	1158	64242
平度市	Pingdu	542112	126999	589	43536
莱西市	Laixi	511215	77581	1831	18816
红岛经济区	Qingdao National High-tech Industrial Development Zone	250217	83502	252	29726
市本级	Municipal Level	487050			64832

8-2 续表
Continued

单位：万元（10 000 yuan）

市、区名称	Region	个人所得税 Personal Income Tax	城市维护建设税 Urban Maintenance and Development Tax	基金预算收入 Funds Budgetary Revenue
全市	**Whole Municipality**	**423571**	**527102**	**5343553**
市南区	Shiman District	113804	42057	
市北区	Shiben District	45683	55934	
李沧区	Licang District	13873	33643	
崂山区	Laoshan District	71900	81492	783180
黄岛区	Huangdao District	73487	144248	1155656
保税港区	Qingdao Free Trade Port Area of China	5257	5645	50809
城阳区	Chengyang District	34837	55662	508876
即墨区	Jimo District	23575	35706	338253
胶州市	Jiaozhou	14226	30819	292956
平度市	Pingdu	10372	18824	87992
莱西市	Laixi	7729	11222	16340
红岛经济区	Qingdao National High-tech Industrial Development Zone	8828	11850	371782
市本级	Municipal Level			1737709

8-3 分市、区公共财政预算支出（2017 年）
PUBLIC FINANCE BUDGET REVENUE BY CITY AND DISTRICT (2017)

单位：万元（10 000 yuan）

市、区名称	Region	公共财政预算支出 Pubic Finance Budget Revenue	一般公共服务支出 General Public Services	公共安全 Public Securty	教育 Education	科学技术 Science and Technology	文化体育与传媒 Culture, Sport and Media
全市	Whole Municipality	14030252	1521288	793851	2538189	385919	193436
市南区	Shiman District	542964	68367	28837	107975	6796	5042
市北区	Shiben District	743571	135466	30002	188316	22749	7577
李沧区	Licang District	724601	51287	19769	127722	109565	6584
崂山区	Laoshan District	911537	78079	27839	115408	40217	5399
黄岛区	Huangdao District	1907601	254622	81696	471413	80610	18979
保税港区	Qingdao Free Trade Port Area of China	77810	22861	2201	32	309	76
城阳区	Chengyang District	789576	72733	35138	200829	13234	6658
即墨区	Jimo District	1282609	118527	37556	293920	12082	23563
胶州市	Jiaozhou	1089059	132455	59573	248275	19223	11903
平度市	Pingdu	969667	100904	38625	280957	9930	8137
莱西市	Laixi	714707	84641	31874	153958	920	4386
红岛经济区	Qingdao National High-tech Industrial Development Zone	191478	26188	4279	27792	19390	15774
市本级	Municipal Level	4085072	375158	396462	321592	50894	79358

8-3 续表
Continued

单位：万元（10 000 yuan）

市、区名称	Region	社会保障和就业 Social Security and Empooyment	医疗卫生 Health Care	节能环保 Environment Protection	城乡社区事务 Urban and Rural Community Affairs	农林水事务 Affairs of Agiculture Forest and Irrigatior	基金预算支出 Funds Budgetary Expenditure
全市	**Whole Municipality**	**1533879**	**861562**	**204246**	**3225681**	**759036**	**6370746**
市南区	Shiman District	70058	36383	3698	174885	42	233693
市北区	Shiben District	116224	56521	3608	134951	75	257052
李沧区	Licang District	66443	30578	42404	244981	2045	86138
崂山区	Laoshan District	32805	32332	2240	403066	62019	782917
黄岛区	Huangdao District	264220	133366	25829	339568	97454	1267796
保税港区	Qingdao Free Trade Port Area of China	4206	153	3	24171		44236
城阳区	Chengyang District	43998	46993	3261	236221	42966	582354
即墨区	Jimo District	144412	97710	9826	350195	99550	440424
胶州市	Jiaozhou	71597	79004	25815	256872	101792	361727
平度市	Pingdu	162228	112384	3568	90197	128097	91970
莱西市	Laixi	85509	77545	11031	74067	84195	42263
红岛经济区	Qingdao National High-tech Industrial Development Zone	11822	7706	5213	25458	8756	315354
市本级	Municipal Level	460357	150887	67750	871049	132045	1864822

8-4　主要年份金融系统人民币存贷款（年末余额）

MAJOR YEAR'S DEPOSITS AND LOANS OF FINANCIAL INSTITUTIONS（YEAR-END BALANCE）

单位：万元（10 000 yuan）

年份 Year	存款合计 Total Deposits	企业存款 Deposits by Enterprises	储蓄存款 Savings Deposits	贷款合计 Total Loans
1949	693	239	28	278
1952	9093	4308	1838	3322
1957	10372	3359	4037	30690
1962	20040	8579	3279	73601
1965	27331	11830	6347	64555
1970	38264	13024	7576	126382
1975	60622	22568	15637	207006
1978	66523	21004	21455	297184
1980	120644	38105	38609	379666
1985	344760	99736	155604	452142
1990	1235562	321542	655895	1535751
1991	1553564	411417	824428	1871462
1992	2076667	612868	1044165	2352449
1993	2747294	835617	1372239	2940658
1994	3769019	1399110	1918734	3610564
1995	5324026	2030382	2687888	4777864
1996	6991289	2630958	3499219	5941281
1997	7385092	2885632	4060259	6508776
1998	8183471	3018063	4591012	7239231
1999	9160001	3454570	4978045	8945730
2000	10560624	4386316	5353215	9564293
2001	12323942	4955336	6187409	10798871
2002	15225733	5819655	7449408	13044792
2003	18920868	7027227	9084693	16783917
2004	22462592	7924690	10894941	18472613
2005	26975372	8226661	13431016	20394792
2006	32453583	10144296	15676197	25779442
2007	38915882	13213434	17020383	30970553
2008	47353803	14641948	21233637	37483209
2009	63019764	21001185	25278658	48735326
2010	76592065	27271963	29123256	58862263
2011	86384994	49189415	31985099	69477500
2012	94348924	50978985	37576007	79465532
2013	109695588	60367185	41405946	88607439
2014	113703085	60791933	44358964	97200532
2015	125330268	45526577	50235905	107718528
2016	140071344	50912759	53263262	118916821
2017	143877550	53835435	53941843	132647913

注：本表数据来源于人民银行，自 2015 年起，人民银行报表指标变化，企业存款指标暂用非金融企业存款，储蓄存款指标暂用住户存款，口径与以前年度不一致。

Note：The data in this table comes from the People's Bank of China. Since 2015, the report index of the People's Bank of China has changed, the enterprise deposit index is temporarily used as the deposit of the enterprise, the savings deposit index is temporarily used for household deposit,The caliber is not consistent with the previous year.

8-5 金融系统人民币存贷款（年末余额）
DEPOSITS AND LOANS OF FINANCIAL INSTITUTIONS（YEAR-END BALANCE）

单位：万元（10 000 yuan）

项目	Item	2017 年	比年初增减数 Incremental/Reductions Compared to the Beginning of the Year
一、存款总计	Total Deposits	143877550	3817220
住户存款	Household Deposits	53941843	687557
非金融企业存款	Non-Financial Corporate Deposits	53835435	2924785
广义政府存款	General Government Deposits	24914406	1943231
非银行业金融机构存款	Non-Banking Financial Institutions's Deposits	10768475	-1707465
二、贷款总计	Total Loans	132647913	13767349
住户贷款	Household Loans	40567470	6694532
#短期贷款	Short-Term Loans	3859558	158769
中长期贷款	Medium And Long-Term Loans	36707912	6535763
非金融企业及机关团体贷款	Non-Financial Enterprises And Institutions/ Organizations' Loans	91726238	6991523
#短期贷款	Short-Term Loans	32090193	1222809
中长期贷款	Medium&Long-term Loans	56201207	7476525
票据融资	Notes Financing	2835554	-2049872
非银行业金融机构贷款	Non-Banking Financial Institution's Loans	213933	103377

注：自 2015 年起，人民银行报表中指标发生变化，本表数据按照新指标提供。
Note：Since 2015，the indexes in the People's Bank of China's statements have changed，the data in the talbe are provided according to the new indexes.

8-6 国内保险业务（2000-2017年）
DOMESTIC INSURANCE BUSINESS (2000-2017)

项目	Item	2000年	2005年	2006年	2008年	2009年
风险保障金额	**Total domestic insurance Value**	**38357485**	**91691581**	**119396881**	**276989344**	**293519697**
国内业务收入	**Domestic Business Income**	**220780**	**495701**	**605143**	**1027258**	**1153101**
1. 保费收入	Premium Income	218714	495701	605143	1027258	1153101
#财产险	Propetry Insurance	85161	159746	199213	280008	339314
农业险	Agiculture Insurance	18	12	19	3135	4066
人身险	Personal Insurance	133535	335943	405911	744115	809721
国内业务支出	**Domestic Business Expenditure**	**94877**	**214148**	**252477**	**423743**	**476377**
1. 赔款支出	Cham Expenditure	62275	111385	131321	196318	219546
#财产险	Property Insurance	58361	92700	115214	164415	188723
农业险	Agriculture Insurance	5	11	3	907	3452
人身险	Personal Insurance	3909	18674	16104	30996	27371
2. 给付支出	Mature Payment	27955	32739	63144	132621	123056
3. 退保	Surrended	4647	70024	58012	94804	133775

注：本表由青岛保监局提供，风险保障金额2012年之前为国内保险总值。
Note: This table was provided by the Qingdao Insurance Regulatory Bureau. The amount of risk protection before 2012 was the total value of domestic insurance.

单位：万元（10 000 yuan）

2010年	2011年	2012年	2013年	2014年	2015年	2016年	2017年
309244255	**380829634**	**447476690**	**491953749**	**611632799**	**836499657**	**1687559828**	**2232390824**
1538526	**1457269**	**1602881**	**1789854**	**2031421**	**2441172**	**3359013**	**3967170**
1538526	1457269	1602881	1789854	2031421	2441172	3359013	3967170
492190	556257	644269	744470	872805	920229	1046908	1062116
3261	3587	5046	6824	8395	12100	12734	15670
1043075	897425	953566	1038560	1150220	1508843	2299371	2889384
497832	**463751**	**592167**	**757404**	**1031415**	**1236281**	**1522375**	**1704218**
279019	307564	360085	432494	492693	539320	681211	733493
250966	286214	328877	392860	442168	492573	526586	554513
2808	1087	1833	3820	5519	9724	16337	18232
25245	20263	29375	35814	45006	37023	138288	160749
109318	156188	154922	194592	274790	340786	455300	470266
109496	69275	77159	130318	263932	356175	376777	500459

主要统计指标解释

财政收入 指国家财政参与社会产品分配所取得的收入，是实现国家职能的财力保证。财政收入所包括的内容几经变化，目前主要包括：

（1）税收收入：包括增值税、营业税、企业所得税、个人所得税、资源税、城市维护建设税、房产税、印花税、城镇土地使用税、土地增值税、车船税、耕地占用税、契税、烟叶税、其他税收收入。

（2）非税收入:包括专项收入、行政事业性收费收入、罚没收入、国有资本经营收入、国有资源有偿使用收入、其他收入。

财政支出 国家财政将筹集起来的资金进行分配使用，以满足经济建设和各项事业的需要，主要包括：

（1）一般公共服务支出：反映政府提供一般公共服务的支出。

（2）公共安全:反映政府维护社会公共安全方面的支出,有关事务包括武装警察、公安、国家安全、检察、法院、司法行政、监狱、劳教、国家保密、缉私警察等。

（3）教育支出：反映政府教育事务支出。有关具体教育事务包括教育行政管理、学前教育、小学教育、初中教育、普通高中教育、普通高等教育、初等职业教育、中专教育、技校教育、职业高中教育、高等职业教育、广播电视教育、留学生教育、特殊教育、干部继续教育、教育机关服务等。

（4）科学技术：反映政府用于科学技术方面的支出。

（5）文化体育与传媒：反映政府在文化、文物、体育、广播电视、新闻出版等方面的支出。

（6）社会保障和就业:反映政府在社会保障与就业方面的支出。有关事项包括社会保障与就业管理事务、民政管理事务、财政对社会保险基金的补助、补充全国社会保障基金、行政事业单位离退休、企业改革补助、就业补助、抚恤、退役安置、社会福利、残疾人事业、城市居民最低生活保障、其他城镇社会救济、农村社会救济、自然灾害生活补助、红十字事务等。

（7）医疗卫生支出：反映政府医疗卫生方面的支出。具体包括医疗卫生管理事务支出、医疗服务支出、医疗保障支出、疾病预防控制支出、卫生监督支出、妇幼保健支出、农村卫生支出等。

（8）环境保护：反映政府环境保护支出。具体包括：环境保护管理事务支出、环境监测与监察支出、污染治理支出、自然生态保护支出、天然林保护工程支出、退耕还林支出、风沙荒漠治理支出、退牧还草支出、已垦草原退耕还草支出。

（9）城乡社区事务：反映政府城乡社区事务支出。具体包括：城乡社区管理事务支出、城乡社区规划与管理支出、城乡社区公共设施支出、城乡社区住宅支出、城乡社区环境卫生支出、建设市场管理与监督支出等。

（10）农林水事务：反映政府农林水事务方面的支出。具体包括农业、林业、水利、扶贫支出、农业综合开发支出等。

存款 指企业、机关、团体或居民根据资金必须收回的原则，把货币资金存入银行或其他信贷机构保管并取得一定利息的一种信用活动形式。根据存款对象或性质的不同可划分为企业存款、财政存款、机关团体存款、基本建设存款、储蓄存款、农村存款、委托存款、其他存款等科目。它是银行信贷资金的主要来源。

贷款 指银行或其他信贷机构根据资金必须归还的原则，按一定利率，为企业、个人等提供资金的一种信用活动形式。我国银行贷款分为短期贷款、中期流动资金贷款、中长期贷款、信托贷款、融资租赁、委托贷款、票据融资、各项垫款等。

承保额 又叫保险金额，指保险人承担赔偿或者给付保险金责任的最高限额。

保费 指投保人为取得保险人在约定范围内所承担赔偿责任而支付给保险人的费用。

Explanatory Notes on Main Statistical Indicators

Government Revenue refers to the revenue of the government finance by means of participating in the distribution of the social products, which is the financial resources for ensuring the government to function. The contents of government revenue have been changed several times. Now it includes the following main items:

(1) Various tax revenues, including value added tax, business tax, enterprise income tax, personal income tax, resources tax, fixed assets investment direction regulating tax, tax on city maintenance and construction, real estate tax, stamp tax, tax on use of urban land, land value added tax, vehicle and vessel tax, tax on occupancy of cultivated land, property tax, tobacco leaf tax, and other tax revenues.

(2) Non-tax Revenues including special revenues, revenues from Administrative and institutional fees, penalty and confiscatory revenues , revenues from state-owned capital operationg,revenues from paid use of state-owned resources, and other revenues.

Government Expenditure refers to the distribution and use of the funds the government finance has raised, so as to meet the needs of economic construction and various causes. It includes the following main items:

(1) Expenditure for general public services: It reflects the expenditure from the government for general public services.

(2) Expenditure on public security: It reflects the expenditure from the government towards safeguarding the public security, including the related affairs of armed police, public security, state security, procuratorial administration,law court, judicial administration, jail , reeducation through labor, state confidentiality, anti-smuggling Patrol,etc.

(3) Expenditure on education: It reflects the expenditure from the government on education, including the related affairs of educational administration management, preschool education, primary education, junior secondary educate, regular senior secondary educate, regular higher education, primary vocational education, specialized secondary educate, technical educate, vocational senior secondary educate, vocational higher education, radio and television education, foreign student educate, special education, cadre continuing education, education institution services,etc.

(4) Expenditure on science and technology: It reflects the expenditure from the government on science and technology.

(5) Expenditure on culture, sport and media: It reflects the expenditure from the government on culture, cultural relics, sport, radio and television, publication, etc.

(6) Expenditure on social security and employment:It reflects the expenditure from the government on social security and employment, including the related affairs of management of social security and employment, civil administration, subsidies to social insurance funds, supplement to national social security funds, retirees of government agencies and institutions, subsidies to enterprises reform, subsidies to employment, pension, settling down demobilized servicemen,social security, disabled person administration, minimum living allowance in urban area, other social relief in urban area, social relief in rural area, subsidies to natural disaster, Red Cross business,etc.

(7) Expenditure on health care: It reflects the expenditure from the government on health care, including expenditure on management of health care, medical services, medical security, disease control and prevention, public health supervision, rural health care,etc.

(8) Expenditure on environment protection: It reflects the expenditure from the government on environment protection, including expenditure on management of environment protection, environment monitoring and supervisory, pollution government, natural ecological protection, project of natural forest protection, returning farmland to forest, sandstorm and wilderness government, returning grazing land to grassland, returning cultivated grassland to grassland, etc.

(9) Expenditure on urban and rural community affairs: It reflects the expenditure from the government on urban and rural community affairs, including expenditure on management of urban and rural community affairs, plan and management of urban and rural community, public utility of urban and rural community, residential buildings of urban and rural community, environmental sanitation of urban and rural community, management and supervision of markets construction, etc.

(10) Expenditure on agriculture, forest and irrigation: It reflects the expenditure from the government on agriculture, forest and irrigation, including expenditure on agriculture, forest, irrigation, poverty alleviation, comprehensive development of agriculture, etc.

Deposit is a form of credit by which enterprises, institutions, organizations or households can put money into banks and other credit institutions for safekeeping and interest earning under the principle of free withdrawal. According to different depositors, deposits are divided into enterprise deposits, treasury deposits, deposits of government agencies and organizations, capital construction deposits, savings deposits, rural saving deposits, entrusted deposits and other deposits. Deposits are major sources of the credit funds of banks.

Loan is a form of credit by which banks and other credit institutions provide funds at certain interest rate to enterprises and individuals in the light of the principle of unconditional repayment. Loans from Chinese banks include circulating capital loans, fixed assets loans, loans to urban and rural individuals engaged in industrial and commercial business and agricultural loans.

Amount Covered which also is known as amount Insured, refers to the maximum that the insurant will get for the claim of the case insured.

Premium is the fee paid by the insurant to the insurer to obtain the obligation of compensation from the insurance within the agreed terms.

价格指数 9

PRICE INDEXES

简要说明

一、本篇资料的主要内容

本篇资料主要包括工业生产者出厂、工业生产者购进、固定资产投资、房地产、居民消费、商品零售等价格指数。

二、本篇资料的来源

1、工业生产者出厂、工业生产者购进、固定资产投资、房地产价格指数分别来源于生产、投资、房地产价格统计调查年报，由国家统计局青岛调查队生产投资价格调查处整理提供。

2、居民消费、商品零售价格指数来源于消费价格统计调查年报，由国家统计局青岛调查队消费价格调查处整理提供。

Brief Introduction

Ⅰ. Main Content

Data in this chapter mainly include producer price indices for manufactured goods, purchasing price indices for industrial producers, price indices of investment in fixed assets, real estate price indices, consumer price indices and retail price indices.

Ⅱ. Source of Data

(1) Data on producer price indices for manufactured goods, purchasing price indices for industrial producers, price indices of investment in fixed assets, real estate price indices are based on annual report of price survey on production, investment, real estate, and provided by the Division of Production Price Survey of Survey Office of the National Bureau of Statistics in Qingdao.

(2) Data on consumer price indices and retail price indices are based on annual report of consumer price survey, and provided by the Division of Consumer Price Survey of Survey Office of the National Bureau of Statistics in Qingdao.

9-1 主要年份居民消费和商品零售价格指数
MAJOR YEAR'S CONSUMER AND RETAIL PRICE INDEXES

（上年价格 = 100） (perceding year = 100)

年份 Year	居民消费价格指数 Consumer Price Index	#食品类 Food	#衣着类 Clothing	#服务项目价格指数 Services Price Index	商品零售价格指数 Retail Price Index
1951	110.5	105.2	112.4		110.5
1952	99.8	99.6	98.7		99.8
1957	101.4	101.3	101.4	99.3	101.4
1962	102.6	102.0	100.2	99.9	102.6
1965	101.2	101.3	98.8	96.9	101.2
1970	98.9	99.7	100.0	99.5	98.9
1975	100.3	100.1	100.0	100.0	100.3
1978	100.5	100.2	99.8	100.0	100.5
1980	105.2	108.5	100.3	100.6	105.5
1985	110.4	115.2	102.3	102.7	110.9
1988	120.7	125.2	117.3	118.3	120.9
1990	104.5	103.4	103.4	118.8	103.6
1991	107.0	107.0	112.1	109.6	106.8
1992	111.4	115.1	108.6	119.9	110.8
1993	123.9	120.9	119.0	158.5	119.8
1994	126.9	135.2	130.1	117.9	122.8
1995	116.2	118.1	122.8	123.2	114.2
1996	112.6	110.1	104.3	130.4	106.0
1997	104.0	101.2	102.3	120.8	100.2
1998	100.0	93.7	94.5	136.2	94.9
1999	100.2	96.7	97.1	115.6	96.6
2000	103.3	100.0	108.3	112.0	99.7
2001	101.0	100.6	98.0	108.7	98.9
2002	98.9	97.8	100.2	101.0	99.5
2003	101.4	104.3	98.4	101.7	98.3
2004	102.1	104.0	103.6	104.7	99.0
2005	102.3	102.1	108.3	101.4	99.3
2006	100.9	101.7	99.4	100.8	99.7
2007	104.5	111.6	99.4	102.4	102.7
2008	104.7	111.7	103.9	99.8	103.9
2009	100.5	101.6	101.4	100.6	98.6
2010	102.2	106.4	101.0	100.4	101.4
2011	105.0	111.1	108.2	103.1	104.5
2012	102.7	104.3	106.3	102.1	101.7
2013	102.5	105.3	104.9	100.7	101.4
2014	102.6	104.4	103.2	101.9	102.3
2015	101.2	101.7	102.8	101.3	100.0
2016	102.5	105.0	100.3	101.8	102.0
2017	102.0	99.6	100.5	103.4	100.8

注：1.2016年起，食品类统计口径有变化，不包括“茶及饮料”和“在外餐饮”两项内容。
2.2016年起，统计分类“服务项目价格指数”改为“服务价格指数”，增加“养老服务”和“金融服务”两项内容。

Note：1. Statistical caliber of food category has changed since 2016. The two sections of Tea and Drinks and Catering Service are not included.
2. The statistical category of “Price Index of Service Item” has been revised to “Price Index of Service” as of 2016 with two additional sections of “Elderly Care Service” and “Financial Service”.

9-2 主要年份居民消费和商品零售价格指数(以1950年价格为100)
MAJOR YEAR'S CONSUMER AND RETAIL PRICE INDEXES (1950 = 100)

年 份 Year	居民消费价格指数 Consumer Price Index	#食品类 Food	#衣着类 Clothing	#服务项目价格指数 Services Price Index	商品零售价格指数 Retail Price Index
1951	110.5	105.2	112.4		110.5
1952	110.3	104.8	110.9		110.3
1957	119.5	120.7	115.3	91.6	119.5
1962	127.4	128.8	115.1	94.2	127.4
1965	133.3	138.7	108.4	81.5	133.3
1970	129.0	137.6	110.3	76.8	129.0
1975	128.8	138.2	110.0	75.7	128.8
1978	129.1	138.7	109.8	75.7	129.1
1980	137.6	154.1	109.3	76.1	138.1
1985	160.8	196.1	103.8	80.5	162.5
1988	223.8	295.2	133.2	100.8	227.6
1990	269.7	333.3	166.8	155.9	269.7
1991	288.6	356.7	187.0	170.9	288.1
1992	321.5	410.5	203.1	204.9	319.2
1993	398.3	496.3	241.7	324.8	382.4
1994	505.4	671.1	314.4	382.9	469.5
1995	587.3	792.5	386.1	471.8	536.2
1996	661.3	872.6	402.7	615.2	568.4
1997	687.8	883.0	412.0	743.1	569.5
1998	687.8	827.4	389.3	1012.1	540.5
1999	689.2	800.1	378.0	1170.0	522.1
2000	711.9	800.1	409.4	1310.4	520.5
2001	719.0	804.9	401.2	1424.4	514.8
2002	711.1	787.2	402.0	1438.7	512.2
2003	721.1	821.0	395.6	1463.1	503.5
2004	736.2	853.9	409.8	1531.9	498.5
2005	753.1	871.8	443.8	1553.4	495.0
2006	759.9	886.6	441.2	1565.8	493.5
2007	794.1	989.5	438.5	1603.4	506.8
2008	831.4	1105.3	455.6	1600.2	526.6
2009	835.6	1123.0	462.0	1609.8	519.2
2010	854.0	1194.9	466.6	1616.2	526.5
2011	896.7	1327.5	504.9	1666.3	550.2
2012	920.9	1384.6	536.7	1701.3	559.6
2013	943.9	1458.0	563.0	1713.2	567.4
2014	968.4	1522.2	581.0	1745.8	580.5
2015	980.0	1548.1	597.3	1768.5	580.5
2016	1004.5	1625.5	599.1	1800.3	592.1
2017	1024.6	1619.0	602.1	1861.5	596.8

注：1. 2016年起，食品类统计口径有变化，不包括“茶及饮料”和“在外餐饮”两项内容。
2. 2016年起，统计分类“服务项目价格指数”改为“服务价格指数”，增加“养老服务”和“金融服务”两项内容。

Note：1. Statistical caliber of food category has changed since 2016. The two sections of Tea and Drinks and Catering Service are not included.
2. The statistical category of “Price Index of Service Item” has been revised to “Price Index of Service” as of 2016 with two additional sections of “Elderly Care Service” and “Financial Service”.

9-3 主要年份生产投资价格指数

MAJOR YEAR'S PRICE INDEXES FOR PRODUCTION AND INVESTMENT

（上年价格 = 100） (perceding year = 100)

年 份 Year	工业生产者出厂价格指数 Producer Price Indexes for Industrial Producers	工业生产者购进价格指数 Purchasing Price Indexes for Industrial Producers	房屋销售价格指数 Sales Price Indexes of Houses	房屋租赁价格指数 Renting Price Indexes of Houses	物业管理价格指数 Property Managerment Price Indexes	固定资产投资价格指数 Price Index for Investment in Fixed Assets
1990	104.33	108.64				
1991	101.68	108.10				
1992	105.46	107.13				
1993	115.49	126.91				
1994	121.62	120.30				
1995	112.70	114.25				
1996	103.81	103.25				
1997	100.22	101.93				
1998	94.96	92.77	100.1	94.0		
1999	96.93	95.88	103.7	104.3		
2000	101.89	106.81	102.3	95.8		
2001	98.00	97.81	104.1	107.0		
2002	97.37	96.78	107.6	94.4		
2003	100.97	106.51	114.6	99.4		
2004	102.92	113.62	115.2	98.6		105.8
2005	101.39	106.52	110.9	103.3	100.2	103.1
2006	101.08	105.80	106.9	110.1	99.8	102.6
2007	101.50	106.69	106.5	108.3	100.4	104.1
2008	105.33	115.91	105.1	106.5	102.1	111.0
2009	95.78	90.35	100.3	103.5	100.4	94.6
2010	103.75	112.21		103.0	100.5	104.9
2011	104.90	109.39				107.0
2012	98.61	97.00				100.0
2013	98.82	96.53				100.1
2014	99.20	97.40				99.9
2015	97.04	94.24				97.1
2016	98.77	97.28				99.8
2017	104.40	110.73				107.3

说明：2010 年之前工业生产者出厂价格为工业品出厂价格；工业生产者购进价格为主要原材料、燃料、动力购进价格。

Note: Producer's Prices at works were the prices of industrial products at words before 2010; producer's purchasing price refers to the purchasing price of main raw materials, fuels and power.

9-4 工业生产者出厂价格指数
PRODUCER PRICE INDEXES FOR INDUSTRIAL PRODUCERS

(上年价格 = 100)

类 别	Item	2000年	2005年	2006年	2008年
总指数	**General Index**	**101.89**	**101.39**	**101.08**	**105.33**
其中：轻工业	Light Industry	98.50	99.78	99.58	102.93
重工业	Heavy Industry	105.62	104.32	103.94	109.17
其中：生产资料	**Means of Production**	**105.03**	**103.24**	**102.49**	**108.76**
采掘	Excavation	95.67	114.74	104.73	115.24
原料	Raw Materials	113.82	106.91	104.05	108.81
加工	Processing	97.58	101.45	101.86	108.59
生活资料	**Means of Livelihood**	**98.25**	**99.13**	**99.74**	**101.72**
食品	Food	96.59	98.80	101.52	108.42
衣着	Clothing	99.37	101.48	102.16	103.36
一般日用品	Articles for Daily Use	104.52	101.97	101.82	103.03
耐用消费品	Durable Consumer Goods	97.70	97.43	97.23	97.13

(perceding year = 100)

2009年	2010年	2011年	2012年	2013年	2014年	2015年	2016年	2017年
95.78	**103.75**	**104.90**	**98.61**	**98.82**	**99.20**	**97.04**	**98.77**	**104.40**
97.21	100.80	103.46	99.70	99.11	99.62	99.85	98.74	101.13
93.45	107.57	105.89	97.87	98.62	98.91	95.10	98.79	106.46
94.25	**106.43**	**105.54**	**97.55**	**98.58**	**98.87**	**95.23**	**98.60**	**106.34**
93.44	130.94	132.07	93.35	91.72	100.65	95.12		
90.67	115.24	111.52	99.05	99.26	98.87	88.59	93.92	112.92
95.34	103.50	103.49	97.20	98.50	98.84	97.06	99.60	104.96
97.45	**99.61**	**103.82**	**100.42**	**99.21**	**99.76**	**100.07**	**99.12**	**100.69**
98.21	105.06	109.71	99.91	95.34	98.34	102.53	102.59	100.55
102.03	101.56	107.44	102.03	102.74	100.34	100.39	100.93	101.54
99.39	99.96	108.02	101.64	101.42	101.01	99.59	100.12	101.63
94.52	93.23	94.34	98.79	98.41	99.65	98.26	94.58	99.78

9-5 工业生产者购进价格指数
PURCHASING PRICE INDEXES FOR INDUSTRIAL PRODUCERS

（上年价格 = 100）

类　别	Item	2000 年	2005 年	2006 年	2008 年
总指数	**General Index**	**106.81**	**106.52**	**105.8**	**115.91**
燃料、动力类	Fuel and Power	113.82	117.34	117.17	126.19
黑色金属材料类	Ferrous Metals	102.66	107.84	95.83	122.19
#钢材	Rolled-steel	105.44	106.57	96.11	119.10
其他	Others	101.1	112.88	94.91	132.40
有色金属材料及电线类	Nonferrous Metals and Electric Wire	106.75	108.06	131.58	93.41
化工原料类	Raw Chemical Materials	106.9	112.47	99.71	123.00
木材及纸浆类	Timber and Paper Pulp	108.98	103.8	104.29	103.58
建筑材料及非金属矿类	Building Materials and Nonmetals	99.5	115.54	92.83	124.52
其他工业原材料及半成品	Other Industrial Raw Materials and Semi-fin-ished Goods	105.32	97.87	103.33	109.65
农副产品	Agricultural Products	92.73	101.55	110.87	117.68
纺织原料类	Textile Materials	104.03	98.15	100.15	101.44

(perceding year = 100)

2009年	2010年	2011年	2012年	2013年	2014年	2015年	2016年	2017年
90.35	**112.21**	**109.39**	**97.00**	**96.53**	**97.40**	**94.24**	**97.28**	**110.73**
90.53	115.43	111.29	100.64	95.18	97.65	88.51	89.94	112.91
82.38	111.97	113.08	93.20	93.76	95.81	87.26	97.23	117.41
85.25	108.67	107.95	92.33	92.87	96.87	89.99	96.89	119.10
72.73	122.64	129.01	94.64	96.57	92.49	78.70	98.41	110.30
86.24	122.65	108.45	93.64	96.23	96.24	92.34	96.29	114.82
87.66	111.04	113.79	96.72	96.47	99.51	96.44	101.00	107.63
89.16	117.06	103.78	93.12	98.79	102.42	98.33	99.93	125.23
100.98	107.61	116.71	102.48	100.13	97.36	95.52	100.91	115.06
92.70	106.41	103.31	98.05	96.65	96.25	96.95	97.50	106.42
88.60	121.30	115.04	98.21	98.54	97.62	99.75	101.53	105.92
98.69	112.90	111.11	95.61	99.60	97.38	95.86	99.81	110.09

9-6 按工业行业分工业生产者出厂价格指数
PRODUCER PRICE INDEXES FOR INDUSTRIAL PRODUCERS BY SECTOR

（上年价格 = 100）

行　业	Sector
工业生产者出厂价格指数	**Producer Price Indexes for Manufactured Manufactured Goods**
黑色金属矿采选业	Mining of Ferrous Metal Ores
有色金属矿采选业	Mining of Non-ferrous Metal Ores
非金属矿采选业	Mining and Processing of Nonmetal Ores
农副食品加工业	Processing of Food from Agricultural Products
食品制造业	Manufacture of Foods
酒、饮料和精制茶制造业	Manufacturing Industry of Alcohol，Beverage and Refined Tea
纺织业	Manufacture of Textile
纺织服装、服饰业	Industry of Textile and Garment，and Apparel
皮革、毛皮、羽毛及其制品和制鞋业	Industry of Leather，Furs，Down and Related Products，and Shoes Making
木材加工和木、竹、藤、棕、草制品业	Processing of Timbers，Manufacture of Wood，Bamboo，Rattan，Palm，and Staw Products
家具制造业	Manufacture of Furniture
造纸和纸制品业	Manufacture of Paper and Paper Products
印刷和记录媒介复制业	Printing，Reproduction of Recording Media
文教、工美、体育和娱乐用品制造业	Industry of Culture and Education，Arts and Crafts，and Entertainment Products Manufacturing
石油加工、炼焦和核燃料加工业	Processing of Petroleum，Coking，Processing of Nucleus Fuel
化学原料和化学制品制造业	Manufacture of Chemical Raw Material and Chemical Products
医药制造业	Manufacture of Medicines
化学纤维制造业	Manufacture of Chemical Fiber
橡胶和塑料制品业	Industry of Rubber and Plastic Products
非金属矿物制品业	Manufacture of Non-metallic Mineral Products
黑色金属冶炼和压延加工业	Smelting and Pressing of Ferrous Metals
有色金属冶炼和压延加工业	Smelting and Pressing of Non-ferrous Metals
金属制品业	Manufacture of Metal Products
通用设备制造业	Manufacture of General Purpose Machinery
专用设备制造业	Manufacture of Special Purpose Machinery
汽车制造业	Vehicle Manufacturing Industry
铁路、船舶、航空航天和其他运输设备制造业	Maufacturing Industry of Railroads，Vessels，Aerospace and Other Transporation Equipment
电气机械和器材制造业	Manufacture of Electrical Machinery&Equipment
计算机、通信和其他电子设备制造业	Computer，Communications and Other Electronic Equipment Manufacturing
仪器仪表制造业	Instruments Manufacturing Industry
其他制造业	Other Manufacturing Industry
金属制品、机械和设备修理业	Industry of Metal Products，and Repair of Machinery and Equipment
电力、热力生产和供应业	Production and Supply of Electric Power and Heat Power
燃气生产和供应业	Production and Supply of Gas
水的生产和供应业	Production and Supply of Water

注：2012 年国民经济行业分类调整，本表中 2011 年— 2017 年数据采用新国民经济行业分类 GB/T 4754-2011。
Note：Classification of national economic industries was adjusted in 2012. The new natinoal economic industries classification by GB/T 4754-2011 applies to data from 2011 to 2017 in this table.

(preceding yrar = 100)

2011年	2012年	2013年	2014年	2015年	2016年	2017年
104.90	**98.61**	**98.82**	**99.20**	**97.04**	**98.77**	**104.40**
104.33	99.93	100.00	99.86	100.00		
111.39	102.48	98.72	95.57	89.94		
145.13	89.33	87.06	102.14	94.85		
111.34	98.69	93.46	97.58	102.47	102.80	101.12
112.52	103.11	103.08	101.78	100.66	100.30	101.40
104.14	105.89	100.48	98.76	99.01	99.97	99.54
105.09	96.15	100.18	100.27	99.41	97.60	103.84
105.43	101.66	104.17	101.74	100.84	100.83	102.17
104.79	102.59	101.83	98.56	99.72	99.81	100.15
108.13	103.21	99.67	100.96	100.35		
101.11	102.00	100.02	100.00	99.91	98.46	98.72
105.71	95.59	96.13	101.96	99.78	99.58	115.83
110.06	107.10	108.65	96.97	95.96	98.45	101.11
100.61	101.47	100.47	100.00	99.96	99.88	101.90
114.95	104.26	99.49	97.38	76.03	91.60	114.48
114.60	89.61	98.04	99.70	96.53	95.20	119.17
107.33	95.05	105.08	127.56	100.73	104.83	101.06
123.72	92.56	95.65	96.69	90.31	89.56	117.03
114.68	99.67	95.40	95.50	94.93	97.60	100.62
108.19	98.39	99.82	100.91	101.62	99.08	114.14
111.00	86.47	93.52	94.45	83.44	99.13	117.16
108.26	89.14	93.87	94.43	87.95	95.29	125.17
99.79	99.82	104.14	96.62	96.59	103.64	106.15
101.39	100.07	103.87	101.02	100.37	98.78	103.45
101.69	101.26	99.99	99.81	99.72	98.36	100.00
99.27	98.97	98.59	102.49	101.04	101.46	100.93
99.17	99.66	97.65	100.96	100.03	99.29	100.16
103.10	98.40	98.82	99.24	98.61	98.96	102.82
84.65	95.43	94.31	98.88	96.31	90.16	102.17
102.01	98.72	98.01	98.43	97.05	100.00	100.09
95.16	98.52	99.94	100.12	99.89	100.87	104.20
102.17	98.43	88.75	91.69	90.21		
101.49	104.36	99.81	99.15	98.10	97.59	97.05
107.34	103.32	102.54	109.38	98.88	101.26	96.32
100.15	100.25	100.05	100.34	103.46	108.78	100.00

9-7 固定资产投资价格指数

PRICE INDEXES FOR INVESTMENT IN FIXED ASSETS

(上年价格 = 100) (preceding yrar = 100)

项目名称	Item	2005	2006	2008	2009	2010	2011	2012	2013	2014	2015	2016	2017
总　计	**Total**	**103.1**	**102.6**	**111.0**	**94.6**	**104.9**	**107.0**	**100.0**	**100.1**	**99.9**	**97.1**	**99.8**	**107.3**
建筑安装、装饰工程	Construction and Installation Project	103.7	103.5	115.5	92.1	107.5	110.1	99.8	100.0	99.6	95.5	99.6	110.7
其中：人工费	Of which：Labor Cost	112.7	110.0	112.7	104.9	112.0	115.9	110.4	107.8	104.8	103.1	101.6	103.0
材料费	Materials Expenses	101.0	100.7	120.5	87.5	107.0	109.6	96.7	97.6	97.7	92	98.8	114.9
机械使用费	Expenses on Machinery Use	104.2	109.1	106.9	100.0	104.3	105.0	102.3	101.0	100.8	100.9	100.1	101.2
设备、工器具购置	Purchase of Equipment，Tools and Instruments	99.7	100.6	102.5	98.0	100.2	101.8	99.2	99.3	99.9	99.2	98.7	100.6
其他费用	Others	105.5	100.9	105.9	98.5	102.2	103.0	102.0	101.4	101.4	101.2	102.2	102.0

9-8 住宅销售价格指数(2017年)

SALES PRICE INDEXES FOR RESIDENCE（2017）

(上年价格 = 100) (preceding yrar = 100)

项　目	Item	2017
新建住宅销售价格指数	**Sales Price Indexes for Newly Constructed Residence**	
一月	January	113.0
二月	February	113.1
三月	March	112.9
四月	April	111.9
五月	May	111.4
六月	June	111.2
七月	July	110.9
八月	August	109.1
九月	September	104.4
十月	October	103.4
十一月	November	103.7
十二月	December	104.1
二手住宅销售价格指数	**Sales Price Indexes for Second-hand Residence**	
一月	January	110.2
二月	February	110.9
三月	March	112.6
四月	April	113.8
五月	May	114.7
六月	June	115.6
七月	July	116.1
八月	August	115.3
九月	September	110.2
十月	October	109.4
十一月	November	109.1
十二月	December	108.9

9-9 居民消费价格分类指数(2017 年)
CONSUMER PRICE INDEXES BY CATEGORY（2017）

(上年价格 = 100) (preceding yrar = 100)

项　目	Item	指数 Indexes
居民消费价格总指数	**Consumer Price Index**	**102.0**
非食品烟酒价格指数	Price index of non-food cigarettes and alcohol	102.4
服务价格指数	Price index of services	103.4
鲜活食品价格指数	Price index of fresh food	97.9
消费品价格指数	Consumer Goods Price Index	101.2
扣除鲜菜鲜果价格指数	Price Index Without Fersh Vegetables and Fresh Fruits	102.0
一、食品烟酒	**Food，cigarettes and liquor**	**100.9**
1. 食品	Food	99.6
(1) 粮食	Grain	104.8
(2) 薯类	Potatoes	97.2
(3) 豆类	Beans	101.8
(4) 食用油	Cooking Oil	105.2
(5) 菜	Vegetables	94.9
(6) 畜肉类	Livestock Products	93.9
(7) 禽肉类	Poultry Products	101.2
(8) 水产品	Aquatic Products	101.0
(9) 蛋类	Eggs	98.3
(10) 奶类	Dairy Products	100.7
(11) 干鲜瓜果类	Dried and Fresh Melons and Fruits	107.4
(12) 糖果糕点类	Candy and Pastry	100.4
(13) 调味品	Flavoring	104.4
(14) 其他食品类	Other Foods	98.1
2. 茶及饮料	Tea and Beverages	101.4
3. 烟酒	Tobacco Liquor	100.4
4. 在外餐饮	Catering service	105.3

注：2016 年起，居民消费价格调查目录进行了调整，新调查目录与居民家庭消费支出目录基本一致。
Note：Since 2016, the consumption price investigation directory has been adjusted, and the new investigation directory is basically consistent with the household consumption expenditure catalogue.

9-9 续表
Continued

项　　目	Item	指数 Indexes
二、衣着	**Clothing**	**100.5**
1. 服装	Garments	100.2
2. 服装材料	Clothing material	100.0
3. 其他衣着及配件	Other clothing and accessories	98.9
4. 衣着加工服务费	Service charge of clothing processing	103.2
5. 鞋类	Shoes	101.2
三、居住	**Residence**	**102.3**
1. 租赁房房租	Rents	103.8
2. 住房保养维修及管理	Maintenance and management of house	101.0
3. 水电燃料	Water，Electricity and Fuels	102.4
4. 自有住房	Private Housing	102.4
四、生活用品及服务	**Article of daily use and service**	**99.7**
1. 家具及室内装饰品	Furniture and interior decoration	102.9
2. 家用器具	Home appliances	96.3
3. 家用纺织品	Home textile	100.7
4. 家庭日用杂品	Daiy Use Household Articles	100.1
5. 个人护理用品	Personal-care supply	99.4
6. 家庭服务	Household Services	103.2
五、交通和通信	**Transportation and Communication**	**100.7**
1. 交通	Transportation	101.1
2. 通信	Communication	99.8
六、教育文化和娱乐	**Education，culture and entertainment**	**101.7**
1. 教育	Education	103.1
2. 文化娱乐	Cultural	100.5
七、医疗保健	**Health Care**	**109.6**
1. 药品及医疗器具	Medicine and medical apparatus	108.5
2. 医疗服务	Medical service	110.7
八、其他用品和服务	**Other articles and services**	**104.1**
1. 其他用品类	Other articles	100.3
2. 其他服务类	Other services	106.9

9-10 商品零售价格分类指数(2017 年)
RETAIL PRICE INDEXES BY CATEGORY（2017）

(上年 = 100) (preceding yrar = 100)

项　目	Iten	指数 Indexes
商品零售价格总指数	**Retail Price Indes**	**100.8**
一、食品	**Food**	**100.5**
1. 粮食	Grain	104.8
2. 薯类	Potatos	97.2
3. 豆类	Beans	101.8
4. 食用油	Edible oil	105.2
5. 菜	Vegetables	94.9
6. 畜肉类	Stock meat	93.9
7. 禽肉类	Poultry meat	101.2
8. 水产品	Aquatic Products	101.0
9. 蛋类	Eggs	98.3
10. 奶类	Dairy	100.7
11. 干鲜瓜果类	Dried and Fresh Melons and Fruits	107.4
12. 糖果糕点类	Sweets and cakes	100.4
13. 调味品	Flavoring	104.4
14. 其他食品类	Other food	98.1
15. 在外餐饮	Catering service	105.3
二、饮料、烟酒	**Beverages，Tobacco and Liquor**	**100.7**
1. 茶及饮料	Tea and Beverages	101.4
2. 烟草	Tobacco	100.0
3. 酒类	Liquor	100.8
三、服装、鞋帽	**Clothing**	**100.4**
1. 服装	Garments	100.2
2. 鞋帽袜	Footgear and Hats	100.9
3. 其他衣着配件	Other clothing and accessories	100.2
四、纺织品	**Textiles**	**101.0**
1. 服装材料	Clothing material	100.0
2. 床上用品	Blend Cloth	101.2
五、家用电器及音像器材	**Household Appliances，Music and Video Equipment**	**96.2**
1. 家庭设备	Household Facilities	96.2
2. 文娱用耐用消费品	Durable Consumer Goods for Cultural and Recreational Use and Services	94.8
3. 专业音像器材	Professional Audio and Video Equipment	101.2

注：2016 年起，商品零售价格调查目录进行了微调。
Note：Contents of survey of retailing price of commodities have been finely adjusted as of 2017.

9-10 续表
Continued

项　　目	Item	指数 Indexes
六、文化办公用品	**Culture and office Articles**	**98.3**
七、日用品	**Articles for Daily Use**	**100.0**
1. 日用百货	General Merchandise for Daily Use	98.9
2. 厨具餐具茶具	Kitchen ware，tableware，tea set	101.6
3. 清洗用品	Cleaning Products	100.3
4. 其他日用品	Other Articles for Daily Use	100.3
八、体育娱乐用品	**Sports and Recreation Articles**	**99.9**
1. 体育户外用品	Sports and outdoors	103.0
2. 娱乐用品	Recreation Articles	98.5
九、交通、通信用品	**Transportation and Communication Appliances**	**98.5**
1. 交通运输机械	Transportation Machines	98.3
2. 通信器材	Communication Equipment	99.2
十、家具	**Furniture**	**104.6**
十一、化妆品	**Cosmetics**	**99.4**
十二、金银饰品	**Gold，Silver and Jewelry**	**101.4**
十三、中西药品及医疗保健用品	**Traditional Chinese and Western Medicals and Health Care Articles**	**108.3**
1. 医疗卫生器具	Medical apparatus	101.1
2. 中药	Herbal medicine	107.3
3. 西药	Western Medicines	109.3
4. 保健器具及用品	Health Care Articles	111.1
十四、书报杂志及电子出版物	**Books，Newspapers，Magazines and Electronic Publications**	**100.2**
1. 教材及参考书	Teaching Material and Reference Books	100.7
2. 书报杂志	Books，Mewspapers and Magazines	100.0
3. 计算机办公软件	Computer office software	98.9
十五、燃料	**Fuels**	**108.0**
1. 煤炭及制品	Coal and Its Products	103.9
2. 石油及制品	Pertoleum and Its Products	108.0
十六、建筑材料及五金电料	**Building Materials and Hardware**	**96.7**
1. 建筑装璜材料	Building Decoration Materials	97.2
2. 五金水暖	Hardware	95.3

主要统计指标解释

居民消费价格指数 是反映一定时期内城乡居民所购买的生活消费品价格和服务项目价格变动趋势和程度的相对数，是对城市居民消费价格指数和农村居民消费价格指数进行综合汇总计算的结果。该指数可以观察和分析消费品的零售价格和服务价格变动对城乡居民实际生活费支出的影响程度。

商品零售价格指数 是反映一定时期内城乡商品零售价格变动趋势和程度的相对数。商品零售价格的变动直接影响到城乡居民的生活支出和国家的财政收入，影响居民购买力和市场供需的平衡，影响到消费与积累的比例关系。因此，该指数可以从一个侧面对上述经济活动进行观察和分析。

工业生产者出厂价格指数 是反映一定时期内全部工业产品出厂价格总水平的变动趋势和程度的相对数，包括工业企业售给本企业以外所有单位的各种产品和直接售给居民用于生活消费的产品。该指数可以观察出厂价格变动对工业总产值及增加值的影响。

工业生产者购进价格指数 是反映工业企业作为生产投入，而从物资交易市场和能源、原材料生产企业购买原材料、燃料和动力产品时，所支付的价格水平变动趋势和程度的统计指标，是扣除工业企业物质消耗成本中的价格变动影响的重要依据。

房地产价格指数 是反映一定时期内房地产价格变动趋势和程度的相对数，包括新建住宅销售价格指数、二手住宅销售价格指数。

Explanatory Notes on Main Statistical Indicators

Consumer Price Indices reflect the trend and degree of changes in prices of consumer goods and services purchased by urban and rural households during a given period. They are obtained by combining the Urban Consumer Price Indices and the Rural Consumer Price Indices. The Indices enable the observation and analysis of the degree of impact of the changes in the prices of retailed goods and services on the actual living expenses of urban and rural residents.

Retail Price Indices reflect the trend and degree of change in retail prices of commodities during a given period. The change in retail prices of commodities directly affect the living expenditure of urban and rural residents, government revenue, purchasing power of residents and the equilibrium of market supply and demand, and the ratio of consumption to accumulation. Therefore, the ratail price indices are useful to analyze the changes of the above economic activities.

Producer Price Indices for Industrial Producers reflect the trend and degree of changes in general ex-factory prices of all industrial products during a given period, including sales of industrial products by an industrial enterprise to all units outside the enterprise, as well as sales of consumer goods to residents. It can be used to analyze the impact of ex-factory prices on gross output value and value-added of the industrial sector.

Purchasing Price Indices for Industrial Producers reflect changes in the level and degree of prices paid by industrial enterprises when they purchase production input such as raw materials, fuels and power from the market or from other energy or raw materials producing enterprises. These indices provide important basis for measuring the material consumption of industrial enterprises after removing influence of price changes.

Price Indices for Real Estate reflect the trend and degree of changes in prices of real estate during a given period, including sales price indices for newly constructed residential buildings and secondhand residential buildings.

人民生活 10

PEOPLE'S LIVING CONDITIONS

简 要 说 明

一、本篇资料的主要内容

本篇资料主要反映了全市居民的家庭收支、居住、家庭消费构成、耐用消费品拥有量等方面的情况。

二、本篇资料的来源

本篇资料中相关数据来源于居民收支调查年报，由国家统计局青岛调查队住户专项调查处整理提供。

Brief Introduction

Ⅰ. Main Content

This section mainly reflects the residents' household income and expenditure, housing, household consumption structure, quantity of durable consumer goods possessed and other information.

Ⅱ. Source of Data

The relevant data in this material comes from the annual report of the residents' income and expenditure survey, which is provided by the Special Investigation Team of the Investigation Team of the National Bureau of Statistics.

10-1 城市居民收支（1978—2014 年）
INCOME AND EXPENDITURE OF URBAN RESIDENTS（1978-2014）

年 份 Year	城市居民人均可支配收入（元） Annual Per Capita Disposable Income of Urban Households（yang）	城市居民人均消费性支出（元） Per Capita Consumption Expenditure of Urban Households（yang）	城市恩格尔系数（%） Engel coefficient（%）
1978	336	321	
1979	380	360	
1980	537	495	
1981	500	490	57.8
1982	528	484	61.6
1983	549	510	63.7
1984	665	580	62.8
1985	733	681	58.6
1986	882	806	59.2
1987	1089	996	58.1
1988	1225	1278	55.9
1989	1455	1439	57.8
1990	1624	1507	58.4
1991	1856	1767	57.4
1992	2138	1956	57.0
1993	2668	2445	51.8
1994	3880	3479	53.2
1995	5357	4606	52.5
1996	5602	5079	51.8
1997	6222	5525	48.2
1998	6554	5565	46.4
1999	7282	5981	44.5
2000	8016	6677	42.5
2001	8731	6849	41.9
2002	8721	7344	40.5
2003	10075	8056	39.3
2004	11089	9002	38.0
2005	12920	9883	37.6
2006	15328	11945	36.4
2007	17856	13376	37.0
2008	20464	14999	37.4
2009	22368	16080	38.5
2010	24998	17531	37.4
2011	28567	19297	37.5
2012	32145	20391	36.5
2013	35227	22060	36.5
2014	38294	24016	35.7

注：2002 年开始城市居民可支配收入为新计算口径。
Note：From 2002 on，disposable income of urban residents are counted by new gauges.

10-2 农村居民收支(1978—2014年)
INCOME AND EXPENDITURE OF RURAL RESIDENTS (1978-2014)

年 份 Year	农民人均纯收入(元) Annual Per Capita Net Income of Rural Households (yuan)	农村居民人均生活消费支出(元) Per Capita Consumption Expenditure of Rural Households (yuan)	农村恩格尔系数(%) Engel coefficient (%)
1978	146	109	59.3
1979	153	129	58.4
1980	209	142	54.9
1981	218	163	44.3
1982	273	199	52.9
1983	399	277	52.8
1984	452	304	50.0
1985	567	376	47.8
1986	647	474	46.4
1987	730	462	42.9
1988	820	439	38.8
1989	876	510	38.9
1990	952	494	41.5
1991	1021	546	41.3
1992	1029	572	41.7
1993	1255	743	42.7
1994	1694	1384	54.5
1995	2225	1641	55.7
1996	2625	2173	50.5
1997	2599	2150	52.9
1998	3177	2119	49.5
1999	3415	2150	47.3
2000	3637	2380	43.2
2001	3901	2618	41.2
2002	4195	2820	38.9
2003	4530	2988	38.0
2004	5080	3353	38.7
2005	5806	3737	37.5
2006	6546	4203	36.6
2007	7477	4736	37.2
2008	8509	5303	37.7
2009	9249	5832	36.4
2010	10550	6662	35.5
2011	12370	7661	36.6
2012	13990	8653	36.2
2013	15731	9786	34.9
2014	17461	10808	33.8

10-3 城乡居民住房面积（1990—2014 年）
HOUSING AREA OF URBAN AND RURAL RESIDENTS（1990–2014）

年 份 Year	城市居民人均现住房建筑面积（平方米） Per Capita Home Floor Area of Urban Residents（square meter）	农村居民人均居住面积（平方米） Per Capita Housing Area of Rural Residents（square meter）
1990	14.16	19.60
1995	17.12	23.03
2000	20.76	25.88
2001	21.86	26.59
2002	22.76	27.00
2003	23.73	27.00
2004	24.22	27.99
2005	22.96	29.54
2006	23.73	30.82
2007	23.72	30.95
2008	26.83	30.73
2009	26.71	31.39
2010	27.42	30.97
2011	27.67	31.73
2012	27.86	32.32
2013	29.12	33.50
2014	29.80	34.20

10-4 全体居民家庭基本情况（2015 年）
BASIC INFORMATION ON ALL HOUSEHOLDS（2015）

指标名称	Name	单位	Unit	2015	2014	2015 年比 2014 年增长（±%）2015/2014（±%）
人均可支配收入	**Per Capita Disposable Income**	**元**	**yuan**	**32885**	**30273**	**8.6**
（一）工资性收入	Income from Wages and Salaries	元	yuan	20068	18348	9.4
（二）经营性净收入	Net Income from Household Operations	元	yuan	6480	6035	7.4
（三）财产性收入	Income from Properties	元	yuan	2522	2396	5.2
（四）转移性收入	Income from Transfers	元	yuan	3815	3494	9.2
人均消费支出	**Per Capita Consumption Expenditure**	**元**	**yuan**	**21326**	**19653**	**8.5**
（一）食品烟酒	Food，Tobacco and Liquor	元	yuan	6459	5970	8.2
（二）衣着	Clothing	元	yuan	2096	1944	7.8
（三）居住	Residence	元	yuan	4584	4316	6.2
（四）生活用品及服务	Household Facilities，Articles and Services	元	yuan	1485	1374	8.1
（五）交通通信	Transportation and Communication	元	yuan	3226	2905	11.0
（六）教育文化娱乐	Education，Cultural and Recreation Services	元	yuan	1830	1654	10.6
（七）医疗保健	Health Care and Medical Services	元	yuan	1115	1002	11.2
（八）其他用品和服务	Other Goods and Services	元	yuan	531	488	8.8
城镇居民人均现住房建筑面积	**Per Capita Building Space in Urban Areas**	**平方米**	**sq.m**	**31.5**		
农村居民人均现住房建筑面积	**Per Capita Living Space in Rural Areas**	**平方米**	**sq.m**	**32.4**		

注：自 2015 年开始，全市城乡住户调查统一使用一体化改革后的数据，与原数据相比，城乡居民收支指标的调查范围和口径均存较大变化。原"城市居民人均可支配收入"调整为"城镇居民人均可支配收入"；原"农民人均纯收入"调整为"农村居民人均可支配收入"。2014 年数据也为新口径，与 2015 年年鉴数据不一致。2014 年农村居民住房为拥有面积，2015 年为现住房建筑面积。

Note：From 2015 on，the data used are statistics of the integrated survey of residents in urban and rural areas. Compared with previous data，there is a significant change in statistic coverage and gauge for indicators of urban and rural residents' income and expenditure. The 'per capita disposable income of residents in cities was changed to' per capita disposable income of urban residents'；the 'pe capita net income of farmers' was changed to 'per capita disposable income of rural residents. Data in 2014 are counted by new gauge and they are different from the data in last yrar's yearbook. As for the statistics of rural resident homes，the owned house area was taken in 2014，but in 2015，the construction area was counted.

10-5 全体居民家庭基本情况（2016 年）
BASIC INFORMATION ON ALL HOUSEHOLDS（2016）

指标名称	Name	单位	Unit	2016	2015	2016 年比 2015 年增长（±%） 2016/2015（±%）
人均可支配收入	**Per Capita Disposable Income**	**元**	**yuan**	**35680**	**32885**	**8.5**
（一）工资性收入	Income from Wages and Salaries	元	yuan	21700	20068	8.1
（二）经营性净收入	Net Income from Household Operations	元	yuan	7011	6480	8.2
（三）财产性收入	Income from Properties	元	yuan	2781	2522	10.3
（四）转移性收入	Income from Transfers	元	yuan	4188	3815	9.8
人均消费支出	**Per Capita Consumption Expenditure**	**元**	**yuan**	**23256**	**21326**	**9.0**
（一）食品烟酒	Food，Tobacco and Liquor	元	yuan	6983	6459	8.1
（二）衣着	Clothing	元	yuan	2271	2096	8.4
（三）居住	Residence	元	yuan	5018	4584	9.5
（四）生活用品及服务	Household Facilities，Articles and Services	元	yuan	1607	1485	8.2
（五）交通通信	Transportation and Communication	元	yuan	3479	3226	7.8
（六）教育文化娱乐	Education，Cultural and Recreation Services	元	yuan	2075	1830	13.4
（七）医疗保健	Health Care and Medical Services	元	yuan	1233	1115	10.6
（八）其他用品和服务	Other Goods and Services	元	yuan	590	531	11.2
城镇居民人均现住房建筑面积	**Per Capita Building Space in Urban Areas**	**平方米**	**sq.m**	**31.7**	**31.5**	**0.6**
农村居民人均现住房建筑面积	**Per Capita Living Space in Rural Areas**	**平方米**	**sq.m**	**33.2**	**32.4**	**2.5**

10-6 全体居民家庭基本情况（2017年）
BASIC INFORMATION ON ALL HOUSEHOLDS（2017）

指标名称	Name	单位	Unit	2017	2016	2017年比2016年增长（±%）2017/2016（±%）
人均可支配收入	**Per Capita Disposable Income**	**元**	**yuan**	38763	**35680**	**8.6**
（一）工资性收入	Income from Wages and Salaries	元	yuan	23514	21700	8.4
（二）经营性净收入	Net Income from Household Operations	元	yuan	7485	7011	6.8
（三）财产性收入	Income from Properties	元	yuan	3082	2781	10.8
（四）转移性收入	Income from Transfers	元	yuan	4682	4188	11.8
人均消费支出	**Per Capita Consumption Expenditure**	**元**	**yuan**	**25232**	**23256**	**8.5**
（一）食品烟酒	Food，Tobacco and Liquor	元	yuan	7489	6983	7.2
（二）衣着	Clothing	元	yuan	2467	2271	8.6
（三）居住	Residence	元	yuan	5454	5018	8.7
（四）生活用品及服务	Household Facilities，Articles and Services	元	yuan	1747	1607	8.7
（五）交通通信	Transportation and Communication	元	yuan	3753	3479	7.9
（六）教育文化娱乐	Education，Cultural and Recreation Services	元	yuan	2347	2075	13.1
（七）医疗保健	Health Care and Medical Services	元	yuan	1350	1233	9.5
（八）其他用品和服务	Other Goods and Services	元	yuan	625	590	6.0
城镇居民人均现住房建筑面积	**Per Capita Building Space in Urban Areas**	**平方米**	**sq.m**	**32.7**	**31.7**	**3.2**
农村居民人均现住房建筑面积	**Per Capita Living Space in Rural Areas**	**平方米**	**sq.m**	**34.8**	**33.2**	**4.8**

10-7　城镇居民家庭基本情况（2015 年）
BASIC CONDITIONS OF URBAN HOUSEHOLDS（2015）

指标名称	Name	单位	Unit	2015	2014	2015 年比 2014 年增长（±%）2015/2014（±%）
人均可支配收入	**Per Capita Disposable Income**	**元**	**yuan**	**40370**	**37346**	**8.1**
（一）工资性收入	Income from Wages and Salaries	元	yuan	25040	23034	8.7
（二）经营性净收入	Net Income from Household Operations	元	yuan	6277	5818	7.9
（三）财产性收入	Income from Properties	元	yuan	3580	3436	4.2
（四）转移性收入	Income from Transfers	元	yuan	5473	5058	8.2
人均消费支出	**Per Capita Consumption Expenditure**	**元**	**yuan**	**26052**	**24122**	**8.0**
（一）食品烟酒	Food，Tobacco and Liquor	元	yuan	7856	7295	7.7
（二）衣着	Clothing	元	yuan	2685	2497	7.5
（三）居住	Residence	元	yuan	5607	5302	5.8
（四）生活用品及服务	Household Facilities，Articles and Services	元	yuan	1819	1686	7.9
（五）交通通信	Transportation and Communication	元	yuan	3810	3455	10.3
（六）教育文化娱乐	Education，Cultural and Recreation Services	元	yuan	2264	2057	10.0
（七）医疗保健	Health Care and Medical Services	元	yuan	1352	1227	10.2
（八）其他用品和服务	Other Goods and Services	元	yuan	659	603	9.3

注：本表数据为新口径，2014 年数据与 2015 年年鉴数据不一致。
Note：The data in this sheet is in line with new statistic caliber，which leads to the inconsistency between the data of 2014 and of 2015.

10-8 城镇居民家庭基本情况（2016 年）
BASIC CONDITIONS OF URBAN HOUSEHOLDS（2016）

指标名称	Name	单位	Unit	2016	2015	2016 年比 2015 年增长（±%） 2016/2015（±%）
人均可支配收入	**Per Capita Disposable Income**	**元**	**yuan**	**43598**	**40370**	**8.0**
（一）工资性收入	Income from Wages and Salaries	元	yuan	26898	25040	7.4
（二）经营性净收入	Net Income from Household Operations	元	yuan	6846	6277	9.1
（三）财产性收入	Income from Properties	元	yuan	3909	3580	9.2
（四）转移性收入	Income from Transfers	元	yuan	5945	5473	8.6
人均消费支出	**Per Capita Consumption Expenditure**	**元**	**yuan**	**28285**	**26052**	**8.6**
（一）食品烟酒	Food, Tobacco and Liquor	元	yuan	8473	7856	7.9
（二）衣着	Clothing	元	yuan	2882	2685	7.4
（三）居住	Residence	元	yuan	6105	5607	8.9
（四）生活用品及服务	Household Facilities, Articles and Services	元	yuan	1962	1819	7.8
（五）交通通信	Transportation and Communication	元	yuan	4089	3810	7.3
（六）教育文化娱乐	Education, Cultural and Recreation Services	元	yuan	2553	2264	12.8
（七）医疗保健	Health Care and Medical Services	元	yuan	1490	1352	10.2
（八）其他用品和服务	Other Goods and Services	元	yuan	731	659	10.8

10-9 城镇居民家庭基本情况(2017年)
BASIC CONDITIONS OF URBAN HOUSEHOLDS (2017)

指标名称	Name	单位	Unit	2017	2016	2017年比2016年增长(±%) 2017/2016(±%)
人均可支配收入	**Per Capita Disposable Income**	**元**	**yuan**	**47176**	**43598**	**8.2**
(一)工资性收入	Income from Wages and Salaries	元	yuan	28992	26898	7.8
(二)经营性净收入	Net Income from Household Operations	元	yuan	7299	6846	6.6
(三)财产性收入	Income from Properties	元	yuan	4297	3909	9.9
(四)转移性收入	Income from Transfers	元	yuan	6588	5945	10.8
人均消费支出	**Per Capita Consumption Expenditure**	**元**	**yuan**	**30569**	**28285**	**8.1**
(一)食品烟酒	Food, Tobacco and Liquor	元	yuan	9059	8473	6.9
(二)衣着	Clothing	元	yuan	3117	2882	8.1
(三)居住	Residence	元	yuan	6605	6105	8.2
(四)生活用品及服务	Household Facilities, Articles and Services	元	yuan	2121	1962	8.1
(五)交通通信	Transportation and Communication	元	yuan	4399	4089	7.6
(六)教育文化娱乐	Education, Cultural and Recreation Services	元	yuan	2875	2553	12.6
(七)医疗保健	Health Care and Medical Services	元	yuan	1624	1490	9.0
(八)其他用品和服务	Other Goods and Services	元	yuan	769	731	5.2

10-10　农村居民家庭基本情况（2015 年）
BASIC CONDITIONS OF RURAL HOUSEHOLDS（2015）

指标名称	Name	单位	Unit	2015	2014	2015 年比 2014 年增长（±%）2015/2014（±%）
人均可支配收入	**Per Capita Disposable Income**	**元**	**yuan**	**16730**	**15434**	**8.4**
（一）工资性收入	Income from Wages and Salaries	元	yuan	9337	8517	9.6
（二）经营性净收入	Net Income from Household Operations	元	yuan	6919	6489	6.6
（三）财产性收入	Income from Properties	元	yuan	236	216	9.3
（四）转移性收入	Income from Transfers	元	yuan	238	212	12.4
人均消费支出	**Per Capita Consumption Expenditure**	**元**	**yuan**	**11127**	**10277**	**8.3**
（一）食品烟酒	Food，Tobacco and Liquor	元	yuan	3442	3188	8.0
（二）衣着	Clothing	元	yuan	826	784	5.3
（三）居住	Residence	元	yuan	2377	2248	5.8
（四）生活用品及服务	Household Facilities，Articles and Services	元	yuan	765	720	6.2
（五）交通通信	Transportation and Communication	元	yuan	1965	1751	12.2
（六）教育文化娱乐	Education，Cultural and Recreation Services	元	yuan	895	809	10.6
（七）医疗保健	Health Care and Medical Services	元	yuan	604	532	13.5
（八）其他用品和服务	Other Goods and Services	元	yuan	253	245	3.3

注：本表数据为新口径，2014 年与去年年鉴数据不一致。
Note：Data in this table are measured by nes gauge and they are different from the figures in last yrar’s yearbook.

10-11 农村居民家庭基本情况（2016年）
BASIC CONDITIONS OF RURAL HOUSEHOLDS（2016）

指标名称	Name	单位	Unit	2016	2015	2016年比2015年增长（±%） 2016/2015（±%）
人均可支配收入	**Per Capita Disposable Income**	**元**	**yuan**	**17969**	**16730**	**7.4**
（一）工资性收入	Income from Wages and Salaries	元	yuan	10074	9337	7.9
（二）经营性净收入	Net Income from Household Operations	元	yuan	7381	6919	6.7
（三）财产性收入	Income from Properties	元	yuan	256	236	8.6
（四）转移性收入	Income from Transfers	元	yuan	258	238	8.2
人均消费支出	**Per Capita Consumption Expenditure**	**元**	**yuan**	**12006**	**11127**	**7.9**
（一）食品烟酒	Food，Tobacco and Liquor	元	yuan	3651	3442	6.1
（二）衣着	Clothing	元	yuan	905	826	9.5
（三）居住	Residence	元	yuan	2586	2377	8.8
（四）生活用品及服务	Household Facilities，Articles and Services	元	yuan	814	765	6.4
（五）交通通信	Transportation and Communication	元	yuan	2113	1965	7.5
（六）教育文化娱乐	Education，Cultural and Recreation Services	元	yuan	1004	895	12.2
（七）医疗保健	Health Care and Medical Services	元	yuan	658	604	9.0
（八）其他用品和服务	Other Goods and Services	元	yuan	275	253	8.8

10-12　农村居民家庭基本情况（2017年）
BASIC CONDITIONS OF RURAL HOUSEHOLDS（2017）

指标名称	Name	单位	Unit	2017	2016	2017年比2016年增长（±%）2017/2016（±%）
人均可支配收入	**Per Capita Disposable Income**	**元**	**yuan**	**19364**	**17969**	**7.8**
（一）工资性收入	Income from Wages and Salaries	元	yuan	10882	10074	8.0
（二）经营性净收入	Net Income from Household Operations	元	yuan	7913	7381	7.2
（三）财产性收入	Income from Properties	元	yuan	280	256	9.0
（四）转移性收入	Income from Transfers	元	yuan	289	258	12.2
人均消费支出	**Per Capita Consumption Expenditure**	**元**	**yuan**	**12928**	**12006**	**7.7**
（一）食品烟酒	Food，Tobacco and Liquor	元	yuan	3869	3651	6.0
（二）衣着	Clothing	元	yuan	971	905	7.3
（三）居住	Residence	元	yuan	2801	2586	8.3
（四）生活用品及服务	Household Facilities，Articles and Services	元	yuan	885	814	8.8
（五）交通通信	Transportation and Communication	元	yuan	2262	2113	7.0
（六）教育文化娱乐	Education，Cultural and Recreation Services	元	yuan	1129	1004	12.4
（七）医疗保健	Health Care and Medical Services	元	yuan	717	658	9.0
（八）其他用品和服务	Other Goods and Services	元	yuan	294	275	6.8

10-13 全体居民家庭消费构成
HOUSEHOLD CONSUMPTION STRUCTURE

项　目	Item	2015年		2016年		2017年	
		年人均支出金额（元）Per Capita Annual Expenditure (yuan)	占消费支出的比重（%）Percentage to Consumption Expenditure (%)	年人均支出金额（元）Per Capita Annual Expenditure (yuan)	占消费支出的比重（%）Percentage to Consumption Expenditure (%)	年人均支出金额（元）Per Capita Annual Expenditure (yuan)	占消费支出的比重（%）Percentage to Consumption Expenditure (%)
消费支出	**Consumption Expenditure**	**21326**	**100**	**23256**	**100**	**25232**	**100**
（一）食品烟酒	Food，Tobacco and Liquor	6459	30.3	6983	30.0	7489	29.7
（二）衣着	Clothing	2096	9.8	2271	9.8	2467	9.8
（三）居住	Residence	4584	21.5	5018	21.6	5454	21.6
（四）生活用品及服务	Household Facilities，Articles and Services	1485	7.0	1607	6.9	1747	6.9
（五）交通通信	Transportation and Communication	3226	15.1	3479	15.0	3753	14.9
（六）教育文化娱乐	Education，Cultural and Recreation Services	1830	8.6	2075	8.9	2347	9.3
（七）医疗保健	Health Care and Medical Services	1115	5.2	1233	5.3	1350	5.4
（八）其他用品和服务	Other Goods and Services	531	2.5	590	2.5	625	2.4

10-14 城镇居民家庭消费构成

COMPOSITION OF URBAN HOUSEHOLDS CONSUMPTION

项　目	Item	2015年		2016年		2017年	
		年人均支出金额（元）Per Capita Annual Expenditure (yuan)	占消费支出的比重（%）Percentage to Consumption Expenditure (%)	年人均支出金额（元）Per Capita Annual Expenditure (yuan)	占消费支出的比重（%）Percentage to Consumption Expenditure (%)	年人均支出金额（元）Per Capita Annual Expenditure (yuan)	占消费支出的比重（%）Percentage to Consumption Expenditure (%)
消费支出	**Consumption Expenditure**	**26052**	**100**	**28285**	**100**	**30569**	**100**
（一）食品烟酒	Food, Tobacco and Liquor	7856	30.2	8473	30.0	9059	29.6
（二）衣着	Clothing	2685	10.3	2882	10.2	3117	10.2
（三）居住	Residence	5607	21.5	6105	21.6	6605	21.6
（四）生活用品及服务	Household Facilities, Articles and Services	1819	7.0	1962	6.9	2121	6.9
（五）交通通信	Transportation and Communication	3810	14.6	4089	14.4	4399	14.4
（六）教育文化娱乐	Education, Cultural and Recreation Services	2264	8.7	2553	9.0	2875	9.4
（七）医疗保健	Health Care and Medical Services	1352	5.2	1490	5.3	1624	5.3
（八）其他用品和服务	Other Goods and Services	659	2.5	731	2.6	769	2.6

10-15 农村居民家庭消费构成
COMPOSITION OF RURAL HOUSEHOLDS CONSUMPTION

项　目	Item	2015年		2016年		2017年	
		年人均支出金额（元）Per Capita Annual Expenditure (yuan)	占消费支出的比重（%）Percentage to Consumption Expenditure (%)	年人均支出金额（元）Per Capita Annual Expenditure (yuan)	占消费支出的比重（%）Percentage to Consumption Expenditure (%)	年人均支出金额（元）Per Capita Annual Expenditure (yuan)	占消费支出的比重（%）Percentage to Consumption Expenditure (%)
消费支出	**Consumption Expenditure**	**11127**	**100**	**12006**	**100**	**12928**	**100**
（一）食品烟酒	Food，Tobacco and Liquor	3442	30.9	3651	30.4	3869	29.9
（二）衣着	Clothing	826	7.4	905	7.5	971	7.5
（三）居住	Residence	2377	21.4	2586	21.5	2801	21.7
（四）生活用品及服务	Household Facilities，Articles and Services	765	6.9	814	6.8	885	6.8
（五）交通通信	Transportation and Communication	1965	17.7	2113	17.6	2262	17.5
（六）教育文化娱乐	Education，Cultural and Recreation Services	895	8.0	1004	8.4	1129	8.7
（七）医疗保健	Health Care and Medical Services	604	5.4	658	5.5	717	5.5
（八）其他用品和服务	Other Goods and Services	253	2.3	275	2.3	294	2.4

10-16 城镇住户每百户家庭主要耐用品拥有量（1980-2017 年）

OWNERSHIP OF MAJOR DURABLE CONSUMER GOODS PER 100 URBAN HOUSEHOLDS（1980-2017）

年 份 Year	家用电脑 （台） Computer （set）	钢琴 （架） Piano （set）	空调器 （台） Air Conditioner （set）	热水器 （台） Water Heater （unit）	洗衣机 （台） Washing Machine （set）	电冰箱（台） Household Refrigerator （set）	家用汽车 （辆） Automobile （unit）	彩色电视机 （台） Color TV （set）	移动电话 （部） Cell Phone （unit）	照相机 （架） Camera （set）
1980										2.0
1981					12.0			1.0		2.0
1982					22.0			2.0		4.0
1983					27.0	1.0		6.0		6.0
1984					30.0	2.0		8.0		8.0
1985					35.5	3.5		17.5		13.5
1986					40.0	4.5		24.5		15.0
1987					51.5	18.0		33.5		17.5
1988					60.5	33.0		47.0		20.5
1989					67.0	50.0		59.0		22.0
1990					66.0	62.0		68.0		26.0
1991					70.0	76.0		82.0		33.0
1992		1.0	0.0	12.5	72.5	83.0		81.0		38.5
1993		2.0	0.5	18.0	82.5	85.5		87.5		49.5
1994		4.0	1.0	17.0	81.0	88.5		92.0		51.0
1995		4.0	3.0	33.5	81.5	89.0		100.0		60.5
1996		4.5	6.5	39.5	83.0	91.5		105.0		63.0
1997	1.0	4.5	9.0	46.5	83.0	93.0		110.5	2.5	63.0
1998	8.3	5.3	16.5	53.0	83.0	91.8		110.8	6.8	69.4
1999	10.5	3.8	21.8	61.3	83.0	93.5		117.3	15.0	68.5
2000	19.3	2.0	24.5	65.8	83.3	94.3		120.0	30.3	69.5
2001	20.0	2.3	24.3	65.8	84.0	92.8		127.5	36.0	68.5
2002	31.5	2.3	38.3	75.3	89.3	93.0	0.5	123.3	80.0	72.8
2003	40.8	3.3	47.5	76.3	90.5	92.8	0.3	124.8	105.5	70.0
2004	46.0	3.0	55.0	79.0	92.5	92.5	2.0	123.5	128.0	68.3
2005	55.0	4.3	69.3	83.8	91.8	94.8	3.8	118.3	152.8	72.3
2006	71.3	7.8	89.3	88.0	97.3	98.5	6.3	124.5	187.0	81.8
2007	75.4	7.4	98.3	93.3	99.8	106.7	7.9	121.8	193.8	82.9
2008	75.0	5.0	93.8	90.3	94.5	102.8	12.8	116.0	190.8	67.0
2009	81.8	6.5	98.3	90.5	96.3	105.0	18.0	117.5	199.0	70.8
2010	86.0	7.5	99.3	90.8	97.3	106.8	20.3	118.5	207.5	71.0
2011	95.0	8.0	103.0	91.5	98.0	108.3	22.0	117.3	218.8	76.5
2012	100.8	9.0	103.5	92.8	97.5	108.0	28.5	115.0	230.5	78.8
2013	105.0	10.0	104.0	93.0	98.0	107.0	32.0	118.0	232.0	79.0
2014	105.0	10.0	104.0	98.0	99.0	105.0	34.0	109.0	235.0	79.0
2015	80.0	9.0	91.0	91.0	91.0	94.0	50.0	101.0	215.0	57.0
2016	86.0		98.0	93.0	90.0	96.0	58.0	100.0	212.0	63.0
2017	80.0		101.0	94.0	91.0	95.0	60.0	100.0	205.0	

10-17 农村住户每百户家庭主要耐用品拥有量(1985-2017 年)

OWNERSHIP OF MAJOR DURABLE CONSUMER GOODS PER 100 RURAL HOUSEHOLDS (1985-2017)

年 份 Year	家用电脑 (台) Computer (set)	空调器 (台) Air Conditioner (set)	热水器 (台) Water Heater (unit)	自行车 (辆) Bicycle (unit)	洗衣机 (台) Washing Machine (set)	电冰箱(台) Household Refrigerator (set)	彩色电视机 (台) Color TV (set)	移动电话 (部) Cell Phone (unit)	照相机 (架) Camera (set)	家用汽车 (辆) Automobile (unit)
1985				147	0.3		3		1	
1986				165	1.1	0.3	4.5		1	
1987				148	2.4	0.5	7		2	
1988				154	2.4	1	9		2	
1989				170	3	1	12		2	
1990				164	4	2	13		2	
1991				173	5	4	16		2	
1992				178	5	7	20		2	
1993				203	7	14	26		2	
1994				204	9	21	35		7	
1995				203	16	28	43		6	
1996				198	13	33	46		8	
1997				191	15	36	56		13	
1998				184	17	39	63		15	
1999				185	20	42	74		10	
2000				165	28	47	86		13	
2001				153	28	53	92		13	
2002				152	36	58	98		16	
2003	6	5	33	137	39	60	100	45	16	2
2004	8	8	39	142	48	68	105	68	21	2
2005	14	14	53	138	57	77	109	91	21	5
2006	17	15	54	116	63	87	112	114	14	7
2007	19	19	63	118	70	94	113	132	17	8
2008	25	23	68	124	76	97	114	148	19	9
2009	28	25	71	127	79	99	115	160	21	11
2010	34	30	75	128	82	102	117	170	21	12
2011	44	32	76	114	85	100	112	202	18	15
2012	55	37	85	119	91	102	114	216	21	16
2013	61	45	88	111	93	105	116	221	26	23
2014	61	49	85		93	102	106	225	24	26
2015	46	54	86		92	105	110	219	21	41
2016	56	70	89		96	107	113	226	21	45
2017	52	78	90		98	106	110	223		48

主要统计指标解释

常住人员　指住户成员中，经常在家居住、或者调查期内居住时间超过一半的人员，以及本住户供养的学生。

可支配收入　指调查户在调查期内获得的、可用于最终消费支出和储蓄的总和，即调查户可以用来自由支配的收入。可支配收入既包括现金，也包括实物收入。按照收入的来源，可支配收入包含四项，分别为：工资性收入、经营净收入、财产净收入和转移净收入。计算公式为：

可支配收入＝工资性收入＋经营净收入＋财产净收入＋转移净收入

居民人均可支配收入是按居民家庭常住人口计算的平均每人可支配收入

消费支出　指住户用于满足家庭日常生活消费需要的全部支出。根据用途不同，消费支出可划分为食品烟酒、衣着、居住、生活用品及服务、交通通信、教育文化娱乐、医疗保健、其他用品及服务八大类。根据来源不同，消费支出可划分为现金消费支出、实物消费支出（含自产自用、来自单位、来自政府和其他社会组织）。

Explanatory Notes on Main Statistical Indicators

Permanent resident　refers to residents that live usually in home or more than half of the survey period and students that are supported by them.

Disposable income　refers to sum of all income earned within the survey period that can be used for deposit and expense on final consumption，which means the income that can be disposed freely by residents. The disposable income includes not only cash，but also income in kinds，which shall be categorized into four kinds according to source of incomes--salary income，net operating income，net property income，net transfer income. Computing formula is as follows：

Disposable income = salary income + net operating income + net property income + net transfer income

Disposable income per capita of residents is the average disposable income per person calculated based on the number of permanent residents of the family.

Consumer spending　refers to all spending of residents to cover daily life consumption demands. According to different usages，the consumer spending shall be classified into eight categories：food，cigarettes and alcohol；clothing；housing；daily use articles and services；transportation & communication；education，culture & entertainment；medical and health care；other articles and services. According to sources，the consumer spending shall be classified as cash consumer spending，consumer spending in kinds（including self-produced，from the unit，from government and other social organization）.

农　业 11

AGRICULTURE

简要说明

一、本篇资料的主要内容

本篇资料主要反映了全市农业生产和农村经济的基本情况，主要包括农林牧渔业总产值、中间消耗、增加值、农村劳动力、耕地、主要农产品产量、农业机械年末拥有量、农业机械化和电气化以及农田水利建设等方面的资料。

二、本篇资料的来源

1、本篇资料中耕地面积资料来源于市国土资源房屋管理局。

2、水产品产量等相关资料来源于市海洋与渔业局。

3、农业机械化等相关资料来源于市农机局。

4、农田水利灌溉等相关资料来源于市水利局。

5、植树造林等相关资料来源于市林业局。

本篇资料由市统计局农村统计处、国家统计局青岛调查队农村调查处整理提供。

Brief Introduction

Ⅰ. Main Content

Data in this chapter show the basic conditions of agricultural production and rural economy，mainly including agricultural output，intermediate consumption，value added，rural labor force，cultivated land，output of main agricultural produces,agricultural. machinery and electrification in rural areas and basic construction on irrigation and drainage.

Ⅱ. Source of Data

（1）Data on area of cultivated land are provided by Qingdao Municipal Bureau of Land Resources and Housing Management.

（2）Data on output of aquatic products are provided by Qingdao Municipal Bureau of Ocean and Fishery.

（3）Data on Agricultural machinery are provided by Qingdao Municipal Bureau of Agricultural Machinery.

（4）Data on farmland water conservancy are provided by Qingdao Municipal Bureau of Water Conservancy.

（5）Data on forest planting are provided by Qingdao Municipal Forestry Bureau.

Data in this chapter are compiled by the Division of Countryside Statistics of Qingdao Municipal Bureau of Statistics and Division of Rural Household Survey of Survey Office of the National Bureau of Statistics in Oingdao.

11-1 农村基本情况（2000-2017 年）
BASIC STATISTICS ON RURAL AREA（2000-2017）

项目	Item	单位	Unit	2000	2005	2006	2008	2009	2010
一、乡村户数人口、劳动力	**Rural Households, Population and Labor Force**								
乡村户数	Rural Households	万户	10 000 households	148	151	151	152	152	155
乡村人口	Rural Population	万人	10 000 persons	483	479	478	480	485	487
乡村劳动力	Rural Labor Force	万人	10 000 persons	255	258	265	271	275	276
男劳动力	Male	万人	10 000 persons	137	138	141	144	146	147
女劳动力	Female	万人	10 000 persons	118	120	123	126	129	129
二、年末实有耕地面积	**Year-end Area of Cultivated Land**	**万公顷**	**10 000 hectares**	**48**	**42**	**41**	**42**	**42**	
三、农用机械总动力	**Total Agricultural Machinery Power**	**万千瓦**	**10 000 kW**	**459**	**620**	**651**	**697**	**719**	**764**
拖拉机	Tractors	台	unit	126981	163032	171155	176156	180171	200208
四、农村用电量	**Electricity Consumed in Rural Areas**	**万千瓦时**	**10 000 kW · h**	**189651**	**372645**	**413762**	**424292**	**426306**	**426819**
五、农用化肥施用量（折纯）	**Consumption of Chemical Fertilizer（convert to pure amount）**	**万吨**	**10 000 tons**	**33**	**33**	**33**	**31**	**30**	**30**
六、有效灌溉面积	**Irrigated Area**	**万公顷**	**10 000 hectares**	**30**	**30**	**30**	**31**	**32**	**33**

11-1 续表
Continued

项目	Item	单位	Unit	2011	2012	2013	2014	2015	2016	2017
一、乡村户数人口、劳动力	**Rural Households, Population and Labor Force**									
乡村户数	Rural Households	万户	10 000 households	155	156	155	157	155	155	140
乡村人口	Rural Population	万人	10 000 persons	489	491	491	494	495	497	453
乡村劳动力	Rural Labor Force	万人	10 000 persons	277	277	277	277	275	273	246
男劳动力	Male	万人	10 000 persons	147	146	147	147	145	145	131
女劳动力	Female	万人	10 000 persons	131	130	131	130	130	128	115
二、年末实有耕地面积	**Year-end Area of Cultivated Land**	**万公顷**	**10 000 hectares**		**53**	**53**	**52**	**52**	**52**	**52**
三、农用机械总动力	**Total Agricultural Machinery Power**	**万千瓦**	**10 000 kW**	**784**	**798**	**809**	**827**	**854**	**698**	**728**
拖拉机	Tractors	台	unit	202022	206290	206300	205065	207809	211689	214799
四、农村用电量	**Electricity Consumed in Rural Areas**	**万千瓦时**	**10 000 kW · h**	**431646**	**426815**	**359139**	**404380**	**401122**	**385434**	**382437**
五、农用化肥施用量(折纯)	**Consumption of Chemical Fertilizer (convert to pure amount)**	**万吨**	**10 000 tons**	**29**	**29**	**29**	**29**	**28**	**28**	**28**
六、有效灌溉面积	**Irrigated Area**	**万公顷**	**10 000 hectares**	**33**	**33**	**30**	**32**	**32**	**33**	**33**

注：农机机械总动力 2017 年为新统计口径，扣除农用运输汽车数据。
Note: Data of total power of agricultural machinery of 2017 is based on the new statistic caliber, deducted by the data of agricultural vehicle.

11-2 农村劳动力（1985-2017 年）
RURAL LABOR FORCE（1985-2017）

单位：万人（10 000 persons）

年份 Year	合计 Total	农林牧渔业 Farming, Forestry, Animal Husbandry and Fishery	工业 Industry	建筑业 Construction
1985	225.09	147.89	32.92	15.62
1988	238.93	146.00	44.46	17.51
1989	242.70	151.16	44.65	16.46
1990	247.29	155.20	44.48	16.17
1991	253.01	160.31	45.49	15.87
1992	258.23	160.04	47.00	17.25
1993	259.18	159.22	44.04	20.20
1994	258.34	155.74	43.70	21.52
1995	258.66	154.08	44.06	22.33
1996	256.34	151.10	43.08	21.80
1997	258.60	153.07	41.66	22.02
1998	258.50	152.79	40.79	21.68
1999	256.82	149.11	42.18	22.32
2000	254.62	143.59	42.76	22.99
2001	253.98	132.46	47.76	24.66
2002	254.08	119.98	53.66	26.52
2003	257.67	118.27	55.65	26.65
2004	258.91	112.05	60.32	28.36
2005	257.87	103.03	65.59	29.03
2006	264.70	102.28	71.46	28.16
2007	268.31	100.63	74.70	30.97
2008	270.71	100.90	74.82	30.87
2009	274.74	102.64	75.42	31.23
2010	276.04	102.45	76.32	32.10
2011	277.24	102.73	76.87	32.57
2012	276.97	102.24	76.82	32.36
2013	277.32	104.48	76.42	31.15
2014	276.90			
2015	274.77			
2016	273.43			
2017	245.92			

11-2 续表
Continued

单位：万人（10 000 persons）

年份 Year	交通运输仓储和邮电业 Transport, Postal and Telecommunication Services	批发零售贸易、餐饮业 Wholesale and Retail Trades and Catering Services	金融保险业 Finance and Insurance	其他劳动力 Other Labor Force
1985	5.23	0.06	19.76	3.61
1988	5.89	0.09	20.40	4.58
1989	6.00	0.12	19.95	4.36
1990	6.11	0.12	20.71	4.50
1991	6.09	0.13	20.52	4.60
1992	7.02	0.16	21.74	5.02
1993	8.93	0.16	20.65	5.98
1994	6.48	10.10		20.80
1995	7.11	10.71		20.37
1996	7.33	11.78		21.25
1997	7.62	12.40		21.83
1998	8.02	13.32		21.90
1999	8.19	14.03		20.99
2000	8.39	16.10		20.79
2001	9.02	17.80		22.28
2002	10.00	20.07		23.85
2003	9.96	20.60		26.54
2004	10.20	24.08		22.96
2005	10.70	25.88		22.34
2006	11.66	25.31		24.37
2007	11.61	27.61		21.16
2008	11.06	28.76		22.09
2009	11.40	29.03		22.75
2010	11.78	28.85		22.01
2011	11.89	29.34		21.02
2012	11.96	29.56		21.11
2013	11.92	29.48		20.33
2014				
2015				
2016				
2017				

11-3 分市、区乡村户数、人口、劳动力(2017年)
RURAL HOUSEHOLDS, POPULATION AND LABOR FORCE BY REGION (2017)

市、区名称	Region	乡村户数(万户) Rural Households (10 000 households)	乡村人口(万人) Rural Popultaion (10 000 persons)	乡村劳动力(万人) Labor Force of Village (10 000 persons)	男劳动力 Male Laborer	女劳动力 Female Laborer	#种植业 Planting
全市	**Whole Municipality**	**140.40**	**453.50**	**245.90**	**130.90**	**115.00**	**73.50**
崂山区	Laoshan District	4.93	14.92	7.92	4.25	3.68	1.99
黄岛区	Huangdao District	21.80	72.63	35.33	18.79	16.55	7.72
城阳区	Chengyang District	11.09	31.03	16.51	8.71	7.81	0.83
即墨区	Jimo District	27.82	93.83	50.56	26.64	23.91	13.14
胶州市	Jiaozhou	17.60	57.32	31.56	17.20	14.36	9.01
平度市	Pingdu	35.79	117.99	66.39	35.44	30.95	26.57
莱西市	Laixi	18.93	58.67	33.68	17.84	15.84	13.61
红岛经济区	Qingdao National High-tech Industrial Development Zone	2.44	7.08	3.96	2.02	1.94	0.57

11-4 主要年份农、林、牧、渔业总产值（按现价计算）
MAJOR YEAR'S GROSS OUTPUT VALUE OF FARMING, FORESTRY, ANINAL HUSBANDRY AND FISHERY（CURRENT PRICE）

单位：万元（10 000 yuan）

年份 Year	农、林、牧、渔业总产值 Gross Output Value of Farming, Forestry, Animal Husbandry and Fishery	农业产值 Farming	林业产值 Forestry	牧业产值 Animal Husbandry	渔业产值 Fishery
1949	16511	14755	325	1200	231
1952	24428	21353	479	1888	708
1957	26189	22717	644	2218	610
1962	15356	13257	230	1243	626
1965	25123	21488	854	2110	671
1970	44078	36889	1851	3817	1521
1975	93213	79208	2144	7923	3938
1978	121497	94397	3112	17293	6695
1980	149436	117547	2953	22215	6721
1985	299139	215729	8986	53894	20530
1987	378981	263066	5949	73271	36695
1989	463952	303679	19134	91885	49254
1990	579877	381287	13801	119208	65581
1991	664779	417111	12875	144909	89884
1992	703433	400471	15252	150942	136768
1993	989763	509601	20845	232143	227174
1994	1424074	763366	23101	356734	280873
1995	1923771	1021413	26765	503999	371594
1996	2317434	1145399	29100	692362	450573
1997	2047712	939922	24052	578443	505295
1998	2386303	1198043	16760	633735	537765
1999	2382320	1169596	17122	618020	577582
2000	2483256	1116397	19102	692782	654975
2001	2615228	1135816	20433	758313	700666
2002	2688532	1110671	23157	796007	758697
2003	2759692	1062576	36183	859915	801018
2004	2967389	1181009	32831	937494	816055
2005	3205057	1265695	25246	1070831	843285
2006	3396096	1360755	23546	1076254	855131
2007	3429877	1483733	20842	975032	830479
2008	4008540	1778404	24452	1214648	856227
2009	4086146	1856753	22264	1160558	898608
2010	4831806	2339238	19241	1264028	1051452
2011	5359343	2365300	19237	1560108	1232720
2012	5665217	2492493	20461	1582549	1370622
2013	6118581	2841323	22178	1640755	1394753
2014	6300421	2998853	22620	1657075	1372771
2015	6601353	3375921	27106	1624718	1300632
2016	6742659	3323396	28292	1753431	1326693
2017	6929219	3476528	30482	1677645	1395309

11-5 分市、区农、林、牧、渔业总产值（2017年，现价）

GROSS OUTPUT VALUE OF FARMING，FORESTRY，ANIMAL HUSBANDRY AND FISHERY BY REGION（2017，CURRENT PRICE）

单位：万元（10 000 yuan）

市、区名称	Region	农、林、牧、渔业总产值 Gross Output Value of Farming, Forestry, Animal Husbandry and Fishery	农业 Farming	林业 Forestry	牧业 Aninal Husbandry	渔业 Fishery	服务业 Services
全市	**Whole Municipality**	**6929219**	**3476528**	**30482**	**1677645**	**1395309**	**349255**
崂山区	Laoshan District	121591	12263	572	2641	91756	14360
黄岛区	Huangdao District	1185569	479764	4674	142093	496507	62531
城阳区	Chengyang District	64432	22542	786	20160	19338	1605
即墨区	Jimo District	1209326	472547	4898	230586	413830	87465
胶州市	Jiaozhou	940627	472169	5859	226086	172665	63848
平度市	Pingdu	1955433	1336118	5742	542588	7985	63000
莱西市	Laixi	1254377	680245	7858	506044	6151	54080
红岛经济区	Qingdao National High-tech Industrial Development Zone	197864	879	93	7448	187078	2366

注：本表按当年价格计算。
Note：Date in this from are calculated at current price.

11-6　农、林、牧、渔业总产值、增加值（2017年）
VALUE-ADDED OF FARMING，FORESTRY，ANIMAL，HUSBANDRYAND FISHERY（2017）

单位：万元（10 000 yuan）

		总计 Total	农业 Farming	林业 Forestry	牧业 Animal Husbandry	渔业 Fishery	服务业 Services
总产值	**Gross Output Value**	**6929219**	**3476527**	**30482**	**1677645**	**1395310**	**349255**
中间消耗	**Intermediate Expenditure**	**2895623**	**1330754**	**14508**	**898891**	**526113**	**125358**
中间物质消耗	Intermediate Expenditure of Matter	2179626	1038269	9193	720955	350128	61080
对非农生产部门的劳动支出	Expenditure of Labor Services to Nonagricultural Production Development	715998	292485	5314	177936	175984	64278

11-7　分市、区农、林、牧、渔业增加值（2017年）
VALUE-ADDED OF FARMING，FORESTRY，ANIMAL HUSBANDRY FISHERY BY REGION（2017）

单位：万元（10 000 yuan）

市、区名称	Region	增加值 Added Value	农业 Farming	林业 Forestry	牧业 Animal Husbandry	渔业 Fishery	服务业 Services
全市	**Whole Municipality**	**4033598**	**2145773**	**15974**	**778753**	**869201**	**223897**
崂山区	Laoshan District	73958	7535	304	1247	55704	9168
黄岛区	Huangdao District	714717	295844	2423	65693	310530	40227
城阳区	Chengyang District	37036	13878	408	9341	12385	1025
即墨区	Jimo District	699339	278380	2701	104914	257249	56095
胶州市	Jiaozhou	553932	294230	3038	106786	108990	40888
平度市	Pingdu	1136417	834466	2977	253565	5064	40346
莱西市	Laixi	697362	420898	4074	233855	3901	34633
红岛经济区	Qingdao National High-tech Industrial Development Zone	120836	543	48	3353	115377	1515

11-8 主要年份耕地面积与播种面积
MAJOR YEAR'S CULTIVATED AND SOWN AREA

单位：万公顷（10 000 hectares）

年份 Year	年末实有耕地面积 Year-end Area of Cultivated Land	农作物播种面积 Sown Area of Farm Crops	#粮食作物 Grain Crops	#经济作物 Economic Crops
1949		93.47	84.00	7.20
1952		97.53	85.07	10.80
1957		97.87	87.07	10.53
1962		81.47	72.53	5.80
1965		82.80	71.80	8.33
1970		80.73	68.27	10.07
1975		79.82	65.84	11.01
1978		77.60	63.60	10.40
1980		75.87	60.33	12.00
1985		78.27	57.33	15.73
1987		76.67	55.87	15.93
1989		74.78	54.28	16.06
1990		76.85	56.99	15.53
1991		76.98	56.89	15.69
1992		76.96	56.37	15.64
1993	56.90	77.75	56.22	15.71
1994		76.61	54.08	16.20
1995		76.54	53.71	15.65
1996	55.01	77.26	54.81	14.90
1997		75.04	52.32	14.40
1998		77.18	53.05	14.54
1999		77.56	50.61	13.24
2000		76.47	45.07	13.98
2001		73.69	41.91	14.54
2002		72.32	40.83	13.95
2003		67.82	36.05	14.50
2004		71.33	41.40	14.11
2005	42.10	75.02	49.93	11.89
2006	41.29	74.86	49.79	11.75
2007	41.31	72.79	47.56	12.11
2008	41.79	74.09	51.06	11.29
2009	41.87	75.00	52.92	11.34
2010		75.39	53.56	11.00
2011		75.70	54.56	10.69
2012	52.81	74.96	54.08	10.69
2013	52.55	70.99	50.04	10.83
2014	52.42	69.96	49.55	9.92
2015	52.22	68.95	49.31	9.19
2016	52.00	68.24	48.02	9.52
2017	51.86	67.88	47.79	9.27

注：2009 年前数据由统计局提供。
Note：Those of before 2009 were provided by the National Bureau of Statistics.

11-9 分市、区耕地面积（2017年）
AREA OF CULTIVATED LAND BY REGION（2017）

单位：公顷（hectare）

市、区名称	Region	年末耕地面积 Year-end Area of Cultivated Land	#旱田 Dry Farmland	当年增加的耕地 Area of Culitivated Land Increased in the Year	#新开荒地 Wasteland Newly Opened up	当年减少的耕地 Area of Cultivated Land Decreased in the Year
全市	**Whole Municipality**	**518625**	**273418**	**366**		**938**
崂山区	Laoshan District	898	866			2
黄岛区	Huangdao District	74150	71820	1		211
城阳区	Chengyang District	6686	5230	85		86
即墨区	Jimo District	99465	86314	1		180
胶州市	Jiaozhou	63764	23516	5		268
平度市	Pingdu	184251	12616	153		129
莱西市	Laixi	89378	73023	121		63

注：1. 2017年数据按照2017年度土地变更调查阶段性成果填写；
　　2. 黄岛区包括保税港区、城阳区包括红岛经济区。

Note：1. The 2017 data is filled in according to the 2017 land change investigation stage results.
　　2. Huangdao District includes Bonded Port Area, and Chengyang District includes Hongdao Economic Zone.

11-10 分市、区农作物播种面积（2017年）
SOWN AREA OF FARM CROPS BY REGION（2017）

单位：万公顷（10 000 hectares）

市、区名称	Region	总播种面积 Total Sown Area	#粮食 Crain	#棉花 Cotton	#花生 Peanut	#烟叶 Tobacco	#蔬菜 Vegetable
全市	**Whole Municipality**	**67.88**	**47.79**	**0.05**	**8.23**	**0.04**	**10.83**
崂山区	Laoshan District	0.06	0.01		0.01		0.03
黄岛区	Huangdao District	7.53	4.73		1.95	0.03	0.76
城阳区	Chengyang District	0.29	0.16		0.01		0.12
即墨区	Jimo District	10.33	7.80	0.00	1.50		0.95
胶州市	Jiaozhou	9.37	6.45		0.68	0.00	2.20
平度市	Pingdu	27.43	19.84	0.05	2.53	0.01	4.65
莱西市	Laixi	12.87	8.80		1.55		2.12

注：城阳区包括红岛经济区。
Note：Chengyang District includes Hongdao Economic Zone.

11-11 分市、区部分农作物产量（2017年）
OUTPUT OF FARM CROPS BY REGION（2017）

单位：吨（ton）

市、区名称	Region	粮食 Grain	棉花 Cotton	花生 Peanut	烟叶 Tobacco	蔬菜 Vegetable
全市	**Whole Municipality**	**2968896**	**767**	**383859**	**1027**	**6012459**
崂山区	Laoshan District	999		271		10737
黄岛区	Huangdao District	244598		98326	783	446437
城阳区	Chengyang District	7757		118		40544
即墨区	Jimo District	426685	10	62241		522206
胶州市	Jiaozhou	375037		29108	15	1089584
平度市	Pingdu	1400714	757	122415	230	2672348
莱西市	Laixi	513105		71346		1230013
红岛经济区	Qingdao National High-tech Industrial Development Zone			34		591

注：城阳区粮食产量包括红岛经济区。
Note：Grain output in Chengyang District includes Hongdao Economic Zone.

11-12　分市、区部分农作物播公顷单产量（2017年）
OUTPUT OF FARM CROPS PER HECTARE BY REGION（2017）

单位：千克（kg）

市、区名称	Region	粮食 Grain	棉花 Cotton	花生 Peanut	烟叶 Tobacco	蔬菜 Vegetable
全市	**Whole Municipality**	**6213**	**1625**	**4667**	**2670**	**55511**
崂山区	Laoshan District	7030		3144		32174
黄岛区	Huangdao District	5171		5037	2624	58925
城阳区	Chengyang District	4937		3296		34427
即墨区	Jimo District	5470	2100	4155		54857
胶州市	Jiaozhou	5814		4269	3015	49439
平度市	Pingdu	7061	1620	4838	2822	57519
莱西市	Laixi	5833		4604		58053

注：城阳区包括红岛经济区。
Note：Chengyang District includes Hongdao Economic Zone.

11-13 主要年份农作物总产量
MAJOR YEAR'S OUPTUT OF FARM CROPS

单位：吨（ton）

年份 Year	粮食 Crain	#小麦 Wheat	#玉米 Corn	棉花 Cotton	花生 Peanut	水果 Fruit	蔬菜 Vegetable
1949	723190	158815	25810	1280	71080	9955	356015
1952	967640	200380	58130	6025	115585	13468	284050
1957	921920	210690	141540	3520	90445	18869	625220
1962	628930	104340	53010	1280	35470	8366	524455
1965	917635	180610	135595	6090	88390	16034	465850
1970	1175985	243945	244530	16490	96280	33907	541145
1975	1899540	430135	420095	15390	98495	59206	693970
1978	1900850	514570	510635	8720	114370	82819	921140
1980	2164415	520045	819930	19630	160670	80840	996565
1985	2331060	961055	739455	19335	475270	200515	1253075
1987	2626029	996165	1030926	13819	394296	249655	1489250
1989	2654334	993406	1084441	14638	391782	288757	1664238
1990	2998246	1265157	1210687	17490	413636	292366	1786041
1991	3180893	1421143	1285043	25965	446880	294349	1837265
1992	2675641	1235755	981490	8160	321145	341415	2030327
1993	3164812	1463759	1248780	15344	419109	383368	2705349
1994	3106562	1392977	1252952	8326	494827	423024	3002318
1995	3291587	1480385	1365167	8177	510662	478685	3221507
1996	3390033	1513479	1466668	4001	486574	505711	3405056
1997	2523064	1584478	743199	2000	308233	438398	3333181
1998	3469821	1627261	1484182	4159	546786	529592	4036992
1999	3331124	1501182	1499775	3668	572941	606800	5459140
2000	2780481	1353445	1169649	2077	534174	651591	6649322
2001	2539257	1143679	1178851	3409	579441	675244	6250361
2002	2383802	1085936	1094731	3755	557714	579703	6847570
2003	2221697	931787	1117704	5324	568798	677361	7305618
2004	2650952	1301791	1202063	7216	580290	748516	6720886
2005	3150203	1535471	1478616	4042	503941	737300	5792110
2006	3039266	1548928	1372166	3954	471853	827755	6051239
2007	3007443	1395643	1497343	4330	495972	793859	6157471
2008	3336643	1620734	1620910	4173	471447	806815	6118876
2009	3539075	1727966	1723279	4529	468022	820887	5679434
2010	3514081	1646745	1795187	3952	441443	803092	5807761
2011	3630046	1653376	1906374	3917	443713	805192	5838183
2012	3699600			4301	459464	798685	5697564
2013	3223879	1518351	1658129	3429	443909	749501	5754180
2014	3230238	1520990	1667630	2467	398028	751757	5953466
2015	3214000	1535245	1636611	2220	345515	1187297	5790950
2016	3049921	1449500	1559121	595	369339	1204244	5698492
2017	2968896	1264073	1666417	767	383859	1183106	6012459

11-13 续表 1
Continued

单位：吨（ton）

市、区名称	Region	蔬菜 Vegetable	#大白菜 Cabbage	#芹菜 Celery	#胡萝卜 Carrot	#马铃薯 Potato
全市	**Whole Municipality**	**6012459**	**1253681**	**178180**	**464484**	**1085777**
崂山区	Laoshan District	10737	4793	69	92	2220
黄岛区	Huangdao District	446437	179162	12004	984	94347
城阳区	Chengyang District	40544	7865	1324		2847
即墨区	Jimo District	522206	139015	13993	43374	79853
胶州市	Jiaozhou	1089584	239034	55920	4222	372944
平度市	Pingdu	2672348	498278	56519	176537	495372
莱西市	Laixi	1230013	185145	38346	239276	38174
红岛经济区	Qingdao National High-tech Industrial Development Zone	591	388	6		19

11-13 续表 2
Continued

单位：吨（ton）

市、区名称	Region	#黄瓜 Cucumber	西红柿 Toamto	#大葱 Green onion	#蒜头 Carlic	#食用菌 Edible fungi
全市	**Whole Municipality**	**380547**	**331718**	**675512**	**156997**	**95479**
崂山区	Laoshan District	375	121	226	41	
黄岛区	Huangdao District	6273	27518	2478	1069	79343
城阳区	Chengyang District	9404	9132	149		343
即墨区	Jimo District	47830	19235	42559	8065	13358
胶州市	Jiaozhou	22417	13408	53778	494	129
平度市	Pingdu	36558	69361	563323	136235	1359
莱西市	Laixi	257683	192937	12997	11092	948
红岛经济区	Qingdao National High-tech Industrial Development Zone	8	6	1	2	

11-14 分市、区猪、羊及家禽存养量（2017年）
HOGS、SHEEP、GOATS AND POULTRY IN STOCK BY REGION（2017）

单位：万只（10 000 head）

市、区名称	Region	年末生猪存养量 Hogs in Stock（year-end）	#母猪 Sow	牛 Cattle and Buffaloes	#奶牛 Cows	年末羊存养量 Sheep and Goats in Stock（year-end）	年末家禽存栏 Poultry stock at the end of the year	#蛋鸡 Egg
全市	**Whole Municipality**	**178.70**	**19.23**	**16.39**	**8.99**	**21.77**	**5524.40**	**1301.62**
崂山区	Laoshan District					0.04		
黄岛区	Huangdao District	31.37	3.06	0.91	0.08	4.38	350.84	114.76
城阳区	Chengyang District	1.68	0.17	0.17	0.17	0.14	39.51	36.91
即墨区	Jimo District	22.76	2.78	1.65	1.15	2.09	806.67	330.80
胶州市	Jiaozhou	25.51	2.58	1.40	0.37	4.92	375.90	245.68
平度市	Pingdu	57.07	6.30	4.09	0.70	5.88	1697.99	261.04
莱西市	Laixi	39.71	4.29	8.14	6.48	4.26	2230.66	295.50
红岛经济区	Qingdao National High-tech Industrial Development Zone	0.61	0.05	0.03	0.03	0.04	22.83	16.93

11-15 分市、区肉、蛋、奶产量（2017年）
OUTPUT OF MEAT，EGGS AND MILK BY REGION（2017）

单位：万吨（10 000 tons）

市、区名称	Region	肉类产量 Output of Meat	#猪肉 Port	#禽肉 Poultry Meat	禽蛋 Poultry Meat	牛羊奶 Milk
全市	**Whole Municipality**	**54.33**	**21.84**	**30.94**	**17.73**	**30.89**
崂山区	Laoshan District					0.01
黄岛区	Huangdao District	5.79	3.62	1.47	1.55	1.14
城阳区	Chengyang District	0.22	0.20	0.02	0.50	0.55
即墨区	Jimo District	5.71	2.56	3.08	4.48	3.88
胶州市	Jiaozhou	4.43	3.23	1.03	3.32	1.72
平度市	Pingdu	17.25	7.11	9.86	3.64	2.64
莱西市	Laixi	20.79	5.02	15.45	4.01	20.85
红岛经济区	Qingdao National High-tech Industrial Development Zone	0.14	0.09	0.04	0.23	0.10

11-16 分市、区渔业养殖面积
AQUACULTURE AREA BY REGION

单位：公顷（hectare）

市、区名称	Region	2017年			2016年		
		养殖面积 Aquaculture Area	#海水 Seawater	#淡水 Fresh Water	养殖面积 Aquaculture Area	#海水 Seawater	#淡水 Fresh Water
全市	**Whole Municipality**	**42793**	**32403**	**10390**	**44840**	**33275**	**11565**
崂山区	Laoshan District	1600	1600		1600	1600	
黄岛区	Huangdao District	13508	11698	1810	13458	11398	2060
城阳区	Chengyang District	8196	6465	1731	9393	7637	1756
即墨区	Jimo District	11163	10889	274	11163	10889	274
胶州市	Jiaozhou	2981	1751	1230	4071	1751	2320
平度市	Pingdu	1400		1400	2083		2083
莱西市	Laixi	3945		3945	3072		3072

注：城阳区包括红岛经济区。
Note：Chengyang District includes Hongdao Economic Zone.

11-17 分市、区水产品总产量(2017年)
OUTPUT OF AQUATIC PRODUCTS BY REGION（2017）

单位：吨（ton）

市、区名称	Region	水产品总产量 Output of Aquatic Products	#养殖产量 Aquaculture Output	#捕捞产量 Catch	#鱼类 Fish	#甲壳类 Crust	#贝类 Shellfish	#藻类 Algae
全市	**Whole Municipality**	**1076091**	**837797**	**238294**	**175378**	**59548**	**750427**	**3680**
崂山区	Laoshan District	65103	20972	44131	49527	11101	22860	1280
黄岛区	Huangdao District	366179	289068	77111	49542	7710	211348	2400
城阳区	Chengyang District	242847	214770	28077	14344	7157	212584	
即墨区	Jimo District	295070	233272	61798	24552	5457	227801	
胶州市	Jiaozhou	101009	73832	27177	16561	6437	67074	
平度市	Pingdu	2019	2019		17000	21686	8760	
莱西市	Laixi	3864	3864					

注：城阳区包括红岛经济区。
Note：Chengyang District includes Hongdao Economic Zone.

11-18 分市、区植树及造林面积（2017 年）
OUTPUT OF AQUATIC PRODUCTS BY REGION（2017）

市、区名称	Region	当年造林面积（公顷）Area of Afforestation in the Year（hectare）	育苗面积（公顷）Seeding Area（hectare）	森林抚育作业面积（公顷）Forest Tending Area（hectare）	零星（四旁）植树（万株）Surrounding Tree Planting（10 000 trees）
全市	**Whole Municipality**	**6905**	**14302**	**15000**	**595.3**
崂山区	Laoshan District	387	120	1333	3.0
黄岛区	Huangdao District	891	1657	2000	58.7
城阳区	Chengyang District	393	540	1333	40.6
即墨区	Jimo District	1009	2733	3067	90.0
胶州市	Jiaozhou	909	1283	2267	20.0
平度市	Pingdu	1917	2219	4000	122.0
莱西市	Laixi	1399	5750	1000	261.0

注：城阳区包括红岛经济区。
Note：Chengyang District includes Hongdao Economic Zone.

11-19 分市、区果园面积、水果总产量（2017 年）
AREA OF FORESTATION AND OUTPUT OF FRUITS BY REGION（2017）

单位：吨（ton），公顷（hectare）

市、区名称	Region	果园总面积 Area of Orchards（hectare）	水果总产量 Output of Fruits（ton）	#园林水果 Garden Fruits	#瓜果类水果 Melon Fruits
全市	**Whole Municipality**	**27470**	**1183527**	**752080**	**431447**
崂山区	Laoshan District	650	6000	5924	77
黄岛区	Huangdao District	5085	114791	90420	24371
城阳区	Chengyang District	798	14547	12912	1635
即墨区	Jimo District	734	53730	16163	37567
胶州市	Jiaozhou	1411	58482	40515	17968
平度市	Pingdu	9864	524894	307681	217213
莱西市	Laixi	8912	410924	278309	132615
红岛经济区	Qingdao National High-tech Industrial Development Zone	16	158	157	2

11-19 续表
Contiuned

单位：吨（ton），公顷（hectare）

市、区名称	Region	# 苹果 Apple	# 梨 Pear	# 桃 Peach	# 葡萄 Grape	# 杏 Apricot	# 山楂 Hawthorn	# 西瓜 Watermelon	# 甜瓜 Muskmelon
全市	**Whole Municipality**	**386944**	**75641**	**90683**	**144124**	**9369**	**2950**	**273726**	**116188**
崂山区	Laoshan District	77	109	1938	11	1486	6		
黄岛区	Huangdao District	46260	4953	16746	3612	356	76	18798	1508
城阳区	Chengyang District	482	86	5076	4145	1762		43	
即墨区	Jimo District	4200	1691	4478	2871	72	41	27140	9668
胶州市	Jiaozhou	16069	3798	10036	4259	5493	60	17179	274
平度市	Pingdu	168848	12489	32056	76954	195	839	192105	3854
莱西市	Laixi	150969	52457	20315	52261	2	1929	18461	100884
红岛经济区	Qingdao National High-tech Industrial Development Zone	39	59	37	10	3			

11-20 分市、区果园、茶园面积和茶叶、蚕茧产量（2017年）
AREA OF ORCHARD AND TEA GARDEN AND PRODUCTION OF TEA BY CTTY AND DISTRICT（2017）

单位：公顷（hectare），吨（ton）

市、区名称	Region	果园面积 Area of Orchards (hectare)	# 苹果园 Apple Orchard	# 梨园 Pear Orchard	# 葡萄园 Vineyand	# 桃园 Peach Orchand	茶园面积（公顷）Area of Tea Plantations (hectare)	茶叶产量（吨）Output of Tea (ton)	蚕茧产量（吨）Cocoon yield(ton)
全市	**Whole Municipality**	**27470**	**11313**	**2211**	**4780**	**4312**	**4017**	**4263**	**4**
崂山区	Laoshan District	650	4	5	1	83	1198	1205	
黄岛区	Huangdao District	5085	1450	159	218	1313	2440	2496	3
城阳区	Chengyang District	798	21	3	164	268	67	124	
即墨区	Jimo District	734	194	49	109	271	292	428	
胶州市	Jiaozhou	1411	413	97	113	407			
平度市	Pingdu	9864	4493	390	2604	1144	19	10	1
莱西市	Laixi	8912	4732	1503	1570	823			
红岛经济区	Qingdao National High-tech Industrial Development Zone	16	6	5		2			

11-21 主要年份主要农业机械拥有量
MAJOR YEAR'S OWNERSHIIP OF AGRICULTURAL MACHINERY

年份 Year	农业机械总动力 （万千瓦） Total Agricultural Machinery Power （10 000 kW）	农用拖拉机 Agricultural Tractors		大、中型机引农具 （万台） Large and Medium Towong Farm Machinery （10 000 sets）	排灌机械 Draingage and Irrigation Machinery	
		混合台 set	千瓦 kW		台 set	万千瓦 10 000 kW
1949						
1952						
1957	0.22	59	2.2	0.01		
1962	2.47	254	11.47	0.06		
1965	3.49	296	13.2	0.08		
1970	10.40	602	7 963	0.07		
1975	43.94	6447	103 476	0.48		
1978	75.45	15576	309 287	1.02		
1980	110.44	24278	502 731	1.72		
1985	174.76	33097	506 217	1.71	67794	54.92
1990	253.52	55363	680 903	2.03	105574	74.63
1991	250.58	57404	691 332	2.20	134900	73.77
1992	253.94	57182	684 182	2.28	124800	82.68
1993	261.24	56335	678 161	2.34	144460	78.96
1994	278.41	58698	688 886	2.39	147259	80.81
1995	289.23	56391	657 025	2.28	138625	73.98
1996	303.57	59698	680 447	2.32	148313	81.53
1997	326.72	66841	744 424	2.42	155629	88.09
1998	364.21	87226	894 985	2	156565	86.68
1999	411.44	105743	1 075 907	3	170875	96.20
2000	459.21	126981	1 253 210	3	182646	108.26
2001	496.27	141409	1 394 114	4	178437	104.18
2002	534.92	152920	1 537 544	5	182799	107.35
2003	560.94	160676	1 666 185	5	192930	109.44
2004	599	168061	1 818 276	5	192144	110
2005	620	163032	1757177	6	188689	112
2006	651	171155	1890402	6	192010	116
2007	680	173326	1958047	7	195050	118
2008	697	176156	2034453	8	208711	134
2009	719	180171	2266697	9	207648	134
2010	764	200208	2331867	10	190770	123
2011	784	202022	2649283	10	189834	127
2012	798	206290	2759004	10	190134	127
2013	809	206309	2968332	10	190433	127
2014	827	205065	2960438	10	190584	128
2015	854	207809	3176870	10	191152	128
2016	698	211689	3372681	10	191283	128
2017	728	214799	3550005	11	191417	128

11-22 主要年份农业机械化用电量、化肥施用量
MAJOR YEAR'S MECHANIZATION, ELECTRICITY AND CHEMICAL FERTILIZER CONSUMPTION

年份 Year	有效灌溉面积（公顷）Irrigated Area (hectare)	配套机电井（眼）Number of Electromechanical Well (well)	机耕面积（公顷）Area of Motorized Cultivation (hectare)	机播面积（公顷）Area of Motorized Planting (hectare)	机收面积（公顷）Area of Motorized Harvesting (hectare)	农村用电量（万千瓦时）Electricity Consumption in Rural Area (10 000 kW·h)	化肥施用量（折纯万吨）Chemical Fertilizer Consumption (convert to 10 000 tons)
1949	8340						
1952	14980						
1957	59353		12800	13			0.19
1962	55213	191	65680	927	927	55	0.10
1965	80000	125	11433	573	247	128	0.55
1970	147613	3947	143700	2527	133	1208	1.76
1975	233980	12820	248867	54507	953	2522	2.77
1978	276660	21017	329213	178533	15060	13975	3.64
1980	296606	22472	444800	187980	55333	20492	12.06
1985	302647	42925	366786	148433	56447	41524	11.66
1990	274680	56821	426680	220593	143133	67616	20.47
1991	281500	58987	431293	254266	192946	81200	22.53
1992	281610	62100	438533	270453	207780	88024	22.60
1993	284080	63954	439300	260287	225807	102501	28.04
1994	286750	64877	436820	262846	238693	121307	28.73
1995	287020	64651	435213	271707	250267	134284	31.45
1996	289320	65237	438947	280480	235933	143740	31.36
1997	292130	66783	442213	308267	266147	150971	28.99
1998	294120	64109	442920	359447	285513	153113	32.0
1999	294790	64734	440967	396180	286367	169337	32.6
2000	295190	65179	439980	346480	292787	189651	32.5
2001	296980	65547	436576	382870	265730	228069	31.7
2002	294310	65588	433660	364680	267690	256453	31.1
2003	292410	65406	415790	404980	256600	299425	31.9
2004	292520	65501	415220	454800	314680	330609	32.5
2005	296450	65303	409610	493240	367740	372644	33.0
2006	303070	65981	403980	493750	398700	413762	32.6
2007	305760	66400	400480	499590	429630	425715	33.9
2008	313920	66828	404080	517540	455120	424292	31.1
2009	322710	67027	404080	538220	481176	426306	30.2
2010	328960	67242	578726	558611	499248	426819	29.9
2011	331690	62104	600451	567947	547108	431646	29.4
2012	333850	62112	610382	627701	566653	426815	29.1
2013	302790	170008	410601	627701	566653	359138	29.1
2014	321670	169491	411355	590798	545360	404380	28.9
2015	323400	155074	417991	640022	600696	401122	28.5
2016	327600	135057	362912	561022	511000	385434	28.37
2017	329620	139342	360085	566264	516763	382437	27.83

11-23 分市、区农业机械化和电气化（2017年）
MECHANIZATION AND ELECTRIFICATION IN AGRICULTURE BY REGION (2017)

市、区名称	Region	农村用电量（万千瓦小时）Electricity Consumed in Rural Areas (10 000 kW·h)	机耕作业面积 Area of Motorized Cultivation (hectare)	机播地面积 Area of Motorized Planting (hectare)	机收面积 Area of Motorized Harvesting (hectare)
			面积 Area（公顷）(hectare)		
全市	**Whole Municipality**	**382437**	**350085**	**566264**	**516763**
崂山区	Laoshan District	8221			
黄岛区	Huangdao District	55471	40019	63544	57419
城阳区	Chengyang District	44675	1867	2007	1623
即墨区	Jimo District	64245	49360	86572	82193
胶州市	Jiaozhou	98864	40149	76571	70912
平度市	Pingdu	70614	149101	229893	208883
莱西市	Laixi	34425	69589	107677	95733
红岛经济区	Qingdao National High-tech Industrial Development Zone	5923			

11-24 分市、区农用化肥施用量（2017年）
CONSUMPTION OF CHEMICAL FERTILIZERS BY REGION (2017)

单位：折纯吨（ton converted to pure amount）

市、区名称	Region	农用化肥施用量 Consumption of Chemical Fertilizers	氮肥 Nitrogenous Fertilizer	磷肥 Phosphate Fertilizer	钾肥 Potash Fertilizer	复合肥 Compound Fertilizer	附：平均每公顷耕地施用化肥量（折纯千克）Annotation: Consumption of Chemical Fertilizer Per Hectare
全市	**Whole Municipality**	**278251**	**43634**	**11292**	**15441**	**207885**	**537**
崂山区	Laoshan District	363	51	18	15	279	404
黄岛区	Huangdao District	33605	6313	2469	3766	21057	453
城阳区	Chengyang District	1016	190	83	87	656	152
即墨区	Jimo District	37912	13949	2320	1144	20499	381
胶州市	Jiaozhou	35531	6268	971	4226	24066	557
平度市	Pingdu	119761	6325	1576	5727	106132	650
莱西市	Laixi	50064	10538	3854	475	35197	560

注：城阳区包括红岛经济区。
Note: Chengyang District includes Hongdao Economic Zone.

11-25 分市、区农田水利（2017年）
FARMLAND WATER CONSERVANCY BY REGION（2017）

市、区名称	Region	有效灌溉面积（公顷）Irrigated Area（hectare）	有效灌溉面积占耕地面积比重（%）Percentage of Irrigated Area to Area of Cultivated Land（%）	农业排灌机械拥有量（万台/万千瓦）Ownership of Drainage and Irrigation Machinery（10 000 sets/10000 kW）	农用水泵（万台）Agricultural Pump（10 000 sets）	节水喷灌机械（万套）Water saving sprinkler irrigation machinery（10 000 set）	机电井数（眼）Number of Electromechanical Well（well）
全市	**Whole Municipality**	**329620**	**63.6**	**19.1/128.3**	**14**	**8.9**	**139342**
崂山区	Laoshan District	520	57.9				1307
黄岛区	Huangdao District	44990	60.7	0.7/6.1	1.2	0.9	10229
城阳区	Chengyang District	3670	54.9	0.6/4.5	0.4	0.3	1027
即墨区	Jimo District	59740	60.1	2.1/14.9	2.1	1.9	37409
胶州市	Jiaozhou	39510	62.0	1.4/11.3	0.8	1.4	17726
平度市	Pingdu	127420	69.2	12.5/80.6	7.1	1.8	44687
莱西市	Laixi	53770	60.2	1.8/10.9	2.4	2.6	26957

注：城阳区包括红岛经济区。
Note：Chengyang District includes Hongdao Economic Zone.

11-26 分市、区主要农业机械拥有量（2017 年）
OWNERSHIP OFMAJOR AGRICULTURAL MACHINERY BY RGION（2017）

市、区名称	Region	农业机械总动力（万千瓦）Agricultural Machinery Power（10 000 kW）	平均每公顷耕地拥有量（千瓦）Power Per Hectare of Cultivated Land（kW）	大中型拖拉机 Large and Medium Trators		小型拖拉机 Small Tractors	
				台 set	千瓦 kW	台 set	千瓦 kW
全市	**Whole Municipality**	**728.0**	**14.0**	**50894**	**2175069**	**163905**	**1374936**
崂山区	Laoshan District						
黄岛区	Huangdao District	85.4	11.5	3890	116820	43464	287941
城阳区	Chengyang District	30.7	45.9	444	14949	1547	10639
即墨区	Jimo District	109.6	11.0	7941	288738	31423	259365
胶州市	Jiaozhou	105.8	16.6	6717	339370	18377	257278
平度市	Pingdu	265.7	14.4	23557	1087684	33723	320365
莱西市	Laixi	130.8	14.6	8345	327508	35371	239348

注：黄岛区包括保税区，城阳区包括红岛经济区。
Note：Huangdao District includes Bonded Port Area, and Chengyang District includes Hongdao Economic Zone.

11-26 续表
Coutinued

市、区名称	Region	种植机械（台）Planting machinery（unit）	机引犁（部）Towing Ploughs（unit）	机引耙（部）Towing Rakes（unit）	粮食加工机械（台）Grain Processing Machinery（unit）	油料加工机械（部）Oill Processing Machinery（unit）	棉花加工机械（部）Cotton Processing Machinery（unit）	饲草料加工机械 Forage processing machinery（unit）
全市	**Whole Municipality**	**62041**	**125710**	**27989**	**25681**	**9144**	**132**	**23074**
崂山区	Laoshan District							
黄岛区	Huangdao District	2202	32920	109	1115	256		3544
城阳区	Chengyang District	772	1200	207	1605	520	17	338
即墨区	Jimo District	12806	19958	1680	3259	1472		1481
胶州市	Jiaozhou	9394	15113	5242	3050	2125		3570
平度市	Pingdu	28430	21850	16500	4372	1421	6	7538
莱西市	Laixi	8437	34669	4251	12280	3350	109	6603

注：城阳区包括红岛经济区。
Note：Chengyang District includes Hongdao Economic Zone.

主要统计指标解释

农业总产值　是以货币表现的农、林、牧、渔业全部产品的总量，它反映一定时期内农业生产的总规模和总成果。

农、林、牧、渔业的统计范围是：

（1）农业包括农作物种植业和其他农业。

农作物种植业包括谷物、豆类、薯类、棉、油料、糖料、麻类、烟叶、蔬菜、药材、瓜类和其他农作物的种植，以及茶园、桑园、果园的生产经营。其他农业包括采集野生植物的果实、纤维、树胶、树脂、油料以及柴草、野生药材、菌类等及农民家庭兼营的商品性工业。

（2）林业包括林木的栽培（不包括茶园、桑园和果园的栽培、管理和收获等活动）、林产品的采集和村及村以下合作经济组织和农户的竹木采伐。

（3）牧业包括除渔业养殖以外的一切动物饲养和放牧，以及野生动物的捕猎和饲养。

（4）渔业包括水生动物和海藻类植物的养殖和捕捞。

粮食产量　指稻谷、小麦、玉米、高粱等谷物及薯类和豆类的全社会产量。包括国有经济经营的、集体统一经营的和农民家庭经营的粮食产量，还包括工矿企业办的农场和其他生产单位的产量。其产量计算方法，豆类按去豆荚后的干豆计算；薯类（包括甘薯和马铃薯，不包括芋头和木薯）按 5 公斤鲜薯折 1 公斤粮食计算。城市郊区作为蔬菜的薯类（如马铃薯等）按鲜品计算，并且不作粮食统计。其他粮食一律按脱粒后的原粮计算。

水产品产量　指人工养殖的水产品和天然生长的水产品的捕捞量。包括海水的鱼类、虾蟹类、贝类和藻类以及内陆水域的鱼类、虾蟹类和贝类，不包括淡水生植物。

猪、牛、羊肉产量　指当年出栏并已屠宰、除去头蹄下水后带骨头肉（即胴体重）的重量。其统计范围为全社会。

农用化肥施用量　指本年内实际用于农业生产的化肥数量，包括氮肥、磷肥、钾肥和复合肥。化肥施用量要求按折纯量计算数量。折纯量是指把氮肥、磷肥、钾肥分别按含氮、含五氧化二磷、含氧化钾的百分之百成分进行折算后的数量。复合肥按其所含主要成分折算。

公式：折纯量＝实物量 × 某种化肥有效成分含量的百分比

农业机械总动力　指用于农、林、牧、渔业生产的各种动力机械的动力总和。动力机械包括耕作、排灌、种植、植物保护、收获、农产品加工、运输、畜牧、渔业、农田水利等各种机械。不包括专门用于乡办工业、基本建设、非农业运输、科学试验和教学等非农业生产方面用的动力机械与作业机械的数量。

Explanatory Notes on Main Statistical Indicators

Gross Output Value of Agriculture　refers to the total volume of products of farming, forestry, animal husbandry, and fishery expressed in the monetary terms. It reflects the overall scale and achievements of agricultural production during a given period of time.

The scope of statistics on farming, forestry, animal husbandry, and fishery are as follows :

Farming includes cultivation of farm crops and other agricultural activities.

Cultivation of farm crops include cultivation of grain crops, legume crops, tuber-crops, cotton, oil-bearing crops, sugar crops, and cultivation and management of tea plantations, mulberry fields and orchards.

Other agricultural activities include harvesting wild fruits, fiber, tree gum, resin, oil-bearing plants, firewood, wild medicinal herbs, fungus, and rural-household commodity industries.

Forestry refers to planting trees of various kinds (excluding tea plantations, mulberry fields and orchards), collection of forestry products and cutting and felling of bamboo and trees by villages and other cooperative organizations under village level.

Animal husbandry refers to raising and grazing of all kinds of farm animals except fishing and aquatic cultivating, and hunting and rising of wild animals.

Fishery refers to cultivation and catching of fish and other aquatic products and cultivation and collection of seaweed and other aquatic plants.

Grain Output refers to the total output of rice, wheat, corn, sorghum, millet and other miscellaneous grains as well as tubers and bean in the whole country including grains produced by states farms, collective unit, industrial enterprises and mines, output of beans refers to dry beans without pods, the output of tubers (sweet potatoes and potatoes, excluding taros and cassava) was converted into that of grain at the ratio 5 : 1, i. e. 5 kilograms of fresh tubers was equivalent to 1 kilogram of grain, tubers supplies as vegetalbe (such as potatoes) in cities and suburbs are calculated as fresh vegetables and their output is not included in the output of grain output of all other grains refers to husked grain.

Output of Aquatic Products refers to catches of both artificially cultured and naturally grown aquatic products, including fish, shrimps, crabs and shellfish in sea and inland water as well as seaweed. Freshwater plants are not included.

Output of Pork, Beef, and Muttonrefers to the meat of slaughtered hogs, cattle, sheep and goats with head, feet, and offal taken away. Data refers to the production of the whole country.

Consumption of Chemical Fertilizers in Agriculture refers to the quantity of chemical fertilizers applied in agriculture in the year, including nitrogenous fertilizer, phosphate fertilizer, potash fertilizer, and compound fertilizer. The consumption of chemical fertilizers in required in calculation to convert the gross weight into weight containing 100% effective component (e. g. 100% nitrogen content in nitrogenous fertilizer, 100% phosphorous pent oxide contents in phosphate fertilizer, 100% potassium oxide contents in potash fertilizer). Compound fertilizer is converted with its major component. The formula is:

Volume of effective component = physical quantity × effective component of certain chemical fertilizer (%)

Total Power of Agriculture Machinery Refers to the total mechanical power of machinery used in farming forestry animal husbandry and fishery, including machines used for ploughing, irrigation and drainage, crop growing, plant protection, harvesting, farm product processing, transport, stock breeding, fishery and water conservancy, Machinery employed for non agricultrual purposes such as township industry, capital construction, non-agricultrual transport, scientific experiments and for teaching is excluded.

工　业　12

INDUSTRY

简要说明

一、本篇资料的主要内容

本篇资料主要反映了全市工业生产和基本效益情况，主要包括工业企业单位数、历年工业总产值、规模以上工业、国有控股工业、集体工业、外商投资和港澳台投资工业、大中型工业企业的主要经济指标、相关的财务分析指标和主要工业产品产量等方面的内容。

二、本篇资料的来源

1、本篇中规模以上工业资料来源于工业统计年报，由市统计局工业统计处整理提供。

2、规模以下工业资料产值与单位数均来源于抽样调查推算，工业单位数除普查年度外无分市（区）数据，由国家统计局青岛调查队工业与投资建筑业调查处整理提供。

Brief Introduction

Ⅰ. Main Content

Data in this chapter show the basic conditions of industrial production and benefit in Qingdao, mainly including the number of industrial enterprises, gross industrial output value and indices, the output of major industrial products and major economic and relevant financial indicators of industrial enterprises. Industrial enterprises include enterprises above designated size, state share-holding enterprises, collective owned enterprises, foreign funded enterprises, enterprises with funds from Hong Kong, Macao and Taiwan, large and medium sized enterprises.

Ⅱ. Source of Data

（1）Data on industry above designated size are based on the annual report of industrial statistics, and prepared by the Division of Industry Statistics of Qingdao Municipal Bureau of Statistics.

（2）Data on output value and unit number of industry below designated size are based on the sample survey, and there is no data on number of enterprises by region except census year. The Data are complied by the Division of Industry, Investment and Construction Survey of Survey Office of the National Bureau of Statistics in Qingdao.

12-1 规模以上工业企业单位数
NUMBER OF INDUSTRIAL ENTERPRISES ABOVE DESIGNATEO SIZE

单位：个（unit）

项　目	Item	1985 年	1990 年	1995 年	2000 年	2005 年	2006 年
总　计	**Total**	**2411**	**2997**	**4987**	**1504**	**3697**	**4567**
一、按隶属关系分	**Grouped by Subordination**						
中央工业	Central Indiustry	24	16	102	18	26	17
省属工业	Provincial Industry	26	22	64	7	37	33
地方工业	Local Industry	2361	2959	4821	1479	3634	4517
二、按经济类型分	**Gronped by Economic Types**						
国有企业	State-owned	502	568	1084	179	76	74
集体企业	Gollective-owned	1907	2386	2731	226	87	72
其他经济类型企业	Other Economic Types	2	43	1172	1099	3534	4421
# 外商及港澳台商投资企业	Foreign Funded Enterprises and Enterprises with Funds from Hong Kong，Macao and Taiwan		35	1027	593	1658	1952
三、按轻重工业分	**Grouped by Light and Heavy Industries**						
轻工业	Light Industry	1398	1730	2858	891	1942	2313
重工业	Heavy Industry	1013	1267	2129	613	1755	2254
四、按企业规模分	**Grouped by Size of Enterprises**						
大型企业	Large	26	42	89	202	51	51
中型企业	Medium	80	168	216	229	441	469
小型企业	Small	2305	2787	4480	1073	3205	4047
五、按行业分	**Grouped by sectors**						
黑色金属矿采选业	Miring of Non-ferrous Metal Ores		4	6	1	2	5
有色金属矿采选业	Mining of Non-ferrous Metal Ores	2	7	9	7	5	5
非金属矿采选业	Mining and Processing of Nometal Ores	43	70	87	29	34	31
食品制造业	Manufacture of Foods	244	324	437	170	121	137
# 粮食及饲料加工	Processing of Gren and Feed	62	57	60	27		
饮料制造业	Manufacture of Beverage	31	44	74	23	29	28
# 饮料酒	Beverage Liquor	20	28	27	19	20	25

注：1. 规模以上工业企业为年主营业务收入 2000 万元及以上的工业法人企业 。
2. 2010 年以前为国有及年主营业务收入 500 万元以上的非国有工业企业。
3. 本表 1998 年以前为乡及乡以上工业企业单位数。
4. 2012 年行业分类按 2011 年发布的《国民经济行业分类》（GB/T4754-2011）重新划分。

Note：1. Industrial enterprises above designated siza refers to industrial enterprises with revenue from pricipal business over 20 millinon yuan.
2. Before 2010，industrial enterprises above designated size refered to all the state-owned enterprises and non-state enterprises with revennie from principal business over 5 million yuan.
3. Before 1998，the number of industrial enterprises refer to those at and above county level.
4.The seetors are grouped by "Classification Code of the Sectors of the National Economy"（GB/T4754-2011）in 2012.

12-1 续表 1
Continued

单位：个（unit）

项 目	Item	2007 年	2008 年	2009 年	2010 年	2011 年
总 计	**Total**	**5032**	**5628**	**5895**	**5674**	**4727**
一、按隶属关系分	**Grouped by Subordination**					
中央工业	Central Indiustry	9	40	44	31	31
省属工业	Provincial Industry	34	28	25	25	17
地方工业	Local Industry	4989	5560	5826	5618	4679
二、按经济类型分	**Gronped by Economic Types**					
国有企业	State-owned	63	65	163	61	147
集体企业	Gollective-owned	72	61	59	53	31
其他经济类型企业	Other Economic Types	4897	5502	5673	5560	4549
# 外商及港澳台商投资企业	Foreign Funded Enterprises and Enterprises with Funds from Hong Kong，Macao and Taiwan	2091	2217	2244	2037	1618
三、按轻重工业分	**Grouped by Light and Heavy Industries**					
轻工业	Light Industry	2489	2704	2805	2635	2131
重工业	Heavy Industry	2543	2924	3090	3039	2596
四、按企业规模分	**Grouped by Size of Enterprises**			0		
大型企业	Large	53	48	50	52	50
中型企业	Medium	489	519	502	525	516
小型企业	Small	4490	5061	5343	5097	4161
五、按行业分	**Grouped by sectors**					
黑色金属矿采选业	Miring of Non-ferrous Metal Ores	7	23	22	12	12
有色金属矿采选业	Mining of Non-ferrous Metal Ores	5	6	6	4	
非金属矿采选业	Mining and Processing of Nometal Ores	33	30	26	26	23
食品制造业	Manufacture of Foods	156	158	174	167	127
# 粮食及饲料加工	Processing of Gren and Feed					
饮料制造业	Manufacture of Beverage	33	40	42	42	36
# 饮料酒	Beverage Liquor					

12-1 续表 2
Continued

单位：个（unit）

项　目	Item	1985年	1990年	1995年	2000年	2005年	2006年
烟草制品业	Manufacture of Tobacco	2	2	5	3	2	2
纺织业	Manufacture of Textile	169	225	330	132	300	327
纺织服装、鞋、帽制造业	Manfacture of Testilee Wearing Apparel. Footware and Caps	171	194	322	95	272	339
皮革、毛皮、羽毛(绒)及其制品业	Manufacture of Leather, Fur, Feather and Related Products	56	64	161	64	167	194
木材加工制品业	Processing of Woon and Wood Prodncts	71	89	116	19	40	53
家具制造业	Manufacture of Furniture	61	72	88	10	72	103
造纸及纸制品业	Manufacture of Paper and Paper Producls	66	74	110	56	102	128
印刷业和记录媒介的复制	Printing, Reproduction of Recording Media	61	81	215	23	44	59
文教体育用品制造业	Manufacture of Articles For Culture, Education and Sport Activities	31	27	93	48	89	91
石油、煤炭及其他燃料加工业	Oil, coal and other fuel processing industries	2	3	13	5	10	6
化学原料及制品	Manufacture of Raw Chemical Materials and Chemical Products	106	156	278	81	178	233
医药制造业	Manufacture of Medicines	16	14	39	20	30	46
化学纤维制造业	Manufacure of Chemical Fibers	2	4	26	15	14	13
橡胶制品业	Manufacture of Rubber	53	57	143	48	116	170
塑料制品业	Manufacture of Plastics	103	131	237	64	153	179
非金属矿物制品业	Manufacture of Non-mettallic Mineral Products	230	245	275	62	161	218
黑色金属压延加工业	Smelting and Pressing of Ferrous Metals	11	13	31	15	41	45
有色金属压延加工业	Smelting and Pressing of Non-ferrous Metals	6	8	19	9	28	40
金属制品业	Manufacture of Metal Products	161	186	372	88	186	250
通用设备制造业	Manufacture of General Purpose Machinery	320	398	320	94	299	397
交通运输制造业	Manufacture of Electrical Machinery and Equipment	104	114	358	52	151	194
电气机械及器材制造业	Manufacture of Electrication Machinery and Equipment	86	96	211	79	214	249
通信设备、计算机及其他电子设备制造业	Manufacture of Communication Equipment, Computers and Other Eleetronic Equipment	32	31	79	34	123	140
仪器仪表及文化、办公用机械制造业	Manufacture of Measuring Instruments and Machinery for Cultural Activity and Office Work	28	33	70	20	40	44
水的生产和供应业	Production and Supply of Water	8	12	12	8	10	10
电力、热力的生产和供应业	Production and Supply of Electric Power and Heat Power	10	16	20	17	27	32
燃气生产和供应业	Production and Supply of Gas	1	4	3	2	5	6
其他工业	Other Industrial Sectors	46	48	209	63	166	534

12-1 续表 3
Continued

单位：个（unit）

项　目	Item	2007年	2008年	2009年	2010年	2011年
烟草制品业	Manufacture of Tobacco	2	2	2	1	1
纺织业	Manufacture of Textile	340	330	322	287	229
纺织服装、鞋、帽制造业	Manfacture of Testilee Wearing Apparel. Footware and Caps	362	418	434	392	295
皮革、毛皮、羽毛(绒)及其制品业	Manufacture of Leather，Fur，Feather and Related Products	197	209	210	211	160
木材加工制品业	Processing of Woon and Wood Prodncts	64	66	68	68	49
家具制造业	Manufacture of Furniture	119	130	133	117	97
造纸及纸制品业	Manufacture of Paper and Paper Producls	126	133	133	138	101
印刷业和记录媒介的复制	Printing，Reproduction of Recording Media	63	74	79	92	58
文教体育用品制造业	Manufacture of Articles For Culture，Education and Sport Activities	97	96	99	90	75
石油、煤炭及其他燃料加工业	Oil, coal and other fuel processing industries	7	7	9	8	7
化学原料及制品	Manufacture of Raw Chemical Materials and Chemical Products	261	276	275	262	231
医药制造业	Manufacture of Medicines	48	49	56	52	44
化学纤维制造业	Manufacure of Chemical Fibers	12	13	14	12	10
橡胶制品业	Manufacture of Rubber	183	211	214	196	187
塑料制品业	Manufacture of Plastics	199	227	234	233	169
非金属矿物制品业	Manufacture of Non-mettallic Mineral Products	259	311	320	327	303
黑色金属压延加工业	Smelting and Pressing of Ferrous Metals	39	24	27	31	29
有色金属压延加工业	Smelting and Pressing of Non-ferrous Metals	40	41	40	35	34
金属制品业	Manufacture of Metal Products	271	347	376	361	294
通用设备制造业	Manufacture of General Purpose Machinery	473	535	592	597	521
交通运输制造业	Manufacture of Electrical Machinery and Equipment	217	264	290	296	263
电气机械及器材制造业	Manufacture of Electrication Machinery and Equipment	274	303	300	281	230
通信设备、计算机及其他电子设备制造业	Manufacture of Communication Equipment，Computers and Other Eleetronic Equipment	152	163	168	167	124
仪器仪表及文化、办公用机械制造业	Manufacture of Measuring Instruments and Machinery for Cultural Activity and Office Work	47	47	55	54	39
水的生产和供应业	Production and Supply of Water	10	13	14	14	11
电力、热力的生产和供应业	Production and Supply of Electric Power and Heat Power	34	36	39	38	36
燃气生产和供应业	Production and Supply of Gas	7	13	13	14	11
其他工业	Other Industrial Sectors	895	1033	1109	1049	921

12-1 续表 4
Continued

单位：个（unit）

项　目	Item	2012 年	2013 年	2014 年	2015 年	2016 年	2017 年
总计	**Total**	**4817**	**4917**	**4790**	**4876**	**4431**	**3569**
一、按隶属关系分	**Grouped by Subordination Relation**						
中央工业	Central Indiustry	15	30	28	33	27	32
省属工业	Provincial Industry	18	16	15	12	6	5
地方工业	Local Industry	4784	4871	4747	4831	4398	3532
二、按经济类型分	**Gronped by Eeonomic Types**						
国有企业	State-owned	144	140	132	141	128	131
集体企业	Gollective-owned	28	24	19	15	11	5
其他经济类型企业	Other Economic Types	4645	4753	4639	4720	4292	3433
#外商及港澳台商投资企业	Foreign Funded Enterprises and Enterprises with Funds from Hong Kong，Macao and Taiwan	1599	1551	1445	1361	1205	1037
三、按轻重工业分	**Grouped by Light and Heavy Industries**						
轻工业	Light Industry	2153	2190	2080	2095	1875	1522
重工业	Heavy Industry	2664	2727	2710	2781	2556	2047
四、按企业规模分	**Grouped by Size of Enterprises**						
大型企业	Large	98	97	91	89	85	78
中型企业	Medium	596	599	568	566	516	459
小型企业	Small	4123	4221	4131	4221	3830	3032
五、按行业分	**Grouped by sectors**						
黑色金属矿采选业	Miring of Ferrous Metal Ores	10	11	8	7	1	0
非金属矿采选业	Mining and processing of Nometal Ores	14	13	7	6	5	2
农副食品加工业	Processing of Food from Agricultural Products	454	468	444	458	419	338
食品制造业	Manufacture of Foods	129	123	109	116	115	111
酒、饮料和精制茶制造业	Manufacture of Liquor，Beverage and Refind Tea	34	35	34	38	33	18
烟草制品业	Manufacture of tobacco	1	1	1	1	0	0
纺织业	Manufacture of Textile	181	175	146	133	111	91
纺织服装、服饰业	Manufacture of Texitile Wearing Apparel	312	283	249	244	206	152
皮革、毛皮、羽毛及其制品和制鞋业	Manufacture of Leather，Fur，Feather & Its Products Footwear	177	148	124	116	89	58

12-1 续表 5
Continued

单位：个（unit）

项　目	Item	2012 年	2013 年	2014 年	2015 年	2016 年	2017 年
木材加工和木、竹、藤、棕、草制品业	Processing of Timbers, Manufacture of Wood, Bamboo, Rattan, Palm and Straw Producls	34	40	32	34	31	27
家具制造业	Manufacture of Furniture	103	107	96	98	88	65
造纸和纸制品业	Manufacture of Paper and Paper Producls	100	71	54	52	50	40
印刷和记录媒介复制业	Printing, Reproduction of Recording Media	80	121	150	156	137	110
文教、工美、体育和娱乐用品制造业	Manufacture of Ariticles for Culture, Ars & Crafts, Sports and Entertaiment	263	335	348	345	310	222
石油、煤炭及其他燃料加工业	Oil, coal and other fuel processing industries	8	8	9	9	9	9
化学原料和化学制品制造业	Manufacture of Chemical Raw Material and Chemical Products	224	240	246	249	223	176
医药制造业	Manufacture of Medicines	45	49	50	54	47	35
化学纤维制造业	Manufacure of Chemical Fibers	9	8	8	8	6	7
橡胶和塑料制品业	Manufacture of Rubber and Plastic	350	345	331	310	281	250
非金属矿物制品业	Manufacture of Non-mettallic Mineral Products	325	333	330	338	315	228
黑色金属冶炼和压延加工业	Smelting and Pressing of Ferrous Metals	105	93	87	83	73	27
有色金属冶炼和压延加工业	Smelting and Pressing of Non-ferrous Metals	37	36	38	39	30	23
金属制品业	Manufacture of Metal Products	399	389	380	388	348	289
通用设备制造业	Manufacture of General Purpose Machinery	362	382	395	402	383	301
专用设备制造业	Manufacture of Special Purpose Machinery	312	322	314	336	311	233
汽车制造业	Manufacture of Vehicle	136	141	145	158	154	156
铁路、船舶、航空航天和其他运输设备制造业	Manufacture of Trarisport Epquipment for Railway, Shipping, Aerospace and other uses	145	146	152	168	156	150
电气机械和器材制造业	Manufacture of Electrical Machinery & Equipment	202	212	217	226	211	184
计算机、通信和其他电子设备制造业	Manufactuter of Computer, Communication Equipment and Other Electronic Equpment	137	136	141	147	140	128
仪器仪表制造业	Manufacture of Measuring Instument	41	49	52	58	50	46
其他制造业	Manufacture of Other Products	18	17	13	15	16	10
废弃资源综合利用业	Reeycling and Disposal of Waste Resources	4	6	6	5	6	3
金属制品、机械和设备修理业	Maintenance of Metal Products, Machinery and Equipment	7	7	7	6	5	6
电力、热力生产和供应业	Production and Supply of Electric Power and Heat Power	36	39	40	43	42	43
燃气生产和供应业	Production and Supply of Gas	12	13	12	14	14	14
水的生产和供应业	Production and Supply of water	11	15	15	16	16	17

注：国家统计局根据《国民经济行业分类》（GB/T 4754-2017），对《三次产业划分规定（2012）》中行业类别进行了对应调整，其中"石油加工、炼焦和核燃料加工业"更名为"石油、煤炭及其他燃料加工业"，并将 2011 版《国民经济行业分类》4500 中部分内容和 4120 全部内容调到此类。

Note：According to the national economic industry classification (GB/ T 4754-2017), the National Bureau of Statistics carries out a corresponding adjustment to the three industries according to the classification of the national economy (GB/ T 4754-2017), in which the petroleum processing, coking and nuclear fuel processing industry is changed to petroleum, coal and other fuel processing industries, and the content of part of the content and 4120 of the 2011 edition of the national economy industry category 4500 are transferred to this category.

12-2 分市、区规模以上工业企业数（2017年）
NUMBER OF ALL INDUSTRIAL ENTERPRISES BY REGION（2017）

单位：个（unit）

市、区名称	Region	规模以上 Above Designated	按轻重工业分 Grouped by Light and Heavy Ind		按企业规模分 Grouped by Size of Enterprises		
			轻工业 Light Industry	重工业 Heavy Industry	大型企业 Large	中型企业 Medium	小型企业 Small
全　市	**Whole Municipality**	**3569**	**1522**	**2047**	**78**	**459**	**3032**
市内三区	Three Districts in Urban Area	142	46	96	10	25	107
崂山区	Laoshan District	79	36	43	6	10	63
黄岛区	Huangdao District	721	213	508	19	112	590
城阳区	Chengyang District	486	200	286	10	63	413
即墨区	Jimo District	526	271	255	12	76	438
胶州市	Jiaozhou	736	332	404	6	75	655
平度市	Pingdu	401	185	216	5	38	358
莱西市	Laixi	332	194	138	4	37	291
红岛经济区	Qingdao National High-tech Industrial Development Zone	109	34	75	1	17	91
保税港区	Qingdao Free Trade Port Area of China	37	11	26	5	6	26

12-2 续表
Contiued

单位：个（unit）

市、区名称	Region	按经济类型分 Grouped by Economic Types			
		国有企业 State-owned	集体企业 Gollective-wned	其他经济 Others	#外资及港澳台商企业 Foreign Funded Entreprises and Enterprises with Funds from Kong Kong, Macao and Taiwan
全　市	**Whole Municipality**	**131**	**5**	**3433**	**1037**
市内三区	Three Districts in Urban Area	28	2	112	38
崂山区	Laoshan District	5		74	23
黄岛区	Huangdao District	35		686	189
城阳区	Chengyang District	13	1	472	185
即墨区	Jimo District	11		515	153
胶州市	Jiaozhou	7		729	169
平度市	Pingdu	15	2	384	117
莱西市	Laixi	5		327	102
红岛经济区	Qingdao National High-tech Industrial Development Zone	12		97	40
保税港区	Qingdao Free Trade Port Area of China			37	21

12-3 历年全部工业总产值
GROSS INDUSTRIAL OUTPUT VALUE OVER THE YEARS

单位：万元（10 000 yuan）

年　份 Year	工业总产值 Gross Industrial Output Value	轻工业产值 Light Industry	重工业产值 Heavy Industry
1949	21605	18494	3111
1950	34010	28720	5290
1951	53538	44600	8938
1952	84295	69258	15037
1953	115222	74716	40506
1954	126064	80604	45460
1955	118935	86956	31979
1956	144833	93809	51024
1957	142920	101202	41718
1958	217648	92407	125241
1959	282610	84376	198234
1960	291451	77043	214408
1962	120738	64233	56505
1963	139542	83630	55912
1964	177273	108884	68389
1965	215536	141765	73771
1966	252896	152304	100592
1967	287739	163627	124112
1968	299814	175791	123489
1969	296814	188860	107954
1970	345212	202903	142309

注：本表按当年价格计算，1995 年开始工业总产值按新规定计算。
Note：The data in this form are calculated at current price. Since 1995， new regulations have been adopted in calcnlating gross industrial output value.

12-3 续表 1
Continued

单位：万元（10 000 yuan）

年 份 Year	工业总产值 Gross Industrial Output Value	轻工业产值 Light Industry	重工业产值 Heavy Industry
1971	365770	216172	149598
1972	378266	230309	147957
1973	377943	245371	132572
1974	237219	154054	83165
1975	402541	261418	141123
1976	439793	278514	161279
1977	490669	296728	193941
1978	565503	336817	228686
1979	625227	379276	245951
1980	677690	442078	235612
1981	707434	479954	227480
1982	732705	474767	257938
1983	816793	513759	303034
1984	918364	569080	349284
1985	1113891	699524	414367
1986	1316230	833864	482366
1987	1703830	1065873	637957
1988	2481594	1451215	1030379
1989	3191643	1857019	1334624
1990	3571845	2057968	1513878

12-3 续表 2
Continued

单位：万元（10 000 yuan）

年 份	Year	工业总产值 Gross Industrial Output Value	轻工业产值 Light Industry	重工业产值 Heavy Industry
1991	1991	3986427	2318257	1668170
1992	1992	4826834	2835728	1991106
1993	1993	5929236	3422107	2507129
1994	1994	8456974	4931262	3525712
1995	1995	9412635	5579637	3832998
1996	1996	11173672	6793007	4380665
1997	1997	13704735	8620710	5084025
1998	1998	15794106	10153634	5640472
1999	1999	16822436	10918827	5903609
2000	2000	19408338	12433214	6975124
2001	2001	22398464	14368582	8029882
2002	2002	25794324	14811106	10983218
2003	2003	31195595	17306539	13889056
2004	2004	39590783	21473202	18117581
2005	2005	50017829	24697792	25320037
2006	2006	59188120	28686826	30501294
2007	2007	74306364	33463071	40843293
2008	2008	89467300	37871227	51596073
2009	2009	102556155	42715781	59840374
2010	2010	116148345	44954630	71193715
2011	2011	132779629	50854938	81924691
2012	2012	153102565	60516341	92546833
2013	2013	168971805	66799317	102172488
2014	2014	174442125	67683545	106758580
2015	2015	180194299	71176748	109017551
2016	2016	174157133	68552071	105605062
2017	2017	130197344	48954201	81243142
“一五”时期合计	“First Five-Year Plan” Peiod	647974	437287	210687
“二五”时期合计	“Second Five-Year Plan” Peiod	1077075	388406	688669
1963-1965 年合计	1963-1965	532351	334279	198072
“三五”时期合计	“Third Five-Year Plan” Peiod	1481941	883485	598456
“四五”时期合计	“Fourth Five-Year Plan” Peiod	1761739	1107324	654415
“五五”时期合计	“Fifth Five-Year Plan” Peiod	2798882	1733413	1065469
“六五”时期合计	“Sixth Five-Year Plan” Peiod	4289187	2737084	1552103
“七五”时期合计	“Seventh Five-Year Plan” Peiod	12265142	7265939	4999204
“八五”时期合计	“Eighth Five-Year Plan” Peiod	32612106	19087323	13524783
“九五”时期合计	“Ninth Five-Year Plan” Peiod	76903287	48919392	27983895
“十五”时期合计	“Tenth Five-Year Plan” Peiod	168996995	92657221	76339774
“十一五”时期合计	“Eleventh Five-Year Plan” Peiod	175336465	73641456	101695009
“十二五”时期合计	“Twelveth Five-Year Plan” Peiod	809490422	317030889	492420143

12-4 分市、区全部工业总产值（2017年）
GROSS INDUSTRIAL OUTPUT VALUE BY REGION（2017）

单位：万元（10 000 yuan）

市、区名称	Region	工业总产值 Gross Industrial Output Value	规模以上 Above Designated Size	外商及港澳台商投资企业 Foreign Funded Entreprises and Enterprises with Funds from Kong Kong，Macao and Taiwan	规模以下 Below Dexignated Size
全 市	**Whole Municipality**	**130197344**	**118953144**	**30290113**	**11244200**
市内三区	Three Districts in Urban Area	7111543	6521703	1831048	589840
崂山区	Laoshan District	5249919	4831919	811649	418000
黄岛区	Huangdao District	44486717	42544317	9684132	1942400
城阳区	Chengyang District	14204607	12419807	3008414	1784800
即墨区	Jimo District	19907915	17889415	4904634	2018500
胶州市	Jiaozhou	18151550	16527050	3750240	1624500
平度市	Pingdu	9632661	8167661	2432055	1465000
莱西市	Laixi	8039503	6745003	2127208	1294500
红岛经济区	Qingdao National High-tech Industrial Development Zone	2474781	2368121	906862	106660
保税港区	Qingdao Free Trade Port Area of Chin	938147	938147	833873	

注：规模以下工业黄岛区包含保税港区。
Note: Huangdao below the scale industry includes bonded port area.

12-5 分市、区规模以上工业总产值（2017 年）
GROSS INDUSTRIAL OUTPUT VALUE ABOVE DESIGNATED SIZE BY REGION（2017）

指标	Indicator	总　计 Total	市内三区 Three Districts in Urban Area	崂山区 Laoshan District	黄岛区 Huangdao District
总　　计	**Total**	**118953144**	**6521703**	**4831919**	**42544317**
按隶属关系分	**Groped by Subordination**				
中央	Centrality	16576754	1658455	98956	7228624
省（自治区、直辖市）	Province（Autonmous Region，Municipality）	102257			51200
市（地级）	Municipality（Local level）	23749676	2581912	3061512	12569434
县级及以下	At and below the county level	2218665	14460		163593
其它	Others	76305792	2266876	1671451	22531466
按登记注册类型分	**Grouped by Status of Registration**				
国有经济	State-owned	29189975	2430289	205738	15786173
集体经济	Collecive-owned	9318929	963446	2603976	5669650
其他经济	Others	80444239	3127968	2022205	21088494
#外资与港澳台企业	Foreign Funded Enterprises and Enterprises with Funds fron Hong Kong，Macao and Taiwan	30290113	1831048	811649	9684132
按轻重工业分	**Grouped by Light and Heavy Industries**				
轻工业	Light Industry	44724236	2926460	3365715	13256041
重工业	Heavy Industry	74228908	3595243	1466204	29288276
按企业规模分	**Grouped by Size of Enterprises**				
大型企业	Large	42194579	3910644	3549955	17528295
中型企业	Medium	27236166	1138891	548493	12695274
小型企业	Small	49522399	1472169	733470	12320747

注：部分数据因四舍五入的原因，存在着分项合计不等的情况。
Note：Some of the data are unequal to subtotal due to rounding.

单位：万元（10 000 yuan）

城阳区 Chengyang District	即墨区 Jimo District	胶州市 Jiaozhou	平度市 Pingdu	莱西市 Laixi	红岛经济区 Qingdao National High-tech Industrial Development Zone	保税港区 Qingdao Free Trade Port Area China
12419807	**17889415**	**16527050**	**8167661**	**6745003**	**2368121**	**938147**
4490675	2878515		7741		213788	
34870			16187			
1505870	1695643	68243	1676279	32252	554116	4417
908713	50367	476465	423577	148453	6948	26089
5479679	13264890	15982343	6043877	6564298	1593270	907641
5204376	3126108	239467	1398696	55301	743827	
59522			22335			
7155909	14763307	16287583	6746630	6689703	1624295	938147
3008414	4904634	3750240	2432055	2127208	906862	833873
1941239	8410343	6488694	3516596	4199724	459006	160417
10478568	9479072	10038356	4651065	2545279	1909115	777730
6229685	5871288	813418	2086246	1366629	273783	564635
2251407	3360029	3159642	1163536	1888495	855112	175286
3938715	8658098	12553990	4917879	3489879	1239226	198226

12-5 续表
Continued

指标	Indicator	总计 Total	市内三区 Three Districts in Urban Area
按行业分	**Grouped by Industrial Sector**	**118953144**	**6521703**
煤炭开采和洗选业	Mining and Washing of Coal		
石油和天然气开采业	Extraction of Petroleum and Natural Gas		
黑色金属矿采选业	Mining of Ferrous Metal Ores		
有色金属矿采选业	Mining of Non-ferrous Metal Ores		
非金属矿采选业	Mining and Processing of Nometal Ores	7805	
开采辅助活动	Auxiliary Activities of Mining		
其他采矿业	Mining of Other Ores		
农副食品加工业	Processing of Food from Agricultural Products	9948592	1001806
食品制造业	Manufacture of Foods	2868153	53954
酒、饮料和精制茶制造业	Manufacture of Liquor, Beverage and Refind Tea	1647659	595556
烟草制品业	Manufacture of Tobacco		
纺织业	Manufacture of Textile	1020774	38517
纺织服装、服饰业	Manufacture of Textile Wearing Apparel	3203639	11888
皮革、毛皮、羽毛及其制品和制鞋业	Processing of Leather, Fur, Feather & Its Products Footwear	1368008	9933
木材加工和木、竹、藤、棕、草制品业	Processing of Timbers, Manufacture of Wood, Bamboo, Rattan, Palm and Straw Products	323038	
家具制造业	Manufacture of Furniture	732953	23231
造纸和纸制品业	Manufacture of Paper and Paper Products	647045	
印刷和记录媒介复制业	Printing, Reproduction of Recording Media	2214668	97602
文教、工美、体育和娱乐用品制造业	Manufacture of Articles for Culture, Arts & Crafts, Sports and Entertainment	5096538	54360
石油、煤炭及其他燃料加工业	Oil, coal and other fuel processing industries	6925864	994421
化学原料和化学制品制造业	Manufacture of Chemical Raw Material and Chemical Products	5650523	143956
医药制造业	Manufacture of Medicines	1521073	20508
化学纤维制造业	Manufacture of Chemical Fibers	137287	
橡胶和塑料制品业	Manufacture of Rubber and Plastic	5363948	52851
非金属矿物制品业	Manufacture of Non-mettallic Mineral Products	3560829	135638
黑色金属冶炼和压延加工业	Smelting and Pressing of Ferrous Metals	2796288	
有色金属冶炼和压延加工业	Smelting and Pressing of Nonferrous Metals	727142	
金属制品业	Manufacture of Metal Products	6289873	20929
通用设备制造业	Manufacture of General Purpose Machinery	6079924	405737
专用设备制造业	Manufacture of Special Purpose Machinery	4654774	82302
汽车制造业	Manufacture of Vehicle	9952867	100954
铁路、船舶、航空航天和其他运输设备制造业	Manufacture of Transport Equipment for Railway, Shipping, Aerospace and other uses	8705958	524337
电气机械和器材制造业	Manufacture of Electrical Machinery & Equipment	15115016	1014931
计算机、通信和其他电子设备制造业	Manufacture of Computer, Communication Equipment and Other Electronic Equipment	8939444	367858
仪器仪表制造业	Manufacture of Measuring Instrument	950719	5553
其他制造业	Manufacture of Other Products	129334	14637
废弃资源综合利用业	Recycling and Disposal of Waste Resources	90032	
金属制品、机械和设备修理业	Manufacture of Metal Products, Machinery and Equipment	141048	4546
电力、热力生产和供应业	Production and Supply of Electric Power and Heat Power	1181220	487925
燃气生产和供应业	Production and Supply of Gas	745888	170979
水的生产和供应业	Production and Supply of Water	215224	86797

单位：万元（10 000 yuan）

崂山区 Laoshan District	黄岛区 Huangdao District	城阳区 Chengyang District	即墨区 Jimo District	胶州市 Jiaozhou	平度市 Pingdu	莱西市 Laixi	红岛经济区 Qingdao National High-tech Industrial Development Zone	保税港区 Qingdao Free Trade Port Area China
4831919	**42544317**	**12419807**	**17889415**	**16527050**	**8167661**	**6745003**	**2368121**	**938147**
					7805			
33300	1826316	316798	1446066	1433686	1667924	2073991	132581	16127
124456	1058357	128757	86583	775928	136772	458592	44752	
275014	385675	2264	25487	42142	296302	25220		
19671	64299	190241	222544	170606	74736	200286	9663	30210
10226	253330	166775	2004738	295489	232260	202960	25973	
7697	141978	35269	564278	265545	55507	287802		
	109321	28246	9805	101477	4805	66165	3218	
	11442	78407	41549	504150	54810	13782	5581	
11251	307967	118300	19469	138187	21051	30822		
6461	475969	166507	1069983	240283	9330	101338	44096	3100
4396	454520	200136	1943935	1363342	737070	312796	5420	20565
	5136851	629000	5196	24747	135649			
66048	2577023	385600	728187	745902	437621	299697	261578	4911
198292	409670	77294	472440	116585	16324	85206	124755	
	11037	19662		79556		27032		
67913	2492003	441515	667075	711613	273583	502836	126016	28545
40130	1139663	303886	280468	962209	290040	365376	25421	17998
	2456364	39789	134224	125265	7540	33105		
	63397	27193	111453	94294	382776		48030	
19009	1152971	494175	2097201	1816892	460113	146640	45900	36045
23519	1732969	288067	437129	2145846	486709	175532	211165	173251
65547	1981481	576201	210974	1318272	98295	135487	118974	67241
31423	3387723	1233740	3367911	430426	262490	760080	285343	92777
135164	1643436	4882849	77309	615966	362645	65881	398370	
3305539	7606345	396146	1028429	1451240	58031	124762	64482	65111
132486	4729450	1003820	500018	149437	1363718	59207	270967	362484
221942	129974	58496	38664	243318	107669	33959	91361	19783
5124	17687	24305		4281	63301			
				20579		69454		
	93901		42601					
27314	448234	31437	60773	31251	44617	35127	14542	
	189624	59772	176923	103511	8281	32386	4412	
	55341	15160	18001	5030	9887	19484	5524	

12-6 规模以上工业企业主要指标（2017 年）
MAN INDICATORS OFINDUSTRIAL ENTERPRISES ABOVE DESIGNATED SIZE（2017）

项　目	Indicator	企业单位数（个）Number of Enterprises（Unit）
总　计	**Total**	**3569**
按注册登记类型分	**Grouped by Status of Registration**	
国有及国有控股企业	State-owned and State-holdinig Enterprises	131
集体企业	Gollective-owned Enterprises	5
股份有限公司	Share-holding Corporations Ltd	100
外商投资企业	Fereign Funded Enterprises	817
港澳台商投资企业	Invested by HongKong，Macao and Taiwan	220
按轻重工业分	**Grouped by Light and Heavy Industries**	
轻工业	Light Industry	1522
重工业	Heavy Industry	2047
按企业规模分	**Grouped by Size of Enterprises**	
大型企业	Large	78
中型企业	Medium	459
小型企业	Small	3032
按所在地分	**Grouped by Location**	
市内三区	Three Districts in Urban Area	142
崂山区	Laoshan District	79
黄岛区	Huangdao District	721
城阳区	Chengyang District	486
即墨区	Jimo District	526
胶州市	Jiaozhou	736
平度市	Pingdu	401
莱西市	Laixi	332
红岛经济区	Qingdao National High-tech Industrial Development Zone	109
保税港区	Qingdao Free Trade Port Area of China	37
按行业分	**Grouped by sector**	
煤炭开采和洗选业	Mining and Washing of Coal	
石油和天然气开采业	Extraction of Petroleum and Natural Gas	
黑色金属矿采选业	Mining of Ferrous Metal Ores	
有色金属矿采选业	Mining of Non-ferrous Metoul Ores	
非金属矿采选业	Mining and Processing of Nometal Ores	2
开采辅助活动	Auxiliary Activities of Mining	
其他采矿业	Mining of Other Ores	

单位：万元（10 000 yuan）

工业总产值 Gross Industrial Output Value	资产合计 Total Assets	流动资产年合计 Total Current Assets	固定资产净值 Net Value of Fixed Assets
118953144	**125919134**	**73892594**	**26401359**
29189975	36590508	23734200	7731617
9318929	27275184	15922475	1925712
10952406	16217782	10692005	1888154
23678003	22355930	14285277	5227034
6612110	4834471	3052728	1260575
44724236	48950502	27171243	8491387
74228908	76968632	46721352	17909972
42194579	66785249	43481105	7211504
27236166	27109450	14639192	7793810
49522399	32024435	15772298	11396045
6521703	10602159	5613030	1974484
4831919	11358317	6819782	1080987
42544317	50764162	30182974	9098082
12419807	15123494	11388455	1486644
17889415	10683531	6122174	2835621
16527050	11835232	4959507	5284767
8167661	6548104	3413071	2031723
6745003	4413534	2458747	1600373
2368121	3824443	2452992	783690
938147	766158	481862	224988
7805	15560	9515	4092

12-6 续表 1
Continued

项　目	Indicator	主营业务收入 Revenue from Principal Business
总　计	**Total**	**122253405**
按注册登记类型分	**Grouped by Status of Registration**	
国有及国有控股企业	State-owned and State-holdinig Enterprises	30050089
集体企业	Gollective-owned Enterprises	11699848
股份有限公司	Share-holding Corporations Ltd	10814379
外商投资企业	Fereign Funded Enterprises	24070336
港澳台商投资企业	Invested by HongKong，Macao and Taiwan	7259059
按轻重工业分	**Grouped by Light and Heavy Industries**	
轻工业	Light Industry	48149964
重工业	Heavy Industry	74103441
按企业规模分	**Grouped by Size of Enterprises**	
大型企业	Large	46155403
中型企业	Medium	27163477
小型企业	Small	48934525
按所在地分	**Grouped by Location**	
市内三区	Three Districts in Urban Area	8154238
崂山区	Laoshan District	5791116
黄岛区	Huangdao District	43577886
城阳区	Chengyang District	12569054
即墨区	Jimo District	17530331
胶州市	Jiaozhou	15810300
平度市	Pingdu	9075527
莱西市	Laixi	6469315
红岛经济区	Qingdao National High-tech Industrial Development Zone	2325917
保税港区	Qingdao Free Trade Port Area of China	949721
按行业分	**Grouped by sector**	
煤炭开采和洗选业	Mining and Washing of Coal	
石油和天然气开采业	Extraction of Petroleum and Natural Gas	
黑色金属矿采选业	Mining of Ferrous Metal Ores	
有色金属矿采选业	Mining of Non-ferrous Metoul Ores	
非金属矿采选业	Mining and Processing of Nometal Ores	8458
开采辅助活动	Auxiliary Activities of Mining	
其他采矿业	Mining of Other Ores	

单位：万元（10 000 yuan）

主营业务成本 Cost of Prinipal Business	主营业务税金及附加 Taxes and Extra Charges on Principal Business	利润总额 Total Profits	全部从业人员年平均人数（人） Annual Average Employed Persons（person）
101367543	**2315793**	**7051004**	**813329**
24834500	1445089	1909384	109849
7654116	104449	1102141	21916
9516610	70106	704805	66796
20170813	270764	1327675	220523
6254673	50838	342783	52106
38876223	450764	2757843	363747
62491321	1865028	4293161	449582
36956556	685789	3069364	240953
22249148	1112418	1505023	252121
42161839	517586	2476618	320255
6674259	352245	277227	37864
3995809	53393	535468	29157
35237564	1299343	2801940	193337
10981131	96484	655215	112497
15292480	202285	925986	138322
12935485	213095	901194	125613
7899812	61835	394877	72347
5762989	17819	278107	66882
1793945	15929	190715	21800
794069	3366	90274	15510
5841	435	663	241

12-6 续表 2
Continued

项　目	Indicator	企业单位数（个）Number of Enterprises（Unit）
农副食品加工业	Processing of Food from Agricultural Products	338
食品制造业	Manufacture of Foods	111
酒、饮料和精制茶制造业	Manufacture of Liquor, Beverage and Refind Tea	18
烟草制品业	Manufacture of Tobacco	
纺织业	Manufacture of Textile	91
纺织服装、服饰业	Manufacture of Texitile Wearing Apparel	152
皮革、毛皮、羽毛及其制品和制鞋业	Processing of Leather, Fur, Feather & Its Products Footwear	58
木材加工和木、竹、藤、棕、草制品业	Processing of Timbers, Manufacture of Wood, Bamboo, Rattan, Palm and Straw Products	27
家具制造业	Manufacture of Furniture	65
造纸和纸制品业	Manufacture of Paper and Paper Products	40
印刷和记录媒介复制业	Printing, Reproduction of Recording Media	110
文教、工美、体育和娱乐用品制造业	Manufacture of Articles for Culture, Arts & Crafts, Sports and Entertainment	222
石油、煤炭及其他燃料加工业	Oil, coal and other fuel processing industries	9
化学原料和化学制品制造业	Manufacture of Chemical Raw Material and Chemical Products	176
医药制造业	Manufacture of Medicines	35
化学纤维制造业	Manufacture of Chemical Fibers	7
橡胶和塑料制品业	Manufacture of Rubber and Plastic	250
非金属矿物制品业	Manufacture of Non-mettallic Mineral Products	228
黑色金属冶炼和压延加工业	Smelting and Pressing of Ferrous Metals	27
有色金属冶炼和压延加工业	Smelting and Pressing of Nonferrous Metals	23
金属制品业	Manufacture of Metal Products	289
通用设备制造业	Manufacture of General Purpose Machinery	301
专用设备制造业	Manufacture of Special Purpose Machinery	233
汽车制造业	Manufacture of Vehicle	156
铁路、船舶、航空航天和其他运输设备制造业	Manufacture of Transport Equipment for Railway, Shipping, Aerospace and other uses	150
电气机械和器材制造业	Manufacture of Electrical Machinery & Equipment	184
计算机、通信和其他电子设备制造业	Manufacture of Computer, Communication Equipment and Other Electronic Equipment	128
仪器仪表制造业	Manufacture of Measuring Instrument	46
其他制造业	Manufacture of Other Products	10
废弃资源综合利用业	Recycling and Disposal of Waste Resources	3
金属制品、机械和设备修理业	Manufacture of Metal Products, Machinery and Equipment	6
电力、热力生产和供应业	Production and Supply of Electric Power and Heat Power	43
燃气生产和供应业	Production and Supply of Gas	14
水的生产和供应业	Production and Supply of Water	17

单位：万元（10 000 yuan）

工业总产值 Gross Industrial Output Value	资产合计 Total Assets	流动资产年合计 Total Current Assets	固定资产净值 Net Value of Fixed Assets
9948592	4412678	2412870	1561053
2868153	2238456	1376668	651313
1647659	2554494	974659	383979
1020774	530538	284296	190289
3203639	2441874	1282613	724930
1368008	575694	331731	177846
323038	226696	66960	107897
732953	489008	234672	197798
647045	340206	198096	120032
2214668	1066926	484232	368157
5096538	1915854	839146	782542
6925864	2788545	1212249	1000282
5650523	5613638	2589679	2054501
1521073	1227627	659537	344379
137287	127996	47809	44884
5363948	5394431	2320740	1157458
3560829	3305176	2130767	891761
2796288	2487328	1351412	935046
727142	528036	156450	344751
6289873	5028088	2358770	1805127
6079924	5568233	3334121	1501747
4654774	3998591	2316605	988189
9952867	12128190	9913432	1293952
8705958	12217490	8771134	1492813
15115016	33799638	20043688	2892917
8939444	7173972	5601899	791733
950719	1181020	858582	176693
129334	200310	172500	17592
90032	40266	8185	32081
141048	45865	19708	19035
1181220	3847482	981384	2125938
745888	1309921	245381	832714
215224	1099310	303106	387842

12-6 续表 3
Continued

项　目	Indicator	主营业务收入 Revenue from Principal Business
农副食品加工业	Processing of Food from Agricultural Products	10640094
食品制造业	Manufacture of Foods	2856004
酒、饮料和精制茶制造业	Manufacture of Liquor, Beverage and Refind Tea	2183929
烟草制品业	Manufacture of Tobacco	
纺织业	Manufacture of Textile	1038489
纺织服装、服饰业	Manufacture of Texitile Wearing Apparel	3152430
皮革、毛皮、羽毛及其制品和制鞋业	Processing of Leather, Fur, Feather & Its Products Footwear	1340769
木材加工和木、竹、藤、棕、草制品业	Processing of Timbers, Manufacture of Wood, Bamboo, Rattan, Palm and Straw Products	315256
家具制造业	Manufacture of Furniture	721536
造纸和纸制品业	Manufacture of Paper and Paper Products	601122
印刷和记录媒介复制业	Printing, Reproduction of Recording Media	2083300
文教、工美、体育和娱乐用品制造业	Manufacture of Articles for Culture, Arts & Crafts, Sports and Entertainment	4994732
石油、煤炭及其他燃料加工业	Oil, coal and other fuel processing industries	6893401
化学原料和化学制品制造业	Manufacture of Chemical Raw Material and Chemical Products	5497156
医药制造业	Manufacture of Medicines	1480970
化学纤维制造业	Manufacture of Chemical Fibers	132848
橡胶和塑料制品业	Manufacture of Rubber and Plastic	5150788
非金属矿物制品业	Manufacture of Non-mettallic Mineral Products	3509003
黑色金属冶炼和压延加工业	Smelting and Pressing of Ferrous Metals	2571340
有色金属冶炼和压延加工业	Smelting and Pressing of Nonferrous Metals	740159
金属制品业	Manufacture of Metal Products	6372564
通用设备制造业	Manufacture of General Purpose Machinery	5989606
专用设备制造业	Manufacture of Special Purpose Machinery	4398534
汽车制造业	Manufacture of Vehicle	9667232
铁路、船舶、航空航天和其他运输设备制造业	Manufacture of Transport Equipment for Railway, Shipping, Aerospace and other uses	8983462
电气机械和器材制造业	Manufacture of Electrical Machinery & Equipment	17677100
计算机、通信和其他电子设备制造业	Manufacture of Computer, Communication Equipment and Other Electronic Equipment	9731761
仪器仪表制造业	Manufacture of Measuring Instrument	1018939
其他制造业	Manufacture of Other Products	144857
废弃资源综合利用业	Recycling and Disposal of Waste Resources	88698
金属制品、机械和设备修理业	Manufacture of Metal Products, Machinery and Equipment	144148
电力、热力生产和供应业	Production and Supply of Electric Power and Heat Power	1168436
燃气生产和供应业	Production and Supply of Gas	736463
水的生产和供应业	Production and Supply of Water	219822

单位：万元（10 000 yuan）

主营业务成本 Cost of Principal Business	主营业务税金及附加 Taxes and Extra Charges on Principal Business	利润总额 Total Profits	全部从业人员年平均人数（人） Annual Average Employed Persons（person）
9765274	55597	259020	68865
2144081	26697	164358	17742
1646871	62877	135200	10304
912834	6770	34342	11542
2745963	29462	133486	69605
1136836	8170	77580	32831
283148	3934	17567	2931
602086	8105	33638	11520
553487	2935	16806	5100
1815845	15676	105533	13200
4281876	63098	304098	42542
4965338	1256109	526976	3073
4651898	37558	314464	29435
989279	14602	193856	10244
109958	1371	6977	986
4470069	53243	172994	46270
2978715	29849	183352	26066
2349306	5591	49750	8183
667771	4137	23058	3408
5466370	89854	305811	47426
5007278	63983	314526	53712
3681559	42646	189323	37355
8548311	88829	523061	48560
7582684	90544	807402	57529
12764012	161083	1415316	65322
8163133	63360	576231	56235
776203	9258	106289	9772
126711	2355	22882	3195
73983	362	7443	645
112637	2326	12838	485
1206862	8680	-119227	12043
538215	2234	145934	2561
243109	4064	-10539	4401

12-7 按行业分国有及国有控股工业企业主要指标（2017 年）

MAIN INDICATORS OF STATE-OWNED AND STATE-HOLDING INDUSTRIAL ENTERPRISES BY INDUSTRIAL SECTOR (2017)

项　目	Indicator	企业单位数（个）Number of Enterprises（Unit）
总　计	**Total**	**131**
煤炭开采和洗选业	Mining and Washing of Coal	
石油和天然气开采业	Extraction of Petroleum and Natural Gas	
黑色金属矿采选业	Mining of Ferrous Metal Ores	
有色金属矿采选业	Mining of Non-ferrous Metal Ores	
非金属矿采选业	Mining and Processing of Nometal Ores	1
开采辅助活动	Auxiliary Activities of Mining	
其他采矿业	Mining of Other Ores	
农副食品加工业	Processing of Food from Agricultural Products	
食品制造业	Manufacture of Foods	3
酒、饮料和精制茶制造业	Manufacture of Liquor, Beverage and Refind Tea	1
烟草制品业	Manufacture of Tobacco	
纺织业	Manufacture of Textile	
纺织服装、服饰业	Manufacture of Textile Wearing Apparel	
皮革、毛皮、羽毛及其制品和制鞋业	Manufacture of Leather, Fur, Feather & Its Products Footwear	1
木材加工和木、竹、藤、棕、草制品业	Processing of Timbers, Manufacture of Wood, Bamboo, Rattan, Palm and Straw Products	
家具制造业	Manufacture of Furniture	
造纸和纸制品业	Manufacture of Paper and Paper Products	1
印刷和记录媒介复制业	Printing, Reproduction of Recording Media	1
文教、工美、体育和娱乐用品制造业	Manufacture of Articles for Culture, Arts & Crafts, Sports and Entertainment	1
石油、煤炭及其他燃料加工业	Oil, coal and other fuel processing industries	3
化学原料和化学制品制造业	Manufacture of Chemical Raw Material and Chemical Products	12
医药制造业	Manufacture of Medicines	2
化学纤维制造业	Manufacture of Chemical Fibers	
橡胶和塑料制品业	Manufacture of Rubber and Plastic	7
非金属矿物制品业	Manufacture of Non-mettallic Mineral Products	10
黑色金属冶炼和压延加工业	Smelting and Pressing of Ferrous Metals	3
有色金属冶炼和压延加工业	Smelting and Pressing of Non-ferrous Metals	4
金属制品业	Manufacture of Metal Products	1
通用设备制造业	Manufacture of General Purpose Machinery	8
专用设备制造业	Manufacture of Special Purpose Machinery	4
汽车制造业	Manufacture of Vehicle	5
铁路、船舶、航空航天和其他运输设备制造业	Manufacture of Transport Equipment for Railway, Shipping, Aerospace and other uses	17
电气机械和器材制造业	Manufacture of Electrical Machinery & Equipment	4
计算机、通信和其他电子设备制造业	Manufacture of Computer, Communication Equipment and Other Electronic Equipment	1
仪器仪表制造业	Manufacture of Measuring Instrument	1
其他制造业	Manufacture of Other Products	1
废弃资源综合利用业	Recycling and Disposal of Waste Resources	
金属制品、机械和设备修理业	Manufacture of Metal Products, Machinery and Equipment	1
电力、热力生产和供应业	Production and Supply of Electric Power and Heat Power	23
燃气生产和供应业	Production and Supply of Gas	4
水的生产和供应业	Production and Supply of Water	11

单位：万元（10 000 yuan）

工业总产值 Gross Industrial Output Value	资产合计 Total Assets	流动资产年合计 Total Current Assets	固定资产净值 Net Value of Fixed Assets
29189975	**36590508**	**23734200**	**7731617**
4921	10507	7001	1553
59405	53417	45393	3185
22457	51628	31934	13111
9933	14024	11027	1720
149982	62701	31236	31465
5249	10570	3924	6010
137492	14167	13001	1166
6665921	2608909	1120164	928479
572959	1639207	525255	879681
240894	239703	150534	56422
612550	1134511	557910	154632
208600	296690	232347	41490
1577139	1803296	866089	770735
69743	299537	25710	270582
17230	59697	19835	39862
224738	511958	318229	75021
110480	218305	103264	110553
5043879	7342413	6663033	422607
5880030	9786325	7303483	947652
765139	856334	564299	75597
5325615	5020636	4142020	290424
954	9436	6179	65
8765	33003	28620	1380
4546	2420	2368	52
993951	2633253	596054	1690358
302512	894092	130240	568875
174891	983771	235053	348942

12-7 续表
Continued

项　目	Indicator	主营业务收入 Revenue from Principal Business
总　计	**Total**	**30050089**
煤炭开采和洗选业	Mining and Washing of Coal	
石油和天然气开采业	Extraction of Petroleum and Natural Gas	
黑色金属矿采选业	Mining of Ferrous Metal Ores	
有色金属矿采选业	Mining of Non-ferrous Metal Ores	
非金属矿采选业	Mining and Processing of Nometal Ores	5945
开采辅助活动	Auxiliary Activities of Mining	
其他采矿业	Mining of Other Ores	
农副食品加工业	Processing of Food from Agricultural Products	
食品制造业	Manufacture of Foods	56202
酒、饮料和精制茶制造业	Manufacture of Liquor, Beverage and Refind Tea	22248
烟草制品业	Manufacture of Tobacco	
纺织业	Manufacture of Textile	
纺织服装、服饰业	Manufacture of Textile Wearing Apparel	
皮革、毛皮、羽毛及其制品和制鞋业	Manufacture of Leather, Fur, Feather & Its Products Footwear	9770
木材加工和木、竹、藤、棕、草制品业	Processing of Timbers, Manufacture of Wood, Bamboo, Rattan, Palm and Straw Products	
家具制造业	Manufacture of Furniture	
造纸和纸制品业	Manufacture of Paper and Paper Products	131192
印刷和记录媒介复制业	Printing, Reproduction of Recording Media	4604
文教、工美、体育和娱乐用品制造业	Manufacture of Articles for Culture, Arts & Crafts, Sports and Entertainment	131948
石油、煤炭及其他燃料加工业	Oil, coal and other fuel processing industries	6610584
化学原料和化学制品制造业	Manufacture of Chemical Raw Material and Chemical Products	593867
医药制造业	Manufacture of Medicines	223993
化学纤维制造业	Manufacture of Chemical Fibers	
橡胶和塑料制品业	Manufacture of Rubber and Plastic	577025
非金属矿物制品业	Manufacture of Non-mettallic Mineral Products	209865
黑色金属冶炼和压延加工业	Smelting and Pressing of Ferrous Metals	1395097
有色金属冶炼和压延加工业	Smelting and Pressing of Non-ferrous Metals	78208
金属制品业	Manufacture of Metal Products	16713
通用设备制造业	Manufacture of General Purpose Machinery	207204
专用设备制造业	Manufacture of Special Purpose Machinery	87593
汽车制造业	Manufacture of Vehicle	4790182
铁路、船舶、航空航天和其他运输设备制造业	Manufacture of Transport Equipment for Railway, Shipping, Aerospace and other uses	6233793
电气机械和器材制造业	Manufacture of Electrical Machinery & Equipment	1042256
计算机、通信和其他电子设备制造业	Manufacture of Computer, Communication Equipment and Other Electronic Equipment	6134182
仪器仪表制造业	Manufacture of Measuring Instrument	4582
其他制造业	Manufacture of Other Products	27106
废弃资源综合利用业	Recycling and Disposal of Waste Resources	
金属制品、机械和设备修理业	Manufacture of Metal Products, Machinery and Equipment	4546
电力、热力生产和供应业	Production and Supply of Electric Power and Heat Power	978832
燃气生产和供应业	Production and Supply of Gas	297759
水的生产和供应业	Production and Supply of Water	174794

单位：万元（10 000 yuan）

主营业务成本 Cost of Principal Business	主营业务税金及附加 Taxes and Extra Charges on Principal Business	利润总额 Total Profits	全部从业人员年平均人数（人） Annual Average Employed Persons（person）
24834500	**1445089**	**1909384**	**109849**
4124	190	185	141
42231	526	7241	821
12417	767	2422	673
7509	159	256	175
125923	213	1160	1011
2852	126	401	151
109214	5027	6032	993
4703715	1254275	523767	2475
498251	4023	22471	3874
104353	2436	49350	1574
526360	2300	-9923	6822
178492	801	10380	1416
1286013	539	8367	3848
58750	2090	2909	1172
12470	288	1386	201
181848	968	-1158	3594
73460	714	1563	944
4319730	58251	243314	8411
5260164	55624	626299	29817
921392	6285	15832	6513
4953918	39240	412666	21019
4545	9	-1859	62
25203	99	241	120
3939		117	44
1050181	7211	-117041	9128
152522	388	122370	930
214928	2540	-19365	3920

12-8 按行业分规模以上外商投资和港澳台商投资工业企业主要指标(2017 年)

MAIN INDICATORS OF FOREIGN FUNEDE ENTERPRISES AND ENTERPRISES WITH FUNDS FROM HONG KONG, MACAO AND TAIWAN ABOVE DESIGNATED SIZE BY INDUSTRIAL SECTOR (2017)

项　目	Indicator	企业单位数(个) Number of Enterprises (Unit)
总　计	**Total**	**1037**
煤炭开采和洗选业	Mining and Washing of Coal	
石油和天然气开采业	Extraction of Petroleum and Natural Gas	
黑色金属矿采选业	Mining of Ferrous Metal Ores	
有色金属矿采选业	Mining of Non-ferrous Metal Ores	
非金属矿采选业	Mining and Processing of Nometal Ores	
开采辅助活动	Auxiliary Activities of Mining	
其他采矿业	Mining of Other Ores	
农副食品加工业	Processing of Food from Agricultural Products	109
食品制造业	Manufacture of Foods	41
酒、饮料和精制茶制造业	Manufacture of Liquor, Beverage and Refind Tea	8
烟草制品业	Manufacture of Tobacco	
纺织业	Manufacture of Textile	34
纺织服装、服饰业	Manufacture of Textile Wearing Apparel	74
皮革、毛皮、羽毛及其制品和制鞋业	Manufacture of Leather, Fur, Feather & Its Products Footwear	35
木材加工和木、竹、藤、棕、草制品业	Processing of Timbers, Manufacture of Wood, Bamboo, Rattan, Palm and Straw Products	4
家具制造业	Manufacture of Furniture	20
造纸和纸制品业	Manufacture of Paper and Paper Products	14
印刷和记录媒介复制业	Printing, Reproduction of Recording Media	27
文教、工美、体育和娱乐用品制造业	Manufacture of Articles for Culture, Arts & Crafts, Sports and Entertainment	95
石油、煤炭及其他燃料加工业	Oil, coal and other fuel processing industries	1
化学原料和化学制品制造业	Manufacture of Chemical Raw Material and Chemical Products	61
医药制造业	Manufacture of Medicines	7
化学纤维制造业	Manufacture of Chemical Fibers	2
橡胶和塑料制品业	Manufacture of Rubber and Plastic	59
非金属矿物制品业	Manufacture of Non-mettallic Mineral Products	41
黑色金属冶炼和压延加工业	Smelting and Pressing of Ferrous Metals	10
有色金属冶炼和压延加工业	Smelting and Pressing of Non-ferrous Metals	2
金属制品业	Manufacture of Metal Products	68
通用设备制造业	Manufacture of General Purpose Machinery	60
专用设备制造业	Manufacture of Special Purpose Machinery	43
汽车制造业	Manufacture of Vehicle	53
铁路、船舶、航空航天和其他运输设备制造业	Manufacture of Transport Equipment for Railway, Shipping, Aerospace and other uses	29
电气机械和器材制造业	Manufacture of Electrical Machinery & Equipment	44
计算机、通信和其他电子设备制造业	Manufacture of Computer, Communication Equipment and Other Electronic Equipment	61
仪器仪表制造业	Manufacture of Measuring Instrument	14
其他制造业	Manufacture of Other Products	5
废弃资源综合利用业	Recycling and Disposal of Waste Resources	1
金属制品、机械和设备修理业	Manufacture of Metal Products, Machinery and Equipment	1
电力、热力生产和供应业	Production and Supply of Electric Power and Heat Power	5
燃气生产和供应业	Production and Supply of Gas	7
水的生产和供应业	Production and Supply of Water	2

单位：万元（10 000 yuan）

工业总产值 Gross Industrial Output Value	资产合计 Total Assets	流动资产年合计 Total Current Assets	固定资产净值 Net Value of Fixed Assets
30290113	**27190401**	**17338005**	**6487609**
3269314	1875742	1124538	627842
1636302	1532779	1055579	357325
1213788	2229846	772611	284629
429754	285311	154796	113203
1037790	868590	534873	244276
671987	291076	183666	94562
66487	51213	6380	44716
273022	139850	76392	42191
192385	162014	108833	43430
684449	512977	272189	172120
2206384	939010	437150	382642
46468	39952	29209	8606
2561004	2072207	1122091	737020
546569	135335	62986	20074
37018	40137	29369	3823
1158576	1093083	552522	439042
597414	667973	389648	228416
491137	245150	158683	77338
48385	42868	27453	15369
2356474	1418617	783437	543229
1704883	1597115	994197	430857
718436	843403	480622	198302
3209364	6253955	5581927	529925
730935	782060	553342	141801
1107909	746421	424672	139747
2271458	1198804	817436	312999
411047	289459	249216	27779
97722	150493	129034	14572
32681	16708	5261	11448
5881	2598	2501	77
22927	166476	31353	78469
429109	435812	169980	83802
23056	63366	16065	37981

12-8 续表
Continued

项　目	Indicator	主营业务收入 Revenue from Principal Business
总　计	**Total**	**31329395**
煤炭开采和洗选业	Mining and Washing of Coal	
石油和天然气开采业	Extraction of Petroleum and Natural Gas	
黑色金属矿采选业	Mining of Ferrous Metal Ores	
有色金属矿采选业	Mining of Non-ferrous Metal Ores	
非金属矿采选业	Mining and Processing of Nometal Ores	
开采辅助活动	Auxiliary Activities of Mining	
其他采矿业	Mining of Other Ores	
农副食品加工业	Processing of Food from Agricultural Products	3703980
食品制造业	Manufacture of Foods	1595624
酒、饮料和精制茶制造业	Manufacture of Liquor, Beverage and Refind Tea	1913357
烟草制品业	Manufacture of Tobacco	
纺织业	Manufacture of Textile	431905
纺织服装、服饰业	Manufacture of Textile Wearing Apparel	1053117
皮革、毛皮、羽毛及其制品和制鞋业	Manufacture of Leather, Fur, Feather & Its Products Footwear	647106
木材加工和木、竹、藤、棕、草制品业	Processing of Timbers, Manufacture of Wood, Bamboo, Rattan, Palm and Straw Products	65696
家具制造业	Manufacture of Furniture	268997
造纸和纸制品业	Manufacture of Paper and Paper Products	182774
印刷和记录媒介复制业	Printing, Reproduction of Recording Media	674252
文教、工美、体育和娱乐用品制造业	Manufacture of Articles for Culture, Arts & Crafts, Sports and Entertainment	2178586
石油、煤炭及其他燃料加工业	Oil, coal and other fuel processing industries	56034
化学原料和化学制品制造业	Manufacture of Chemical Raw Material and Chemical Products	2506729
医药制造业	Manufacture of Medicines	519513
化学纤维制造业	Manufacture of Chemical Fibers	38885
橡胶和塑料制品业	Manufacture of Rubber and Plastic	1187943
非金属矿物制品业	Manufacture of Non-mettallic Mineral Products	610365
黑色金属冶炼和压延加工业	Smelting and Pressing of Ferrous Metals	458931
有色金属冶炼和压延加工业	Smelting and Pressing of Non-ferrous Metals	50425
金属制品业	Manufacture of Metal Products	2465954
通用设备制造业	Manufacture of General Purpose Machinery	1711674
专用设备制造业	Manufacture of Special Purpose Machinery	691196
汽车制造业	Manufacture of Vehicle	3191954
铁路、船舶、航空航天和其他运输设备制造业	Manufacture of Transport Equipment for Railway, Shipping, Aerospace and other uses	699554
电气机械和器材制造业	Manufacture of Electrical Machinery & Equipment	1084272
计算机、通信和其他电子设备制造业	Manufacture of Computer, Communication Equipment and Other Electronic Equipment	2295057
仪器仪表制造业	Manufacture of Measuring Instrument	435168
其他制造业	Manufacture of Other Products	95092
废弃资源综合利用业	Recycling and Disposal of Waste Resources	32559
金属制品、机械和设备修理业	Manufacture of Metal Products, Machinery and Equipment	5881
电力、热力生产和供应业	Production and Supply of Electric Power and Heat Power	24653
燃气生产和供应业	Production and Supply of Gas	429109
水的生产和供应业	Production and Supply of Water	23056

单位：万元（10 000 yuan）

主营业务成本 Cost of Principal Business	主营业务税金及附加 Taxes and Extra Charges on Principal Business	利润总额 Total Profits	全部从业人员年平均人数（人） Annual Average Employed Persons（person）
26425485	**321602**	**1670459**	**272629**
3399770	17427	74637	24036
1097179	16695	79676	7920
1430726	56316	117467	7332
376308	2281	11615	5496
925940	10490	35118	27130
578982	4126	15968	21088
58379	389	3134	294
228553	2981	12385	3504
169128	774	3978	1561
575497	5018	33399	5731
1854821	22514	134159	22925
48915	149	2977	138
2116013	13751	131249	11125
433887	3393	35489	1292
31305	179	454	351
997146	22375	40208	13156
500805	5312	41075	5795
415203	2532	15583	1759
42123	80	-3744	218
2100559	36998	121382	18140
1417067	9027	97017	17923
560943	5012	31881	6947
2636769	53023	293283	20406
548898	7074	62626	6754
946542	6903	55275	11304
2079056	9006	101368	22357
327958	3545	67405	3143
83146	2053	19750	2585
28222		3651	271
3538	57	944	125
16612	411	4357	187
381790	1228	21379	1389
13707	487	5317	247

12-9 按行业分大中型工业企业主要指标（2017 年）

MAIN INDICATORS OF LARGE AND MEDIUM-SIZED INDUSTRIAL ENTERPRISES BY INDUSTRIAL SECTOR (2017)

项　目	Indicator	企业单位数（个）Number of Enterprises（Unit）
总　计	**Total**	**537**
煤炭开采和洗选业	Mining and Washing of Coal	
石油和天然气开采业	Extraction of Petroleum and Natural Gas	
黑色金属矿采选业	Mining of Ferrous Metal Ores	
有色金属矿采选业	Mining of Non-ferrous Metal Ores	
非金属矿采选业	Mining and Processing of Nometal Ores	
开采辅助活动	Auxiliary Activities of Mining	
其他采矿业	Mining of Other Ores	
农副食品加工业	Processing of Food from Agricultural Products	44
食品制造业	Manufacture of Foods	19
酒、饮料和精制茶制造业	Manufacture of Liquor, Beverage and Refind Tea	5
烟草制品业	Manufacture of Tobacco	
纺织业	Manufacture of Textile	5
纺织服装、服饰业	Manufacture of Textile Wearing Apparel	39
皮革、毛皮、羽毛及其制品和制鞋业	Manufacture of Leather, Fur, Feather & Its Products Footwear	20
木材加工和木、竹、藤、棕、草制品业	Processing of Timbers, Manufacture of Wood, Bamboo, Rattan, Palm and Straw Products	1
家具制造业	Manufacture of Furniture	7
造纸和纸制品业	Manufacture of Paper and Paper Products	2
印刷和记录媒介复制业	Printing, Reproduction of Recording Media	7
文教、工美、体育和娱乐用品制造业	Manufacture of Articles for Culture, Arts & Crafts, Sports and Entertainment	32
石油、煤炭及其他燃料加工业	Oil, coal and other fuel processing industries	3
化学原料和化学制品制造业	Manufacture of Chemical Raw Material and Chemical Products	19
医药制造业	Manufacture of Medicines	11
化学纤维制造业	Manufacture of Chemical Fibers	1
橡胶和塑料制品业	Manufacture of Rubber and Plastic	33
非金属矿物制品业	Manufacture of Non-mettallic Mineral Products	15
黑色金属冶炼和压延加工业	Smelting and Pressing of Ferrous Metals	5
有色金属冶炼和压延加工业	Smelting and Pressing of Non-ferrous Metals	2
金属制品业	Manufacture of Metal Products	34
通用设备制造业	Manufacture of General Purpose Machinery	42
专用设备制造业	Manufacture of Special Purpose Machinery	24
汽车制造业	Manufacture of Vehicle	35
铁路、船舶、航空航天和其他运输设备制造业	Manufacture of Transport Equipment for Railway, Shipping, Aerospace and other uses	34
电气机械和器材制造业	Manufacture of Electrical Machinery & Equipment	35
计算机、通信和其他电子设备制造业	Manufacture of Computer, Communication Equipment and Other Electronic Equipment	34
仪器仪表制造业	Manufacture of Measuring Instrument	8
其他制造业	Manufacture of Other Products	2
废弃资源综合利用业	Recycling and Disposal of Waste Resources	
金属制品、机械和设备修理业	Manufacture of Metal Products, Machinery and Equipment	
电力、热力生产和供应业	Production and Supply of Electric Power and Heat Power	14
燃气生产和供应业	Production and Supply of Gas	2
水的生产和供应业	Production and Supply of Water	3

单位：万元（10 000 yuan）

工业总产值 Gross Industrial Output Value	资产合计 Total Assets	流动资产年合计 Total Current Assets	固定资产净值 Net Value of Fixed Assets
69430745	**93894700**	**58120297**	**15005314.2**
3986963	2032372	1158310	745183.3
1308912	1415277	1004983	278991.7
1471480	2318976	832993	313853.9
231417	103677	62108	34246.8
2134287	1662415	921429	405046.2
1045108	432399	242587	148691.2
7018	36097	3770	
115599	136558	80292	45710.9
220864	78590	34980	43610
327534	237729	140822	72560
1443764	707840	353465	296741.9
6665921	2608909	1120164	928478.9
2539433	3575319	1543357	1351705.3
764397	940126	543527	219001.3
17356	29574	23691	2531.5
2331985	3655584	1517006	720292.1
533229	832455	604124	161366.4
1735756	2076513	1067171	825320.8
37474	208662	6513	198216.3
1877342	2230160	1084419	514985.1
2302374	2906108	1963551	531631.2
1536559	1398796	978213	245182.3
8380771	10928065	9249521	989626.5
6763647	10698851	7971109	1074376.3
12861964	31869305	19057644	2348534.1
7052192	6192137	4984446	539114.3
517561	719557	573690	91292.2
68071	66578	46853	13729.6
880320	2549957	672128	1426961.8
170979	463124	123281	162501.3
100469	782991	154149	275831

12-9 续表
Continued

项　目	Indicator	主营业务收入 Revenue from Principal Business
总　计	**Total**	**73318880**
煤炭开采和洗选业	Mining and Washing of Coal	
石油和天然气开采业	Extraction of Petroleum and Natural Gas	
黑色金属矿采选业	Mining of Ferrous Metal Ores	
有色金属矿采选业	Mining of Non-ferrous Metal Ores	
非金属矿采选业	Mining and Processing of Nometal Ores	
开采辅助活动	Auxiliary Activities of Mining	
其他采矿业	Mining of Other Ores	
农副食品加工业	Processing of Food from Agricultural Products	4475192
食品制造业	Manufacture of Foods	1281568
酒、饮料和精制茶制造业	Manufacture of Liquor, Beverage and Refind Tea	1982032
烟草制品业	Manufacture of Tobacco	
纺织业	Manufacture of Textile	232592
纺织服装、服饰业	Manufacture of Textile Wearing Apparel	2031036
皮革、毛皮、羽毛及其制品和制鞋业	Manufacture of Leather, Fur, Feather & Its Products Footwear	1011232
木材加工和木、竹、藤、棕、草制品业	Processing of Timbers, Manufacture of Wood, Bamboo, Rattan, Palm and Straw Products	7002
家具制造业	Manufacture of Furniture	113839
造纸和纸制品业	Manufacture of Paper and Paper Products	196506
印刷和记录媒介复制业	Printing, Reproduction of Recording Media	324939
文教、工美、体育和娱乐用品制造业	Manufacture of Articles for Culture, Arts & Crafts, Sports and Entertainment	1419192
石油、煤炭及其他燃料加工业	Oil, coal and other fuel processing industries	6610584
化学原料和化学制品制造业	Manufacture of Chemical Raw Material and Chemical Products	2439966
医药制造业	Manufacture of Medicines	747553
化学纤维制造业	Manufacture of Chemical Fibers	19223
橡胶和塑料制品业	Manufacture of Rubber and Plastic	2259390
非金属矿物制品业	Manufacture of Non-mettallic Mineral Products	539461
黑色金属冶炼和压延加工业	Smelting and Pressing of Ferrous Metals	1549146
有色金属冶炼和压延加工业	Smelting and Pressing of Non-ferrous Metals	38015
金属制品业	Manufacture of Metal Products	1854672
通用设备制造业	Manufacture of General Purpose Machinery	2368595
专用设备制造业	Manufacture of Special Purpose Machinery	1437664
汽车制造业	Manufacture of Vehicle	8096209
铁路、船舶、航空航天和其他运输设备制造业	Manufacture of Transport Equipment for Railway, Shipping, Aerospace and other uses	7146333
电气机械和器材制造业	Manufacture of Electrical Machinery & Equipment	15554273
计算机、通信和其他电子设备制造业	Manufacture of Computer, Communication Equipment and Other Electronic Equipment	7873336
仪器仪表制造业	Manufacture of Measuring Instrument	501509
其他制造业	Manufacture of Other Products	68325
废弃资源综合利用业	Recycling and Disposal of Waste Resources	
金属制品、机械和设备修理业	Manufacture of Metal Products, Machinery and Equipment	
电力、热力生产和供应业	Production and Supply of Electric Power and Heat Power	868109
燃气生产和供应业	Production and Supply of Gas	170979
水的生产和供应业	Production and Supply of Water	100411

单位：万元（10 000 yuan）

主营业务成本 Cost of Principal Business	主营业务税金及附加 Taxes and Extra Charges on Principal Business	利润总额 Total Profits	全部从业人员年平均人数（人） Annual Average Employed Persons（person）
59205704	**1798207**	**4574387**	**493074**
4156834	15317	71688	40754
819959	9026	72620	8153
1494110	58820	120086	8490
207660	980	5615	2632
1779053	15376	79749	55859
854224	5302	61026	27137
5259		840	549
94642	1302	930	3449
186267	456	5272	1422
273398	2030	16652	3223
1195617	13962	82861	19311
4703715	1254275	523767	2475
2121772	10029	112114	13481
366219	9854	134625	7211
16811	97	-384	333
1908215	17240	77781	24969
450652	3704	28420	8004
1395296	2180	25965	6188
21806	1265	2812	1246
1594693	21754	100726	20445
1986794	16111	114833	25899
1201887	7452	48266	17025
7194769	76045	458439	34242
6008381	66566	685620	46918
11005141	128403	1298410	49572
6514314	46362	504749	43339
368592	4909	57560	4815
62400	592	-1614	2480
924393	6439	-105026	9419
146778	637	7780	1241
146056	1722	-17790	2793

12-10 按行业分规模以上工业企业主要经济效益指标（2017 年）

MAIN INDICATORS ON ECONOMIC BENEFIT OF INDUSTRIA ENTERPRISES ABOVE DESIGNATED SIZE BY INDOUSTRIAL SECTOR（2017）

项　目	Indicator	总资产贡献率（%）Ratio of Total Assets to Industrial Output Value（%）
总　计	**Total**	**10.18**
按轻重工业分	**Grouped by Light and Heavy Industries**	
轻工业	Light Industry	9.08
重工业	Heavy Industry	10.87
按行业分	**Grouped by sector**	
煤炭开采和洗选业	Mining and Washing of Coal	
石油和天然气开采业	Extraction of Petroleum and Natural Gas	
黑色金属矿采选业	Mining of Ferrous Metal Ores	
有色金属矿采选业	Mining of Non-ferrous Metal Ores	
非金属矿采选业	Mining and Processing of Nometal Ores	11.23
开采辅助活动	Auxiliary Activities of Mining	
其他采矿业	Mining of Other Ores	
农副食品加工业	Processing of Food from Agricultural Products	11.17
食品制造业	Manufacture of Foods	12.25
酒、饮料和精制茶制造业	Manufacture of Liquor，Beverage and Refind Tea	11.14
烟草制品业	Manufacture of Tobacco	
纺织业	Manufacture of Textile	11.84
纺织服装、服饰业	Manufacture of Textile Wearing Apparel	11.13
皮革、毛皮、羽毛及其制品和制鞋业	Manufacture of Leather，Fur，Feather & Its Products Footwear	20.95
木材加工和木、竹、藤、棕、草制品业	Processing of Timbers，Manufacture of Wood，Bamboo，Rattan，Palm and Straw Products	12.39
家具制造业	Manufacture of Furniture	13.25
造纸和纸制品业	Manufacture of Paper and Paper Products	10.86
印刷和记录媒介复制业	Printing，Reproduction of Recording Media	15.65
文教、工美、体育和娱乐用品制造业	Manufacture of Articles for Culture，Arts & Crafts，Sports and Entertainment	25.48
石油、煤炭及其他燃料加工业	Oil, coal and other fuel processing industries	75.21
化学原料和化学制品制造业	Manufacture of Chemical Raw Material and Chemical Products	8.75
医药制造业	Manufacture of Medicines	23.97
化学纤维制造业	Manufacture of Chemical Fibers	7.87
橡胶和塑料制品业	Manufacture of Rubber and Plastic	6.63
非金属矿物制品业	Manufacture of Non-mettallic Mineral Products	10
黑色金属冶炼和压延加工业	Smelting and Pressing of Ferrous Metals	5.14
有色金属冶炼和压延加工业	Smelting and Pressing of Non-ferrous Metals	7.35
金属制品业	Manufacture of Metal Products	11.71
通用设备制造业	Manufacture of General Purpose Machinery	9.95
专用设备制造业	Manufacture of Special Purpose Machinery	9.44
汽车制造业	Manufacture of Vehicle	6.68
铁路、船舶、航空航天和其他运输设备制造业	Manufacture of Transport Equipment for Railway，Shipping，Aerospace and other uses	8.92
电气机械和器材制造业	Manufacture of Electrical Machinery & Equipment	6.02
计算机、通信和其他电子设备制造业	Manufacture of Computer，Communication Equipment and Other Electronic Equipment	13.13
仪器仪表制造业	Manufacture of Measuring Instrument	13.11
其他制造业	Manufacture of Other Products	16.29
废弃资源综合利用业	Recycling and Disposal of Waste Resources	23.02
金属制品、机械和设备修理业	Manufacture of Metal Products，Machinery and Equipment	42.58
电力、热力生产和供应业	Production and Supply of Electric Power and Heat Power	-1.83
燃气生产和供应业	Production and Supply of Gas	17.36
水的生产和供应业	Production and Supply of Water	0.52

资产负债率（%） Assets-Liability Ratio （%）	流动资产周转次数（次/年） Number of Times of Annual of Turnover Current Assets（time/year）	工业成本费用利润率（%） Ratio of Profits to Industrial Costs（%）	产品销售率（%） Ratio of Sales to Output （%）
60.17	**1.68**	**6.05**	**98.69**
64.16	1.79	6.03	98.9
57.64	1.62	6.06	98.57
73.35	0.92	8.85	91.38
55.74	4.46	2.48	99.37
56.18	2.11	6.34	98.63
36.79	2.38	6.08	148.72
57.68	3.67	3.44	98.77
54.76	2.48	4.41	99.61
53.26	4.05	6.16	95.51
42.43	4.71	5.89	99.59
53.59	3.09	4.92	98.75
58	3.07	2.86	95.3
47.48	4.31	5.31	97
42.1	5.96	6.54	99.13
58.29	5.74	10.19	99.93
50.82	2.16	5.98	95.67
36.82	2.25	15.14	96.37
66.77	2.78	5.64	99.05
55.37	2.26	3.44	99.42
54.97	1.66	5.51	100.24
75.1	2.05	1.86	99.99
61.37	4.76	3.23	101.89
38.91	2.71	5.07	97.68
50.89	1.82	5.51	98.9
47.81	1.92	4.5	96.87
66.12	1	5.58	97.84
63.99	1.03	9.2	98.03
70.63	0.88	8.59	94.28
53.74	1.88	5.75	101.25
67.95	1.2	11.47	103.37
55.96	0.84	16.15	99.98
17.55	10.84	9.2	98.09
44.31	7.31	9.8	92.29
70.14	1.24	-8.77	97.23
50.57	3.18	23.17	74.56
63.77	0.8	-3.56	99.02

12-11 按行业分国有控股工业企业主要经济效益指标(2017年)

MAIN INDICATORS ON ECONOMIC BENEFIT OF STATE-OWNED AND STATE-HOLDING INUSTRIAL ENTERPRISES BY INDUSTRIAL SECTOR (2017)

项　目	Indicator	总资产贡献率(%) Ratio of Total Assets to Industrial Output Value (%)
总　计	**Total**	**12.04**
煤炭开采和洗选业	Mining and Washing of Coal	
石油和天然气开采业	Extraction of Petroleum and Natural Gas	
黑色金属矿采选业	Mining of Ferrous Metal Ores	
有色金属矿采选业	Mining of Non-ferrous Metal Ores	
非金属矿采选业	Mining and Processing of Nometal Ores	9.30
开采辅助活动	Auxiliary Activities of Mining	
其他采矿业	Mining of Other Ores	
农副食品加工业	Processing of Food from Agricultural Products	
食品制造业	Manufacture of Foods	17.67
酒、饮料和精制茶制造业	Manufacture of Liquor, Beverage and Refind Tea	7.85
烟草制品业	Manufacture of Tobacco	
纺织业	Manufacture of Textile	
纺织服装、服饰业	Manufacture of Textile Wearing Apparel	
皮革、毛皮、羽毛及其制品和制鞋业	Manufacture of Leather, Fur, Feather & Its Products Footwear	5.56
木材加工和木、竹、藤、棕、草制品业	Processing of Timbers, Manufacture of Wood, Bamboo, Rattan, Palm and Straw Products	
家具制造业	Manufacture of Furniture	
造纸和纸制品业	Manufacture of Paper and Paper Products	6.55
印刷和记录媒介复制业	Printing, Reproduction of Recording Media	8.63
文教、工美、体育和娱乐用品制造业	Manufacture of Articles for Culture, Arts & Crafts, Sports and Entertainment	91.82
石油、煤炭及其他燃料加工业	Oil, coal and other fuel processing industries	80.19
化学原料和化学制品制造业	Manufacture of Chemical Raw Material and Chemical Products	2.77
医药制造业	Manufacture of Medicines	27.00
化学纤维制造业	Manufacture of Chemical Fibers	
橡胶和塑料制品业	Manufacture of Rubber and Plastic	0.65
非金属矿物制品业	Manufacture of Non-mettallic Mineral Products	6.25
黑色金属冶炼和压延加工业	Smelting and Pressing of Ferrous Metals	4.05
有色金属冶炼和压延加工业	Smelting and Pressing of Non-ferrous Metals	2.85
金属制品业	Manufacture of Metal Products	3.98
通用设备制造业	Manufacture of General Purpose Machinery	0.81
专用设备制造业	Manufacture of Special Purpose Machinery	2.27
汽车制造业	Manufacture of Vehicle	5.30
铁路、船舶、航空航天和其他运输设备制造业	Manufacture of Transport Equipment for Railway, Shipping, Aerospace and other uses	8.05
电气机械和器材制造业	Manufacture of Electrical Machinery & Equipment	4.70
计算机、通信和其他电子设备制造业	Manufacture of Computer, Communication Equipment and Other Electronic Equipment	14.29
仪器仪表制造业	Manufacture of Measuring Instrument	-17.29
其他制造业	Manufacture of Other Products	4.56
废弃资源综合利用业	Recycling and Disposal of Waste Resources	
金属制品、机械和设备修理业	Manufacture of Metal Products, Machinery and Equipment	8.79
电力、热力生产和供应业	Production and Supply of Electric Power and Heat Power	-2.68
燃气生产和供应业	Production and Supply of Gas	21.64
水的生产和供应业	Production and Supply of Water	-0.74

资产负债率（%） Assets-Liability Ratio （%）	流动资产周转次数（次/年） Number of Times of Annual of Turnover Current Assets（time/year）	工业成本费用利润率（%） Ratio of Profits to Industrial Costs（%）	产品销售率（%） Ratio of Sales to Output （%）
64.72	**1.32**	**6.59**	**98.65**
82.23	0.85	3.39	90.33
33.34	1.35	13.58	94.84
32.50	0.70	12.47	99.07
55.33	0.91	2.66	100.04
57.90	4.20	0.89	87.48
5.65	1.17	9.75	87.72
44.81	10.15	4.99	100
58.45	5.96	10.72	100.04
52.47	1.15	3.86	99.19
24.92	1.50	28.12	102.97
82.65	1.11	-1.56	101.32
75.45	0.94	5.03	103.8
83.13	1.81	0.55	98.62
67.57	3.23	3.67	115.49
62.38	0.84	9.22	100
60.69	0.70	-0.50	86.95
81.32	0.86	1.79	69.31
66.42	0.75	5.13	96.6
66.64	0.85	10.07	97.91
62.80	1.87	1.53	102.72
54.40	1.66	6.30	103.33
99.84	0.74	-30.81	100
70.37	0.95	0.89	100
84.03	1.92	2.68	99.34
76.94	1.70	-10.16	96.9
41.89	2.40	66.43	37.32
66.10	0.84	-7.41	99.69

12-12 按行业分规模以上外商及港澳台商投资工业企业主要经济效益指标(2017年)

MAIN INDICATORS ON ECONOMIC BENEFIT OF FOREIGN FUNDED ENTERPRISES AND ENTERPRISES WITH FUNDS FROM HONG KONG, MACAO AND TAIWAN ABOVE DESIGNATED SIZE BY INDUSTRIAL SECTOR (2017)

项　目	Indicator	总资产贡献率(%) Ratio of Total Assets to Industrial Output Value (%)
总　计	**Total**	**9.92**
煤炭开采和洗选业	Mining and Washing of Coal	
石油和天然气开采业	Extraction of Petroleum and Natural Gas	
黑色金属矿采选业	Mining of Ferrous Metal Ores	
有色金属矿采选业	Mining of Non-ferrous Metal Ores	
非金属矿采选业	Mining and Processing of Nometal Ores	
开采辅助活动	Auxiliary Activities of Mining	
其他采矿业	Mining of Other Ores	
农副食品加工业	Processing of Food from Agricultural Products	8.22
食品制造业	Manufacture of Foods	8.59
酒、饮料和精制茶制造业	Manufacture of Liquor, Beverage and Refind Tea	11.20
烟草制品业	Manufacture of Tobacco	
纺织业	Manufacture of Textile	6.61
纺织服装、服饰业	Manufacture of Textile Wearing Apparel	8.66
皮革、毛皮、羽毛及其制品和制鞋业	Manufacture of Leather, Fur, Feather & Its Products Footwear	10.67
木材加工和木、竹、藤、棕、草制品业	Processing of Timbers, Manufacture of Wood, Bamboo, Rattan, Palm and Straw Products	10.21
家具制造业	Manufacture of Furniture	16.41
造纸和纸制品业	Manufacture of Paper and Paper Products	5.45
印刷和记录媒介复制业	Printing, Reproduction of Recording Media	10.16
文教、工美、体育和娱乐用品制造业	Manufacture of Articles for Culture, Arts & Crafts, Sports and Entertainment	22.98
石油、煤炭及其他燃料加工业	Oil, coal and other fuel processing industries	10.06
化学原料和化学制品制造业	Manufacture of Chemical Raw Material and Chemical Products	9.62
医药制造业	Manufacture of Medicines	47.35
化学纤维制造业	Manufacture of Chemical Fibers	3.22
橡胶和塑料制品业	Manufacture of Rubber and Plastic	8.28
非金属矿物制品业	Manufacture of Non-mettallic Mineral Products	9.66
黑色金属冶炼和压延加工业	Smelting and Pressing of Ferrous Metals	9.93
有色金属冶炼和压延加工业	Smelting and Pressing of Non-ferrous Metals	-5.43
金属制品业	Manufacture of Metal Products	15.51
通用设备制造业	Manufacture of General Purpose Machinery	7.85
专用设备制造业	Manufacture of Special Purpose Machinery	6.06
汽车制造业	Manufacture of Vehicle	6.89
铁路、船舶、航空航天和其他运输设备制造业	Manufacture of Transport Equipment for Railway, Shipping, Aerospace and other uses	12.71
电气机械和器材制造业	Manufacture of Electrical Machinery & Equipment	10.72
计算机、通信和其他电子设备制造业	Manufacture of Computer, Communication Equipment and Other Electronic Equipment	10.27
仪器仪表制造业	Manufacture of Measuring Instrument	31.23
其他制造业	Manufacture of Other Products	17.85
废弃资源综合利用业	Recycling and Disposal of Waste Resources	24.15
金属制品、机械和设备修理业	Manufacture of Metal Products, Machinery and Equipment	52.42
电力、热力生产和供应业	Production and Supply of Electric Power and Heat Power	2.99
燃气生产和供应业	Production and Supply of Gas	4.94
水的生产和供应业	Production and Supply of Water	11.50

资产负债率（%） Assets-Liability Ratio （%）	流动资产周转次数（次/年） Number of Times of Annual of Turnover Current Assets（time/year）	工业成本费用利润率（%） Ratio of Profits to Industrial Costs（%）	产品销售率（%） Ratio of Sales to Output （%）
50.30	**1.84**	**5.59**	**101.14**
58.61	3.31	2.06	98.16
62.00	1.56	5.60	98.44
31.81	2.64	5.95	166.92
57.71	2.81	2.77	98.91
49.73	1.98	3.46	98.37
52.58	3.52	2.54	97.78
57.08	10.30	5.04	100.34
50.11	3.52	4.89	98.4
54.53	1.72	2.18	94.88
51.80	2.48	5.24	98.98
36.11	4.99	6.62	100.12
74.85	1.94	5.58	100
55.61	2.28	5.44	91.05
33.87	8.26	7.37	94.53
67.51	1.32	1.20	105.04
43.35	2.17	3.54	99.84
33.70	1.60	7.14	102.07
35.05	2.94	3.48	97.05
41.67	1.84	-8.11	129.54
46.65	3.17	5.17	97.65
47.21	1.77	5.85	99.88
40.98	1.44	4.86	98.75
57.00	0.58	10.03	101.33
55.99	1.28	9.79	99.27
42.59	2.56	5.38	99.02
48.99	2.85	4.55	98.22
56.40	1.77	18.10	99.73
56.27	0.74	20.82	100.26
19.36	6.19	12.63	99.63
49.94	2.35	19.41	100
60.73	0.79	19.97	103.43
60.96	2.57	5.05	100
46.08	1.44	30.21	100

12-13 按行业分大中型工业企业主要经济效益指标(2017年)

MAIN INDICATORS ON ECONOMIC BENEFIT OF LARGE AND MEDICM-SIZED INDUSTRIAL ENTERPRISES BY INDUSTRIAL SECTOR (2017)

项　目	Indicator	总资产贡献率(%) Ratio of Total Assets to Industrial Output Value (%)
总　计	**Total**	**8.98**
煤炭开采和洗选业	Mining and Washing of Coal	
石油和天然气开采业	Extraction of Petroleum and Natural Gas	
黑色金属矿采选业	Mining of Ferrous Metal Ores	
有色金属矿采选业	Mining of Non-ferrous Metal Ores	
非金属矿采选业	Mining and Processing of Nometal Ores	
开采辅助活动	Auxiliary Activities of Mining	
其他采矿业	Mining of Other Ores	
农副食品加工业	Processing of Food from Agricultural Products	7.65
食品制造业	Manufacture of Foods	7.98
酒、饮料和精制茶制造业	Manufacture of Liquor, Beverage and Refind Tea	11.00
烟草制品业	Manufacture of Tobacco	0.00
纺织业	Manufacture of Textile	7.15
纺织服装、服饰业	Manufacture of Textile Wearing Apparel	10.28
皮革、毛皮、羽毛及其制品和制鞋业	Manufacture of Leather, Fur, Feather & Its Products Footwear	20.92
木材加工和木、竹、藤、棕、草制品业	Processing of Timbers, Manufacture of Wood, Bamboo, Rattan, Palm and Straw Products	3.56
家具制造业	Manufacture of Furniture	5.07
造纸和纸制品业	Manufacture of Paper and Paper Products	13.58
印刷和记录媒介复制业	Printing, Reproduction of Recording Media	10.76
文教、工美、体育和娱乐用品制造业	Manufacture of Articles for Culture, Arts & Crafts, Sports and Entertainment	18.38
石油、煤炭及其他燃料加工业	Oil, coal and other fuel processing industries	80.19
化学原料和化学制品制造业	Manufacture of Chemical Raw Material and Chemical Products	4.76
医药制造业	Manufacture of Medicines	21.93
化学纤维制造业	Manufacture of Chemical Fibers	-0.85
橡胶和塑料制品业	Manufacture of Rubber and Plastic	4.47
非金属矿物制品业	Manufacture of Non-mettallic Mineral Products	5.96
黑色金属冶炼和压延加工业	Smelting and Pressing of Ferrous Metals	4.48
有色金属冶炼和压延加工业	Smelting and Pressing of Non-ferrous Metals	3.10
金属制品业	Manufacture of Metal Products	7.55
通用设备制造业	Manufacture of General Purpose Machinery	6.24
专用设备制造业	Manufacture of Special Purpose Machinery	6.33
汽车制造业	Manufacture of Vehicle	6.35
铁路、船舶、航空航天和其他运输设备制造业	Manufacture of Transport Equipment for Railway, Shipping, Aerospace and other uses	8.36
电气机械和器材制造业	Manufacture of Electrical Machinery & Equipment	5.71
计算机、通信和其他电子设备制造业	Manufacture of Computer, Communication Equipment and Other Electronic Equipment	13.36
仪器仪表制造业	Manufacture of Measuring Instrument	11.32
其他制造业	Manufacture of Other Products	-0.36
废弃资源综合利用业	Recycling and Disposal of Waste Resources	
金属制品、机械和设备修理业	Manufacture of Metal Products, Machinery and Equipment	
电力、热力生产和供应业	Production and Supply of Electric Power and Heat Power	-2.63
燃气生产和供应业	Production and Supply of Gas	1.78
水的生产和供应业	Production and Supply of Water	-1.16

资产负债率（%） Assets-Liability Ratio （%）	流动资产周转次数（次/年） Number of Times of Annual of Turnover Current Assets（time/year）	工业成本费用利润率（%） Ratio of Profits to Industrial Costs（%）	产品销售率（%） Ratio of Sales to Output （%）
64.44	**1.29**	**6.52**	**98.97**
57.39	3.96	1.59	98.51
64.13	1.32	6.49	98.44
34.72	2.53	5.91	156.84
0.00	0.00	0.00	0
50.97	3.76	2.48	100.5
57.67	2.23	4.06	100.08
56.57	4.18	6.43	93.53
22.07	1.86	13.80	100
69.31	1.46	0.81	96.34
56.95	5.62	2.76	90.17
38.12	2.32	5.42	99.41
37.66	4.03	6.25	100.01
58.45	5.96	10.72	100.04
55.33	1.61	4.72	91.31
36.63	1.38	22.08	95.99
55.83	0.81	−2.05	110.76
59.45	1.53	3.48	100.15
63.91	0.91	5.47	101.83
78.10	1.63	1.54	100.49
57.80	6.16	7.52	100
34.54	1.73	5.74	98.18
59.38	1.23	5.01	99.19
62.19	1.50	3.44	95.55
67.43	0.90	5.85	97.54
66.63	0.90	9.69	98
72.33	0.82	8.96	93.57
53.38	1.73	6.14	102.37
85.61	0.89	12.91	99.38
83.03	1.47	−2.31	100.37
72.99	1.36	−10.19	96.52
65.46	1.68	3.78	100
64.15	0.76	−10.11	99.47

12-14 主要年份主要工业产品产量

MAJOR YEAR'S PRODUCTS OUTPUT OF INDUSTRY ABOVE DESIGNATED SIZE

年份 Year	原盐 （万吨） Salt （10 000 tons）	发电量 （亿千瓦小时） Electricity （100 million kW·h）	饮料酒 （万吨） Beverage Liquour （10 000 tons）	#啤酒 Beer	卷烟 （万箱） Cigarettes （10 000 cases）	罐头 （吨） Canned Food （ton）	化学纤维 （吨） Chemical Fiber （ton）	纱 （吨） Yarn （ton）
1949	15.16	1.21	0.18	0.12	2.36			27447
1952	35.08	2.11	0.37	0.18	12.27			59674
1957	44.34	2.92	0.96	0.58	23.41			50699
1962	38.60	3.86	1.58	0.79	16.59		28	17939
1965	41.34	6.80	2.04	1.34	31.34		205	68082
1970	29.96	10.57	3.39	2.55	42.16		621	85591
1975	34.52	10.98	5.30	2.98	36.00		357	79516
1978	60.68	13.63	6.25	3.75	44.00	4743	1413	85233
1980	41.19	12.50	8.49	4.84	48.79	3521	2116	83389
1985	47.34	26.97	13.76	10.05	51.81	6400	1747	91839
1988	53.28	29.35	26.61	15.58	57.01	27200	3393	107720
1990	35.70	40.22	29.18	19.61	61.94		2900	100381
1991	31.39	54.60	36.75	27.38	56.19	130510	5200	96271
1992	46.24	58.63	44.59	37.01	59.37	3200	6000	99043
1993	48.88	59.39	54.74	45.92	63.46	1900	27100	91351
1994	53.02	59.62	60.00	50.92	69.20	2300	21400	86744
1995	50.84	64.69	60.85	54.16	70.96	4609	20973	79492
1996	41.39	83.02	61.79	54.40	73.04	1719	22945	66832
1997	34.11	95.12	66.64	56.06	88.32	554	26300	70402
1998	19.08	79.65	47.33	42.79	77.10		23858	66504
1999	30.30	82.00	126.21	120.10	149.00	379	29967	56431
2000	41.83	90.84	211.47	206.50	148.10	225	65362	69561
2001	31.40	85.73	279.37	274.28	142.95	99	89989	72933
2002	42.50	89.70	323.20	320.60	138.10	11690	91394	70888
2003	36.85	87.69	353.90	351.80	148.00		101752	65919
2004	34.36	89.01	393.30	390.60	147.10	10889	115187	71931
2005	10.00	98.63	439.70	435.20	150.70	10097	95887	72140
2006	15.30	124.54	101.60（本地）	95.60（本地）	95.16（本地）	1668	72381	56128
2007	19.23	155.30	118.10（本地）	112.50（本地）	100.08（本地）	1850	68746	47850
2008	15.90	164.58	132.07（本地）	124.75（本地）	100.02（本地）	1510	51751	43102
2009	5.90	172.66	137.21（本地）	127.12（本地）	100.08（本地）	4706	59852	38566
2010	11.25	181.93	144.66（本地）	141.65（本地）	102.55（本地）	1092	68654	35278
2011		173.69	164.04（本地）	156.50（本地）	104.51（本地）	41204	38640	18556
2012		174.72	174.03（本地）	163.95（本地）	106.03（本地）	35026	32371	19404
2013	1.28	180.11	194.22（本地）	185.17（本地）	108.36（本地）	30203	23647	33687
2014		178.29	169.85（本地）	164.59（本地）	112.06（本地）	23970	22053	32336
2015		173.53	162.66（本地）	157.83（本地）	111.48（本地）	36179	17419	27721
2016		175.40	168.82（本地）	164.27（本地）		53139	14839	33416
2017		181.80	163.41（本地）	159.97（本地）		85942	11565	26493

注：1998 年以前为乡及乡以上工业。

Note：Before 1998，the data refer to those at and above county level.

12-14 续表 1
Continued

年 份 Year	布 （万米） Cloth （10 000 m）	印染布 （万米） Printed Fabric （10 000 m）	机制纸及纸板（万吨） Machine-made Paper and Paperboards （10 000 tons）	硫酸 （万吨） Sulfuric Acid （10 000 tons）	烧碱 （万吨） Caustic Soda （10 000 tons）	纯碱 （万吨） Soda Ash （10 000 tons）
1949	10608	2947	0.98		0.01	
1952	30069	13658	0.44		0.17	
1957	27806	16053	1.54		0.74	
1962	7444	7375	1.45	0.06	0.89	
1965	29538	13670	2.22		1.66	5.32
1970	33660	21994	3.14	0.04	2.14	12.01
1975	31242	22828	3.10	0.53	2.36	9.15
1978	36877	25797	4.55	1.32	3.61	14.04
1980	34937	22900	5.25	4.11	4.33	18.18
1985	34998	17679	6.20	3.34	5.52	26.03
1988	35890	21213	7.42	4.88	6.62	31.12
1990	34066	21446	6.02	4.86	6.73	30.48
1991	34076	19999	5.99	5.62	5.99	29.50
1992	33682	21534	5.95	6.70	5.62	34.60
1993	35912	16606	8.84	6.96	6.07	40.43
1994	43241	16387	12.36	8.33	6.48	43.36
1995	41170	17864	11.06	9.69	7.90	43.20
1996	39023	16881	11.31	10.12	7.30	46.91
1997	43615	15722	7.78	10.16	8.45	50.55
1998	40440	9864	6.91	10.33	9.25	52.80
1999	39576	4340	7.77	12.56	8.96	53.70
2000	41783	3526	10.96	12.96	10.24	56.20
2001	40640	3402	23.05	13.03	11.44	58.47
2002	47609	5592	29.92	5.00	13.80	60.70
2003	35922	10131	31.76	4.50	13.53	62.50
2004	50111	7718	36.38	14.70	14.86	60.80
2005	51307	16027	31.95	14.80	16.10	62.50
2006	55093	20867	15.50	7.00	15.90	63.95
2007	44251	18708	24.04	9.22	14.91	71.02
2008	48399	58907	22.41	13.02	12.78	72.03
2009	31048	27998	34.59	1.40	12.24	68.21
2010	17457	29631	35.43	4.07	13.87	69.35
2011	49617	28449	32.28	5.06	13.20	70.07
2012	48987	32478	22.27	7.22	13.71	63.35
2013	51646	34381	17.95	4.32	11.06	61.66
2014	44593	33653	18.26			67.85
2015	28040	25458	18.29			68.95
2016	24973	28661	18.17		11.33	
2017	23550	21530	17.39		33.89	

12-14 续表 2
Continued

年 份 Year	合成氨 （万吨） Synthetic Ammonia （10 000 tons）	化学肥料 （万吨） Chemical Fertilizer （10 000 tons）	化学农药 （吨） Chemical Peticides （ton）	油漆 （吨） Paint （ton）	染料 （吨） Dye （ton）
1949				30	599
1952				480	2855
1957			1226	1247	4307
1962		0.45	213	910	3560
1965		1.42	2	4727	8667
1970	0.98	5.89	2313	6380	9347
1975	3.46	12.46	4439	7016	5967
1978	7.17	23.66	9714	8786	5877
1980	7.24	7.82	8333	14556	2159
1985	6.31	5.16	2000	26055	4448
1988	8.72	9.41	2400	28943	5527
1990	7.56	7.55	2500	29075	5119
1991	8.52	8.04	2800	33548	5263
1992	10.45	7.85	3400	35058	4821
1993	10.70	8.02	3600	33054	4550
1994	13.04	12.39	3600	29437	5097
1995	14.98	12.62	4934	37772	7185
1996	18.67	12.62	4976	26762	7668
1997	16.94	12.52	4600	19743	11189
1998	22.36	15.30	6755	17594	8274
1999	26.09	20.19	4480	3730	7866
2000	24.64	20.04	3758	693	9306
2001	35.53	28.07	3915	1349	9757
2002	20.30	9.80	4020	1701	9826
2003	21.55	9.70	2039	2106	10734
2004	30.30	19.60	5061	1955	3961
2005	33.80	22.10	6524	1687	13979
2006	33.30	21.30	12544		26544
2007	28.22	25.70	16433	2957	28269
2008	17.93	21.51	12848	12105	18263
2009	17.71	21.23	49684		24893
2010	16.84	14.10	16450		41383
2011	10.78	9.26	23286		
2012	7.71	6.98	28801		
2013	6.48	5.10	27715		
2014			27160		
2015			36853		
2016		14.33	34993		
2017		7.38	18911		

12-14 续表 3
Continued

年 份 Year	化学原料药 （吨） Chemical Medicines （ton）	水泥 （万吨） Cement （10 000 tons）	平板玻璃 （万重量箱） Plate Glass （10 000 weight cases）	耐火材料 （万吨） Refractory Material （10 000 tons）	粗钢 （万吨） Crude Steel （10 000 tons）	钢材 （万吨） Rolled-steel （10 000 tons）
1949						0.06
1952				0.78	0.36	0.41
1957				3.39	1.77	4.30
1962		2.09		2.41	4.59	2.94
1965		6.59		2.91	11.72	8.43
1970		7.35	16.31	3.23	19.38	14.56
1975	55	20.93	19.44	4.88	21.25	20.01
1978	185	35.40	8.86	5.93	31.06	27.61
1980	123	44.66	70.13	5.38	37.14	32.82
1984	7228	70.27	91.25	7.98	37.81	32.43
1985	4222	82.70	77.00	4.35	37.51	32.68
1988	7655	141.00	108.81	4.56	50.17	38.26
1990	6913	139.48	83.13	3.91	54.55	38.04
1991	4754	165.66	96.90	3.71	56.96	39.02
1992	5743	191.50	120.00	3.86	63.75	50.09
1993	6566	221.30	148.71	3.55	61.75	44.88
1994	4238	246.50	145.12	3.06	60.82	46.95
1995	1993	213.82	426.40	3.88	67.27	49.60
1996	5505	181.45	423.60	3.54	72.02	50.60
1997	1693	208.04	570.85	2.45	75.71	51.06
1998	910	131.51	509.38	0.99	84.02	64.93
1999	1691	149.41	576.50	0.59	108.10	86.58
2000	2131	137.52	556.58	0.62	101.17	93.35
2001	2534	148.67	421.51	0.51	124.45	119.77
2002	2712	140.30	405.40	0.45	145.90	142.20
2003	3288	154.90	361.40	0.47	204.80	204.30
2004	4394	181.19	163.30	0.69	225.70	230.97
2005	4430	210.80	297.50	1.04	309.70	330.30
2006	32232	232.72	418.74	1.21	325.82	375.52
2007	14139	425.53	397.79	2.38	327.00	365.55
2008	17910	363.57	599.87	3.65	300.19	350.14
2009	19086	397.66	681.02	18.46	307.89	349.63
2010	26170	442.66	662.04	8.17	300.04	333.46
2011	29337	588.08	510.05	20.02	318.27	325.89
2012	49290	556.57	494.54	33.44	252.78	274.67
2013	49081	575.66	610.21	42.34	235.53	230.39
2014	50713	597.35	612.40	39.37	214.43	212.79
2015	45923	532.36	534.99	41.13	154.56	140.63
2016	2248	600.56	576.16	108.76	188.04	191.37
2017	2775	525.42	557.44	109.84	280.96	291.85

12-14 续表 4
Continued

年份 Year	金属切削机床（台） Metal-cutting Machine Tools (unit)	锻压机械（台） Metal Forming Machinery (unit)	汽车（辆） Motor Vehicles (set)	交流电动机（万千瓦） AC Motors (10 000 kW)
1949				0.02
1952	105			0.50
1957	76			3.61
1962	167	77		3.85
1965	526	111	13	6.48
1970	2353	531	120	14.53
1975	3213	788	490	15.56
1978	2558	379	22	21.72
1980	595	444	1644	20.11
1985	900	607	4575	26.08
1988	1336	737	3722	39.60
1990	1049	440	2317	34.28
1991	869	764	1514	44.17
1992	1018	982	3287	61.08
1993	1532	919	4828	64.13
1994	1505	860	2793	37.71
1995	972	2563	5210	39.18
1996	1084	584	12247	22.65
1997	449	416	13020	20.74
1998	280		15475	6.43
1999	251		20038	11.10
2000	384		30053	38.70
2001	472	2477	40658	42.72
2002	588		70079	68.25
2003	990		65612	95.63
2004	1287		62572	96.13
2005	1347		31055	63.50
2006	3636		50278	702.02
2007	3392	1869	61016	119.23
2008	8381	1230	70161	96.89
2009	668		458900	728.03
2010	1120		566211	101.10
2011	1194		488330	74.08
2012	1014		574729	104.48
2013	2689		708966	126.82
2014	2563		770245	114.46
2015	618		861250	104.30
2016	588		816839	98.70
2017	610		741455	202.79

12-14 续表 5
Continued

年 份 Year	钢芯铝绞线（吨） Steel-cored Aluminum Stranded Wire （ton）	家用电冰箱 （万台） Home Refrigerators （10 000 sets）	家用洗衣机 （万台） Home Washing Machines （10 000 sets）	彩色电视机 （万部） Color TV Sets （10 000 sets）
1949				
1952				
1957				
1962				
1965	250			
1970	34			
1975	188			
1978	684			
1980	1232			
1985	2327	1.66	0.48	6.60
1988	1571	15.22	42.38	17.00
1990	1880	27.41	45.86	18.50
1991	2463	31.51	45.70	22.27
1992	2248	54.84	46.31	28.07
1993	1144	50.48	56.59	36.08
1994	287	62.50	71.34	60.15
1995	1659	107.91	64.34	60.53
1996	2265	193.80	100.94	56.68
1997	2616	257.10	171.95	124.86
1998	1725	219.23	183.67	96.83
1999	2805	259.60	256.30	285.20
2000	4202	311.10	318.50	379.40
2001	4498	396.30	367.89	455.40
2002	5825	518.20	408.60	593.20
2003	4940	598.30	471.50	671.70
2004	6608	815.03	575.06	957.90
2005	116592	908.80	614.90	1324.30
2006	46974	1290.00	649.40	1205.60
2007	22564	1421.40	769.40	1243.10
2008	29507	723.19	407.54	836.66
2009		827.21	488.72	1064.70
2010		801.22	580.87	1111.19
2011		718.54	604.55	1154.20
2012		575.01	583.60	1439.98
2013		524.35	606.65	1512.05
2014		610.07	590.95	1714.93
2015		872.09	595.11	1736.20
2016		882.22	606.74	2111.71
2017		818.65	603.4	1703.01

12-15　规模以上工业主要产品产量
OUTPUT OF MAJOR INDUSTRIAL PRODUCTS OF INDUSTRY ABOVE DESIGNATED SIZE

产品名称	Name	计量单位	Unit	2017年	2016年	2017年比2016年（±%）2017/2016（±%）
冶金工业产品	**Products of Metallurgical Industry**					
粗钢	Crude Steel	万吨	10 000 tons	280.96	188.04	49.41
钢材	Rolled-steel	万吨	10 000 tons	291.85	213.04	37
耐火材料制品	Refractory Material	万吨	10 000 tons	109.84	99.53	10.36
电力工业产品	**Products of Electricity Industry**					
发电量	Electricity	亿千瓦小时	100 million kW·h	181.8	175.4	3.7
化学工业产品	**Products of Chemical Industry**					
原油加工量	Processing Amount of Crude Oill	万吨	10 000 tons	1522.9	1518.8	1
汽油	Petrol	万吨	10 000 tons	456.1	460.5	–1
柴油	Diesel Oill	万吨	10 000 tons	408.1	419.3	–2.7
燃料油	Fuel Oil	万吨	10 000 tons	12.1	12.6	–4
化学农药	Chemical Pesticides	万吨	10 000 tons	1.89	1.43	32.58
塑料制品	Plastic	万吨	10 000 tons	26.79	25.41	5.45
化学药品（原料）	Chemical Medicines（Paw Materials）	万吨	10 000 tons	0.28	0.22	23.42

12-15 续表 1
Continued

产品名称	Name	计量单位	Unit	2017 年	2016 年	2017 年比 2016 年（±%） 2017/2016（±%）
橡胶轮胎外胎	Tires	万条	10 000 tires	5452.86	5034.19	8.32
机械工业产品	**Products of Machinery Industry**					
工业锅炉	Industrial Boiler	蒸发量吨	ton （evaporation amunt）	14680.67	12554.92	16.93
交流电动机	AC Motors	万千瓦	10 000 kW	202.79	207.82	–2.42
金属切削机床	Metal-cutting Machine	台	set	610	588	3.74
汽车	Motor Vehicles	辆	set	741455	636809	16.43
改装汽车	Refitted Motor Vehicles	辆	set	20982	15511	35.27
民用钢质船舶	Civil Steel Ships	载重吨	syn-ton	103207	189459	–45.53
电子产品	**Electronic Products**					
彩色电视机	Color TV sets	万台	10 000 sets	1703.00	2111.71	–19.35
电子元件	Electronice	万只	10 000 Units	371556.23	397264.13	–6.47
建材工业产品	Products of Construction Industry					
水泥	Cement	万吨	10 000 tons	525.42	596.11	–11.86
平板玻璃	Plate Glass	万重量箱	10 000 weight cases	557.44	576.16	–3.25
砖（折标准砖）	Bricks	万块	10 000 piecces	70438.00	43218.00	62.98

12-15 续表 2
Continued

产品名称	Name	计量单位	Unit	2017 年	2016 年	2017 年比 2016 年 (±%) 2017/2016 (±%)
纺织工业产品	**Products of Textile Industry**					
纱	Yarn	吨	ton	26493.18	28833.22	-8.12
布	Cloth	万米	10 000 m	23550.30	24021.66	-1.96
印染布	Printed Fabric	万米	10 000 m	21530.00	28446.00	-24.31
化学纤维	Chemical Fibers	吨	ton	11564.40	14842.28	-22.08
轻工产品	**Products of Light Industry**					
机制纸及纸板	Machine-made Paper and Paperboards	万吨	10 000 tons	17.39	18.17	-4.31
家用洗衣机	Home Washing Machines	万台	10 000 sets	603.40	606.74	-0.55
糖果	Sugar	吨	ton	11545.00	11552.00	-0.06
食用植物油	Vegetable Oil	万吨	10 000 tons	43.63	47.73	-8.59
饮料酒	Beverage Liquor	万千升	10 000 KL	161.47	166.81	-3.20
# 白酒	Wine	万千升	10 000 KL	1.97	1.89	3.85
啤酒	Beer	万千升	10 000 KL	158.07	162.32	-2.62
塑料制品	Plastic Products	万吨	10 000 tons	26.79	25.41	5.45
家具	Furniture	万件	10 000 articles	672.85	666.81	0.91
家用电冰箱	Home Refrigerators	万台	10 000 sets	818.65	882.22	-7.21
皮革鞋靴	Leather Shoes	万双	10 000 pairs	4276.20	4554.88	-6.12
服装	Chothing	万件	10 000 articles	58353.18	64115.09	-8.99

12-16　规模以上工业主要产品生产能力
PRODUCTION CAPACITY OF MAJOR PRODUCTS OF INDUSTRY ABOVE DESIGNATED SIZE

产品名称	Name	计量单位	Unit	2017年生产能力 Production Capacity of 2017	2016年生产能力 Production Capacity of 2016
发电设备容量总计 / 发电量	Total Capacity of Generation Equipment	万千瓦 / 万千瓦小时	10 000 kW/ 10 000 kW · h		
化学纤维	Chemical Fiber	吨	ton	14800	14800
棉纺锭 / 纺纱量	Knitting Spindle	锭 / 吨	spindle/ton	178716	143032
棉布织机 / 布	Cotton Cloth Loom	台 / 万米	set/10 000 m	9833.3	11093
焦炭	Coke	吨	ton	1600000	1600000
农用氮、磷、钾化学肥料总计（折纯）	Chemical Fertilizer	吨	ton	80000	80000
水泥	Cement	吨	ton	9200000	9200000
平板玻璃	Plate Glass	重量箱	weight cases	6200000	6200000
生铁	Pig Iron	吨	ton	3220000	3220000
粗钢	Crude Steel	吨	ton	3125000	3000000
钢材	Rolled-steel	吨	ton	4255602	4265000
金属切削机床	Metal-cutting Machine	台	set	1799	1880
汽车	Motor Vehicles	辆	set	102000	102000
家用电冰箱	Home Refrigerators	台	set	11917700	13550000
房间空气调节器	Air Conditioner	台	set	10900000	10040000
移动通信手持机（手机）	Cell Phone	台	set	33500000	35000000
彩色电视机	Color TV Sets	台	set	20700000	22700000

主要统计指标解释

工业总产值　是以货币表现的工业企业在一定时期内生产的已出售或可供出售工业产品总量，它是反映一定时间内工业生产的总规模和总水平。

工业销售产值　是以货币表现的工业企业在一定时期内销售的本企业生产的工业产品产量。包括已销售的成品、半成品价值，以及对外提供的工业性作业价值和对本单位基本建设部门、生活福利部门等提供的产品和工业性作业及自制设备的价值。

工业增加值　指工业企业在报告期内以货币表现的工业生产活动的最终成果。是企业全部生产活动的总成果扣除了在生产过程中消耗或转移的物质产品和劳务价值后的余额，是企业生产过程中新增加的价值。

资产总计　指企业拥有或控制的能以货币计量的经济资源，包括各种财产、债权和其他权利。资产按其流动性（即资产的变现能力和支付能力）划分为：流动资产、长期投资、固定资产、无形资产、递延资产和其他资产。

负债合计　指企业所承担的能以货币计量，将以资产或劳务偿付的债务，偿还形式包括货币、资产或提供劳务。负债一般按偿还期长短分为流动负债和长期负债。

利润总额　指企业生产经营活动的最终成果，是企业在一定时期内实现的盈亏相抵后的利润总额（亏损以“–”号表示），它等于营业利润加上补贴收入加上投资收益加上营业外净收入再加上以前年度损益调整。

Explanatory Notes on Main Statistical Indicators

Gross Industrial Output Value　is the total volume of final industrial products produced and industrial services provided during a given period. It reflects the total achievements and overall scale of industrial production during a given period.

Sales Output Value of Industry　refers to total sales of products produced by industrial enterprises during a given period, including sales of fished goods, value of semi-products, value of industrial services provided to other units, value of products, industrial services provided for capital construction sector, welfare and self produced equipments within enterprise.

Value-added of Industry　rdfers to the final results of industrial production of industrial enterprises in money terms during the reference period.

Total Assets　refer to all economic resources, in monetary terms, that in owned or controlled by enterprises, including properties, creditors equity and other economic rights of all forms. Classified by the degree of equitability, total assets include circulating assets, long-term investment, fixed assets, intangible assets and deferred assets, and other assets.

Total Liabilities　refer to payable liabilities of enterprises that have to repay in terms of money, assets or labour services. In terms of payment, it can be divided into liquid liabilities and long-term liabilities.

Total Profits　refer to the final achievements of production and operation of the enterprises, represented by the total profits after deducting losses (loss is expressed by the negative figure) . It is the sum of profits from operation, income from subsidies, investment earnings, net income from activities other than operation, and adjustment of profits and losses of previous years.

建筑业 13
CONSTRUCTION

简要说明

一、本篇资料的主要内容

本篇资料主要反映了全市建筑业基本情况，主要包括建筑业总产值、增加值、建筑企业生产指标、财务指标、重点建筑企业名单等方面的内容。

二、本篇资料的来源

本篇资料来源于建筑业统计年报，由市统计局固定资产投资统计处整理提供。

Brief Introduction

Ⅰ. Main Content

Data in this chapter show the basic conditions of construction of the whole city, mainly including the gross output value of construction, value added, major production and financial indicators and list of key enterprises of construction, etc.

Ⅱ. Source of Data

Data in this chapter are based on the annual report of construction industry, and complied by the Division of Investment and Construction Statistics of Qingdao Municipal Bureau of Statistics.

13-1 建筑业企业生产情况（2017 年）
PRODUCTION SITUATION OF CONSTRUCTION ENTERPRISES（2017）

项　目	Item	单位	Unit	合计 Total	#中央 of which：Central Enterprises	国有企业 State-owned Enterprises	集体企业 Collectiveowned Enterprises	其他所有制企业 Other Ownership Enterprises
施工企业单位数	Number of Construction Enterpises	个	unit	679	11	22	8	649
建筑业总产值	Gross Output Value of Construction	万元	10000 yuan	18 793 842	3 005 414	631 272	20 758	18 141 812
#建筑工程	of which：Construction	万元	10000 yuan	16 554 703	2 469 352	421 262	20 087	16 113 354
安装工程	Installation	万元	10000 yuan	1 675 155	501 610	182 998	561	1 491 596
建筑业增加值	Value Added of Construction	万元	10000 yuan	6 022 200				
全年竣工产值	Output Value of Buildings Completed in the Year	万元	10000 yuan	7 880 503	1 221 104	377 226	11 111	7 492 166
施工房屋面积	Floor Spece of Buildings under Construction	万平方米	10000 sp.m	13 892	1 604	16	28	13 848
#新开工	of which：Newly Operating	万平方米	10000 sp.m	4 640	505	9	7	4 624
竣工房屋面积	Floor Space of Buildings Completed	万平方米	10000 sp.m	2 539	184	9	10	2 520
#住宅	of which：Residential Buildings	万平方米	10000 sp.m	1 490	100		9	1 481
计算建筑业劳动生产率平均人数	Average Number of Persons for Calculating the Labor Productivity	人	person	607 990	66 380	9 809	1 065	597 116

13-2 建筑业企业财务状况（2017年）
FINANCIAL SITUATION OF CONSTRUCTION ENTRPRISES（2017）

项 目	Item	单位	Unit	合计 Total
流动资产	Circulating Funds	万元	10000 yuan	19 711 600
#存货	of which：Inventory	万元	10000 yuan	3 702 153
年末固定资产原价	Original Value of Fixed Assets（year-end）	万元	10000 yuan	1 939 175
本年固定资产折旧	Depreciation of Fixed Assets in the Year	万元	10000 yuan	116 468
年末资产合计	Total Assets（year-end）	万元	10000 yuan	23 380 947
年末负债合计	Total Liabilities（year-end）	万元	10000 yuan	17 702 798
所有者权益合计	Total Owners' Equity	万元	10000 yuan	5 678 149
#实收资本	Paid-in Capitals	万元	10000 yuan	3 254 311
主营业务收入	Revenue from Principal Business	万元	10000 yuan	19 089 834
主营业务成本	Cost of Principal Business	万元	10000 yuan	17 277 203
主营业务税金及附加	Taxes and Extra Charges on Principal Business	万元	10000 yuan	114 573
管理费用	Management Expenses	万元	10000 yuan	604 057
利润总额	Total Profits	万元	10000 yuan	557 504
利税总额	Total Pre-tax Profits	万元	10000 yuan	969 978
年末应收工程款	Account Receivable（year-end）	万元	10000 yuan	6 862 898

#中央 of which：Central Enterprises	国有企业 State-owned Enterprises	集体企业 Gollective-owned Enterprises	其他所有制企业 Other Ownership Enterprises
4 866 020	1 902 216	8 898	17 800 486
1 228 450	464 165	1 696	3 236 292
652 048	116 816	4 247	1 818 112
49 114	6 403	67	109 998
5 517 851	2 124 421	13 100	21 243 426
4 780 957	1 811 567	6 047	15 885 184
736 894	312 854	7 053	5 358 242
438 539	189 667	5 424	3 059 220
4 253 894	1 347 732	23 053	17 719 049
3 953 986	1 257 019	20 597	15 999 587
8 254	1 961	884	111 728
152 937	44 127	971	558 959
110 414	29 620	478	527 406
158 058	37 188	1 879	930 911
1 190 134	219 937	2 707	6 640 254

13-3 建筑业企业主要经济效益指标(2017年)
MAIN INDICATORS ON ECONOMIC BENEFIT OF CONSTRUCTION ENTERPRISES (2017)

项　目	Item	单位	Unit	合计 Total	#中央 of which: Central Enterprises	国有企业 State-owned Enterprises	集体企业 Collectiveowned Enterprises	其他所有制企业 Other Ownership Enterprises
建筑业劳动生产率	**Labor Productivity of Construction**							
按总产值计算	In Terms of Gross Output Value	元/人	yuan/person	309 114	452 759	643 564	194 912	303 824
竣工率	**Rate of Buildings completd**							
按产值计算	In Terms of Gross output Value	%		41.9	40.6	59.8	53.5	41.3
产值工资率	Ratio of Wages to Gross Output Value	%		13.3	11.6	18.9	25.1	13.1
资金利润率	Ratio of Profit to Funds	%		2.7	1.6	1.5	2.4	2.8
产值利润率	Ratio of Profit to Gross Output Value	%		2.9	3.7	4.6	2.3	2.8
流动比率	Current Ratio	%		111.3	101.7	105.0	147.1	112.1
资产负债率	Assets-Liability Ratio	%		75.7	86.6	85.2	46.2	74.7

13-4 建筑业增加值（2017 年）
VALUE ADDED OF CONSTRUCTION（2017）

单位：亿元（100 million yuan）

市、区名称	Region	增加值 Value Added
全　市	**Whole Municipal**	**602.22**
市南区	Shinan District	54.01
市北区	Shiber District	71.35
李沧区	Licang District	13.65
崂山区	Laoshan District	82.22
黄岛区	Huangdao District	162.42
城阳区	Chengyang District	15.71
即墨区	Jimo District	68.51
胶州市	Jiaozhou	71.11
平度市	Pingdu	16.23
莱西市	Laixi	43.03
红岛经济区	Qingdao National High-tech Industrial Development Zone	3.98

注：黄岛区含保税港区数据。
Note：The Huangdao District contains the data of the bonded harbor area.

13-5 重点建筑企业一览表（2017 年）
LIST OF KEY CONSTRUCTION ENTERPRISES（2017）

序　号 Precedence	企业单位名称	Name	所在地区 Location	资质等级 Qualification Criteria
1	青建集团股份公司	Qingjian Group Co., Ltd.	市北区 Shibei District	A001
2	中青建安建设集团有限公司	Zhongqing Jianan Construction Group Co., Ltd.	市南区 Shinan District	A001
3	荣华建设集团有限公司	Ronghua Construction Group Co., Ltd.	莱西市 Laixi	A001
4	中建八局第四建设有限公司	Fourth Construction of China Construction Eight Bureau Co., Ltd.	市南区 Shinan District	A001
5	中启胶建集团有限公司	Zhongqi Rubber Construction Group Co., Ltd.	胶州市 Jiaozhou	A001
6	东亚装饰股份有限公司	East Asia Decoration Limited by Share Ltd.	市南区 Shinan District	B103
7	中铁二十局集团第四工程有限公司	Fourth Engineering of China Railway twenty Bureau Group Co., Ltd.	崂山区 Laoshan District	A103
8	青岛一建集团有限公司	Qingdao Yi Jian Group Co., Ltd.	市北区 Shibei District	A001
9	中建筑港集团有限公司	Zhongjian Zhu Gang Group Co., Ltd.	市北区 Shibei District	A104
10	青岛海川建设集团有限公司	Qingdao Hai Chuan Construction Group Co., Ltd.	市北区 Shibei District	A001
11	山东莱钢建设有限公司	Shandong Laiwu Iron and Steel Construction Co., Ltd.	市南区 Shinan District	A101
12	青岛海尔家居集成股份有限公司	Qingdao Haier Integrated Limited by Share Ltd.	胶州市 Jiaozhou	B103
13	青岛博海建设集团有限公司	Qingdao Bohai Construction Group Co., Ltd.	市南区 Shinan District	A001
14	青岛温泉建设集团有限公司	Qingdao Hot Spring Construction Group Co., Ltd.	即墨区 Jimo District	A101
15	中铁建工集团山东有限公司	China Railway Construction Engineering Group Shandong Co., Ltd.	崂山区 Laoshan District	A301
16	山东电力建设第三工程有限公司	Third Engineering Co., Ltd. of Shandong Electric Power Construction	崂山区 Laoshan District	A006
17	青岛即建建设集团有限公司	Qingdao JiJian Construction Group Co., Ltd.	即墨区 Jimo District	A101
18	中铁二十五局集团第五工程有限公司	Fifth Engineering Co., Ltd. of China Railway twenty-five Bureau Group	崂山区 Laoshan District	A110
19	中交一航局第二工程有限公司	Second Engineering Company Co., Ltd. of China Communications Central Airlines	市南区 Shinan District	A104
20	山东兴华建设集团有限公司	Shandong Xinghua Construction Group Co., Ltd.	黄岛区 Huangdao District	A001
21	青岛中建联合建设工程有限公司	Qingdao Zhongjian United Construction Engineering Co., Ltd.	崂山区 Laoshan District	A101
22	青岛滨海建设集团有限公司	Qingdao Binhai Construction Group Co., Ltd.	黄岛区 Huangdao District	A101
23	青岛亿联集团股份有限公司	QingdaoYilian Group Limited by Share Ltd.	黄岛区 Huangdao District	A101
24	青建国际集团有限公司	Qingjian International Group Limited	市北区 Shibei District	A101
25	青岛中嘉建设集团有限公司	Qingdao Zhongjia Construction Group Co., Ltd.	市北区 Shibei District	A201
26	中铁十局集团青岛工程有限公司	China Railway Ten Bureau Group Qingdao Engineering Co., Ltd.	市北区 Shibei District	A110
27	德才装饰股份有限公司	Decai Decoration Limited by Share Ltd.	崂山区 Laoshan District	B103
28	山东荣泰建筑工程集团有限公司	Shandong Rongtai Construction Engineering Group Co., Ltd.	黄岛区 Huangdao District	A101
29	青岛恒生源集团建设有限公司	Qingdao Hengshengyuan Group Construction Co., Ltd.	即墨区 Jimo District	A101
30	青岛公路建设集团有限公司	Qingdao Highway Construction Group Co., Ltd.	崂山区 Laoshan District	A102
31	青岛福瀛建设集团有限公司	Qingdao Fu ying Construction Group Co., Ltd.	黄岛区 Huangdao District	A101
32	青岛第一市政工程有限公司	Qingdao First Municipal Engineering Co., Ltd.	市北区 Shibei District	A110
33	青岛土木建工集团有限公司	Qingdao Civil Engineering Group Co., Ltd.	黄岛区 Huangdao District	A101
34	中石化第十建设有限公司	Sinopec tenth Construction Company Limited	黄岛区 Huangdao District	A109
35	青岛瑞源工程集团有限公司	Qingdao Ruiyuan Engineering Group Co., Ltd.	黄岛区 Huangdao District	A105

13-5 续表 1
Continued

序号 Precedence	企业单位名称	Name	所在地区 Location	资质等级 Qualification Criteria
36	青岛安装建设股份有限公司	Qingdao Installation and Construction Limited by Share Ltd.	市北区 Shibei District	A112
37	中国石油天然气第七建设有限公司	China Petroleum and Natural Gas Seventh Construction Co., Ltd.	崂山区 Laoshan District	A109
38	青岛海德路桥工程股份有限公司	Qingdao Hyde Road and Bridge Engineering Limited by Share Ltd.	市南区 Shinan District	A210
39	青岛城建集团有限公司	Qingdao Urban Construction Group Co., Ltd.	市北区 Shibei District	A110
40	青岛胶城建设集团有限公司	Qingdao Rubber City Construction Group Co., Ltd.	胶州市 Jiaozhou	A101
41	青岛建设集团有限公司	Qingdao Construction Group Co., Ltd.	市南区 Shinan District	A201
42	青岛平建建筑安装股份有限公司	Qingdao Ping Jian Building and Installation Limited by Share Ltd.	平度市 Pingdu	A101
43	青岛登科市政工程有限公司	Qingdao Dengke Municipal Engineering Co., Ltd.	城阳区 Chengyang District	A110
44	青岛市政空间开发集团有限责任公司	Qingdao Municipal Space Development Group Ltd	市南区 Shinan District	A110
45	青岛市房屋建筑集团股份有限公司	Qingdao Housing Construction Group Limited by Share Ltd.	市北区 Shibei District	A101
46	青岛新华友建工集团股份有限公司	Qingdao Xinhuayou Construction Engineering Group Limited by Share Ltd.	崂山区 Laoshan District	A101
47	青岛德泰建设工程有限公司	Qingdao de Tai Construction Engineering Co., Ltd.	黄岛区 Huangdao District	A101
48	青岛营上建设集团有限公司	Qingdao Yingshang Construction Group Co., Ltd.	即墨区 Jimo District	A101
49	青岛颐金建筑装饰工程有限公司	Qingdao Yijin Building Decoration Engineering Co., Ltd.	市南区 Shinan District	B103
50	青岛建工集团有限公司	Qingdao Construction Engineering Group Co., Ltd.	崂山区 Laoshan District	A102
51	青岛营海建设集团有限公司	Qingdao Ying hai Construction Group Co., Ltd.	胶州市 Jiaozhou	A101
52	青岛青房建安集团有限公司	Qingdao Qingfang Jianan Group Co., Ltd.	市南区 Shinan District	A101
53	青岛胶州湾建设集团有限公司	Qingdao Jiaozhou Bay Construction Group Co., Ltd.	胶州市 Jiaozhou	A101
54	青岛建祥建设集团有限公司	Qingdao Jian Xiang Construction Group Co., Ltd.	胶州市 Jiaozhou	A101
55	青岛高新建筑安装工程有限公司	Qingdao Hi tech Huilding Installation Engineering Co., Ltd.	崂山区 Laoshan District	A101
56	青岛港务局港务工程公司	Qingdao Port Bureau Port Engineering Company	黄岛区 Huangdao District	A204
57	山东天诚市政公路工程有限公司	Shandong Tiancheng Municipal Highway Engineering Co., Ltd.	崂山区 Laoshan District	A110
58	青岛鑫兴泰建筑工程有限公司	Qingdao xinxingtai Construction Engineering Co., Ltd.	城阳区 Chengyang District	A201
59	青岛新城发展建筑工程有限公司	Qingdao New Town Development Engineering Co., Ltd.	市北区 Shibei District	A101
60	青岛艺高城市建设工程有限公司	Qingdao Yi Gao City Construction Engineering Co., Ltd.	市北区 Shibei District	B237
61	中铁建港航局集团第三工程有限公司	China Railway Construction Group Third Engineering Co., Ltd.	李沧区 Licang District	A110
62	青岛东捷建设工程有限公司	Qingdao Dong jie Construction Engineering Co., Ltd.	市北区 Shibei District	A101
63	青岛西海岸市政集团市政工程公司	Qingdao West Coast municipal Group Municipal Engineering Company	黄岛区 Huangdao District	A310
64	山东国建工程集团有限公司	Shandong State Construction Engineering Group Co., Ltd.	崂山区 Laoshan District	A101
65	青岛环城建工集团有限公司	Qingdao Ring City Construction Engineering Group Co., Ltd.	黄岛区 Huangdao District	A201
66	青岛地矿岩土工程有限公司	Qingdao Geotechnical Engineering Co., Ltd.	市南区 Shinan District	B101
67	青岛环海工程贸易发展有限公司	Qingdao Huanhai Engineering & Trade Development Co., Ltd.	市北区 Shibei District	A201

13-5 续表 2
Continued

序号 Precedence	企业单位名称	Name	所在地区 Location	资质等级 Qualification Criteria
68	山东省路通工程集团有限公司	Shandong Lutong Engineering Group Co., Ltd.	崂山区 Laoshan District	A102
69	山东奥华建筑安装工程有限公司	Shandong Ao Hua Construction and Installation Engineering Co., Ltd.	市南区 Shinan District	A101
70	青岛万怡东方建设集团有限公司	Qingdao Wan Yi Oriental Construction Group Co., Ltd.	黄岛区 Huangdao District	A101
71	青岛凌云建设集团有限公司	Qingdao Lingyun Construction Group Co., Ltd.	胶州市 Jiaozhou	A201
72	青岛市崂山区古建建筑工程有限公司	Qingdao Laoshan ancient building engineering Co., Ltd.	崂山区 Laoshan District	A101
73	青岛金楷装饰工程有限公司	Qingdao Jin Kai decoration Engineering Co., Ltd.	市北区 Shibei District	B202
74	青岛鑫隆建设集团有限公司	Qingdao Xinlong Construction Group Co., Ltd.	黄岛区 Huangdao District	A101
75	青岛九龙建设集团有限公司	Qingdao Jiulong Construction Group Co., Ltd.	胶州市 Jiaozhou	A201
76	青岛世纪阳光建筑装饰工程有限公司	Qingdao Shiji Sunshine Building Decoration Engineering Co., Ltd.	市南区 Shinan District	B213
77	青岛东建建设有限公司	Qingdao Dongjian Construction Co., Ltd.	李沧区 Licang District	A201
78	青岛建设集团建兴工程有限公司	Qingdao construction group LITE-ON Engineering Co., Ltd.	红岛经济区 Qingdao National Hightech Industrial Development Zone	A101
79	青岛市益水工程股份有限公司	Qingdao Yi Shui project Limited by Share Ltd.	市南区 Shinan District	A210
80	青岛三星工程有限公司	Qingdao Sanxing Engineering Co., Ltd.	城阳区 Chengyang District	A110
81	青岛恒辉建设集团有限公司	Qingdao Heng Hui Construction Group Co., Ltd.	黄岛区 Huangdao District	A201
82	青岛三林建筑工程有限公司	Qingdao Sanlin Construction Engineering Co., Ltd.	黄岛区 Huangdao District	A201
83	青岛太行园林建设有限公司	Qingdao Taihang Garden Construction Co., Ltd.	黄岛区 Huangdao District	A210
84	青岛金星科技工程有限公司	Qingdao Jinxing Science and Technology Engineering Co., Ltd.	市南区 Shinan District	B111
85	青岛恒华机房设备工程有限公司	Qingdao Heng Hua machine Room Equipment Engineering Co., Ltd.	市南区 Shinan District	B123
86	青岛恒源送变电工程有限公司	Qingdao Hengyuan transmission and Transformation Engineering Co., Ltd.	城阳区 Chengyang District	A201
87	青岛福海洋建设集团有限公司	Qingdao Fu Ocean Construction Group Co., Ltd.	胶州市 Jiaozhou	A201
88	青岛金沙滩建设集团有限公司	Qingdao Jinshatan Construction Group Co., Ltd.	黄岛区 Huangdao District	A101
89	青岛泰能工程股份有限公司	Qingdao Taineng Engineering Limited by Share Ltd	市北区 Shibei District	A210
90	鲁建集团股份有限公司	Lu Jian Group Limited by Share Ltd.	崂山区 Laoshan District	A202
91	青岛盛泽建设工程有限公司	Qingdao Shengze Construction Engineering Co., Ltd.	胶州市 Jiaozhou	A201
92	青岛柏高市政园林建设集团有限公司	Qingdao BOGAO Municipal Garden Construction Group Co., Ltd.	市南区 Shinan District	A110
93	青岛万福建筑工程有限公司	Qingdao Wanfu Construction Engineering Co., Ltd.	莱西市 Laixi	A301
94	胶南市建筑工程公司	Jiaonan Construction Engineering Co., Ltd.	黄岛区 Huangdao District	A101
95	青岛市黄岛区园林绿化工程有限公司	Huangdao of Qingdao Landscaping Engineering Co., Ltd.	黄岛区 Huangdao District	B101
96	青岛建国工程集团有限公司	Qingdao Jianguo Engineering Group Co., Ltd.	黄岛区 Huangdao District	A201
97	青岛亿佰建工集团有限公司	Qingdao Yibai Construction Group Co., Ltd.	黄岛区 Huangdao District	A201
98	青岛华商工程有限公司	Qingdao Huashang Engineering Co., Ltd.	莱西市 Laixi	A301
99	青岛昶德建设集团有限公司	Qingdao Changde Construction Group Co., Ltd.	胶州市 Jiaozhou	A101
100	青岛田横建筑工程有限公司	Qingdao Tianheng Construction Engineering Co., Ltd.	即墨区 Jimo District	A201

主要统计指标解释

建筑业统计单位 指从事房屋、构筑物建造和设备安装活动的法人企业。建筑业法人企业应具有建筑业资质并能够独立核算，同时其应具备以下条件：①依法成立，有自己的名称、组织机构和场所，能够承担民事责任；②独立拥有和使用资产，承担负债，有权与其他单位签订合同；③独立核算盈亏，能够编制资产负债表。

建筑业总产值 是以货币形式表现的建筑业企业在一定时期内生产的建筑业产品和提供的服务的总和。建筑业总产值包括：

（1）建筑工程产值：指列入建筑工程预算内的各种工程价值。

（2）安装工程产值：指设备安装工程价值，不包括被安装设备本身的价值。

（3）其他产值：建筑业总产值中除建筑工程、安装工程以外的产值。包括房屋构筑物修理产值、非标准设备制造产值、总包企业向分包企业收取的管理费以及不能明确划分的施工活动所完成的产值。

建筑业增加值 指建筑业企业在报告期内以货币形式表现的建筑业生产经营活动的最终成果。

建筑业现价增加值 按生产法和分配法（收入法）两种方法计算，以收入法的计算结果为准，即从收入的角度出发，根据生产要素在生产过程中应得的收入份额计算。具体计算方法：经济普查年度建筑业增加值按照《经济普查年度 GDP 核算方案》计算，非经济普查年度建筑业增加值按照《非经济普查年度 GDP 核算方案》计算。

Explanatory Notes on Main Statistical Indicators

Statistical Unit in Construction refers to corporate enterprise engaged in the construction of buildings and structures and in the installation of equipment. A corporate construction enterprise should have qualification certificates with independent accounting system, and should meet the following 3 requirements : a) being set up in line with relevant legal basis, having its full name, organization and location, and capable of taking civil liabilities ; b) independently possessing and using its assets and assuming its liabilities, and entitled to sign contracts with other institutions ; and c) making independent accounts of its profits and losses, and capable of compiling its own balance sheet.

Gross Output Value of Construction refers to total of construction products and services, expressed in money terms, produced or rendered by construction and installation enterprises during a given period of time. It includes :

(1) Output value of construction projects, that is the value of projects covered by the project budgets ;

(2) Output value of installation projects, that is the value of the installation of equipment, (excluding the value of the equipment to be installed) ;

(3) Output value of others, that is the output value of construction industry excluding that of construction projects and installation projects. It includes : output value of repair of buildings and structures ; output value of non-standard equipment manufacturing ; overhead expenses received by contracted enterprises to the sub-contracted enterprises and the completed output value of construction activities that have no clear definition.

The added value of the building industry refers to the final results of production and operation activities of enterprises in the building industry, expressed in monetary form, during the reporting period.

The construction industry's added value at current price is calculated by the production method and distribution method (income method), based on the result of income method, that is from the point of view of income, the calculation is based on the share of income to be received by the production factors during the production process. The specific calculation method : For the economic census year, construction industry's added value is based on the Economic Census Year's GDP Accounting Scheme ; for the non-economic census year, construction industry's added value is based on the Non-economic Census Year's GDP Accounting Scheme.

Added value of building industry refers to the final achievement within the report period indicated in currency of all production and operation activities of building enterprises.

Added value at current prices of building industry shall be calculated in such two ways as production and distribution (income), while the result of latter shall be taken as the norm, which means, from the point of view of income, it shall be calculated according to the income that the production factors deserve in the process of production. Detailed calculation of added value of building industry of economic census year shall follow the guidance of Accounting Method of GDP in Economic Census Year, while the one of non-economic census year shall be as in Accounting Method of GDP in Non-Economic Census Year.

运输、邮电 14

TRANSPORT，POSTAL AND TELECOMMUNICATION SERVICES

简 要 说 明

一、本篇资料的主要内容

本篇资料主要反映了全市交通运输业和邮电业通讯业发展的基本情况，主要包括客货运输及港口吞吐量、民用汽车拥有量、独立核算运输邮电单位主要财务指标、邮电通讯基本情况等方面的内容。

二、本篇资料的来源

1、本篇资料中交通运输资料来源于全市交通运输业统计年报。

2、邮电通讯业资料来源于邮电通讯基本情况统计年报。

3、民用汽车拥有量资料来源于青岛市公安局交警支队车辆管理所。

本篇资料由市统计局服务业统计处整理提供。

Brief Introduction

Ⅰ. Main Content

Data in this chapter show the basic conditions of the development of transport, post and telecommunications in Shandong Province, mainly including the freight traffic and passenger traffic, cargo handled at port, possession of civil motor vehicles, major financial indices and basic conditions of transport, postal and telecommunication services.

Ⅱ. Source of Data

(1) Data on transport are based on the annual report of transport.

(2) Data on postal and telecommunication are based on the annual report of postal and telecommunication.

(3) Data on possession of civil motor vehicles are provided by Traffic Police Office of Vehicle Management of Qingdao Municipal Bureau of Public Security.

Data in this article is cleared up and provided by Department of Statistics for Service Industry affiliated to Municipal Statistics Bureau.

14-1 主要年份客货运输及港口吞吐量
MAJOR YEAR'S PASSENGER & FREIGHT TRAFFIC AND HANDLING CAPACITY OF THE PORTS

年份 Year	客运量（万人） Passenger Traffic（10000 persons）				货运量（万吨） Freight Traffic（10000 tons）				港口吞吐量（万吨） Cargo Handled at Ports（10000 tons）	集装箱吞吐量（万标箱） Containers（10000 TEU）
	铁路 Railways	公路 Highways	海运 Waterways	航空 Civil Aviation	铁路 Railways	公路 Highways	海运 Waterways	航空 Civil Aviation		
1949	327	14	9		386	162	22		73	
1952	571	49	13		447	399	44		181	
1957	1054	149	13		747	548	118		269	
1962	3100	141	39		909	524	97		391	
1965	1424	230	19		1257	690	158		524	
1970	1329	373	20		1856	736	232		695	
1975	1803	159	30		2325	817	282		1542	
1978	1986	274	49		2917	1561	528		2081	
1980	1896	713	73		2596	1642	941		1779	
1985	2063	1 894	86	1.0	3009	2303	919	0.03	2610	
1988	2083	3 300	234	8.8	3418	6486	1160	0.04	3153	
1990	1488	3 639	316	14.1	3741	6433	1556	0.20	3068	
1991	1453	4144	366	19.0	3774	6896	1789	0.31	3194	
1992	1488	4965	437	27.0	3899	6822	1981	0.45	3240	
1993	1499	6436	499	35.3	4044	7685	1910	0.64	3650	
1994	1564	6787		47.0	4112	8336	1804		4331	
1995	1480	9785		66.6	4205	11788	2185		5165	
1996	1230	10738		79.9	4415	10749	474		6056	81.1
1997	1308	11855			4466	11232	544		6944	103.3
1998	1549	11754			4028	14311	1792	1.44	7044	121.3
1999	1674	12103			3919	14550	1926	1.96	7282	154.3
2000	1780	12145		124.1	4256	17234	2998	2.30	8661	212.0
2001	1678	13686		143.0	4778	20906	3432	2.40	10423	264.0
2002	1530	14516	777	163.7	5079	24480	2530	3.00	12252	341.0
2003	1366	13132	786	174.7	4929	27241	2773	3.60	14135	424.0
2004	1496	16420	862	241.9	5119	29937	3503	5.30	16303	514.0
2005	552	17212	972	280.9	2299	31009	4471	4.60	18727	630.7
2006	810	17752	999	320.2	2790	32047	4768	5.10	22438	770.0
2007	1101	18800	1080	733.8	2781	33336	4019	5.90	26507	946.6
2008	1278	19909	1055	755.8	3225	34172	5080	7.20	30029	1037.7
2009	1425	19612	1145	881.8	3772	16297	4332	7.19	31668	1027.6
2010	1537	20460	1302	1010.9	5031	17525	4407	8.44	35012	1201.0
2011	1693	21560	791	1074.8	5697	19208	4220	8.93	37971	1302.0
2012	1881	22724	414	1173.1	6126	21312	1791	9.06	41465	1450.0
2013	2056	23588	333	1572.4	6266	23270	1313	9.31	45782	1552.0
2014	2301	5588	324	1641.2	5564	19043	1434	10.22	47701	1658.0
2015	2421	5370	288	1820.2	5486	20073	1456	20.80	49749	1743.0
2016	2701	4532	225	2050.5	5569	20701	1685	23.07	51463	1805.0
2017	3179	4534	215	2321.1	6021	24716	1800	23.20	51314	1830.9

注：从2014年公路客、货运量统计口径进行调整，与以前年度不可比。

Note: In 2014, the Ministry of Transportation made an adjustment to the statistical gauge for highway passenger and freight transportation and the data are not comparable directly.

14-2 民用车辆拥有量(2017年底)
ROSSESSION OF CIVIL MOTOR VEHICLES（END OF 2017）

单位：辆（unit）

项　目	Item	合计 Total	#个人 of which：Private Vehicles
		辆数 Number	辆数 Number
一、汽车	**Automobile**	**2464514**	**2122629**
1. 载客汽车	Passenger Vehicles	2228986	1994003
其中：轿车	of which：Sedan	1454637	1317120
2. 载货汽车	Trucks	219533	118259
3. 其他汽车	Other Automobile	15995	10367
二、电车	**Tram**	**63**	
三、摩托车	**Motorcycle**	**123561**	**122164**
四、农用运输车	**Agricultural Camion**		
五、挂车	**Trailer Trucks**	**26325**	**322**
六、其他类型车	**Other Vehicles**	**81**	**2**

补充资料：机动车驾驶员（3288096人）Motor drivers（3288096 person）
其中：汽车驾驶员（3239153人）of which：Automobile drivers（3239153 person）

14-3 客货运输及港口吞吐量(2017年)
PASSENGER & FREICHT TRAFFIC AND HANDLING CAPACITY OF THE PORTS (2017)

单位：辆（unit）

项　目	Item	货运量（万吨）Freight Traffic (10000 tons)	货物周转量（亿吨公里）Freight Ton-kilometers (100 million tons·km)	客运量（万人）Passenger Traffic (10000 persons)	旅客周转量（亿人公里）Passenger-Kilometers (100 milion persons-km)	旅客吞吐量（万人）Volume of Passenger Handled (10000 persons)	货物吞吐量（万吨）Volume of Freight Handled (10000 tons)	集装箱（万标箱）Containers (10000 TEU)
总　计	**Total**	**32537**	**1507.05**	**7928**	**171.59**	**2337**	**51337**	**1831**
铁路	Railways	6021	183.04	3179	96.95			
公路	Highways	24716	515.91	4534	74.42			
水运	Weterways	1800	808.09	215	0.22			
机场	Civil Aviation					2321	23	
港口	Ports					16	51314	1831

14-4 规模以上运输邮电单位主要财务指标(2017年)
MAJOR FINANCIAL INDICATORS OF TRANSPORTATION, POST AND TELECOMMUNICATION UNITS ABOVE DESIGNATED SCALE (2017)

单位：万元（10 000 yuan）

项　目	Item	营业收入 Revenue from principal Business	营业成本 Cost of principal Business	营业利润 Operating Profits	营业税金及附加 Business taxes and surtax	利润总额 Total Profits
总　计	**Total**	**8558547**	**6057644**	**1755318**	**75183**	**1983760**
铁路	Railways					
公路	Highways	1125189	1152303	-193951	7323	-39819
水运	Waterways	3206254	2056805	931513	39436	973830
航空	Civil Aviation	334486	256723	38617	2156	56006
港口	Ports	2495926	1705080	658484	20562	669954
邮政	Postal Services	287585	245259	11756	1329	11367
电信	Telecommunication Services	1109107	641475	308899	4377	312421

14-5 邮电通讯基本情况(2017年)
BASIC CONDITIONS OF POSTAL AND TELECOMMUNICATION SERVICES（2017）

市、区名称	Region	邮电局（处）Post Office（unit）	#提供邮政全功能服务的 of which：Providing Omni-directional Services	邮路总长度（公里）Length of Postal Routes（km）	邮运汽车（辆）Vehicles for Postal Services（unit）	信筒、信箱（个）Post Boxes（unit）
总　计	**Total**	**454**	**217**	**7324**	**394**	**750**
市　区	Urban Area	254	113	6095	282	504
#崂山区	Laoshan District	23	8	127	35	56
黄岛区	Huangdao District	79	38	670	69	86
即墨区	Jimo District	64	34	522	49	75
胶州市	Jiaozhou	54	29	295	41	63
平度市	Pingdu	96	50	636	38	127
莱西市	Laixi	50	25	298	33	56

14-5 续表 1
Continued

市、区名称	Region	固定电话市话交换机容量（门） Capacity of Urban Fixed Telephone Exchanges（line）	固定电话市话用户数（户） Urban Fixed Telephone Subscribers（subscriber）	固定电话农村交换机容量（门） Capacity of Rural Fixed Telephone Exchanges（line）	固定电话农村用户数（户） Rural Fixed Telephone Subscribers（subscriber）	移动电话交换机容量（户） Capacity of Mobile Telephone Exchanges（subscriber）	年末移动电话用户（户） Mobile Telephone Subscribersat Year-end（subscriber）
总　计	**Total**	**2164115**	**1180662**	**819604**	**329521**	**28130000**	**12913824**
市　区	Urban Area	121064	1039725	21569	256897	1470000	9771214
#崂山区	Laoshan District	3829	67798	1275	15042	3890000	730658
黄岛区	Huangdao District	43830	164854	14910	42491	4105000	2241357
即墨区	Jimo District	16892	65384	5383	57732	2566000	1455293
胶州市	Jiaozhou	19044	68749	2439	24124	1790000	1073796
平度市	Pingdu	13524	37642	1168	34386	1727000	1306464
莱西市	Laixi	14898	34546	1048	14114	1130000	762350

14-5 续表 2
Continued

市、区名称	Region	函件（万件）Number of Letters (10000 pcs)	邮政储蓄期末余额（万元）Balance of Postal Savings at Termend (10000 yuan)	特快专递（万件）Express Mail Services (10000 pcs)	邮电业务总量（万元）Business Volume of Post and Telecommunication Services (10000 yuan)	报纸期发份数（万份）Issue of Newspapers (10000 copies)	杂志期发份数（万份）Issue of Magazine (10000 copies)
总　计	**Total**	**2603807**	**3499005**	**74**	**3031725**	**57**	**36**
市　区	Urban Area	2165966	1753853	54	2229107	40	26
#崂山区	Laoshan District	125316	120778	8	172746	5	4
黄岛区	Huangdao District	341455	570589	20	476710	9	5
即墨区	Jimo District	200940	746723	7	359007	6	3
胶州市	Jiaozhou	172136	586242	9	277977	6	4
平度市	Pingdu	175048	821944	5	337110	6	4
莱西市	Laixi	90658	336966	6	187531	5	2

主要统计指标解释

货（客）运量 指在一定时期内，各运输部门实际运送的货物（旅客）数量。是反映运输业为国民经济和人民生活服务的数量指标，也是制定和检查运输生产计划，研究运输发展规模和速度的重要指标。货运按吨计算，客运按人计算。货物不论运输距离长短，货物类别，均按实际重量统计；旅客不论行程远近或票价多少，均按一人一次作为客运量统计。半价票、小孩票也按一人统计。

货物（旅客）周转量 指在一定时期内，由各种运输工具运送的货物（旅客）数量与其相应运输距离的乘积之总和，是反映运输业生产总成果的重要指标，也是编制和检查运输生产计划，计算运输效益、劳动生产率以及核算运输单位成本的主要基础资料。通常以吨公里和人公里为计算单位。 计算货物周转量通常按发出站与到达站之间的最短距离，也就是计费距离计算。

港口货物吞吐量 指经水运进出沿海主要港区范围，并经过装卸的货物数量，包括邮件及办理托运手续的行李、包裹以及补给运输船舶的燃、物料和淡水。货物吞吐量按货物流向分为进口、出口吞吐量，按货物交流性质分为外贸货物吞吐量和国内贸易货物吞吐量。货物吞吐量的货类构成及其流向，是衡量港口生产能力大小的重要指标。

邮电业务总量 指以货币表现的邮电部门用于传递信息和提供其他邮电服务的总数量。它综合反映了一定时期邮电工作的总成果，是研究邮电业务量构成和发展趋势的重要指标。它用各种邮电分类业务量，如函件件数、快递业务量、市内电话和农村电话的年均户数、订销报刊累计份数等，分别乘以相应的平均单位（不变价），加总后再加上出租电路和设备的收入、代用户维护电话交换机和线路等设备的收入、其他业务收入求得。

Explanatory Notes on Main Statistical Indicators

Freight (Passenger) Traffic refers to the volume of freight (passenger) transported with various means. Freight transport is calculated in tons and passenger traffic is calculated in the number of persons. Despite the type of freight and traveling distance, the freight transport is calculated in the actual weight of the goods : and despite the traveling distance and ticket price, the passenger traffic is calculated by the principle that one person can be counted only once in one travel. The passengers who travel with a half price ticket or a child ticket is also calculated as one person. The freight (passenger) traffic provides a quantitative measure to show how the transport industry serves the national economy and people, and is also an important indicator for planning the transport industry and for studying the development scale and speed of the transport industry.

Freight Ton-kilometers (Passenger-kilometers) refers to the sum of the products of the volume of transported cargo (passengers) multiplying by the transport distance. It is an important indicator to reflect the achievement of transportation industry. Normally, the shortest distance between the departure station and the destination station (i. e., the payable distance) is the basis to calculate the freight ton-kilometers. This is an important indicator to show the total results of the transport industry, to prepare and examine the transport plan and to measure the efficiency, the labour productivity and the unit cost of transport.

Volume of Freight Handled in Ports refers to the volume of cargo passing in and out the harbor area of the major coastal ports and having been loaded and unloaded. The volume includes that of the postal matters, registered luggage and fuels, materials and fresh water as supplies of the ships. The volume of freight handled may be classified by direction of flow as freight for import and freight for export, or by nature of cargo as freight for domestic trade and freight for foreign trade. As an important indicator, the volume of freight handled by type of cargo and by main flow direction reflects the production capacity of ports.

Businesss Volume of Postal and Telecommunication Services refers to the total amount of the information delivered and other post and telecommunication services provided by the post and telecommunication departments for the customers. It is arrived by first multiplying the business volume of different types, such as number of letters, telegrams, long distance calls, city and rural telephone (fixed price) and then adding these products together, plus the income from maintenance of telephone switchboards and lines, and the income from other business operations. The service revenue of posts and telecommunications reflects the total achievements by the post and telecommunication departments during a given period of time in a comprehensive way, and is an important indicator to study the composition and development of the post and telecommunication business.

批发和零售业 15

WHOLESALE AND RETAIL TRADES

简 要 说 明

一、本篇资料的主要内容

本篇资料主要反映了全市批发和零售业经营情况和效益情况，主要包括批发和零售业商品流转及财务情况、亿元以上商品交易市场、社会消费品零售总额等内容。

二、本篇资料的来源

本篇资料来源于批发和零售业统计年报和定期报表统计资料。由市统计局外经贸易统计处整理提供。

Brief Introduction

Ⅰ. Main Content

Data in this chapter show the development of wholesale and retail trade of the whole city, mainly including the circulation and financial indices of commodities in the wholesale and retail trade, commodity exchange markets over 100 million yuan, Total retail sales of consumer goods, etc.

Ⅱ. Source of Data

Data in this chapter are based on annual report and regular reports of wholesale and retail trade.

Data in this chapter are prepared and compiled by the Division of Trade and External Economic Relations Statistics of Qingdao Municipal Bureau of Statistics.

15-1 社会消费品零售总额(1985-2017 年)

TOTAL RETAIL SALES OF CONSUMER GOODS (1985-2017)

单位：万元(10 000 yuan)

年 份 Year	消费品零售总额 Total Retail Sales of Consumer Goods	批发零售业 Wholesale and Retail Trades	住宿餐饮业 Hotels and Catering Services	其他行业 Othres
1985	307222	231477	16996	18753
1986	364091	269418	21384	27118
1987	432569	310658	23319	32617
1988	590538	434572	32304	45449
1989	619941	450812	34083	56303
1990	658264	484770	35568	67863
1991	760562	566767	43320	56812
1992	888411	666911	53045	67392
1993	1384533	1031794	80077	96759
1994	1880654	1352073	127313	202937
1995	2376776	1637349	186028	305947
1996	2708527	1873008	220322	321325
1997	3008981	2105728	241928	361248
1998	3368736	2322209	277696	411210
1999	3762754	2715635	315307	391388
2000	4282871	3116990	387944	403854
2001	4911735	3561731	507012	433851
2002	5574364	4162676	638358	402654
2003	6455113	5283584	849032	322497
2004	7475022	6266750	1017193	191079
2005	8701057	7304660	1176539	219858
2006	10163457	8458226	1443120	262111
2007	12162246	9995772	1837754	328720
2008	14922153	12995842	1554086	372225
2009	17302231	14232954	2549203	520074
2010	19611331	17151504	2459827	
2011	23023703	20153079	2870624	
2012	26356180	23043005	3313175	
2013	29868133	26142405	3725728	
2014	33617217	29435856	4181361	
2015	37136940	32459539	4677401	
2016	41049345	35840499	5208846	
2017	45410086	39669946	5740140	

注：1. 自 2003 年开始消费品零售总额不再包括制造业零售额和农民对非农居民的销售额分组。
2. 自 2005 年起，住宿业从其它行业调整到住宿餐饮业中。
3. 根据第二次经济普查结果，对 2005 年以来的历史数据进行了调整。

Note：1.Since 2003，retail sales of manufacturing and retail sales of rural residents to urban residents are excluded in total retail sales of consumer goods.
2.Since 2005，hotels is adjusted to hotels and catering services from the others.
3.Historical data since 2005 have been adjusted according to results of the Second China Economic Census.

15-2 分市、区社会消费品零售总额（2017年）
TOTAL RETAIL SALES OF CONSUMER GOODS BY REGION（2017）

单位：万元（10 000 yuan）

市、区名称	Region	消费品零售总额 Total Retail Sales of Consumer Gddos	按行业分 批发零售业 Wholesale and Retail Trades	住宿餐饮业 Hotels and Catering Services
全　市	**Whole Municipal**	**45410086**	**39669946**	**5740140**
市南区	Shinan District	5963162	4963447	999715
市北区	Shibei District	7605908	6688873	917035
李沧区	Licang District	4252272	3820030	432242
崂山区	Laoshan District	2395210	2232384	162826
黄岛区	Huangdao District	5795362	4922437	872925
城阳区	Chengyang District	2631718	2295111	336607
即墨区	Jimo District	4623807	4195512	428295
胶州市	Jiaozhou	4357173	3766090	591083
平度市	Pingdu	4214878	3711704	503174
莱西市	Laixi	3238058	2771054	467004
红岛经济区	Qingdao National Hightech Industrial Development Zone	163473	138766	24707
保税港区	Qingdao Free Trade Port Area of China	169065	164538	4527

15-3 限额以上批发和零售业商品购销存总额（2017 年）

TOTAL PURCHASES，SALES AND STOCK OF ENTERPRISES ABOVE DESIGNATED SIZE OF WHOLESALE AND RETAIL TRADES（2017）

单位：万元（10 000 yuan）

项 目	Item	商品销售总额 Total Sales Value	#批发总额 Wholesale Value	零售总额 Retail Value	库存总额 Stock
总 计	**Total**	**67718515.0**	**53477733.0**	**14240782.0**	**3425789.3**
国有企业	State-owned Enterprises	76807.2	48243.8	28563.4	16872.1
集体企业	Collective-owned Enterprises	68622.9	309.8	68313.1	384.8
其它企业	Other Enterprises	67573084.9	53429179.4	14143905.5	3408532.4
农、林、牧产品批发	Wholesale of Farm Produce and Livestock Products	994577.3	983828.2	10749.1	64180.4
食品、饮料及烟草制品批发	Wholesale of Food，Beverages and Tobaccos	3530495.5	3404758.1	125737.4	292384.4
纺织、服装及家庭用品批发	Retail of Textiles，Garments and Daily Consumer Articles	11145979.6	10839496.7	306482.9	308152.9
文化、体育用品及器材批发	Wholesale of Culture，Sports Appliances and Equipments	537645.7	511744.0	25901.7	30435.9
医药及医疗器材批发	Wholesale of Medicines and Medical Appliances	2096248.9	1976970.5	119278.4	158648.4
矿产品、建材及化工产品批发	Wholesale of Machinery，Hardware and Electronic Equipment	31450245.1	31106606.3	343638.8	880935.0
机械设备、五金产品及电子产品批发	Wholesale of Machinery，Hardware and Electronic Equipment	3362844.3	3284590.3	78254.0	199811.2
贸易经纪与代理	Trade Broker and Agency	1111.4	1111.4		34.6
其它批发业	Other Wholesale not Classified Elsewhere	296005.8	295815.8	190.0	16328.6
综合零售	Integrated Retail Trade	3338987.4	30197.4	3308790.0	224089.0
食品、饮料及烟草制品专门零售	Retail of Food，Beverages and Tobaccos	199257.5	84703.6	114553.9	23416.5
纺织、服装及日用品专门零售	Retail of Textiles，Garments and Daily Consumer Articles	991945.8	203768.9	788176.9	283094.6
文化、体育用品及器材专门零售	Retail of Culture，Sports Appliances and Equipments	339389.8	129093.0	210296.8	100752.0
医药及医疗器材专门零售	Retail of Medicines and Medical Appliances	668860.3	91834.0	577026.3	85604.2
汽车、摩托车、燃料及零配件专门零售	Retail of Motor Vehicles，Motorcycles，Fuel and Parts	5458155.6	201366.8	5256788.8	494622.8
家用电器及电子产品专门零售	Retail of Household Electric Appliances and Electronic Products	1654736.7	141382.6	1513354.1	247637.9
五金、家具及室内装饰材料专门零售	Retail of Hardware，Furniture and Decoration Materials	67997.4	27775.6	40221.8	13000.2
货摊、无店铺及其他零售业	Non-shop and Other Retails	1584030.9	162689.8	1421341.1	2660.7

15-4 限额以上批发和零售业商品分类销售额(2017 年)

SALES VALUE OF ENTERPRISES ABOVE DESIGNATED SIZE OF WHOLESALE AND RETAIL TRADES BY CATEGORY OF COMMODITIES (2017)

单位：万元（10 000 yuan）

项目	Item	销售总额 Total Sales Value	#批发总额 Wholesale Value	零售总额 Retail Value
销售总额	**Total Sales Value**	**63433860.8**	**48655883.5**	**14777977.3**
1. 粮油、食品类	Grain & Oil and Food	4022131.1	2566277.7	1455853.4
其中：粮油类	Grain and Oil	1209717.3	1045007.1	164710.2
肉禽蛋类	Meat, Poultry and Eggs	381474.5	185688.5	195786
水产品类	Aquatic Products	203987.8	120106.9	83880.9
蔬菜类	Vegetable and Fruit	214319.1	144294.6	70024.5
干鲜果品类	Dried and Fresh Fruit	580675.8	409331.9	171343.9
2. 饮料类	Beverages	276221.1	97727.3	178493.8
3. 烟酒类	Tobacco and Liquor	2030657.9	1668084.1	362573.8
4. 服装、鞋帽、针纺织品类	Clothing, Shoes, Hats and Textiles	3384755.9	1839640.8	1545115.1
（1）服装类	Clothing	1793209.6	835003.4	958206.2
（2）鞋帽类	Shoes and Hats	706346.7	188370.6	517976.1
（3）针纺织品类	Knitwear and Textiles	885199.6	816266.8	68932.8
5. 化妆品类	Cosmetics	280082.0	66889.0	213193.0
6. 金银珠宝类	Gold, Silver and Jewellery	376370.8	79460.1	296910.7
7. 日用品类	Articles for Daily Use	938956.8	353668.5	585288.3
其中：儿童玩具类	Children toys	45470.3	7899.0	37571.3
8. 五金、电料类	Hardware and Electrical Materials	425180.4	352367.5	72812.9
9. 体育、娱乐用品类	Sports and Recreation Articles	112760.9	16313.1	96447.8
其中：照相器材类	Photographic Apparatus	8427.7	358.0	8069.7
10. 书报杂志类	Newspapers and Magazines	144803	59044.9	85758.1
11. 电子出版物及音像制品类	E-journals and Video Products	7761.2	3128.1	4633.1
12. 家用电器和音像器材类	Household Appliances and Video Appilances	9789968.3	7342577	2447391.3
13. 中西药品类	Traditional Chinese and Western Medicines	2137787.2	1661233.5	476553.7
其中：西药类	Western Medicines	1874217.5	1516234.8	357982.7
中草药及中成药类	Traditional Chinese Medicines	176326.5	115776.2	60550.3
14. 文化办公用品类	Cultural and Offices Appliances	679479.1	259593.8	419885.3
其中：计算机及其配套产品	Computer and Related Products	214065.4	128307.6	85757.8
15. 家具类	Furniture	82748.6	14764.5	67984.1
16. 通讯器材类	Communication Appliances	847592.6	428087.7	419504.9
17. 煤炭及制品类	Coal and Related Products	2208092.9	2197969	10123.9
18. 木材及制品类	Wood and Wooden Products	372900.0	372900.0	
19. 石油及制品类	Petroleum and Related Products	13402540.0	11567246.3	1835293.7
20. 化工材料及制品类	Chemical Materials and Related Products	3643772.9	3643772.9	
其中：化肥类	Fertilizers	313498.7	313498.7	
21. 金属材料类	Metal Materials	9007137.5	9007137.5	
22. 建筑及装潢材料类	Building and Decoration Materials	722363.5	605594.0	116769.5
23. 机电产品及设备类	Mechanical and Electrical Products	1674859.5	1613308.0	61551.5
其中：农机类	Agricultural Machineries	62801.1	62801.1	
24. 汽车类	Automobiles	4796572.9	911618.6	3884954.3
25. 种子饲料类	Seeds and Feedstuff	463767.0	463767.0	
26. 棉麻类	Cotton, Hemp	224330.8	224330.8	
27. 其他类	Others	1380266.9	1239381.8	140885.1

注：此表为定期报表数据。

Note: The data are from regular reports.

15-5 限额以上批发业财务状况（2017 年）
FINANCIAL POSITION OF ENTERPRISES ABOVE DESIGNATED SIZE OF WHOLESALE TRADE（2017）

单位：万元（10 000 yuan）

指标	Indicator	合计 Total	国有经济 State-owned Enterprises	集体经济 Collective-owned Enterprises	外商及港澳台经济 Foreign Funded Enterprises and Enterprises with Funds from Hong Kong，Macao and Taiwan	其它 Other Enterprises
单位数	**Number of Emterprises**	**1140**	**6**	**1**	**50**	**1083**
年末资产负债	**Year-end Assets-Liability**					
资产总计	Total Assets	20706338	61723	41347	1444525	19158743
流动资产合计	Sub-total of Current Assets	18610965	46024	40337	1331523	17193081
负债合计	Total Liabilities	17089085	43807	34677	1064681	15945920
所有者权益合计	Total Owners' Equities	3617253	17916	6670	379844	3212824
损益及分配	**Loss，Profits and Distributon**					
主营业务收入	Revenue from Principal Business	46601548	52273	62746	3608187	42878342
主营业务成本	Cost of Principal Business	44487025	51409	56584	3471976	40907057
主营业务税金及附加	Taxes and Extra Charges on Principal Business	190446		120	3947	186379
营业利润	Profits from Principal Business	494091	-1860	159	60995	434797
其他业务利润	Profits from other Business	164673	840	101	30701	133031
销售费用	Operating Costs	918527	932	298	34485	882812
管理费用	Management Expenses	474862	1833	5685	33567	433777
财务费用	Financial Expenses	175847	933	-16	9426	165504
利润总额	Total Profits	543719	456	162	63508	479594
经济效益	**Economic Benefit**					
商品经营费用率 %	Ratio of Operating Costs to Revenue from Principal Business	1.97	1.78	0.47	0.96	2.06
商品销售利润率 %	Ratio of Profit to Sales Revenue	1.17	0.87	0.26	1.76	1.12

15-6 限额以上零售业财务状况（2017年）
FINANCIAL POSITION OF ENTERPRISES ABOVE DESIGNATED SIZE OF RETAIL TRADE（2017）

单位：万元（10 000 yuan）

指标	Indicator	合计 Total	国有经济 State-owned Enterprises	集体经济 Collective-owned Enterprises	外商及港澳台经济 Foreign Funded Enterprises and Enterprises with Funds from Hong Kong, Macao and Taiwan	其它 Other Enterprises
单位数	**Number of Enterprises**	**721**	**5**	**2**	**37**	**677**
年末资产负债	**Year-end Assets-Liability**					
资产合计	Total Assets	7110874	32979	3311	892195	6182388
流动资产合计	Sub-total of Current Assets	5026104	31107	3255	699709	4292033
负债合计	Total Liabilities	5790470	30164	2729	678199	5079379
所有者权益合计	Total Owners' Equities	1653262	2815	582	213996	1435868
损益及分配	**Loss, Profits and Distributon**					
主营业务收入	Revenue from Principal Business	12304576	22011	5023	1756451	10521092
主营业务成本	Cost of Principal Business	11025387	17622	4406	1447504	9555856
主营业务税金及附加	Taxes and Extra Charges on Principal Business	37199	110	12	9012	28067
营业利润	Profits from Principal Business	213558	1930	18	78167	133444
其他业务利润	Profits from other Business	146336	3	0	32461	113872
销售费用	Operating Costs	808829	232	65	182503	626028
管理费用	Management Expenses	375303	2086	520	90417	282280
财务费用	Financial Expenses	67431	18	2	2921	64490
利润总额	Total Profits	227357	1927	21	76881	148529
经济效益	**Economic Benefit**					
商品经营费用率 %	Ratio of Operating Costs to Revenue from Principal Business	6.57	1.06	1.30	10.39	5.95
商品销售利润率 %	Ratio of Profit to Sales Revenue	1.85	8.75	0.41	4.38	1.41

15-7 分市、区城乡亿元商品交易市场分布情况（2017年）
BASIC STATISTICS ON COMMODITY EXCHANGE MARKETS OF TRANSACTION VALUE OVER 100 NILLION YUAN BY REGION（2017）

单位：万元（10 000 yuan）

市、区名称	Region	亿元商品交易市场数量（个） Number of Commodity Exchange Markets of Transaction Value over 100 Million Yuan（unit）			亿元商品交易市场成交额（亿元） Turnover of Commodity Exchange Markets of Transaction Value over 100 Million yuan（100 million yuan）		
		合计 Total	# 综合市场 Integrated Markets	# 专业市场 Special Markets	合计 Total	# 综合市场 Integrated Markets	# 专业市场 Special Markets
全　市	**Whole Municipality**	**60**	**12**	**48**	**1305.4**	**490.6**	**814.8**
市南区	Shinan District						
市北区	Shibei District	9	1	8	92.4	43.1	49.3
李沧区	Licang District	5	1	4	50.5	15.3	35.2
崂山区	Laoshan District	2		2	2.7		2.7
黄岛区	Huangdao District	8	2	6	88.8	20.0	68.8
城阳区	Chengyang District	2	1	1	216.9	215.7	1.2
即墨区	Jimo District	12	1	11	612.5	130.4	482.1
胶州市	Jiaozhou	12	4	8	152.5	52.6	99.9
平度市	Pingdu	10	2	8	89.1	13.5	75.6
莱西市	Laixi						
红岛经济区	Qingdao National High-tech Industrial Development Zone						
保税港区	Qingdao Free Trade Port Area of China						

主要统计指标解释

社会消费品零售总额 指各种经济类型的批发和零售业、住宿和餐饮业以及其他行业对城乡居民和社会集团的消费品零售额总和。该指标从2003年开始不再包括制造业零售额和农民对非农居民的零售额。

商品购进总额 指从本企业（单位）以外的单位和个人购进（包括从国外直接进口）作为转卖或加工后转卖的商品。这个指标反映批发零售贸易业从国内、国外市场上购进商品的总量。商品购进总额包括：（1）从工农业生产者购进的商品；（2）从出版社、报社的出版发行部门购进的图书、杂志和报纸；（3）从各种类型的批发零售贸易企业（单位）购进的商品；（4）从其他单位购进的商品，如从机关、团体、企业、单位购进的剩余物资，从餐饮业、服务业购进的商品，从海关、市场管理部门购进的缉私和没收的商品，向居民收购的废旧商品等;（5）从国（境）外直接进口的商品，但不包括企业（单位）为自身经营用和未通过买卖行为而收入的商品以及销售退回、商品损益等。

商品销售总额 指对本企业（单位）以外的单位和个人出售（包括对国（境）外直接出口）的商品。这个指标反映批发零售贸易业在国内市场上销售商品以及出口商品的总量。商品销售总额包括:（1）售给城乡居民和社会集团消费用的商品；（2）售给工业、农业、建筑业、运输邮电业、批发零售贸易业、餐饮业、服务业等作为生产、经营使用的商品；（3）售给批发零售贸易业作为转卖或加工后转卖的商品；（4）对国（境）外直接出口的商品。不包括：出售本企业（单位）自用的废旧包装用品，未通过买卖行为付出的商品，经本单位介绍，由买卖双方直接结算，本单位只收取手续费的业务，购货退出的商品以及商品损耗和损失等。

Explanatory Notes on Main Statistical Indicators

Total Retail Sales of Consumer Goods refers to the sum of ratail sales of consumer goods sold by all sectors of the national economy to urban and rural residents and social groups. Sectors of the national economy include wholesale and retail trade, accommodation and catering trade and others. Since 2003, retail sales of manufacture and retail sales of rural residents to urban residents are excluded in total retail sales.

Total Purchases of Commodities refer to the total value of purchases of commodities by the enterprises (establishments) from other establishments or individuals (including direct import from abroad) for the purpose of re-selling, either with or without further processing of the commodities purchased. This indicator is used to show the total value of purchases of commodities by wholesale and retail establishments from domestic and overseas markets. The total purchases include: (1) agricultural and industrial products purchased from producers; (2) books, magazines and newspapers purchased from distribution departments of the publishers; (3) commodities purchased from wholesale and retail establishments of different status of registration; (4) commodities purchased from other units, such as surplus materials purchased from government agencies, enterprises or institutions, commodities purchased from catering and service establishments, confiscated goods purchased from customs authorities or market management agencies, second-hand goods and wastes purchased from residents; and (5) commodities directly imported from abroad. Excluded are commodities purchased by enterprises (establishments) for use in their own business operation, commodities obtained without buying or selling procedures, rejected commodities, ets.

Total Sales of Commodities refer to value of commodities sold by the establishments to other establishments and individuals (including direct export). This indicator is used to show the total value of sales of commodities at domestic markets and export. The total sales include: (1) commodities sold to urban and rural residents and social groups for their consumption; (2) commodities sold to establishments in industry, agriculture, construction, transportation, post and telecommunications, wholesale and retail trades, hotels and catering services, and public utility for their production and operation; (3) commodities sold to wholesale and retail establishments for re-selling, with or without further processing; and (4) commodities for direct export to other countries. Excluded are selling of waste packaging materials used by the establishments (units) themselves, commodities transferred without buying or selling procedures, commission income from brokerage in transactions for which settlement is directly handled by buyers and sellers, rejected commodities in the purchase, loss in commodities, etc.

住宿、餐饮业和旅游 16

HOTELS，CATERING SERVICES AND TOURISM

简 要 说 明

一、本篇资料的主要内容

本篇资料主要反映了全市住宿和餐饮业的经营情况和效益情况以及旅游的基本情况，主要包括住宿和餐饮业经营情况和财务情况、涉外以及国内旅游基本情况等方面的内容。

二、本篇资料的来源

本篇资料中住宿和餐饮业经营情况和财务情况资料来源于住宿和餐饮业统计年报和定期报表统计资料；旅游资料来源于市旅游局。由市统计局外经贸易统计处整理提供。

Brief Introduction

Ⅰ. Main Content

Data in this chapter show the development of wholesale and retail trade and tourism of the whole city, mainly including the circulation and financial indices of hotels and catering services, international and domestic tourism, etc.

Ⅱ. Source of Data

Data on hotels and catering services are based on annual report and regular reports of hotels and catering services. Data on international tourism are provided by Qingdao Tourism Bureau. The above data are prepared and compiled by the Division of Trade and External Economic Relations Statistics of Qingdao Municipal Bureau of Statistics.

16-1 限额以上住宿和餐饮业法人企业经营情况（2017 年）

BUSINESS CONDITIONS OF ENTERPRISES OF HOTELS AND CATERING SERVICES ABOVE DESIGNATED SIZE (2017)

单位：万元（10 000 yuan）

项目	Item	营业额 Turnover	#客房收入 Income from Guest Rooms	餐费收入 Catering Income	商品销售收入 Income from Commodity Sales	其他收入 Other Income
总　计	**Total**	**978229.9**	**262350.0**	**653222.1**	**22064.7**	**40593.1**
一、住宿业	**Hotels**	**463581.0**	**228454.1**	**187788.3**	**10795.8**	**36542.8**
国有企业	State-owned Enterprises	79597.4	32829.3	36315.5	969.0	9483.6
集体企业	Collective-owned Enterprises	0.0	0.0	0.0	0.0	0.0
其他企业	Other Enterprises	383983.6	195624.8	151472.8	9826.8	27059.2
独立门店	Freestanding Stores	421084.7	200223.9	175813.4	10283.4	34764.0
连锁总店	General Chain Stores	450.7	399.3	0.0	38.2	13.2
连锁直营店	Chain Store	3126.6	2411.7	0.0	0.0	714.9
连锁加盟店	Chain Store	4047.8	3911.2	53.1	17.7	65.8
其他	Others	34871.2	21508.0	11921.8	456.5	984.9
五星	Five Star Class	133910.5	62394.7	58799.9	1454.9	11261.0
四星	Four Star class	92667.5	40524.0	45000.1	915.2	6228.2
三星	Three Star class	50068.8	23699.7	21151.6	1541.4	3676.1
二星	Two Star class	6716.6	2000.5	4367.7	212.7	135.7
其他	Others	180217.6	99835.2	58469.0	6671.6	15241.8
二、餐饮业	**Catering Services**	**514648.9**	**33895.9**	**465433.8**	**11268.9**	**4050.3**
国有企业	State-owned Enterprises	5821.9	3321.0	2349.0	76.4	75.5
集体企业	Collective-owned Enterprises	2766.4	396.7	738.2	1617.1	14.4
其他企业	Other Enterprises	506060.6	30178.2	462346.6	9575.4	3960.4
独立门店	Freestanding Stores	196865.7	28858.8	156421.1	7710.6	3875.2
连锁总店	General Chain Stores	238429.2	164.5	236621.5	1643.2	0.0
连锁直营店	Chain Store	5962.2	0.0	5961.0	0.0	1.2
连锁加盟店	Chain Store	35777.6	0.0	35777.6	0.0	0.0
其他	Others	37614.2	4872.6	30652.6	1915.1	173.9

16-2 限额以上住宿业财务状况（2017 年）
FINANCIAL SITUATION OF HOTELS ABOVE DESIGNATED SIZE（2017）

单位：万元（10 000 yuan）

指标	Indicator	合计 Total	国有经济 State-owned Enterprises	集体经济 Collective-owned Enterprises	外商及港澳台经济 Foreign Funded Enterprises and Enterprises with Funds from Hong Kong, Macao and Taiwan	其它 Other Enterprises
单位数	**Number of Enterprises**	**173**	**17**		**11**	**145**
年末资产负债	**Year-end Assets-Liability**					
资产总计	Total Assets	1191155	112666		344628	733861
流动资产合计	Sub-total of Current Assets	442378	45054		82206	315118
负债合计	Total Liabilities	934653	65098		279236	590319
所有者权益合计	Total Owners' Equities	256501	47568		65391	143542
损益及分配	**Loss, Profits and Distributon**					
主营业务收入	Revenue from Principal Business	448830	74604		88186	286041
主营业务成本	Cost of Principal Business	131552	19436		15836	96281
主营业务税金及附加	Taxes and Extra Charges on Principal Business	5231	528		1629	3073
营业利润	Profits from Principal Business	-11755	444		4784	-16983
其他业务利润	Profits from other Business	24022	2110		1296	20616
销售费用	Operating Costs	147477	33746		20425	93306
管理费用	Management Expenses	161624	20754		43119	97752
财务费用	Financial Expenses	24457	318		11527	12612
利润总额	Total Profits	-10498	2069		3550	-16117
其他	**Others**					
应付职工薪酬	Total Wages Payble in This Year	122114	29821		21873	70420
主营业务利润率	Profitability of Principal	-2.34	2.77		4.03	-5.63

16-3　限额以上餐饮业财务状况（2017 年）
FINANCIAL SITUATION OF CATERING SERVICES ABOVE DESIGNATED SIZE（2017）

单位：万元（10 000 yuan）

指标	Indicator	合计 Total	国有经济 State-owned Enterprises	集体经济 Collective-owned Enterprises	外商及港澳台经济 Foreign Funded Enterprises and Enterprises with Funds from Hong Kong, Macao and Taiwan	其它 Other Enterprises
单位数	**Number of Enterprises**	**184**	**5**	**2**	**19**	**158**
年末资产负债	**Year-end Assets-Liability**					
资产总计	Total Assets	581196	7798	477	130242	442679
流动资产合计	Sub-total of Current Assets	338849	2711	388	33211	302539
负债合计	Total Liabilities	459050	4340	530	104346	349834
所有者权益合计	Total Owners' Equities	122146	3459	-53	25896	92845
损益及分配	**Loss, Profits and Distributon**					
主营业务收入	Revenue from Principal Business	494956	5679	2522	227896	258858
主营业务成本	Cost of Principal Business	243293	2930	2276	107754	130334
主营业务税金及附加	Taxes and Extra Charges on Principal Business	2154	78	2	257	1817
营业利润	Profits from Principal Business	30603	-99	44	21769	8889
其他业务利润	Profits from other Business	1066	19	0	138	909
销售费用	Operating Costs	149172	1586	190	70722	76674
管理费用	Management Expenses	66215	1203	9	25883	39120
财务费用	Financial Expenses	2873	4	1	507	2361
利润总额	Total Profits	30733	-96	45	21699	9086
其他	**Others**					
应付职工薪酬	Total Wages Payble in This Year	93563	1886.6	301	27029	64346
主营业务利润率	Profitability of Principal	6.21	-1.69	1.77	9.52	3.51

16-4 入境旅游人数(2000－2017年)
NUMBER OF OVERSEA VISITOR ARRIVALS (2000-2017)

项 目	Item	2000年	2005年	2006年	2008年
总 计	**Total**	**260592**	**684407**	**854462**	**800455**
一、外国人	**Foreigner**	**177098**	**596177**	**751403**	**697391**
#韩国	Korea	69878	295111	373712	340648
日本	Japan	67215	177121	221542	210090
美国	United States	10384	23284	32256	28998
俄罗斯	Russia	4820	12062	17457	3774
德国	Germany	3820	10646	14440	11261
新加坡	Singapore	6321	6060	8332	10683
英国	United Kingdom	2798	5744	10047	10657
加拿大	Canada	1865	4397	5727	5467
法国	France	2491	5166	7377	6067
意大利	Italy	1555	3963	4022	3871
澳大利亚	Australia	1817	4257	7106	7940
菲律宾	Philippines	7947	3459	1812	2075
泰国	Thailand	780	3261	2464	2236
印尼	Indonesia	1 241	2349	2301	1589
新西兰	New Zealand	442	710	980	1161
二、港澳和台湾同胞	**Chinese Compatriots from Hong Kong, Macao and Taiwan**	**60367**	**88230**	**103059**	**103064**

16-5 入境旅游收入(2000-2017年)
EARNINGS FROM INTERNATIONAL TOURISM (2000-2017)

项 目	Item	2000年	2005年	2006年	2008年
总 计	**Total**	**118164**	**340899**	**434100**	**347645**
旅游购物	Shopping	20742	67047	78882	66053
住宿费	Accommodation	17443	37277	44011	37198
餐饮费	Dining	11223	33557	39611	33374
交通费	Transportation	35252	128112	140831	9039
邮电费	Postal and Telecommunication	5502	18394	21654	17382
文化娱乐费	Culture and Entertainment	6894	20240	23900	20163
游览	Sightseeing				18773
其他	Other Services		36272	85210	145663

单位：人次（person-time）

2009年	2010年	2011年	2012年	2013年	2014年	2015年	2016年	2017年
1000670	**1080511**	**1156391**	**1270113**	**1282814**	**1280526**	**1338098**	**1410494**	**1443715**
801424	**826628**	**809043**	**877593**	**905415**	**951732**	**996191**	**1042213**	**1056800**
363181	382225	298096	338383	338191	366584	389832	68010	432430
261553	242082	216755	185613	146080	135179	140762	151832	164095
28745	35539	45842	48431	54178	57907	62771	68010	73905
9525	15793	15750	26432	26519	25356	28529	30534	32540
14735	21626	26178	26311	19014	21723	23425	25456	26636
17453	13444	16626	16316	16305	19975	21310	23713	25257
9103	17639	23955	28385	19496	22817	23812	26133	28006
7741	9279	12007	11678	9727	9483	10659	11592	12544
7030	11766	12019	15595	21422	17828	19388	21836	23507
3747	3867	7028	5622	5679	7705	8747	9234	10627
6641	8223	15465	16644	11149	15339	16798	18839	20304
7800	14140	14259	7546	18630	6668	7300	7891	8489
3685	2572	3271	2369	3692	4803	5331	5784	6628
4221	7863	8128	4571	10011	6568	5692	6220	7388
2029	1597	6265	6448	1452	2549	2872	3352	4230
199246	**253883**	**347348**	**392520**	**377399**	**328794**	**342511**	**368281**	**386915**

单位：万元（10 000 yuan）

2009年	2010年	2011年	2012年	2013年	2014年	2015年	2016年	2017年
377000	**399688**	**441171**	**519495**	**511158**	**503900**	**566742**	**656966**	**694103**
70763	74104	80823	93872	94055	109246	122473	141970	129381
41093	43933	59823	59378	58577	62232	69879	81004	77184
36569	38747	40191	51378	51065	44041	49589	57483	68091
9877	145551	134425	170238	180945	160492	180791	209573	249113
18812	19081	16720	23014	22950	19400	21593	25031	33248
22394	24032	36132	32832	32103	33409	36271	42045	42201
21037	22978	51705	32832	32152	44192	49930	57879	40674
29745	31262	21353	55951	39311	30888	36216	41982	54211

16-6　国内旅游人数及收入（2017年）
NUMBER OF DOME STTC TOURISM INCOME（2017）

指　　标	Indicator	单位	Unit	2017年
国内旅游人数	Number of Domestic Toursts	万人次	10000 person-times	8672
1. 过夜旅游者人数	Number of Overnight Tourists	万人次	10000 person-times	4838
（1）旅游住宿设施国内旅游人数	Domestic Tourists Staying Overnight at Hotels	万人次	10000 person-times	2032
（2）住亲友家去景点的国内旅游人数	Domestic Tourists Staying Overnight at Relatives and Friends' s Home	万人次	10000 person-times	2806
2. 不过夜旅游者（一日游人数）	Number of Same-day（One-day Sightseeing）Tourists	万人次	10000 person-times	3834
旅游景点接待一日游人数	One-day Sightseeing Tourists Received by Tour Scenes	万人次	10000 person-times	3834
（1）本地一日游人数	Number of Local One-day Sightseeing Tourists	万人次	10000 person-times	2486
（2）外地一日游人数	Number of One-day Sightseeing Tourists from Outside Areas	万人次	10000 person-times	1348
国内旅游人均花费	Per Capita Expenditure of Domestic Tourist	元	yuan	1693
国内旅游收入	Earings from Domestic Tourism	亿元	100 million yuan	1468
1. 接待过夜旅游者收入	Earings from Overnight Tourists	万元	10000 yuan	1307
2. 接待不过夜旅游者（一日游）收入	Earings from Same-day（One-day Sightseeing）Tourists	万元	10000 yuan	161

主要统计指标解释

住宿餐饮业营业额 指住宿和餐饮业法人企业、产业活动单位在经营活动中因提供服务或销售商品等取得的收入，包括客房收入、餐费收入、商品销售收入和其他收入。客房收入指住宿和餐饮业法人企业、产业活动单位在经营活动中因提供住宿服务取得的客房收入。餐费收入指住宿和餐饮业法人企业、产业活动单位因为顾客提供就餐服务取得的收入，包括经烹饪、调制加工后出售的各种食品，如主食、炒菜、凉拌菜等的收入。商品销售收入指住宿和餐饮业法人企业、产业活动单位伴随服务而出售商品所取得的收入。其他收入指营业收入中除客房收入、餐费收入、商品销售收入以外的其他收入，包括娱乐、健身和商务服务等。

国内旅游者 是指不以谋求职业、获取报酬为目的，离开惯常居住环境，到国内其它地方从事参观、游览、度假等旅游活动（包括外出探亲、疗养、考察、参加会议和从事商务、科技、文化、教育、宗教活动过程中的旅游活动），出行距离超过 10 公里，出游时间超过 6 小时，但不超过 12 个月的我国大陆居民。

入境旅游者 指来我国参观、访问、旅行、探亲、访友、休养、考察、参加会议和从事经济、科技、文化、教育、体育、宗教等活动的外国人、华侨、港澳和台湾同胞的人数。不包括外国在我国的常驻机构，如领事馆、通讯社、企业办事处的工作人员；来我国常住的外国专家、留学生以及在岸逗留不过夜人员。

Explanatory Notes on Main Statistical Indicators

Business Revenue of Hotels and Catering Services refer to revenue received from providing services or selling commodities by corporate enterprises and establishments engaged in hotel and catering services, including income from hotel rooms, from catering services, from selling of commodities and from other services. Income from hotel rooms refers to income of corporate enterprises and establishments by providing lodging services. Income from catering services refers to income of corporate enterprises and establishments by providing catering services, including selling of cooked or prepared foods such as stable food, cooked dishes or cold dishes. Income from selling of commodities refers to income of corporate enterprises and establishments by selling commodities that accompany the services they provide. Income from other activities fefers to income received other than income from hotel rooms, catering services or selling of commodities, such as income from providing recreation, fitness or business services.

Domestic Tourists refers to residents in mainland China who are not for the purpose of seeking employment, remuneration, and leaving the usual living environment, elsewhere to engage in domestic visitors, sightseeing, vacation travel (including to go out to visit relatives, infirmary, observing, participate in the meeting and engage in business, science and technology, culture, education, religious activities in the course of tourism activities), trip distance of more than 10 km, trips longer than six hours, but not more than 12 months.

Entrance Tourists refers to foreigners, overseas Chinese, Chinese compatriots from Hong Kong, Macao and Taiwan coming to China for sight-seeing, visits, tours, family reunions, vacations, study tours, conferences and other activities of a business, scientific and technological, cultural, educational and religious nature. It does not include representatives and employees of resident institutions of foreign countries in China such as embassies, consulates, news agencies and offices of foreign companies and organizations, nor does it include long-term foreign experts or students residing in China, or persons in transition without spending a night in China.

教育、科技和文化 17

EDUCATION SCIENCE & TECHNOLOY AND CULTURE

简要说明

一、本篇资料的主要内容

本篇资料主要反映了全市教育、科技和文化事业基本情况。教育部分主要包括高等教育、中等教育、初等教育、成人教育、职业教育、幼儿园等方面的基本情况。科技部分主要包括科研机构、科学技术奖励、大中型工业企业技术开发情况。文化部分主要包括文化、文物、广播、电视、报纸杂志出版、图书出版等方面的发展状况。

二、本篇资料的来源

1、教育部分，技工学校的资料来源于市人力资源和社会保障局，其他资料来源于市教育局。

2、科技部分，科研机构及科技奖励资料来源于市科技局，大中型工业企业科技活动资料来源于市统计局统计调查年报。

3、文化部分，图书、杂志、报纸出版有关资料来源于青岛出版集团、海大出版社其他资料来源于市文化广电新闻出版局。

本篇资料由市统计局人口和社会科技统计处整理提供。

Brief Introduction

Ⅰ. Main Content

Data in this chapter show the basic conditions of education, science & technology and culture, Data on education, show the development of higher education, secondary education, primary education, adult education, vocational education and kindergartens. Data on science & technology show the basic conditions of science research institutions, scientific and technological achievements and prizes, scientific & technological activities of large and medium-size industrial enterprises. Data on culture show the basic conditions of arts, cultural relics, broadcasting, television and publication of newspapers, magazines and books.

Ⅱ. Source of Data

（1）In education component, data on the basic conditions of technical schools are provided by Qingdao Municipal Bureau of Human Resources and Social Security, and the other dtat on education are provided by Qingdao Municipal Bureau of Education.

（2）In science & technology component, data on science research institutions and scientific & technological achievements and prizes are provided by Qingdao Municipal Bureau of Science and Technology. Data on scientific and technological activities are from the annual report of scientific and technological activities, which is provided by Qingdao Municipal Bureau of Statistics.

（3）In culture component, data on publication of books, magazines and newspapers are provided by Qingdao Publishing Group and Ocean University Press. the other data are provided by Qingdao municipal Bureau of Cluture, Broadcasting, Television, Press and Publication.

Data in this chapter are provided and compiled by the Division of Population and Science & Technology of Qingdao Municipal Bureau of Statistics.

17-1 各级各类学校基本情况（2017年）
BASIC STATISTICS ON SCHOOLS BY LEVEL AND TYPE OF SCHOOL（2017）

项目	Item	学校数（所）Schools（unit）	毕业生数（人）Graduates（person）	招生数（人）New Students Enrollment（person）	在校学生数（人）Students Enrollment（person）	教职工数（人）Teachers and Staff（person）	#专任教师 of which：Full-time Teachers
研究生	Postgraduates		9435	13933	37058		
普通高等学校	Regular Institutions of Higher Education	25	95006	98983	346238	32013	21231
中等专业学校	Specialized Secondary Schools	6	10400	10450	32882	899	664
技工学校	Technical Schools	23	6880	9828	33179	2302	1712
职业学校	Vocational Schools	42	13488	17981	52539	7191	5844
普通中学	Regular Secondary Schools	311	115875	132399	372196	40196	34667
初中	Junior Secondary Schools	241	78685	92750	255016	25025	23177
高中	Senior Secondary Schools	70	37190	39649	117180	15171	11490
小学	Primary Schools	722	93107	94414	550540	36151	34713
特殊教育学校	Special Education Schools	13	295	248	1738	631	541
幼儿园	Kindergartens	2097	79170	95331	252765	29074	19640
成人高等学校	Adult Institutions of Higher Education	1	64026	37234	86134	121	65
成人中等学校	Adult Institutions of Higher Education	2	1419	181	2495	36	27
成人初等学校	Adult Primary Education Schools						

注：1. 研究生栏中专任教师指的是指导教师。
2. 成人中等学校仅包括成人中学和成人中专。

Note：1. Adult secondary education schools refer to adult secondary schools and adult specialized secondary schools.
2. Adult secondary school includes adult middle school and adult secondary technical education.

17-2 主要年份各级各类学校在校学生数

MAJOR YEAR'S STUDENTS ENROLLMENT OF SCHOOLS BY LEVEL AND TYPE OF SCHOOL

单位：人（person）

年份 Year	普通高等学校 Pegular Institutions of Higher Education	中等学校 Secondary Schools	中等专业学校 Specialized Secondary Schools	普通中学 Regular Secondary Schools	职业中学 Vocational Schools	技工学校 Technical Schools	小学 Primary Schools
1949	1 007	13 804	1 600	12 204			213 470
1952	2 761	27 951	3 770	24 181			413 286
1957	3 133	56 689	4 985	51 604	100		482 397
1962	4 381	62 646	2 791	58 639	243	973	522 921
1965	2 987	99 605	9 405	88 187	1 490	523	788 485
1970	320	222 521	105	220 262	2 154		728 433
1975	1 151	350 309	3 144	346 403		762	928 153
1978	3 465	464 584	4 269	457 460	2 000	865	634 905
1980	6 783	325 935	5 195	318 193	1 344	1 203	816 970
1985	10 631	327 446	11 475	279 915	33 945	2 111	691 341
1988	14 408	352 576	11 819	306 943	28 933	4 881	629 212
1990	15 433	351 365	15 118	296 163	34 568	5 516	632 314
1991	15 491	353 410	14 618	298 568	34 421	5 803	612 772
1992	16 470	367 480	14 763	307 903	38 242	6 572	585 381
1993	23 858	383 043	16 877	318 179	40 743	7 244	583 585
1994	25 018	420 077	20 582	347 667	43 734	8 094	593 419
1995	24 908	450 212	23 744	372 335	46 044	8 089	595 891
1996	26 076	468 561	26 951	382 760	50 131	8 719	607 284
1997	27 434	463 619	28 543	362 305	61 640	11 131	626 749
1998	29 507	442 525	28 757	336 918	65 989	10 861	625 308
1999	33 681	459 520	26 955	352 238	70 236	10 091	583 594
2000	46 131	497 391	25 192	398 458	63 894	9 847	534 922
2001	60 728	542 400	25 358	443 693	62 003	11 346	499 147
2002	82 539	575 599	27 421	467 628	67 085	13 465	478 634
2003	168 439	586 704	28 948	461 435	75 221	21 100	467 560
2004	201 739	598 804	30 881	436 117	101 553	30 253	476 897
2005	239 761	569 230	33 522	391 148	106 400	38 160	479 781
2006	260 339	554 308	32 051	365 192	116 487	40 578	483 892
2007	264 917	558 527	28 011	360 410	130 156	39 950	484 775
2008	269 314	582 932	25 330	373 884	143 126	40 592	477 230
2009	275157	564476	22739	377427	127792	36518	465031
2010	284788	535079	24014	380025	98560	32480	462722
2011	291453	505051	25905	373226	74892	31028	479513
2012	296645	489103	27005	369580	65419	27099	484985
2013	300246	484025	28389	365110	61594	28932	496343
2014	313486	479260	28751	362599	58170	29740	516529
2015	322260	467231	33038	355401	48590	30202	536492
2016	340875	470333	32710	356107	50927	30589	547231
2017	346328	490796	32882	372196	52539	33179	550540

17-3　主要年份普通高等学校基本情况
MAJOR YEAR'S BASIC STATISTICS ON REGULAR INSTTUTIONS OF HIGHER EDUCATION

单位：人（person）

年份 Year	学校数（所） Schools （unit）	毕业生数 Graduates	招生数 New Students Enrollment	在校学生数 Students Enrollment	教职工数 Teachers and Staff	#专任教师 of which：Full-time Teachers
1949	1		250	1 007	779	226
1952	2	262	565	2 761	12 530	308
1957	2	356	755	3 133	1 308	622
1962	5	647	653	4 381	1 866	749
1965	3	741	529	2 987	1 539	623
1970	2	684		320	1 178	486
1975	2	460	473	1 151	1 353	582
1978	4	739	1 782	3 465	2 829	1 176
1980	6	431	1 717	6 783	4 182	1 606
1985	7	1 828	3 823	10 631	5 561	2 181
1988	7	3 496	4 687	14 408	6 875	2 499
1990	7	4 495	4 745	15 433	7 305	2 624
1991	7	4 880	4 954	15 491	7 282	2 489
1992	7	4 458	5 428	16 470	7 344	2 523
1993	7	3 140	9 449	23 858	7 366	2 520
1994	4	7 059	8 042	25 018	7 466	2 650
1995	4	7 828	7 978	24 908	7 545	2 682
1996	4	6 691	7 956	26 076	7 606	2 745
1997	4	7 091	8 503	27 434	7 790	2 813
1998	4	6 912	8 849	29 507	7 662	2 907
1999	4	7 202	11 584	33 681	7 662	2 928
2000	6	7 128	18 427	46 131	8 030	3 278
2001	6	8 991	22 787	60 728	8 706	4 058
2002	7	13 053	29 731	82 539	9 517	4 723
2003	25	25 747	61 975	168 439	18 911	10 293
2004	25	34 860	70 022	201 739	21 437	12 347
2005	25	46 114	79 725	239 761	23 078	13 894
2006	25	55 931	79 094	260 339	24 881	15 195
2007	25	68 354	78 728	264 917	25 956	16 005
2008	25	75 198	86 878	269 314	26 654	16 805
2009	25	69475	81025	275157	26983	16870
2010	25	70450	82220	284788	28145	16996
2011	22	79466	84434	291453	28151	17120
2012	22	79791	87981	296645	29445	18183
2013	22	78974	85707	300246	28958	18396
2014	22	77503	90127	313486	28944	18587
2015	24	79784	92251	322260	29620	19213
2016	26	86270	100525	340875	30390	20151
2017	25	95006	98983	346238	32013	21231

17-4 各类成人教育基本情况(2017年)
BASIC STATISTICS ON ADULT EDUCATION (2017)

单位：人（person）

各类学校	Schools by Type of School	学校数（所）Schools (unit)	毕业生数 Graduates	招生数 New Students Enrollment	在校学生数 Students Enrollment	教职工数 Teachers and Staff	#专任教师 of which: Full-time Teachers
总　计	**Total**	**3**	**65445**	**37415**	**88629**	**157**	**92**
成人高等教育	Adult Higher Education	1	64026	37234	86134	121	65
广播电视大学	Broadcasting and TV Universities	1	314	538	764	121	65
职工、农民大学	Universities of Vocational and Agricultural Education						
函授、夜大学	Correspondence and Evening College Education						
管理干部学校	Cadre Management Schools						
成人中等教育	Adult Secondary Education	2	1419	181	2495	36	27
成人中等专业学校	Adult Specialized Secondary Schools	2	1419	181	2495	36	27

17-5 分市、区普通中学情况(2017年)
BASIC STATISTICS ON REGULAR SECONDARY SCHOOLS BY REGION (2017)

单位：人（person）

市、区名称	Region	普通高中 Regular Senior Secondary Schools				普通初中 Regular Junior Secondary Schools			
		学校数 Schools (unit)	毕业生数 Graduates	招生数 New Students Enrollment	在校生数 Students Enrollment	学校数 Schools (unit)	毕业生数 Graduates	招生数 New Students Enrollment	在校生数 Students Enrollment
全　市	**Whole Municipality**	**70**	**37190**	**39649**	**117180**	**241**	**78685**	**92750**	**255016**
市　直	Municipal Level	22	8858	10161	29350	3	2742	2574	7700
市南区	Shinan District					10	3052	2961	7829
市北区	Shibei District	1		152	152	24	6341	7529	19834
李沧区	Licang District	1		20	20	13	3507	4203	10851
崂山区	Laoshan District	2				9	2269	2551	6764
黄岛区	Huangdao District	11	6056	6046	18910	39	12713	16269	42893
城阳区	Chengyang District	6	2689	2770	8224	16	5549	7367	18896
即墨区	Jimo District	9	5403	6306	17789	29	12854	15151	39166
胶州市	Jiaozhou	7	4358	4446	12998	22	9082	12034	31979
平度市	Pingdu	6	6877	6171	19798	43	12806	14534	38728
莱西市	Laixi	4	2949	3509	9871	29	7113	6824	28330
红岛经济区	Qingdao National High-tech Industrial Development Zone	1		68	68	4	657	753	2046

注：黄岛区含保税港区数据。
Note: The Huangdao District contains the data of the bonded harbor area.

17-6 分市、区职业中学、小学情况(2017 年)

BASIC STATISTICS ON VOCATIONAL SECONDARY SCHOOLS AND PRIMARY SCHOOLS BY REGION（2017）

单位：人(person)

市、区名称	Region	职业中学 Vocational Secondary Schools				小学 Primany School			
		学校数 Schools (unit)	毕业生数 Graduates	招生数 New Students Enrollment	在校生数 Students Enrollment	学校数 Schools (unit)	毕业生数 Graduates	招生数 New Students Enrollment	在校生数 Students Enrollment
全　市	**Whole Municipality**	**42**	**13488**	**17981**	**52539**	**722**	**93107**	**94414**	**550540**
市　直	Municipal Level	22	2863	3063	9615				
市南区	Shinan District					28	4724	5715	31138
市北区	Shibei District					67	8045	9748	56049
李沧区	Licang District					35	4485	6494	34103
崂山区	Laoshan District					26	2889	4382	22972
黄岛区	Huangdao District	11	4713	5873	16528	89	16419	16800	96993
城阳区	Chengyang District	3	8	1149	2934	46	7564	11175	56789
即墨区	Jimo District	2	1668	2099	6450	171	14988	12794	83248
胶州市	Jiaozhou	1	1868	2505	7278	78	11749	9831	61179
平度市	Pingdu	1	1308	1673	5360	106	14640	10753	69780
莱西市	Laixi	2	1060	1619	4374	72	6818	5833	33502
红岛经济区	Qingdao National High-tech Industrial Development Zone					4	786	889	4787

注：黄岛区含保税港区数据。

Note：The Huangdao District contains the data of the bonded harbor area.

17-7 分市、区中小学教职工情况(2017 年)

BASIC STATSTICS ON TEACHERS AND STAFF IN SECONDARY AND PRIMARY SCHOOLS BY REGION（2017）

单位：人（person）

市、区名称	Region	普通中学 Regular Secondary Schools		职业中学 Vocational Secondary Schools		小学 Primary Schools	
		教职工数 Teachers and Staff	#专任教师 of which：Full-time Teachers	教职工数 Teachers and Staff	#专任教师 of which：Full-time Teachers	教职工数 Teachers and Staff	#专任教师 of which：Full-time Teachers
全　市	**Whole Municipality**	**40196**	**34667**	**7191**	**5844**	**36151**	**34713**
市　直	Municipal Level	4082	3264	2513	1837		
市南区	Shinan District	1051	839			2074	1977
市北区	Shibei District	2311	1914			3546	3373
李沧区	Licang District	1348	1049			1910	1836
崂山区	Laoshan District	946	789			1541	1480
黄岛区	Huangdao District	6663	5836	1431	1229	6141	5916
城阳区	Chengyang District	2825	2240	675	599	2846	2712
即墨区	Jimo District	6206	5453	717	614	5618	5429
胶州市	Jiaozhou	4196	3780	672	495	4020	3914
平度市	Pingdu	6074	5551	667	624	5492	5244
莱西市	Laixi	4044	3633	516	446	2676	2549
红岛经济区	Qingdao National High-tech Industrial Development Zone	450	319			287	283

注：黄岛区含保税港区数据。

Note：The Huangdao District contains the data of the bonded harbor area.

17-8 分市、区幼儿园基本情况(2017年)
BASIC STATISTICS ON KINDERGARTENS BY REGION (2017)

单位：人(person)

市、区名称	Region	幼儿园(所) Kindergartens (unit)	幼儿数 Children	教职工数 Teachers and Staff	#专任教师 of which: Full-time teachers
全 市	**Whole Municipality**	**2097**	**252765**	**29074**	**19640**
市南区	Shinan District	61	14103	2256	1089
市北区	Shibei District	109	28706	3153	1918
李沧区	Licang District	48	19193	2270	1150
崂山区	Laoshan District	107	14147	2120	1283
黄岛区	Huangdao District	373	43502	5597	3997
城阳区	Chengyang District	149	25825	3524	2363
即墨区	Jimo District	314	30838	3197	2399
胶州市	Jiaozhou	369	28470	2950	2217
平度市	Pingdu	400	31027	2352	1834
莱西市	Laixi	140	14273	1288	1071
红岛经济区	Qingdao National High-tech Industrial Development Zone	27	2681	367	319

注：黄岛区含保税港区数据。
Note: The Huangdao District contains the data of the bonded harbor area.

17-9 科研机构基本情况(1978-2017 年)
BASIC STATISTICS ON SCIENTIFIC RESEARCH INSTITUTIONS（1978-2017）

年 份 Year	独立自然科研结构(个) Independent Institutions of Natural Scientific Research (unit)	独立自然科研结构中科技人员(个) Personnel of Independent Institutions of Natural Scientific Research (person)	完成科研项目(项) Number of Scientific Research Projects Completed (item)	取得科技成果(项) Number of Achievements in S&T (item)
1978	31	2701	306	306
1980			481	297
1982	41	2345	451	451
1983	48	3182	530	530
1984	53	3312	507	507
1985	52	3673	552	552
1986	63	3998	577	577
1988	101	5199	544	510
1990	141	6046	414	931
1991	72	5665	753	753
1992	71	5726	659	659
1993	69	5545	546	546
1994	69	5540	467	467
1995	59	5286	441	441
1996	58	4738	613	613
1997	54	4577	418	418
1998	52	4142	517	517
1999	58	3771	606	606
2000	54	3637	621	621
2001	50	3191	457	457
2002	52	3248	406	406
2003	53	3246	589	589
2004	50	3226	506	506
2005	50	3234	438	438
2006	50	3291	548	548
2007	50	3432	506	506
2008	42	3709	416	416
2009	43	3727	572	572
2010	44	4088	472	472
2011	47	4548	345	345
2012	48	4967	304	304
2013	48	6057	433	433
2014	50	5438	415	415
2015	54	6037	639	639
2016	57	5722	606	606
2017	57	6017	588	588

注：1991 年以后不包括民办科研机构。
Note：Since 1991，private institutions of scientific research are not included.

17-10 独立科学研究机构情况(2017年)
BASIC STATISTICS ON INDEPENDENT INSHUTIONS OF SCIENTIFIC RESEARCH（2017）

项目	Item	计量单位	Unit	总计 Total	中央属 Central	地方属 Local
机构数	Number of Institutions	个	unit	57	22	35
职工人数	Staff and Workers	人	person	8215	5955	2260
科技人员	Personnel Engaged in S&T	人	person	6017	4463	1554
经费收入	Funding for S&T	万元	10 000 yuan	322871.9	267727.3	55144.6
经费支出	Expenditures for S&T	万元	10 000 yuan	309776.5	259037.1	50739.4

17-11 科学技术奖励情况(2017年)
AWARD STATISTICS ON SCIENCE AND TECHNOLOGY（2017）

项目	Item	单位	unit	自然科学奖 Natural Science Prizes Awarded	技术发明奖 Invention Prizes Awarded	科技进步奖 Scientific and Technological Progress Prizes Awarded	科学技术功勋奖 Scientific and Technolgical Credit Prizes Awarded	国际科技合作奖 International S&T Cooperation Prizes Award	最高奖 Highest Prizes Award
国家级	National Level	项	item		3	6			
特等	Special Grade								
#一等	First Prize	项	item			1			
二等	Second Prize	项	item		3	5			
省级	Provincial Level	项	item	7	3	41			1
#一等	First Prize	项	item		2	7			
二等	Second Prize	项	item	7	1	22			
三等	Third Prize	项	item			12			
市级	Municipal Level	项	item	8	9	126		2	
#一等	First Prize	项	item	2		9			
二等	Second Prize	项	item	6	3	53			
三等	Third Prize	项	item		6	64			

注：国际科技合作奖、最高奖不分等级。
Note：There is no grade in international scientific and technological cooperation prizes award and highest prizes award.

17-12 大中型工业企业技术开发主要相对指标(2011-2017年)

MAJOR RELATIVE INDICATORS FOR TECHNOLOGICAL DEVELOPMENT OF LARGE AND MEDIUM-SIZED INDUSTRIAL ENTERPRISES（2011-2017）

项　目	Item	单位	2011年	2012年	2013年	2014年	2015年	2016年	2017年
企业技术开发人员占全部职工比重	The proportion of enterprise technology developers to the total staff and workers	%	7.7	7.4	8.3	8.5	6.3	7.0	8.2
设有开发机构的企业占企业总数比重	Enterprises with development institutions account for the total number of enterprises	%	28.1	26.7	25.1	25.8	24.0	27.8	28.9
新产品产值比重	Proportion of new product output value	%	28.8	26.0	25.3	28.1	27.6	15.8	25.1
新产品销售额比重	Proportion of new product sales	%	29.3	27.0	27.2	28.0	28.3	16.8	24.0

17-13 文化、文物事业机构、人员数(2017年)

NUMBER OF INSTITUTIONS AND PERSONNEL IN CUUTURE（2017）

项目	Item	文化机构数（个） Number of Cultural Institutions（unit）		文化人员数（人） Number of Cultural Personnel（Person）	
		2017年	2016年	2017年	2016年
一、艺术事业	**Art**	**26**	**27**	**832**	**1085**
1.艺术表演团体	Art Peformance Troupes	8	9	575	819
2.艺术表演场所	Art Centers	10	10	197	202
3.艺术展览创作机构	Art Creation Institutions	5	5	33	35
4.艺术研究机构	Art Research Institutions				
5.艺术展览机构	Art Exhibition Institutions				
6.其他	Others	3	3	27	29
二、图书馆事业	**Libraries**		**12**		**274**
公共图书馆	Publie Libraries	12	12	275	274
#县(区)级图书馆	County Libraries	11	11	175	170
三、群众文化事业	**Nass Culture**	**148**	**148**	**725**	**746**
1.群众艺术馆	Nass Art Centers				
2.文化馆	Cultural Palaces	12	12	225	224
3.文化站	Cultural Centers	136	136	500	522
4.其他	Others				

17-14 文化部门艺术剧团情况(2017 年)
STATISTICS ON ART TROUPES OF CULTURAL DEPARTMENT（2017）

项 目	Item	剧团数（个）Number of Troupes (unit)	职工人数（人）Stalf and Workers (person)	演出场次（场）Number of Performances (show)	观众人数（万人次）Number of Spectators (10000 person-times)	演出收入（万元）Income from Ticket Sales (10000 yuan)	#财政补贴（万元）Apporopriation Funds (10000 yuan)
总 计	**Total**	**8**	**575**	**1891**	**125.1**	**11364.7**	**9481.7**
一、按隶属关系分	**Grouped by Administrative Relationship**						
国营剧团	State-run Troupes	8	575	1891	125.1	11364.7	9481.7
集体经营剧团	Collective-owned Troupes						
二、按剧种分	**Grouped by Type of Drama**						
1. 话剧团	Drama Troupes	1	110	275	13.8	1743.6	1344.1
2. 歌舞团	Song and Dance Troupes						
3. 戏曲剧团	Local Opera Troupes	6	369	1546	105.3	6368.7	5289.1
#京剧	of which：Beijing Opera	1	88	173	6.9	1788.2	1560.2
4. 曲艺团	Recitation and Ballad Troupes						
5. 文工团（艺术团）	Cultural and Performance Troupes	1	96	70	6.0	3252.4	2848.5

17-15 图书馆、文化馆情况
STATISTICS ON LIBRARIES AND CULTURAL CENTERS

项 目	Item	单位	2017 年		2016 年	
			全市合计 Total	#市区 Urban Area	全市合计 Total	#市区 Urban Area
公共图书馆	**Pubilc Libraries**	个	**12**	**9**	**12**	**8**
工作人员	Staff and Workers	人	275	225	274	202
藏书册数	Colicetion Books	千册	6996	6108	6463	5381
阅览席位	Seating Capacity of Reading Rooms	张	6412	5351	6279	4655
读者人数	Readers	万人次	482.1	419.3	587.1	506
文化馆	**Cultural Centers**	个	**12**	**9**	**12**	**8**

主要统计指标解释

普通高等学校　指按照国家规定的设置标准和审批程序批准举办，通过国家统一招生考试，招收高中毕业生为主要培养对象，实施高等教育的全日制大学、独立设置的学院和高等专科学校、短期职业大学。

成人高等学校　指按照国家有关规定审批，招收通过全国成人高教统一招生考试的具有高中毕业或同等学历的在职从业人员，利用脱产、半脱产、业余或函授等多种形式对其实施高等学历教育，培养高等教育专科或本科毕业水平的专门人才，修业年限、课程设置和总学时数均按高等学历教育要求付诸实施的学校。包括广播电视大学、职工高等学校、农民高等学校、管理干部学院；教育学院、独立设置的函授学院等。

科技活动人员　指直接从事科技活动、以及专门从事科技活动管理和为科技活动提供直接服务，累计的实际工作时间占全年制度工作时间 10% 及以上的人员。

文化事业机构　指从事专业文化工作和为专业文化工作服务的独立建制的单独核算的单位。不包括这些单位另外举办独立核算的其他机构和各部门的业余文化组织。

Explanatory Notes on Main Statistical Indicators

Regular Institutions of Higher Education　refer to educational establishments set up according to the government evaluation and approval procedures，enrolling graduates from senior secondary schools and providing higher education courses and training for senior professionals. They include full-time universities，colleges，high professional schools，high professional vocational schools and others.

Adult Institutions of Higher Education　refers to educational establishments，set up in line with relevant urles approved by the government，enrolling staff and workers with senior secondary schoos or equivalent education，and providing higher education courses in many forms of correspondence，spare time，or full time for adults. Professionals thus trained receive a qualification equivalent to graduates studying regular courses at regular universities，colleges and professional colleges. Institutions of higher learning for adults include schools of high education for staff and workers，schools of high education for peasants，colleges for management cadres，pedagogical colleges，independent correspondence colleges，Radio and TV universities and other educational establishments.

Personnel Engaged in S&T Activities　refer to personnel directly engaged in S&T activities，in the management of S&T activities，and in providing direct service to S&T activities，who spend over 10% of the total working hours in a year in S&T activities.

Cultural Institutions　refer to units，which have their own organizational system and independent accounting system and specialize in or serve cultural development. They exclude other establishments run by these cultural institutions and amateur cultural groups established by various departments.

18 体育、卫生和民政、司法

SPORTS，PUBLIC HEALTH AND CIVIL AFFAIRS，JUDICIAL AFFAIRS

简要说明

一、本篇资料的主要内容

本篇资料反映了全市体育、卫生、民政、司法等社会事业的基本情况。体育部分主要包括主要年份运动员、教练员、裁判员发展人数、体育运动破纪录、获奖情况。卫生部分主要包括各类卫生机构及其人员、床位数。民政部分主要包括婚姻登记、社会救济、社会福利事业基本情况、殡葬服务情况。司法部分主要包括律师、公证、调解、社会治安基本情况。

二、本篇资料的来源

1、体育部分来源于市体育局。

2、卫生部分来源于市卫生局。

3、民政部分来源于市民政局。

4、司法部分，社会治安资料来源于市公安局，其他资料来源于市司法局，

本篇资料由市统计局人口和社会科技统计处整理提供。

Brief Introduction

Ⅰ. Main Content

Data in this chapter show the basic conditions of sports，public health，civil affairs and judicial affairs. Data on sports are mainly including the number of athletes，coaches and referees，conditions of record and awards. Data on public health are mainly including the number of health institutions，personnel and beds. Data on civil affairs are mainly including the conditions of marriage registration，social relief，social welfare and funeral services. Data on judicial affairs are mainly including the conditions of lawyers，notarization，mediation and social order.

Ⅱ. Source of Data

（1）Data on sports are provided by Qingdao Municipal Bureau of Physical.

（2）Data on public health are provided by Qingdao Municipal Bureau of Health.

（3）Data on civil affairs are provided by Qingdao Municipal Bureau of Civil Affairs.

（4）In judicial affairs component，data on social order are provided by Qingdao Municipal Bureau of Public Security and the other data are provided by Qingdao Municipal Bureau of Justice.

Data in this chapter are provided and compiled by the Division of Population and Science & Technology of Qingdao Municipal Bureau of Statistics.

18-1 体育事业情况(2000-2017年)
STATISTICS ON SPORTS（2000-2017）

单位：人（person）

项　目	Item	2000	2005	2006	2007	2008	2009	2010	2011	2012	2013	2014	2015	2016	2017
体育部门职工人数	**Staff and Workers in Sports Commissions**	**849**	**834**	**848**	**772**	**1210**	**910**	**1015**				**847**	**795**	**857**	**654**
# 运动员	Athletes	90	87	81	55	452	512	287				287	259		284
教练员	Coaches	174	235	221	211	173	106	170	136					120	133
重点体校	Key Sports School	126	117	166	249	109	97	115	129						1061
业余体校	Sparetime Sports Schools	142	223	220	145		160								1537
体育专业队	Professional Sports Teams	135	132	154	121		144	192	87	84	42	38	17	17	5
优秀运动员	Exeellent Athletes	90	87	81	55	71	72	146	57						
优秀运动队专职教练员	Full-time Coaches of Excellennt Sports Teams	18	23	48	47	106	92	97	54				89	120	
等级裁判员发展人数	**Certified Referees**	**1114**	**275**	**1068**	**781**	**205**	**292**	**212**	**510**	**558**	**512**	**514**	**490**	**167**	
# 二级	Second Grades	451	275	1068	781	181	252	169	510	484	463	514	490	116	
三级	Third Grades	616													
等级运动员发展人数	**Certified Athletes**	**343**	**260**	**267**	**108**	**310**	**512**	**229**	**436**	**362**	**362**	**283**	**259**		**176**
# 二级	Second Grades	209	260	267	108	281	448	229	436	256	362	283	259		176
三级	Third Grades	46													
少年级	Juvenile	88													

18-1 续表
Contiuned

单位：人（person）

项　目	Item	单位	Unit	2000	2005	2006	2007	2008	2009	2010	2011	2012	2013	2014	2015	2016	2017
全年获得奖牌数	**Number of Medals Won in the Year**	枚	**unit**	**347.5**	**669**	**829**	**481**	**494**	**602**	**754**	**829**	**746**	**659**	**576.5**	**596**	**729.5**	**3032**
#国家级金牌	Golden Medals at National Level	枚	unit	45	62	71	61	26	30	14	105	88	90	48	51	101	104
国家级银牌	Silver Medals at National Level	枚	unit	28	48	54	38	21	23	7	49	100	44	21	44	56	91
省级金牌	Golden Medals at Provincial Level	枚	unit	116.5	187	363	116	168	207	459	225	193	174.5	202.5	149	219.5	214.5
省级银牌	Silver Medals at Provincial Level	枚	unit	62	174	144	93	122	149	116	155	110	111.5	121.5	126	135	140
体育运动破全国记录	**Records Broken the National Records**																
项目	Number of Events	项	item		2		1		1	1	2	1					
人数	Number of Persons	人	person		2		1		1	1	2	1					
次数	Number of Times	人次	person-tims		4		1		1	1	2	1					
体育运动破全省记录	**Records Broken the Provincial Records**																
项目	Number of Events	项	item	7	3	5		2		1							
人数	Number of Persons	人	person	7	1	3		2		1							
次数	Number of Times	人次	person-tims	7	3	5		2		1							

18-2 主要年份卫生事业基本情况
MAJOR YEAR'S BASIC STATISTICS ON PUBLIC HEALTH

年 份 Year	卫生机构数（个）Health Institutions (unit)	#医院 of which: Hospitals	医疗床位数（张）Beds in Health Institutions (bed)	#医院 of which: Hospitals	卫生技术人员（人）Medical and Technical Personnel (person)	#医生 of which: Doctors	每千人口拥有医生数（人）Number of Doctors per 1000 Population (person)	每千人口拥有床位数（张）Number of Hospital Beds per 1000 Population (bed)
1949	80	26	1079	970	2637	1292	0.32	0.27
1952	260	34	2943	1691	3748	1559	0.37	0.70
1957	624	45	5163	2656	6941	2578	0.53	1.07
1962	849	149	7167	4526	8279	2972	0.64	1.55
1965	912	162	8428	5003	9051	3586	0.73	1.72
1970	712	170	8613	6603	9591	3761	0.70	1.60
1975	959	181	10902	9078	13558	4566	0.80	1.90
1978	1192	212	13084	10709	16921	5893	1.01	2.24
1980	1253	212	14170	11345	19265	6781	1.14	2.38
1985	1517	219	18469	13214	23413	9694	1.55	2.95
1990	1563	235	23541	16586	27932	13761	2.08	3.56
1991	1579	235	23727	16796	27772	13227	1.98	3.54
1992	1562	236	24765	17269	28305	13157	1.95	3.67
1993	1540	237	24885	17469	28705	13312	1.97	3.68
1994	1335	242	24732	17882	28938	13535	1.99	3.64
1995	1347	228	25282	18126	29816	13840	2.02	3.69
1996	2216	228	24334	18344	30048	13790	2.00	3.53
1997	2193	239	25201	19046	31121	14400	2.07	3.62
1998	2190	237	24887	19083	31623	14327	2.05	3.56
1999	2185	235	25481	19798	31965	14453	2.06	3.62
2000	2911	231	24392	20057	32160	14860	2.10	3.45
2001	3199	217	24755	20313	32765	15772	2.22	3.48
2002	3050	213	21370	20662	31469	13371	1.87	2.99
2003	3111	213	23980	21605	32337	13452	1.87	3.33
2004	2923	219	25432	23465	32937	13953	1.91	3.48
2005	2609	235	30627	28564	33942	15008	2.03	4.13
2006	2834	232	28724	26653	34360	15451	2.06	3.83
2007	2006	251	30062	28107	33807	15018	1.98	3.97
2008	1985	249	32350	29874	36574	16260	2.14	4.25
2009	2017	252	32803	30527	40217	16734	2.19	4.30
2010	2147	254	36066	33383	43285	17696	2.32	4.72
2011	2549	280	39980	35600	47347	18310	2.39	5.22
2012	2607	288	47254	41186	54488	21593	2.81	6.14
2013	2936	285	44876	39725	59961	24113	3.12	5.80
2014	3126	297	47081	42961	62738	24946	3.20	6.03
2015	3146	308	48601	45066	65264	26270	3.35	6.20
2016	7564	322	50649	47309	87733	27675	3.49	6.39
2017	7927	410	55798	46282	76146	30867	3.84	6.94

注：自 2016 年起，卫生机构及人员包含村卫生室。
Note: Health agency and personnel includes village clinic as of 2016.

18-3 各类卫生机构、床位、人员数（2017 年底）
NUMBER OF HEALTH INSTITUTIONS，BEDS AND EMPLOYED PERSONS（END OF 2017）

项　　目	Item	机构数（个）Health Institutions（unit）	床位数（张）Beds in Health Institutions（bed）	人员数（人）Personnel（person）
总　　计		**7927**	**55798**	**95591**
一、医院合计	**Sub-total of Hospitals**	**410**	**53341**	**66372**
1. 医院	Hospitals	306	46282	58854
#综合医院	General Hospitals	172	29641	39298
中医医院	Hospitals Specialized in Traditional Chinese Medicine	36	6050	7587
中西医结合医院	Hospitals of Combination of Chinese and Western Medicine	7	645	684
专科医院	Specialized Hospitals	87	9726	11205
#口腔医院	Stomatological Hospitals	7	78	427
眼科医院	Ophthalmology Hospitals	7	538	745
肿瘤医院	Tumor Hospitals	3	514	590
心血管病医院	Cardiovascular Diseases Hospitals	4	1086	1069
精神病医院	Mental Hospitals	12	2534	1384
传染病医院	Infectious Disease Hospitals	2	640	504
皮肤病医院	The Skin Disease Hospital	2	52	70
骨科医院	Orthopaedics Hospitals	6	451	343
2. 卫生院	Sanitation Stations	104	7059	7518
二、社区卫生服务中心	**Neighborhood Service Centers**	**71**	**506**	**2794**
三、门诊部	**Outpatient Service Stations**	**332**	**305**	**4926**
四、诊所	**Clinics**	**2027**	**0**	**7039**
五、卫生所、医务室、护理站	**Medical Houses Nursing Station**	**311**	**0**	**902**
六、社区卫生服务站	**Neighborhood Service Stations**	**218**	**237**	**2638**
七、急救中心	**First Aid Centers**	**2**	**0**	**143**
八、采供血机构	**Institutions of Blood Collection and Supply**			
九、妇幼保健院（所、站）	**Maternity and Child Care Centers**	**12**	**460**	**1521**
十、专科疾病防治院（所、站）	**Specialized Disease Prevention & Treatment Institutions**	**6**	**291**	**237**
十一、疾病预防控制中心（防疫站）	**Centers for Disease Control and Prevention（Epidemic Prevention Stations）**	**25**	**0**	**839**
十二、卫生监督所	**Sanitation Control Stations**	**11**	**0**	**375**
十三、卫生监督检验所（站）	**Sanitation Control and Test Stations**			
十四、计划生育技术服务机构	**Family Planning Service Institutions**	**25**	**0**	**148**
十五、临床检验中心（所、站）	**Clinical Laboratory Center**	**3**	**0**	**268**
十六、健康教育所（站、中心）	**Health Education Stations**			
十七、其它卫生机构	**Other Health Institutions**	**36**	**0**	**279**
十八、疗养院	**Sanatoriums**	**5**	**658**	**476**
十九、村卫生室	**Village clinic**	**4433**	**0**	**6634**

# 卫生技术人员 Medical and Technical Personnel	# 医生 Doctos	注册护士 Registered Nurses	药剂人员 Pharmacists	检验人员 Laboratory Technicians
76146	**30867**	**33985**	**3862**	**2470**
55795	**19976**	**27141**	**3072**	**1914**
49225	17308	24886	2555	1627
33273	11746	16938	1647	1090
6527	2375	3111	460	209
566	253	225	59	21
8822	2915	4601	387	306
367	170	143	6	1
570	176	342	17	13
499	162	276	18	13
872	279	424	48	29
1154	271	747	54	30
423	139	217	27	29
54	23	18	9	4
249	71	102	14	10
6570	2668	2255	517	287
2360	**979**	**861**	**202**	**88**
4005	**2019**	**1453**	**206**	**168**
6904	**4263**	**2513**	**78**	**8**
875	**524**	**326**	**11**	**2**
2163	**1030**	**789**	**196**	**52**
81	**33**	**46**	**1**	**1**
1178	**443**	**483**	**46**	**86**
186	**79**	**53**	**16**	**16**
635	**325**	**41**	**13**	**58**
272	**0**	**0**	**0**	**0**
47	**25**	**6**	**0**	**0**
106	**9**	**5**	**0**	**60**
206	**110**	**51**	**6**	**4**
273	**116**	**93**	**15**	**13**
1060	**936**	**124**	**0**	**0**

18-4 分市、区各类卫生机构、床位、人员数(2017 年底)

NUMBER OF HEALTH INSTITUTIONS, BEDS AND EMPLOYED PERSONS BY REGION (END OF 2017)

市、区名称	Region	机构数（个）Instiutions (unit)	医院小计 Sub-total of Hospitals	#医院 Hospitals	#卫生院 Sanitation Staions
全　市	**Whole Municpality**	**7927**	**410**	**306**	**104**
市南区	Shinan District	391	29	29	
市北区	Shibei District	706	73	73	
李沧区	Licang District	421	19	19	
崂山区	Laoshan District	422	24	21	3
黄岛区	Huangdao District	1269	56	40	16
城阳区	Chengyang District	727	26	21	5
即墨区	Jimo District	1075	51	30	21
胶州市	Jiaozhou	970	37	23	14
平度市	Pingdu	1122	55	26	29
莱西市	Laixi	824	40	24	16

注：黄岛区含保税港区数据；城阳区含红岛经济区数据。
Note: The Huangdao District contains the data of the bonded harbor area. Chengyang District contains red island economic zone data.

18-4 续表 1

Continued

市、区名称	Region	采供血机构 Institutions of Blood Collection and Supply	妇幼保健院（所、站）Maternity and Child Care Centers	专科疾病防治院（所、站）Specialized Disease Prevention & Treatment Institutions
全　市	**Whole Municipality**		**12**	**6**
市南区	Shinan District		1	1
市北区	Shibei District		2	
李沧区	Licang District		1	
崂山区	Laoshan District		1	
黄岛区	Huangdao District		2	2
城阳区	Chengyang District		1	
即墨区	Jimo District		1	1
胶州市	Jiaozhou		1	
平度市	Pingdu		1	2
莱西市	Laixi		1	

注：黄岛区含保税港区数据；城阳区含红岛经济区数据。
Note: The Huangdao District contains the data of the bonded harbor area. Chengyang District contains red island economic zone data.

社区卫生服务中心 Neighborhood Service Centers	社区卫生服务站 Neighborhood Service Stations	门诊部 Outpatient Service Stations	诊所、卫生所、医务室、护理站 Clinics Medical Houses	急救中心 First Aid Centers
71	**218**	**332**	**2338**	**2**
9	31	41	268	
17	50	75	484	1
13	48	28	310	
3	28	28	188	
11	18	46	375	
10	1	64	178	1
2	36	9	152	
4		15	177	
		25	165	
2	6	1	41	

疾病预防控制中心（防疫站） Centers for Disease Control and Prevention（Epidemic Prevention Stations）	卫生监督所 Sanitation Control Stations	村卫生室 Village health room	计划生育技术服务机构 Family Planning Service Institutions
25	**11**	**4433**	**25**
1	1		
2	2		
1	1		
1	1	146	
6	1	751	
9	1	427	9
1	1	780	16
1	1	730	
1	1	870	
2	1	729	

18-4 续表 2
Continued

市、区名称	Region	健康教育所（站、中心）Health Education Station	临床检验中心（站、所）Clinical Laboratory Center	其他卫生机构 Other Health Institutions	疗养院 Sanatoriums	床位数（张）Beds in Health Institutions（bed）
全　市	**Whole Municpality**		**3**	**36**	**5**	**55798**
市南区	Shinan District			4	5	6847
市北区	Shibei District					13721
李沧区	Licang District					2993
崂山区	Laoshan District		2			1293
黄岛区	Huangdao District		1			6811
城阳区	Chengyang District					3133
即墨区	Jimo District			25		5634
胶州市	Jiaozhou			4		5723
平度市	Pingdu			2		5287
莱西市	Laixi			1		4356

注：黄岛区含保税港区数据；城阳区含红岛经济区数据。
Note：The Huangdao District contains the data of the bonded harbor area. Chengyang District contains red island economic zone data.

18-4 续表 3
Continued

市、区名称	Region	专科疾病防治院（所、站）Specialized Disease Centers	人员数（人）Personnel（person）	卫生技术人员 Medical and Technical Personnel
全　市	**Whole Municpality**		**95591**	**76146**
市南区	Shinan District		12958	10542
市北区	Shibei District		22149	18956
李沧区	Licang District		7641	6613
崂山区	Laoshan District		4090	3071
黄岛区	Huangdao District		12377	9915
城阳区	Chengyang District		7183	5517
即墨区	Jimo District		8331	6052
胶州市	Jiaozhou		7814	5978
平度市	Pingdu		7407	5427
莱西市	Laixi		5641	4075

注：黄岛区含保税港区数据；城阳区含红岛经济区数据。
Note：The Huangdao District contains the data of the bonded harbor area. Chengyang District contains red island economic zone data.

医院小计 Sub-total of Hospitals	# 医院 Hospitals	# 卫生院 Sanitation Stations	门诊部 Outpatient Service Stations	妇幼保健院（所、站） Maternity and Child Care Centers
53341	**46282**	**7059**	**305**	
6178	6178		9	
13643	13643		9	
2901	2901			
1179	1132	47	34	
6236	4986	1250	5	
3023	2892	131	26	
5499	4155	1344	6	
5528	4451	1077	4	
4858	2905	1953	212	
4296	3039	1257		

执业（助理）医师 Certified（Assistant）Doctors	注册护士 Registered Nurses	药剂人员 Pharmacists	检验人员 Laboratory Technicians	其他人员 Other Personnel
30867	**33985**	**3862**	**2470**	**4588**
4180	4929	471	352	697
7764	8682	997	572	1083
2829	3047	309	180	365
1370	1246	178	131	160
3963	4474	478	322	626
2269	2312	295	184	463
2395	2506	362	195	385
2288	2752	275	184	284
2217	2261	281	207	283
1592	1776	216	143	242

18-5 收养性社会福利单位情况（2017年）
BASIC STATICTICS ON SOCIAL WELFARE INSTITUTIONS（2017）

市、区名称	Region	单位数（个）Number of Institutions（unit）	年末职工人数（人）Number of Staff and Workers at Year-end（person）	年末床位数（张）Number of Beds at Year-end（bed）
全　市	**Whole Municpality**	**296**	**6078**	**43271**
市本级	Municipal Level	31	2175	8438
市南区	Shinan District	16	363	3496
市北区	Shibei District	51	1107	9147
李沧区	Licang District	32	682	3373
崂山区	Laoshan District	9	243	1732
黄岛区	Huangdao District	20	475	2731
城阳区	Chengyang District	15	161	3041
即墨区	Jimo District	21	134	3408
胶州市	Jiaozhou	9	102	2499
平度市	Pingdu	80	346	2505
莱西市	Laixi	12	290	2901

注：1. 年末在院人数仅包括老年人与残疾人服务机构。2. 黄岛区含保税港区数据；城阳区含红岛经济区数据。
Note：1. At the end of the year, the number of people in hostitals includes the elderly and disabled service organizations only.
2. The Huangdao District contains the data of the bonded harbor area. Chengyang District contains red island economic zone data.

18-6 社会救济情况（2017年）
BASIC STATISTICS ON SOCLAL RELIEF（2017）

市、区名称	Region	城镇居民最低生活保障人数（人）Number of Persons Receiving Minimun Living Allowance in Urban Area（Person）	城镇居民最低生活保障家庭数（户）Number of Households Receiving Minimum Living Allowance in Urban Area（household）	城镇低保资金计划支出（万元）Planned Expense of Funds for Minimum Living Allowance in Urban Area（10 000 yuan）
全　市	**Whole Municpality**	**24220**	**15520**	**23,815.6**
市南区	Shinan District	3837	2530	4,115.3
市北区	Shibei District	13854	8751	13,445.8
李沧区	Licang District	2891	1723	2,989.1
崂山区	Laoshan District	140	82	158.2
黄岛区	Huangdao District	782	542	754.7
城阳区	Chengyang District	215	144	224.8
即墨区	Jimo District	1008	710	852.8
胶州市	Jiaozhou	762	524	661.9
平度市	Pingdu	502	345	422.7
莱西市	Laixi	229	169	190.3

注：1. 全市农村低保资金计划支出中包含市本级数据。2. 黄岛区含保税港区数据；城阳区含红岛经济区数据。
Note：1. The municipal level data shall be included in the expenditure of the rural low-insurance fund plan of the whole city.
2. The Huangdao District contains the data of the bonded harbor area. Chengyang District contains red island economic zone data.

年末在院人数（人） Residences at Year-end （person）	老年人 Senior Citizens	青壮年 Young and middle-aged	少年儿童 Youth
25460	**18499**	**409**	**418**
8250	1707	397	412
1264	1264	0	0
6255	6255	0	0
2481	2481	0	0
526	520	6	0
1583	1457	6	0
1053	1053	0	0
750	706	0	0
792	671	0	0
1280	1186	0	0
1226	1199	0	6

农村居民最低生活保障人数（人） Number of Persons Receiving Minimum living Allowance in Rural Area（person）	农村居民最低生活保障家庭数（户） Number of Households Receiving Minimum Living Allowance in Rural Area（household）	农村低保资金计划支出（万元） Rural low-insurance fund plan expenditure （10 000 yuan）
87141	**57860**	**53,121.3**
1907	1019	1,692.6
14225	9440	10,276.7
3379	2145	2,676.6
19672	13161	12,532.0
14474	9260	7,996.6
23699	15719	13,086.2
9785	7116	4,860.6

18-7 分市、区婚姻登记情况(2017年)
BASIC STATISTICS ON MARRIAGE REGISTRATION BY REGION (2017)

市、区名称	Region	准予登记结婚 Registered Marriages		
		合计(对) Total (couple)	初婚(人) First Marriages (person)	恢复结婚(对) Resumed Marriages (couple)
全　市	**Whole Municipality**	**58404**	**83498**	**116**
市本级	Municipal Level	222	271	
市南区	Shinan District	6003	9294	11
市北区	Shibei District	7049	9498	9
李沧区	Licang District	2942	4118	5
崂山区	Laoshan District	2685	4291	
黄岛区	Huangdao District	9893	13809	
城阳区	Chengyang District	3695	5592	
即墨区	Jimo District	7056	10445	14
胶州市	Jiaozhou	5729	7940	
平度市	Pingdu	8630	12056	77
莱西市	Laixi	4500	6184	

注：黄岛区含保税港区数据；城阳区含红岛经济区数据。
Note: The Huangdao District contains the data of the bonded harbor area. Chengyang District contains red island economic zone data.

再婚（人）Remariages（person）		准予登记离婚（对）Registered Divorces（couple）	涉外婚姻登记（对）Registered Marriages with Foreigner（couple）
男 Male	女 Female		
16626	**16684**	**23624**	**222**
91	82	42	222
1445	1267	2211	
2410	2190	3814	
917	849	1416	
566	513	754	
2962	3015	4571	
914	884	1150	
1810	1857	2118	
1723	1795	2658	
2434	2770	3407	
1354	1462	1483	

18-8 律师、公证、调解、社会治安基本情况(2000-2017年)

BASIC STATISTICS ON LAW YERS, NOTARIZATION, MEDIATION AND SOCIAL ORDER（2000-2017）

项 目	Item	单位	Unit	2000年	2005年	2006年	2008年	2009年
一、律师工作	**Lawyers**							
律师事务所	Law Offices	个	Unit	76	116	122	159	203
律师工作者	Lawyers	人	person	1439	1941	2218	2915	3144
专职	Full-time Lawyers	人	person	971	1542	1616	1855	1934
兼职(含特邀)	Part-time Lawyers	人	person	150	73	75	90	86
请常年法律顾问单位	Units with Permanent Legal Advisors	个	Unit	2508	3564	4032	4086	4457
全年办理民事代理	Agent of Civil Gases	件	case	5571	11104	10556	20547	29025
刑事辩护	Defender of Criminal Cases	件	case	1755	3003	2917	3655	3758
非诉讼事件	Agent of Non-litigious Legal Affairs	件	case	5251	6501	10049	5467	5897
解答法律询问	Agent of Legal Advisory Services	件	case	58385	27880	26518	31571	30123
代写法律事务文书	Agent of Legal Documents Written on Behalf of Clients	件	case	9335	8595	8171	9077	6015
二、公证工作	**Notarization**							
公证处	Notary Offices	个	Unit	15	15	15	13	13
公证人员	Notarial Personnel	人	person	152	196	209	214	214
公证员	Notaries	人	person	106	112	117	117	118
办理公证文书	Notarized Documents	件	case	120849	105787	100513	101766	97019
三、人民调解	**People' s Mediation**							
人民调解委员会	People' s Mediation Committees	个	Unit	9750	11480	10897	11223	9643
调解人员	Mediators	人	person	34714	46735	34487	33875	32675
调解民间纠纷	Civil Disputes Mediated	件	case	18501	13658	14094	12803	14660
四、社会治安	**Social Order**							
交通事故发生次数	Traffic Accidents	次	time	15601	7051	5559	3025	2570
死亡人数	Deaths	人	person	1371	776	689	489	402
受伤人数	Injuries	人	person	8620	6639	5685	3273	2943
经济损失	Losses	万元	10000 yuan	4815.70	2208.20	1514.00	991.50	854.80
火灾发生次数	Fire Accidents	次	time	3088	1948	1400	840	773
死亡人数	Deaths	人	person	10	3	8	16	5
受伤人数	Injuries	人	person	43	3	5	13	
经济损失	Losses	万元	10000 yuan	1531.06	550.40	544.00	979.70	865.50

2010年	2011年	2012年	2013年	2014年	2015年	2016年	2017年
222	247	266	285	322	337	355	371
2487	2801	3130	3143	3637	3896	4260	4839
2377	2643	2944	2980	3443	3728	4134	4578
94	105	107	93	110	112	123	127
4779	5180	5228	5374	5647	6101	6294	6952
26935	27702	30586	31147	36317	39640	42216	47679
3964	4535	4935	4858	5370	5107	4560	4936
4274	3576	4251	4133	4833	4900	4624	5386
21102	42428	45388	53775	33717	34003	40884	55320
6210	6762	6388	7376	5961	6272	7326	7112
13	13	13	13	13	12	12	12
214	221	225	244	249	242	250	264
117	119	118	113	119	129	125	127
94077	88506	87703	99852	100553	96085	104423	105200
8014	8486	8426	8448	8027	7708	7861	7413
27820	28094	27421	27035	25646	25222	26318	23918
20550	22882	23999	19525	23737	23552	30084	
2313	2164	1951	1896	1857	1814	1759	1847
393	374	343	333	321	313	308	324
2504	2240	1913	1840	1796	1785	1770	1828
811.27	861.05	652.10	609.80	561.80	509.1	506.6	528.7
683	369	366	742	1170	1001	1654	1458
9	1	6	7	12	10	8	13
4	2	2	11	9	3	10	9
5566.11	598.20	601.90	2348.10	1725.50	1491.0	1433.2	2739.7

18-9 分区、市殡葬服务情况(2017年)

BASIC STATISTICS ON FUNERAL SERVICES（2017）

区、市名称	Region	单位数（个）Number of Institutions（unit）	年末职工人数（人）Number of Staff and Workers at Year-end（person）	火化炉数（台）Number of Cremators（unit）	处理遗体数（具）Number of Remains Cremated（body）
全　市	**Whole Municpality**	**10**	**206**	**51**	**62747**
市本级	Municipal Level	1	47	14	12914
市南区	Shinan District				
市北区	Shibei District				
李沧区	Licang District				
崂山区	Laoshan District				
黄岛区	Huangdao District	2	23	7	9445
城阳区	Chengyang District	1	19	5	6130
即墨区	Jimo District	1	11	7	9538
胶州市	Jiaozhou	1	9	5	6495
平度市	Pingdu	2	30	7	11867
莱西市	Laixi	2	67	6	6358

注：黄岛区含保税港区数据；城阳区含红岛经济区数据。
Note：The Huangdao District contains the data of the bonded harbor area. Chengyang District contains red island economic zone data.

18-9 续表
Continued

区、市名称	Region	穴位数（个）Number of Graves (unit)	本年销售穴位数 Number of Graves Saled in the Year	安葬数（具）Number of Remains Buried (body)	本年安葬数 Number of Remains Buried in the Year
全　市	**Whole Municipality**	**24299**	**300**	**6791**	**671**
市本级	Municipal Level	20118	125	3585	520
市南区	Shinan District				
市北区	Shibei District				
李沧区	Licang District				
崂山区	Laoshan District				
黄岛区	Huangdao District				
城阳区	Chengyang District				
即墨区	Jimo District				
胶州市	Jiaozhou				
平度市	Pingdu	1644	99	1669	101
莱西市	Laixi	2537	76	1537	50

注：黄岛区含保税港区数据；城阳区含红岛经济区数据。
Note: The Huangdao District contains the data of the bonded harbor area. Chengyang District contains red island economic zone data.

主要统计指标解释

卫生机构 包括医疗机构、疾病预防控制中心（防疫站）、采供血机构、卫生监督及监测（检验）机构、医学科研和在职培训机构、健康教育所等。

医疗机构 包括医院、社区卫生服务中心（站）、疗养院、卫生院、门诊部、诊所（卫生所、医务室）、妇幼保健院（所、站）、专科疾病防治院（所、站）、急救中心（站）和临床检验中心。医疗机构分为非赢利性医疗机构和赢利性医疗机构。

医院 包括综合医院、中医医院、中西医结合医院、民族医院、各类专科医院和护理院。

医生 指在医疗、预防保健机构工作且取得《执业医师证书》的执业医师和执业助理医师。

卫生技术人员 指卫生事业机构中现任职务为卫生技术工作的人员。包括中医师、西医师、中西医结合高级医师、护师、中药师、西药师、检验师、其他技师、中医士、西医士、护士、助产士、中药剂士、西药剂士、检验士、其他技士、其他中医、护理员、中药剂员、西药剂员、检验员、其他初级卫生技术人员。

社会福利事业单位 指集中收养社会孤老、残、幼的机构，包括由民政部门管理的社会福利院、儿童福利院、精神病人福利院和城镇集体举办的福利院及农村集体举办的敬老院以及优抚医院和具有收养能力的社区服务中心等。

Explanatory Notes on Main Statistical Indicators

Health Care Institutions include: medical institutions，disease prevention and control centers（epidemic prevention stations），blood gathering and supplying institutions，health supervision and inspection（check up）institutions，medicinal scientific research and onjob training institutions，health education and so on.

Medical Organizations include: hospitals，health service centers（stations）of communities，nursing homes，health centers，clinics，clinics（health stations and infirmaries），maternity and child care agencies（centers and stations），special disease prevention and curing agencies（centers and stations），first aid centers（stations）and clinical inspection centers. Medical organizations are grouped by two types：profit–making and non–profit–making medical organizations.

Hospitals include: polyclinics，traditional Chinese medical hospitals，hospitals integrated with traditional Chinese therapeutics and western therapeutics，ethical hospitals，various specialties hospitals and nursing hospitals.

Doctors refer to certified physicians and certified assistant physicians with certifications working in medical and health care and prevention agencies.

Medical Technical Personnel refers to those medical workers employed institutions，including doctors of Chinese and Western medicine，senior doctors of integrated Chinese-Western medicine，head nurses，pharmacists of Chinese and Western medicine，laboratory specialists，other specialists，junior doctors of Chinese and Western medicine，nurses，midwives，druggists of Chinese and Western medicine，laboratory technicians，other technicians，other practitioners of Chinese medicine，nursing attendants，pharmacological workers of Chinese and Western medicine，laboratory workers，and other primary medical personnel.

Social Welfare Institutions refer to institutions taking care of old people without children，handicapped people and orphans. They include social welfare institutions run by civil affairs departments，children welfare institutions，socoal welfare institutions for mental patients，collective-owned old people's homes in rural areas，convalescent homes and community service centers with the capacity of receiving those people.

附　录

APPENDIX

2017 年省内各市主要经济指标对比情况
MAJOR ECONOMIC INDICATORS ON CTTIES OF THE PROVINCE（2017）

指 标 Indicator	单位 Unit	山东省 Shandong	青岛市 Qingdao	济南市 JIman	淄博市 Zibo	枣庄市 Zaozhuang	东营市 Dongying
生产总值（GDP）	亿元 （100 million yuan）	72678.2	11037.3	7202.0	4781.3	2315.9	3801.8
比上年增长 YOY Growth	%	7.4	7.5	8.0	7.4	6.7	6.4
规上工业增加值 YOY Growth of Industrial Added Value above Designated Size	%	6.9	7.5	9.8	5.7	6.8	7.2
固定资产投资额 Investment Fixed Assets	亿元 （100 million yuan）	54236.0	7777.1	4363.6	3135.1	1797.5	2557.5
比上年增长 YOY Growth	%	7.3	7.4	13.5	3.4	5.7	5.8
进出口总额 Imports and Exports	亿元 （100 million yuan）	17823.9	5033.5	765.5	677.7	100.2	1311.6
比上年增长 YOY Growth	%	15.2	15.7	6.8	29.6	12.2	31.2
#出口 Exports	亿元 （100 million yuan）	9965.4	3031.8	508.4	372.3	88.1	334.0
比上年增长 YOY Growth	%	10.1	7.5	5.0	7.7	9.3	11.0
进口 Imports	亿元 （100 million yuan）	7858.5	2001.7	257.1	305.4	12.0	977.7
比上年增长 YOY Growth	%	22.2	30.8	10.4	72.2	39.2	39.9
社会消费品零售总额 Total Retail Sales of Consumer Goods	亿元 （100 million yuan）	33649.0	4541.0	4146.1	2374.0	982.1	862.3
比上年增长 YOY Growth	%	9.8	10.6	10.1	10.2	10.1	9.2
一般公共预算收入 General Public Budget Revenue	亿元 （100 million yuan）	6098.5	1157.1	677.2	361.6	145.2	232.9
比上年增长 YOY Growth	%	6.6	7.1	10.5	6.1	1.2	8.6
全体居民人均可支配收入 Disposable income per capita of all residents	元 yuan	26930	38763	36872	32038	22420	34830
比上年增长 YOY Growth	%	9.1	8.6	8.7	8.7	8.6	8.2
城镇居民人均可支配收入 Per Capita Disposable Income of Urban Households	元 yuan	36789	47176	46642	39410	29924	44763
比上年增长 YOY Growth	%	8.2	8.2	8.3	8.2	8.0	7.7
农村居民人均可支配收入 Per Capital Net Income of Rural Households	元 yuan	15118	19364	16594	16953	14164	16252
比上年增长 YOY Growth	%	8.3	7.8	8.1	8.2	8.8	8.4

烟台市 Yantai	潍坊市 Weifang	济宁市 Jining	泰安市 Taian	威海市 Weihai	日照市 Rizhao	莱芜市 Laiwu	临沂市 Linyi	德州市 Dezhou	聊城市 Liaocheng	滨州市 Binzhou	菏泽市 Heze
7339.0	5858.6	4650.6	3585.3	3480.1	2002.7	896.0	4345.4	3140.2	3064.1	2612.9	2820.2
6.5	7.0	7.1	6.8	8.1	9.0	8.1	7.9	7.3	7.5	6.2	8.5
5.9	6.0	7.1	6.7	8.1	10.2	9.8	6.2	7.1	7.2	5.4	10.5
5594.2	4855.5	3473.5	2992.5	2941.9	1691.2	668.1	3765.7	2641.0	2470.1	2187.9	1323.6
8.5	0.5	8.4	7.2	8.7	9.5	5.5	8.0	8.0	10.7	5.6	9.5
3073.7	1456.6	409.9	152.2	1402.0	908.9	106.7	666.1	244.4	456.8	671.5	395.7
6.2	17.2	14.6	14.8	19.0	10.6	–5.1	16.9	16.4	22.5	16.4	12.9
1736.6	945.7	236.5	117.3	852.8	349.3	69.9	491.8	179.5	233.9	270.1	156.7
6.0	16.1	6.5	10.0	10.5	25.3	8.4	25.7	21.4	21.3	8.9	–2.5
1337.1	510.9	173.4	35.0	549.2	559.6	36.8	174.4	64.9	222.9	401.4	239.1
6.5	19.4	27.9	34.3	35.2	3.1	–23.3	–2.4	4.7	23.7	22.1	25.9
3273.1	2737.9	2259.2	1608.3	1607.9	720.3	380.0	2721.6	1537.1	1278.8	968.7	1650.4
10.0	8.9	9.0	10.0	10.4	9.1	9.3	9.4	10.2	9.0	8.9	9.8
600.3	539.1	385.7	207.1	273.1	141.3	56.0	285.3	187.5	186.5	226.3	186.6
6.4	6.9	3.0	3.9	9.5	12.7	10.2	3.9	6.9	2.0	5.5	6.1
32299	27823	23847	25244	33788	23286	27012	23528	19083	18183	24552	17222
8.6	9.2	9.1	8.8	9.2	9.4	9.1	8.9	9.3	9.5	8.6	10.0
41837	36286	32420	32739	42703	30790	34889	33266	24640	25231	32919	24116
8.0	8.0	8.1	8.1	8.5	8.6	7.8	7.8	8.3	8.4	7.6	9.0
18051	17434	14845	15674	18963	14540	16144	12613	13389	12415	14907	11753
8.0	8.3	9.0	8.6	7.9	8.7	8.7	8.3	9.3	9.0	8.5	9.8

2017 年十五个副省级城市主要经济指标情况

MAJOR ECONOMIC INDICATORS ON CTTIES UNDER PROVINCIAL LEVELS（2017）

指　标 Indicator	单位 Unit	青岛 Qingdao	沈阳 Shenyang	大连 Dalian	长春 Changchun	哈尔滨 Harbin
全市生产总值（GDP）	亿元 （100 million yuan）	11037.3	5865.0	7363.9	6530.0	6355.0
比上年增长 YOY　Growth	%	7.5	3.5	7.1	8.0	6.7
第一产业 Primary Industry	亿元 （100 million yuan）	381.0	268.2	477.1	315.1	688.8
比上年增长 YOY　Growth	%	3.2	3.6	4.4	3.8	3.7
第二产业 Secondary Industry	亿元 （100 million yuan）	4546.2	2261.4	3052.6	3175.2	1820.7
比上年增长 YOY　Growth	%	6.8	2.7	8.3	7.5	3.6
第三产业 Tertiary Industry	亿元 （100 million yuan）	6110.1	3335.4	3834.3	3039.7	3845.5
比上年增长 YOY　Growth	%	8.4	4.0	6.4	9.0	9.0
三产占比 Three-yield ratio	%	55.4	56.9	52.1	46.5	60.5
规上工业增加值 YOY Growth of Industrial Added Value above Designated size	%	7.5	2.8	11.2	9.0	5.0
固定资产投资额 Investment in Fixed Assets	亿元 （100 million yuan）	7777.1	1484.0	1652.8	5194.8	5395.5
比上年增长 YOY　Growth	%	7.4	-9.0	15.1	11.5	7.1
社会消费品零售总额 Total Retail Sales of Consumer Goods	亿元 （100 million yuan）	4541.0	3989.8	3722.5	2922.8	4044.8
比上年增长 YOY　Growth	%	10.6	0.1	9.2	10.3	8.0
进出口总额 Imports and Exports	亿元 （100 million yuan）	5033.5	867.6	4132.2	952.5	223.5
比上年增长 YOY　Growth	%	15.7	15.9	21.7	1.9	-14.1
# 出口 Exports	亿元 （100 million yuan）	3031.8	317.7	1745.8	129.8	98.2
比上年增长 YOY　Growth	%	7.5	13.4	8.5	2.8	-11.3
进口 Imports	亿元 （100 million yuan）	2001.7	549.9	2386.4	822.7	125.3
比上年增长 YOY　Growth	%	30.8	17.4	33.6	1.8	-16.2
一般公共预算收入 General Public Budget Revenue	亿元 （100 million yuan）	1157.1	656.2	657.7	450.1	368.1
比上年增长 YOY　Growth	%	7.1	5.7	7.5	8.3	8.4
城镇居民人均可支配收入 Per Capita Disposable Income of Urban Households	元（yuan）	47176	41359	40587		35546
比上年增长 YOY　Growth	%	8.2	6.1	6.7		7.1
农村居民人均可支配收入 Per Capltal Net Income of Rural Households	元（yuan）	19364	15461	16865		15614
比上年增长 YOY　Growth	%	7.8	7.5	7.7		8.1
居民消费价格指数 Consumer Price Index	%	102.0	101.4	102.1	101.3	101.6

注：部分城市收入数据尚未最终确定。

Note：Some of the urban income data has not been finalized.

南京 Nanjing	杭州 Hangzhou	宁波 Mingbo	厦门 Xiamen	济南 Jinan	武汉 Wuhan	广州 Guangzhou	深圳 Shenzhen	成都 Chengdu	西安 Xian
11715.1	12556.2	9846.9	4351.2	7202.0	13410.3	21503.2	22438.4	13889.4	7469.9
8.1	8.0	7.8	7.6	8.0	8.0	7.0	8.8	8.1	7.7
263.0	311.7	314.1	23.2	317.4	408.2	233.5	18.5	500.9	281.1
1.2	1.9	2.4	2.1	3.3	2.8	-1.0	52.8	3.9	4.6
4454.9	4387.2	5105.5	1815.9	2569.2	5861.4	6015.3	9266.8	5998.2	2596.1
5.1	5.3	7.9	7.2	8.4	7.1	4.7	8.8	7.5	5.5
6997.2	7857.3	4427.4	2512.0	4315.3	7140.8	15254.4	13153.0	7390.3	4592.7
10.3	10.0	8.1	7.9	8.2	9.2	8.2	8.8	8.9	9.2
59.7	62.6	45.0	57.7	59.9	53.2	70.9	58.6	53.2	61.5
6.0	7.0	9.6	8.1	9.8	7.7	1.0	9.3	9.0	5.8
6215.2	5856.7	5009.6	2381.5	4363.6	7871.7	5919.8	5147.3	9404.2	7556.5
12.3	1.4	3.5	10.3	13.5	11.0	5.7	23.8	12.3	12.9
5604.7	5717.4	4047.8	1446.7	4146.1	6196.3	9402.6	6016.2	6403.5	4329.5
10.2	10.5	10.4	12.7	10.1	10.4	8.0	9.1	11.5	10.5
4143.0	5085.1	7600.1	5816.0	765.5	1936.2	9714.4	28011.5	3941.8	2545.4
24.8	13.3	21.3	14.3	6.8	23.2	13.7	6.4	45.4	39.1
2333.0	3455.6	4984.1	3253.7	508.4	1157.6	5792.2	16533.6	2064.9	1552.4
19.3	4.3	14.3	5.2	5.0	27.8	12.3	5.5	42.3	63.9
1810.0	1629.5	2616.0	2562.4	257.1	778.6	3922.2	11477.9	1876.9	993.0
32.8	38.8	37.3	28.4	10.4	17.0	16.0	7.9	48.8	12.5
1271.9	1567.4	1245.3	696.8	677.2	2677.7	1533.1	3332.1	1275.5	654.5
11.9	17.4	10.9	11.0	10.5	10.5	10.9	10.1	11.3	9.8
54538	56276	55656	50019	46642	43405	55400		38918	38536
9.1	7.8	7.9	8.1	8.3	9.2	8.8		8.4	8.2
23133	30397	30871	20460	16594	20887	23484		20298	16522
9.3	8.9	8.0	8.3	8.1	9.1	9.5		9.1	8.8
101.9	102.5	101.8	102.0	102.0	101.9	102.3	101.4	102.0	102.0

2017 年副省级城市之外部分城市主要经济指标情况

THE MAIN ECONOMIC INDICATORS OF SOME OTHER CITIES THAN THE SUB-PROVINCIAL CITY FOR (2017)

指标名称 Zndicator	单位 Unit	北京 Beijing	天津 Tianjin	上海 Shanghai	重庆 Chongqing	苏州 Suzhou	无锡 Wuxi
全市生产总值（GDP）	亿元（100 million yuan）	28000.4	18595.4	30133.9	19500.3	17319.5	10511.8
同比增长 Year-on-year growth	%	6.7	3.6	6.9	9.3	7.1	7.4
# 第一产业 Primary Industry	亿元（100 million yuan）	120.5	218.3	99	1339.6	222	135.2
同比增长 Year-on-year growth	%	-6.2	2.0	-9.5	4	0.8	0.8
第二产业 Secondary Industry	亿元（100 million yuan）	5310.6	7590.4	9251.4	8596.6	8235.9	4964.4
同比增长 Year-on-year growth	%	4.6	1.0	5.8	9.5	6	7.3
第三产业 Tertiary Industry	亿元（100 million yuan）	22569.3	10786.7	20783.5	9564.0	8861.6	5412.2
同比增长 Year-on-year growth	%	7.3	6.0	7.5	9.9	8.2	7.7
第三产业增加值占 GDP 比重 Proportion taken by the added value in GDP for the Tertiary Industry	%	80.6	58.0	69.0	49.0	51.2	51.5
规模以上工业增加值同比增长 YOY Growth of Industrial Added Value above Designated Size	%	5.6	2.3	6.8	9.6	6.7	8.6
固定资产投资额 Investment in Fixed Assets	亿元（100 million yuan）	8948.1	11274.7	7246.6	17440.6	5629.6	4967.5
同比增长 Year-on-year growth	%	5.7	0.5	7.3	9.5	0.3	4.7
社会消费品零售总额 Total Retail Sales of Consumer Goods	亿元（100 million yuan）	11575.4	5729.7	11830.3	8067.7	5442.8	3458.0
同比增长 Year-on-year growth	%	5.2	1.7	8.1	11	10.3	10.9
进出口总额 Imports and Exports	亿元（100 million yuan）	21923.9	7646.9	32237.8	4508.3	21394.9	5502.5
同比增长 Year-on-year growth	%	17.5	12.8	12.5	8.9	18.5	19.4
# 出口总额 Exports	亿元（100 million yuan）	3962.5	2952.4	13120.3	2883.7	12670.5	3354.6
同比增长 Year-on-year growth	%	15.5	1.2	8.4	7.8	17.2	18.4
一般公共预算收入 General Public Budget Revenue	亿元（100 million yuan）	5430.8	2310.1	6642.3	2252.4	1908.1	930.0
同比增长 Year-on-year growth	%	6.8	-10.4	9.1	3	10.3	6.3
城镇居民人均可支配收入 Per Capita Disposable Income of Urban Households	元（yuan）	62406	40278	62596	32193	58806	52659
同比增长 Year-on-year growth	%	9.0	8.5	8.5	8.7	8.2	8.3
农村居民人均可支配收入 Per Capital Net Income of Rural Households	元（yuan）	24240	21754	27825	12638	29977	28358
同比增长 Year-on-year growth	%	8.7	8.4	9.0	9.4	8.3	8.4
居民消费价格指数 Consumer Price Index	%	101.9	102.1	101.7	101.0	101.7	101.9

青岛西海岸新区统计指标表
QINGDAO WEST COAST NEW DISTRICT STATISTICAL INDICATOR TABLE

指　标	Indicator	单位	Unit	2014	2015	2016	2017
年末常住人口	Resident population at the end of the year	万人	10 000 persons	148.42	149.36	151.59	153.92
国民经济各部门就业人员人数	Number of employed persons in various sectors of the national economy	万人	10 000 persons	55.6	61.2	63.2	69.3
公共财政预算收入	Public Budget Revenue	亿元	100 million	175.3	197.79	223.3	243.7
公共财政预算支出	Public Budget Expenditure	亿元	100 million	163.53	180.48	192.7	198.5
生产总值	Total output value	亿元	100 million	2404.74	2648.79	2942.09	3212.71
第一产业	Primary Industry	亿元	100 million	60.24	61.7	63.26	67.45
第二产业	Secondary Industry	亿元	100 million	1219.53	1296.64	1366.60	1474.33
#工业	Industy	亿元	100 million	1101.49	1170.27	1234.28	1315.48
第三产业	Tertiary Industry	亿元	100 million	1124.97	1290.45	1512.22	1670.93
生产总值增长速度	Total output value growth rate	%	%	9.8	12.2	12.3	11.0
生产总值构成	Total output value composition	%	%	100	100	100	100
第一产业	Primary Industry	%	%	2.50	2.33	2.15	2.1
第二产业	Secondary Industry	%	%	50.72	49.0	46.45	45.89
#工业	Industy	%	%	45.80	44.18	41.95	40.95
第三产业	Tertiary Industry	%	%	46.78	48.72	51.40	52.01
规模以上工业主营业务收入	Main business income of above scale industry	亿元	100 million	4516.27	5203.69	4871.86	4452.76
规模以上工业利润总额	Total industrial profits above Designated Size	亿元	100 million	196.12	254.43	287.42	289.22
固定资产投资额	Investment in Fixed Assets	亿元	100 million	1444.10	1714.66	2008.60	2262.00
#房地产开发	Investment in Real Estate Development	亿元	100 million	228.11	233.16	210.75	275.54
#住宅	Residential Buildings	亿元	100 million	148.08	146.12	142.97	155.06
社会消费品零售额	Total Retail Sales of Consumer Goods	亿元	100 million	418.2	476.6	533.4	596.4
农林牧渔业总产值	Gross Output Value of Farming, Forestry, Animal Husbandry and Fishery	亿元	100 million	105.75	110.73	112.77	118.56
粮食产量	Grain production	吨	ton	276000	252500	248000	244598
肉类产量	meat production	吨	ton	87336	88906	87625	89712
水产品总产量	Output of Aquatic Products	吨	ton	347712	349496	349496	366200

中国统计出版社最新图书简目

（仅供参考，以实际出版为准）

统计资料

中国统计年鉴　中国统计摘要　中国第三产业统计年鉴

中国第三次全国农业普查综合资料　国际统计年鉴　金砖国家联合统计手册

中国－东盟国家统计手册　中国农村统计年鉴　中国县域统计年鉴

中国农产品价格调查年鉴　中国城市统计年鉴　中国价格统计年鉴

中国贸易外经统计年鉴　中国零售和餐饮连锁企业统计年鉴　中国商品交易市场统计年鉴

大中型批发零售和住宿餐饮企业统计年鉴　中国住户调查年鉴　中国工业统计年鉴

中国环境统计年鉴　中国能源统计年鉴　中国建筑业统计年鉴

中国房地产统计年鉴　中国固定资产投资统计年鉴　中国对外直接投资统计公报

中国人口和就业统计年鉴　中国劳动统计年鉴　中国社会统计年鉴

中国科技统计年鉴　中国高技术产业统计年鉴　全国企业创新调查年鉴

中国文化及相关产业统计年鉴　2018 年时间利用调查资料　中国妇女儿童状况统计资料

中国基本单位统计年鉴　中国教育统计年鉴　中国教育经费统计年鉴

中国民族统计年鉴　中国残疾人事业统计年鉴

省级综合统计年鉴系列

北京　天津　河北　山西　内蒙古　辽宁　吉林　黑龙江　上海　江苏　浙江　安徽　福建　江西　山东　河南　湖北　湖南　广东　广西　海南　重庆　四川　贵州　云南　西藏　陕西　甘肃　青海　宁夏　新疆　新疆生产建设兵团

市（县）级综合统计年鉴系列

滨海新区　石家庄　唐山　邯郸　保定　沧州　邢台　廊坊　承德　衡水　秦皇岛　张家口　太原　大同　阳泉　长治　晋城　朔州　晋中　运城　忻州　临汾　吕梁　呼和浩特　呼和浩特新城区　鄂尔多斯　包头　沈阳　大连　长春　吉林　延吉　四平　通化　松原　哈尔滨　齐齐哈尔　黑龙江垦区　上海浦东新区　南京　无锡　徐州　常州　苏州　南通　连云港　淮安　盐城　扬州　镇江　泰州　宿迁　江阴　丹阳　海门　杭州　宁波　温州　嘉兴　湖州　绍兴　金华　衢州　舟山　台州　丽水　合肥　安庆　马鞍山　福州　厦门　宁德　漳州　龙岩　南昌　九江　上饶　新余　抚州　萍乡　赣州　吉安　景德镇　济南　青岛　潍坊　枣庄　日照　滕州　郑州　洛阳　平顶山　三门峡　商丘　信阳　济源　汝州　武汉　十堰　荆州　宜昌　荆门　咸宁　长沙　广州　深圳　惠州　东莞　汕尾　南宁　柳州　桂林　梧州　来宾　河池　防城港　海口　三亚　成都　贵阳　黔南　毕节　昆明　西安　咸阳　延安　宝鸡　安康　铜川　汉中　榆林　兰州　庆阳　银川　乌鲁木齐　兵团一师　兵团十师

调查年鉴系列

天津　内蒙古　上海　浙江　福建　河南　湖北　湖南　广东　广西　重庆　四川　云南　甘肃　宁夏

统计方法应用／实用手册

实用 SAS 统计分析教程　Python 数据分析基础　统计公文知识问答　领导干部统计知识问答

乡镇统计人员岗位知识培训系列教材：辅助调查员岗位基础知识　乡镇统计人员岗位基础知识

县级统计人员岗位知识培训系列教材：Excel 在统计工作中的应用　简明统计分析

地市级统计人员岗位知识培训系列教材：统计报告与演示　中国国民经济核算体系（2016）基础知识

全国统计专业技术资格考试系列考试用书：统计业务知识（第四版）　统计业务知识学习指导与习题

全国统计专业技术资格考试系列考试用书：统计相关知识（第四版）　统计相关知识学习指导与习题

统计通俗读物／统计科普图书

我国 20 个统计指标的历史变迁　联合国工业发展组织：2016 年工业发展报告　中国古代统计发展史　理解国民账户

重点图书

波澜壮阔四十年　砥砺奋进铸就辉煌——改革开放 40 年与时俱进的中国统计

新编英汉汉英统计大词典　中国国民经济核算体系 2016　国民经济行业分类注释

挑大学选专业 2019—考研择校指南　挑大学选专业 2019—高考志愿填报指南　中华医学统计百科全书

中国统计出版社发行部电话：（010）63376907　63376908　同棏行书店电话：68783171　68783172

地址：北京市丰台区西三环南路甲 6 号　邮政编码：100073　网址：http://www.zgtjcbs.com